The

ALMANAC

of

POLITICAL CORRUPTION,

SCANDALS,

and

DIRTY POLITICS

An unjust scale representing corrupt legislation. One section of a
five-part mural in the Jefferson Building in the Library of Congress,
Washington, D.C., painted in 1898 by Elihu Vedder.

The
ALMANAC
of
POLITICAL CORRUPTION,
SCANDALS,
and
DIRTY POLITICS

KIM LONG

Delacorte Press

THE ALMANAC OF POLITICAL CORRUPTION,
SCANDALS, AND DIRTY POLITICS
A Delacorte Press Book

Published by
Bantam Dell
A Division of Random House, Inc.
New York, New York

Book design by Kim Long
Cover design by Tom McKeveny
Illustration credits can be found on pages 333–335

ISBN-13: 978-0-7394-9571-1

Printed in the United States of America

To the majority of politicians, local and national, who are elected honestly, lead without corruption, and behave ethically

The purification of politics is an
iridescent dream. Politics is a battle for
supremacy. The Decalogue and the
Golden Rule have no place in a political
campaign. The object is success.

—Senator John Ingalls, 1890

Scandals in Government are not a new
phenomena. What seems to be new
about these scandals is the moral
blindness or callousness which allows
those in responsible positions to accept
the practices which the facts reveal.
It is bad enough for us to have
corruption in our midst, but it is worse
if it is to be condoned and accepted as
inevitable.

—Senator J. William Fulbright, 1951

CONTENTS

INTRODUCTION

For many American adults, contemporary political history has been defined more by negatives than positives. In the past thirty-odd years, major scandals have marked the executive and legislative branches of the federal government in a relentless parade of revealing headlines. Keywords now brand the recent presidencies: Iran-Contra, Watergate, Abscam, Whitewater, Monica Lewinsky. The collective response has been to lower our approval rating for the very officials who require the highest confidence.

When first exposed, any scandal now seems to have the potential to be career threatening, and too few voters are willing to take a politician's avowal of innocence at face value. Worse, many Americans believe that all politicians are tainted—with scandal, unethical standards, corrupt behavior, or similar substandard character—and the country is gradually regressing, losing its traditional values, and spiraling downward toward a degraded, immoral finale.

Is this perception appropriate, much less accurate? One of the goals of this project is to provide a new measuring rod with which to gauge the breadth and depth of the current political environment, both the activities of politicians and the process of electing them. A chronological history—from our colonial roots onward—provides just such a unique barometer of reality. And it becomes quickly apparent, once this approach is under way, that the past provides a considerable wealth of evidence to support the folk saying, "The more things change, the more they stay the same."

Pick any category of modern political wrongdoing—sins of the flesh, theft, bribery, extortion, lies, cover-ups, election fraud—and historical precedents are easy to find. Add an element missing from most political activity in the past few decades, bloodshed, and the historical record often outshines today's antics.

Yet our human inclination to focus on the sensational does us a disservice. Even in colonial America, people read newspapers, the main source of information about current events, but then, as now, "normal" isn't news. As the saying goes, it's only news when the man bites the dog. The current and historical record of political misdoings covers just that, misdoings, not the standard, mundane, day-to-day operations that keep local and national systems operational.

Consider the bigger picture. Since the first Congress, just under 12,000 individuals have served in the U.S. House and Senate, but far less than one percent of these have been expelled, indicted, or tried for criminal activity. Only two presidents out of forty-two have been impeached, and neither of those was convicted. Out of more than 2,100 governors, only fifteen have been impeached, with only seven convicted after impeachment. A similar record holds for federal judges: more than 3,100 have served and only seven have been convicted after impeachment. Politicians who screw up are the exception, not the rule.

Even when politicians have erred and elections have been rigged, life goes on. The country and the Constitution have survived. Rules have been added to reduce opportunities for malfeasance, to remove barriers for participation in both politics and voting, and to provide fairer platforms for both. Those who do not play by the rules—then or now—are individuals who may be "good people making bad decisions," sinister manipulators, or followers more willing to imitate their peers than do what is right. But these miscreants have one thing in common: they are all in the minority.

Here we focus on that minority with the knowledge that their brethren were tending to business while they were screwing up or screwing around. It's an equal opportunity exposé, with plenty of room for participation regardless of party affiliation, wealth, intelligence, age, race, ethnicity, gender, or geographical location.

Most important, the story of this group of misfits is much more entertaining than that of their mainstream colleagues. And it is a story that is unlikely to end. With that in mind, we wrote the last line first... to be continued.

A political cartoon entitled "Election Day." *McClure's Magazine*, March 1905.

PRE–1776

The United States created a demonstrably unique form of government after its independence from England, but it can't take credit for the concept of political corruption and scandal. British officials who were appointed to positions in the American colonies committed misdeeds from graft to bribery to extortion. One estimate of the loss to the British Treasury in the year 1765 due to corrupt colonial officials was £700,000 ($132 million in today's dollars).[1] They had their share of scandals as well. Lord Cornbury (Edward Hyde), the appointed governor of the colonies of New York and New Jersey, was rumored to wear women's clothes, although some contemporary scholars believe this was false information spread by his political enemies. While his dressing habits may have given his subjects cause for concern, what got him in real trouble was his significant personal debt, a serious issue in those days. Because of this failing, he was stripped of his position by Queen Anne and locked up in an American debtors' prison.

PRE
1776

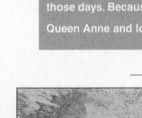

Colonial authorities burn votes from towns in Long Island.

Francis Lovelace (1621–1675), colonial governor of New York, was credited with introducing important improvements during his term of leadership. But he also had his share of trouble. In 1670, residents of the colony's towns were requested to vote to approve a new tax to help expand the fortifications that protected New York City. Some towns in Long Island voted against the tax, which prompted Lovelace to have their votes publicly burned. He also benefited personally from the profits of a tavern that he built adjoining city hall, an establishment carefully designed to benefit from its location. The pub had a door that offered a direct connection to the courtroom next to it.[2]

Edmund Andros

In 1689, the residents of New England deposed and imprisoned colonial governor Sir Edmund Andros (1637–1714) in a revolt against his harsh leadership. Charges against him included restraining freedom of the press, arbitrary taxes, high taxes, and "exorbitant charges" for residents to obtain titles to their own property. He was shipped back to England, but not before escaping twice. In England, British authorities declined to put him on trial and instead sent him back to the new country as governor of the Virginia colony. He was subsequently recalled from

PRE 1776

there as well. Earlier, he held the governorship for the colony of New York and New Jersey, but was recalled from there in 1681, also because of complaints.[3]

Benjamin Fletcher (1640–1703), royal governor of New York, was investigated and removed from office in 1697 by the Board of Trade, acting under the authority of the British government. Fletcher was found guilty of "abetting

Edmund Andros escaped from captivity twice, once disguised as a woman.

piracy," conspiring with pirates to use the city's port in exchange for sizable bribes. One notorious pirate, Edward Coates, testified at Fletcher's trial that he paid the governor £1,800 ($320,000 in today's dollars) in exchange for safe entry for a ship; the governor reportedly shared this income with his council. At that time, the annual revenue from the pirate trade in New York was estimated to be up to £100,000 ($18 million in today's dollars). According to some sources, Fletcher did not limit his quest for extra income to the port trade but had his hand in a variety of other schemes as well. A rival of Fletcher's wrote,

"To recount all his arts of squeezing money both out of the publick and private purses would make a volume instead of a letter."[4]

In 1700, the British parliament passed a law entitled "An Act to Punish Governors of Plantations in this Kingdom for Crimes by Them Committed in the Plantations." This legislation came in response to an increasing number of complaints—from colonials as well as officials— pertaining to abuse of power. This was the first type of formal recourse with which misdeeds by governors could be addressed, not counting offenses such as that committed by Benjamin Fletcher. Previously, the colonial rulers—as direct representatives of the monarchy—were an- swerable solely to the English king. However, the act was put into prac- tice only once, and not on the American mainland. It was used to punish Walter Douglas, governor of the Leeward Islands, in 1711, on a variety of charges, including the theft of the royal silver communion service.[5]

Lord Cornbury (1662–1723), provincial governor of New York and New Jersey, was recalled to England in 1708 by order of Queen Anne. The governor, born Edward Hyde, was targeted by political enemies, who sent letters back to England describing Cornbury's shortcomings as well as his eccentric- ities. In one letter it was written, "My Lord Cornbury has and dos still make use of an unfor- tunate Custom of dressing himself in Womens Cloaths and of exposing himself in that Garb upon the Ramparts to the view of the public." Although repeated in history texts for centuries, this may have been a fiction made up to discredit him. There is no corroborating evidence from contemporary publications, personal journals, or letters, and the single portrait of him dressed in a gown is now thought to be a forgery. More sub- stantive was the charge he borrowed money that

Edward Hyde (Lord Cornbury) was rumored to wear women's clothes, but the rumor was likely only a political attack. This portrait, with Hyde in a dress, is likely a forgery.

he did not repay. He was jailed as a debtor in New York City before he was allowed to leave the country.[6]

In 1730, Jonathan Belcher (1682–1757) was appointed royal governor of Massachusetts and the province of New Hampshire. Belcher had ongoing problems with the residents, including charges of corruption. The legislature refused to grant him an annual salary, although this was an issue based more on colonial vs. British rights than a personal affront; the assembly refused the same request for twelve other governors. He remained in office until 1741, when he was forced out for receiving a bribe, a charge he successfully defended against. He later served as the governor of the Province of New Jersey and is credited as the founder of Princeton University.[7]

In 1734, George Burrington (1680–1759), royal governor of North Carolina, was sent back to England because of complaints about his leadership. Burrington had previously been the Lord Proprietor of North Carolina (1724–1725) before the territory was made a colony. While there, he had incurred charges of improper conduct, including an indictment for assaulting the previous governor. Some—or all—of the dislike for his rule may have been politically motivated. In any case, there was no shortage of vindictive descriptions of his character and activities. The slurs included: "notorious ignorance and profligacy," "vileness of character," "mad extravagence of behaviour," "drunken and quarrelsome," "character unadorned by a single virtue," and "dirty rogue and villain." One of his political enemies circulated a story that while in England, he had been convicted and imprisoned for physically attacking an old woman. He was reportedly killed in a street brawl in London.[8]

At the end of the colonial era in America, 130 governors had served as heads in the colonies, including those in the Caribbean Islands. Of those, forty died in office and the rest served terms of varying length before they were replaced. The record for the longest term was twenty-five years, for Benning Wentworth in New Hampshire. The record for the shortest term was two days, for Sir Danvers Osborn in New York, who killed himself two days after his inauguration. Average term: about five years.[9]

1776–1779

The American Revolution began in 1776 with the publication of the Declaration of Independence, the jumping-off point for the history that follows. George Washington became the country's first president in 1789, the first year when nationally elected officials can be held accountable within this chronology (though Washington was not elected by voters, but the Electoral College). But things were stirring even before this. During the war, as commander of the American army, Washington was the subject of many rumors, including one that suggested he had conducted an extramarital affair with a cleaning woman in Philadelphia. He was also scolded for using alcohol to tempt voters, even though during colonial days, politicians routinely used free alcohol as an enticement for voters. In the national elections of 1792, the *Gazette of the United States* commented "That the Voice of the People, was the Voice of Grog." Physical attacks were also employed against other politicians in this era, as when the representative from Vermont, slighted by the representative from Connecticut, spat a mouthful of tobacco juice at him.

On May 16, 1777, Button Gwinnett (1735–1777), acting governor of Georgia, dueled with General Lachlan McIntosh (1725–1806), a delegate from Georgia, near Savannah. The men had been feuding about McIntosh's brother, who had been arrested by Gwinnett on "suspicion of treachery," as well as McIntosh's own inefficient actions in leading Continental troops against the British. During an official state inquiry into the latter, McIntosh publicly called Gwinnett a "scoundrel

Button Gwinnett

and a lying rascal," sufficient instigation for a duel. Both McIntosh and Gwinnett were wounded in the fight; Gwinnett died from his wounds several days later.[1]

A popular war hero, George Washington (1732–1799) was also a popular president. Yet he had detractors who were happy to spread rumors diminishing his stature. Among the barbs: he had an illegitimate son named Lawrence Posey, a resident of a farm near Mount Vernon; another illegitimate son was reported to be Alexander Hamilton, Washington's secretary of the treasury; and during Washington's com-

George Washington

mand of the American troops in the war, he had a mistress who was a British supporter. The British themselves circulated a bogus letter—supposedly written by Washington—which suggested the general was intimate with a young maid, whom he called "pretty little Kate, the Washer-woman's daughter." Benjamin Franklin Bache, Benjamin Franklin's grandson, was an outspoken critic and used his position as editor of an influential newspa-per to publish this kind of anti-Washington content. At various times, he called the first president a "despotic, anemic counterfeit of the English Georges," deceptive, and guilty of having "treacherous mazes of passion."[2]

Henry Osborne (1751–1800), superior court judge in Georgia, was expelled from office in December 1791 by the state senate because of fraud during the election of Anthony Wayne to the U.S. House. Osborne was charged and convicted of altering the results—from a total of twenty-five votes to eighty-nine votes—with an increase of sixty-four for Wayne. Osborne had previously held several state positions in Pennsylvania but was expelled there as well, in June 1783, after he was found to be a bigamist.[3]

During the gubernatorial election of 1792 in New York State, Federalist John Jay (1745–1829) received the majority of votes but lost the election. The ruling Democratic-Republican party seized all of the ballots in three counties and declared them invalid, citing irregularities in how the ballots had been collected. Although none was found to be fraudulent, the action resulted in the runner-up, incumbent George Clinton (1739–1812), being declared the winner. Clinton—who became known as the father of New York after serving a total of twenty-two years as governor—later went on to be elected vice president of the United States. Jay won the following election for governor and later was appointed Chief Justice of the Supreme Court.[4]

In 1792, an informal group of U.S. congressmen investigated allegations that Secretary of the Treasury Alexander Hamilton (1757–1804) had used confidential information about government activities to enrich his investments. Their inquiry did not substantiate this charge, but it did uncover a previously unknown scandal involving Hamilton as the victim of a blackmail plot. A woman named Maria Reynolds had a sexual tryst with Hamilton in Philadelphia while Hamilton's wife was home in New York. The event turned out to be a setup, a trap set by James Reynolds, Maria's husband, who encouraged the continuation of the affair in exchange for hush money from Hamilton. Hamilton

Alexander Hamilton

ended the affair a year later when Mr. Reynolds upped his demands and demanded a government job in return for silence. The report of Hamilton's blackmail was kept secret until 1796, when a political rival learned of it and published an account in a pamphlet, creating a public scandal. In the interim, Maria Reynolds divorced her husband, relying on attorney Aaron Burr to do the legal work. In 1804, Burr and Hamilton fought a fatal duel over a different issue.[5]

Albert Gallatin (1761–1849) was the first U.S. senator denied a seat after an election. On February 28, 1794, a committee of the Senate voted to keep him from serving on the grounds that he failed to meet the Constitution's requirement for residency. He had emigrated from Switzerland in 1780 but had not been a citizen for a minimum of nine years at the time he was elected in 1793 because the "start date" was

Albert Gallatin

considered the ratification date of the Constitution, 1788. But the real issue behind the ouster was that Gallatin, a Republican from Pennsylvania, was a leader in opposing the financial policies of Alexander Hamilton and the majority Federalist party. His politics gave the Federalists the motivation to remove him from power. The committee voted along party lines—fourteen to twelve—to keep him out.[6]

Kensey Johns (1759–1848), Federalist senator from Delaware, was removed from office on March 28, 1794, by a majority vote of the Senate. Johns committed no wrong but was an early victim of national politics, in this case having been appointed to replace George Read (another Federalist, and a signer of the Declaration of Independence) by the governor of Delaware, Joshua Clayton. The vote to unseat Johns was motivated by party politics—Republicans angry at the recent successful ouster of one of their own, Albert Gallatin—and focused on a technicality. In this case, Clayton was found to have made the appointment while the Delaware state legislature was in recess, a violation of a provision in the U.S. Constitution.[7]

On July 8, 1797, the full Senate voted to expel William Blount (1749–1800), a Republican from Tennessee. The case focused on Blount's questionable activities in the acquisition of land. The evidence included a letter he wrote attempting to instigate an attack on the Florida and Louisiana territories with the hope that Great Britain might acquire the land, benefiting Blount's real estate investments there. The Senate voted to expel him on the grounds of disloyalty but failed in a later attempt to impeach him, because of a technicality in the impeachment rules.[8]

On January 30, 1798, Congress engaged in a debate about potential American involvement in a war then under way in Europe. In the House of Representatives, an argument between Matthew Lyon (1749–1822), Republican from Vermont, and Roger Griswold

(1762–1812), Federalist from Connecticut, escalated to a shouting match. Lyon, a tobacco chewer—like many members of Congress in that era—spat in the face of Griswold. The House voted on expelling Lyon, but failed to reach the two-thirds majority necessary for this action. It was the first recorded case of an attempt to discipline a congressman and the first recorded case of violence in the House. On February 15, Griswold resorted to his own retribution and attacked Lyon with a hickory cane; Lyon used a pair of fireplace tongs to return the blows. A recommendation to expel both parties was brought to the floor, but not enough votes were raised to pass the resolution.[9]

In July 1798, Congress passed the Sedition Act, a Federalist-sponsored bill that outlawed speech that was critical of Congress or the president. Matthew Lyon opposed this move and took action. He wrote a letter to a prominent newspaper in his home state, stating that President Adams had "a continual grasp for power...unbounded thirst for ridiculous pomp, foolish adulation and selfish avarice." Shortly thereafter, he was the first person arrested under the Sedition Act. In court, his defense was that the act was unconstitutional. The jury—all Federalists—found him guilty and sent him to prison for four months. Out of jail in time for the elections of 1798, he was reelected.[10]

"He in a trice struck Lyon thrice / Upon his head, enrag'd sir, / Who seiz'd the tongs to ease his wrongs, / And Griswold thus engag'd, sir." A 1798 print of the Lyon–Griswold fight.

PROFILE | XYZ Affair

In 1798, in Paris, U.S. diplomats were targeted in a scheme to extort money from the United States in exchange for a diplomatic agreement to solve problems between the two countries. Three French agents were involved in the deal. To provide a cover of secrecy when communicating this development to Washington, the American representatives dubbed the French agents X, Y, and Z, which provided a label for the ensuing scandal, thereafter known as the XYZ Affair. When news of this unethical activity was published, some politicians attacked President Adams and the Federalist party

because they believed the whole thing was a political ploy. The evidence, in the form of the official *1776 1799* correspondence from the diplomats abroad, proved otherwise, and the focus of the attack shifted to the French. The result was escalating military confrontations, which lasted until a treaty was negotiated, one with no bribes involved.[11]

A satirical 1798 British print about the XYZ Affair, with Frenchmen musing over a female "America," with other Europeans looking on.

After George Washington's death in 1799, George Washington Bowen claimed to be the son of George and Betsy "Elixa" Bowen, a former prostitute, who later married Aaron Burr. Born in 1794, Bowen instituted a lawsuit after his mother died because he had not been the beneficiary of her estate. His case lasted thirteen years and ended in the Supreme Court, which decided against him. In the interim, coverage of the proceedings prolonged the scandal about the former president, but it was eventually proven that Bowen was unrelated to Washington. Another scandal involved Washington's wife, Martha, whose family was reported to have sired children with black slaves on the Mount Vernon estate. These descendants, with the family name Syphax, were sometimes linked to the president as well.[12]

1800–1819

I n this era, electoral votes were the key to national politics, making them an attractive target for corruption. In the 1800 election, a tie vote between Thomas Jefferson and Aaron Burr for president required a lengthy debate—and thirty-five separate ballots—in the House of Representatives before Jefferson emerged the winner. As president, he wrestled with various scandals, including patronage, fathering an illegitimate child with one of his slaves, and rumor-mongering. Jefferson and his allies reportedly spread the word that John Adams, a political rival, had sent a friend to England to acquire four young women as mistresses. In this period, the first federal judge was impeached for "tyrannical conduct" and an associate justice of the U.S. Supreme Court was impeached (although later acquitted), the first of a wave of attacks on judicial conduct that continues to the present day.

1800
1819

By the time that Thomas Jefferson (1743–1826) was elected president in 1800, the practice of attacking the character and personal activities of elected politicians—even the president—was well established. In Jefferson's case, the mudslinging began while he was minister to France, with rumors of "libertine" behavior in circulation back in the States. Among the charges: he made sexual advances on the wife of a friend when he was younger; he had several affairs with married women while he was posted in France; and he had fathered one or more children with Sally Hemings, one of his own slaves. At least some of this turned out to be true, although it was not publicly proven in his lifetime. The last of the charges was a long-running contention

Thomas Jefferson

that endured more than two hundred years of speculation. Recent DNA tests on the descendants of Hemings found a strong match with Jefferson's legitimate descendants.[1]

Aaron Burr

Shortly after being elected vice president, Aaron Burr (1756–1836), a Democratic Republican, was the target of attacks by Federalists in New York. At one point they published a handbill accusing him of being immoral, against the Constitution, and guilty of political intrigue. The charge of immorality was addressed in some detail, for example: "His abandoned profligacy, and the numerous unhappy wretches who have fallen victims to this accomplished and but too successful debauchee, have indeed been long known to those whom similar habits of vice, or the amiable office of humanity have led to the wretched haunts of female prostitution." Specifics were added—all untrue—including his seduction of a young woman during his trip to the inauguration.[2]

1800 1819

On July 31, 1802, DeWitt Clinton (1769–1828), the Democratic Republican senator from New York, fought a duel in which his opponent, John Swartwout, was hit twice in the leg. The two were allies of Aaron Burr and had argued over political patronage, a dispute that escalated from a quarrel to the duel. Clinton was elected governor in 1817, and George Clinton, his brother, became the vice president in 1804. Swartwout also had a political lineage: his brother Samuel became the collector of customs for the Port of New York, a patronage position, and was the focus of a major scandal in the administration of President Jackson.[3]

On September 5, 1802, Richard Dobbs Spaight (1758–1802), a former anti-Federalist representative from North Carolina, was wounded in a duel and died the following day. His adversary was John Stanly (1774–1834), leader of the Federalist party in North Carolina. Spaight had been a member of the Continental Congress as well as the Constitutional Convention, governor of North Carolina, and had just been defeated in his bid for reelection to Congress by Stanly. The duel, held in New Bern, North Carolina, was instigated by an exchange of handbills between the two, a method favored at the time for exchanging public insults. In Spaight's words, "I must now gentlemen, declare to you, that in my opinion, Mr. Stanley [*sic*] is both a lyar [*sic*] and a scoundrel." Stanly responded, "To your disappointment, this letter informs you, that humiliating as it is to my feelings, to fight a man who can descend to the filth contained in your handbill, I shall expect that you will meet me as soon as may be convenient."[4]

On December 16, 1806, William Harris Crawford (1772–1834), state representative in Georgia, fought a duel with General John Clark, in which a shot from Clark's pistol shattered his left wrist. Crawford had fought an earlier duel in 1802, in which he had killed Peter Lawrence Van Alen, a political foe. A long-simmering feud with Van Alen's political colleagues festered and eventually led to the encounter with Clark. Crawford survived his wound and went on to bigger accomplishments, in both politics and scandals.[5]

In March 1807, President Jefferson removed James Wilkinson (1757–1825) as governor of the Louisiana territory. Wilkinson, who had previously been the senior officer in the U.S. Army, was implicated in a plot to form a separate country from the northeastern states, making him an unsound government appointee. Aaron Burr, former vice president, was also implicated. But Wilkinson was also involved in other suspect activity, including receiving secret payments from the government of Spain in exchange for information and advice on boundary rules from the U.S. government, diplomatic plans, and military readiness. In 1808, two formal investigations dealt with this issue, one by a

James Wilkinson

military court of inquiry and one by the U.S. House. Neither found enough evidence to charge him; written proof of his activities did not surface until the 1900s.[6]

On August 3, 1807, a trial for Aaron Burr, former vice president of the United States, opened in Richmond, Virginia. Burr had been arrested on a charge of treason, specifically, conspiring to remove western states from the country. He and others concocted a plan to lead an armed assault on Mexican territory, then ruled by Spain, with the goal being the creation of a new country. Because the prosecution was unable to provide two witnesses to any explicit act of treason—a written rule required by the judge, Chief Justice John Marshall of the U.S. Supreme Court—the jury voted for acquittal.[7]

1800 1819

In 1807, the U.S. Senate investigated one of its members, John Smith (1735–1824), Republican senator from Ohio, on charges he had conspired with Aaron Burr in a plot to generate a revolt in the western territories. The Senate voted not to expel Smith—the outcome was one vote shy of the two-thirds majority required—but facing extreme negative publicity because of the charges and the link to Burr, he resigned his seat on April 25, 1808.[8]

Bladensburg, Maryland, about eight miles north of Washington, D.C., was a favored site for duels because of its proximity and its isolation. It was also the site of a battle in the War of 1812.

On March 2, 1808, Barent Gardenier (?–1822), Federalist U.S. representative from New York, faced George Washington Campbell (1769–1848), Democratic Republican U.S. representative from Tennessee, in a duel in Bladensburg, Maryland, just north of Washington, D.C. The two men had a vigorous debate in Congress over the effects of a recently initiated embargo on British trade; when the debate escalated to personal abuse, Gardenier challenged Campbell to a duel. The duel was originally scheduled to be held in Georgetown, but a large crowd of spectators deterred the combatants, who preferred to settle their grievances privately. Both men survived the final confrontation, although Gardenier was wounded.⁹

On February 26, 1808, Vice President George Clinton (1739–1812) read to an open session of the Senate from diplomatic dispatches about pending embargoes between the United States and Great Britain. The dispatches, which were marked confidential, indicated that war with England was likely. Clinton, a Democratic Republican, later claimed that he had made a mistake, not noticing the warning about confidentiality, but the public disclosure was widely reported, diminishing his stature and credibility.¹⁰

George Clinton

1800 1819

On January 25, 1809, Josiah Quincy (1772–1864), Federalist U.S. representative from Massachusetts, initiated a scandal in the administration of President Jefferson by claiming the president had committed a "high misdemeanor." If substantiated, this charge was an impeachable offense and could have resulted in Jefferson's expulsion from office. Quincy's charge was that Jefferson had refused to accept an offer of resignation from the government customs collector for the Port of Boston because Jefferson wanted to hold it for a later date, when he could award it to his then secretary of war, Henry Dearborn. A debate in the House concluded that the charge represented too little merit to be considered, and the issue was dropped.¹¹

Samuel Smith (1752–1839), Republican senator from Maryland, was accused—along with his brother, Robert Smith—of misuse of government funds. The charges were made by a political rival, who was also a Republican politician. Although not found guilty of this charge, Smith lost a reelection race early in 1809 because of the negative publicity attached to the issue. Robert Smith, his brother, was secretary of state at the time, an appointed position, and may have triggered the attack on

PROFILE Burr–Hamilton Duel

On July 11, 1804, the second-highest-ranking American politician confronted another prominent politician in a deadly duel. Vice President Aaron Burr faced Alexander Hamilton, former secretary of the treasury, near Weehawken, New Jersey. The two men had once been friends but had fallen out over a clash of political philosophy and ambitions. Burr was a Democratic Republican, and Hamilton, a leading force among the Federalists. In a campaign for governor of New York, one of Hamilton's friends opposed Burr, who lost the election, causing further friction. This and other political differences fueled a personal animosity that led Burr to challenge Hamilton to a duel. In their encounter on July 11, he shot and wounded Hamilton, who died the following day. The dueling pistols used in this confrontation had also been used in 1801 by Philip Hamilton, Alexander's son, in another duel triggered by a political argument; the Hamilton heir was killed in that fight. According to legend, these guns were used in a total of eleven fatal duels. In the ethics of the day, duels were common but illegal and the official response, if any, varied. In this case, a grand jury in New York City indicted Burr for a misdemeanor ("challenging to a duel"). In the New Jersey county where the action took place, another grand jury indicted him for murder. The vice president ignored both charges and returned to his duties in Washington, D.C. No further legal action on either charge was ever pursued.[12]

his brother because of the position, which was coveted by others. Then, as now, accusations of wrongdoing were sometimes used as a political tactic. Samuel regained his seat in an election held in late 1809.[13]

Humphrey Marshall (1760–1841), Federalist member of the Kentucky state legislature and formerly a U.S. senator (he was also a cousin of John Marshall, Chief Justice of the Supreme Court) opposed a state

resolution sponsored by Henry Clay (1777– 1852), a Republican and at the time secretary of state of Kentucky. Clay's resolution required state legislators to wear suits made of homespun fabric instead of imported British cloth. An angry debate led to Clay hitting Marshall in the face, then challenging him to a duel. Both men were wounded in this confrontation. During his earlier term in Congress, Marshall was accused of fraudulent activity, but the Senate voted not to deal with the issue because it had occurred before Marshall had been elected.[14]

Henry Clay

On December 4, 1809, John George Jackson (1777–1825), Republican representative from Virginia, engaged in a duel with Joseph Pearson (1776–1834), Federalist representative from North Carolina. Pearson was seriously wounded, and Jackson was permanently crippled from a shot to the leg during the encounter. The fight involved political disagreements in Congress over negotiations with Spain about the Yazoo Lands. Jackson offered other challenges related to the same issue, but no others resulted in violence.[15]

In 1809, just after leaving office as president, Thomas Jefferson was sued by Edward Livingston (1764–1836), a politician from Louisiana and formerly from New York, where he had been a U.S. representative and senator, as well as mayor of New York City. Livingston owned land near New Orleans, but was evicted by the federal government in 1805

PROFILE   Yazoo Land Fraud

The so-called Yazoo Lands spanned most of present-day Alabama and Mississippi. The area, about 35 million acres, was claimed by the state of Georgia as well as several Native American tribes. The Georgia legislature sold the entire parcel in 1795 to four companies for about one and a half cents an acre. The land was then carved up and resold in smaller parcels at a huge profit to the original speculators. The buyers included groups of businessmen from Georgia and other states, as well as state and national elected officials. To help push the deal through the Georgia state legislature, shares of land were offered as bribes. The following year, news of the sale triggered major negative publicity because of the corrupt politics involved. A new reform legislature was elected as a result, and it promptly nullified the sale. The original bill authorizing the sale was symbolically burned as a public statement of this cleansing. In 1802, the entire Yazoo territory was ceded by Georgia to the federal government, ultimately leading to the creation of two new states, Alabama and Mississippi. However, in the interim, some parcels were bought and sold several times over, and ownership of large chunks ended up in the hands of New England businesses, all potential losers if a nullification of the Georgia sale could be engineered. In 1806, the U.S. House opened an investigation into the issue, because several senators and congressmen were beneficiaries of the original sale. In 1810, the is-

1800 1819

sue landed in the U.S. Supreme Court, which ruled that Georgia had to honor its original contracts, a contentious ruling because it turned out that at least one Supreme Court justice had benefited from Yazoo investments.[16]

"Burning the Yazoo Act," an illustration published in Georgia school textbooks in the 1800s.

because of nonpayment of federal funds. In lieu of payment, the land reverted to the government. After years of legal wrangling, Livingston's claim was upheld—although his suit against Jefferson was dismissed—and upon payment of his debt, he got the land back. In 1831, he was appointed U.S. secretary of state.[17]

On August 28, 1816, two politicians in St. Genevieve, Missouri territory, settled their differences with firearms. Auguste De Mun and William McArthur were both running for seats in the legislature when McArthur challenged De Mun to a duel because his opponent suggested he had ties to counterfeiters. De Mun, however, followed the prevailing cultural code, which did not allow a gentleman such as himself to fight an honorable duel with someone who was lower in social rank—namely, his opponent. Instead, De Mun confronted McArthur in the St. Genevieve town square in a less formal encounter. In the ensuing exchange of pistol shots, he was shot and killed.[18]

Daniel Tompkins

At the end of the gubernatorial campaign of 1816 in New York, incumbent Republican governor, Daniel D. Tompkins (1774–1825), was reelected. During the campaign, the opposing Federalist party accused Tompkins of misusing both state and federal funds. The allegations involved transactions Tompkins undertook with his own money to support the War of 1812. The charges brought about a long-running series of hearings in New York over what was owed and who owed it, eventually resulting in a trial in U.S. district court in 1822, after Tompkins had been elected vice president of the United States. He was completely vindicated in this trial, but when he died a few years later, broke, he had still not been paid back.[19]

Before Missouri became a state and Thomas Hart Benton (1782–1858) was elected a U.S. senator (in 1821), he was involved in several duels while he was practicing law. One of these occurred on August 12,

1817. He was opposed by Charles Lucas, a lawyer and son of a noted Missouri judge who had argued a case against Benton. Disagreements from their legal battle escalated into a personal confrontation, ending in the August duel, in which Lucas was hit in the throat by a bullet and almost died. Benton, slightly wounded in the encounter, demanded a rematch. On September 23, after Lucas had recovered sufficiently, the two opposed each other again on "Bloody Island," a notorious dueling site on the Mississippi River, across from St. Louis. Firing at each other with pistols at a distance of ten feet, Lucas was hit by a fatal shot.[20]

1800 1819

Thomas Hart Benton

In 1816, Armistead Thomson Mason (1787–1819), former Democratic Republican senator from Virginia, moved and ran for office in a new district. In a notably bitter campaign, political arguments triggered several duels, the last of which resulted in Mason's death on February 6, 1819. His final fight was at the Bladensburg, Maryland, dueling grounds outside of Washington, D.C. His opponent was John Mason McCarty, his brother-in-law.[21]

On March 12, 1804, John Pickering (1737–1805) became the first federal official to be removed from office by impeachment. Pickering, a U.S. district court judge in New Hampshire, had been appointed by President Washington but was targeted for replacement by Jefferson in a move to control the judiciary. The judge's peculiar behavior provided a rationale for attack, as well as a complex issue for the first use of the impeachment standard. Pickering might have been clinically insane by the standards of any era—among his known symptoms were hypochondria and a fear of crossing water—and he attracted animosity from both friends and foes because of his belligerent behavior, not the least of which was the frequent use of profanity while hearing cases. Plus, he was a heavy drinker. During one of his federal trials, Pickering postponed the proceedings in order to have time to get

PROFILE   Dueling Politicians

By the late 1700s, dueling was an entrenched part of the culture of the upper classes even though it was often outlawed and shunned by many individuals. The culture of the duel came to the United States from Europe, where the "code duello" provided twenty-six rules of proper dueling etiquette. It was not universally acceptable to participate in a duel, either by challenging or by accepting a challenge, and by the 1800s, most states had laws that prohibited the activity. Among elected officials, duels played a noticeable role in local and national politics up to the Civil War, mostly in the southern states. Although typically fought in private, duels by politicians were often well publicized—in advance and after the fact—even if, as in most cases, they ended with a handshake before any violence took place.[22]

1800 1819

Some politicians killed in duels:

• Delegate to the Continental Congress Button Gwinnett (Georgia), 1777.

• Governor George Wells (Georgia), 1780.

• State Senator Richard Spaight (North Carolina), 1802.

• Former Secretary of the Treasury Alexander Hamilton, 1804.

• U.S. Senator Armistead Mason (Virginia), 1819.

• U.S. District Attorney Joshua Barton (Missouri), 1823.

• Territorial Supreme Court Justice Joseph Selden (Arkansas), 1824.

• U.S. Representative Robert Vance (North Carolina), 1827.

• Territorial Representative Henry Conway (Arkansas), 1827.

• U.S. Representative Spencer Pettis (Missouri), 1831.

• U.S. Representative Jonathan Cilley (Maine), 1838.

• State Representative Augustus Alston (Georgia), 1839.

• U.S. Senator George Waggaman (Louisiana), 1843.

• U.S. Representative Edward Gilbert (California), 1852.

• U.S. Senator Solomon Downs (Louisiana), 1854.

• U.S. Senator David Broderick (California), 1859.

• State Representative William Lake (Mississippi), 1861.

sober; the questionable ruling in this case was one of the issues examined in the House hearings. With no other recourse to remove a federal judge from office, impeachment was reserved for cases of treason, bribery, high crimes, and misdemeanors, leaving Pickering—who refused to resign—with a singular defense: insanity. That is, if considered insane, he could not be removed because this condition did not fit any of the prescribed causes for conviction. A letter from his son claimed the judge was "for more than two years before, and ever since has been, and now is, insane, his mind wholly deranged, and altogether incapable of transacting any kind of business which requires the exercise of judgment, or the faculties of reason." Nevertheless, both the Senate and the House voted to expel him.[23]

Samuel Chase

1800 1819

In 1805, Samuel Chase (1741–1811), associate justice of the U.S. Supreme Court, was impeached by the House. Chase was accused of misconduct during several critical court cases involving treason and sedition. According to some elected officials—including President Jefferson—he appeared to make decisions based on a political preference, and in one instance included political content in a presentation to a grand jury. The House found this adequate grounds to begin the impeachment process, but when his case moved to the Senate, the vote came up short of the two-thirds majority necessary for conviction. In essence, he was acquitted because his actions did not meet the standards of a criminal act, a decision that set an important precedent for future impeachments.[24]

1820–1839

In 1832, President Jackson vehemently vetoed a controversial bill rechartering the national bank, declaring it a "hydra of corruption," as well as un-American. In the campaign leading up to the bill's passage, politics and corruption played key roles. Jackson's veto, the act of a president thought to be above corruption himself, brought an abrupt and surprising end to this event. In this same period, however, Jackson engineered the Indian Removal Act, which provided federal muscle—and legal grounds—to transfer most Native Americans in the South to land west of the Mississippi. The "Trail of Tears" that resulted from this forced transplant stood in stark contrast to the land speculation that it made possible, speculation that played a role in the removal. Jackson is not known to have accepted bribes for his leadership in this event, but bore responsibility. On a lesser scale, he was also the one responsible for appointing Samuel Swartwout to be collector of the Port of New York. When Swartwout abruptly left the country for England in 1838, he had the distinction of being the first person to steal more than $1 million from the U.S. government.

On June 30, 1823, a duel was held on "Bloody Island" in the Mississippi River in St. Louis, Missouri. The duelists were Joshua Barton, U.S. district attorney and previously the first secretary of state of Missouri, and Thomas Rector, standing in for his brother, General William Rector, the U.S. surveyor for the region. Barton had previously accused the general of corruption, prompting the challenge. The duel ended with Barton dead.[1]

Joseph Selden, justice of the Arkansas territorial supreme court, was killed on May 26, 1824, in a duel with Andrew Scott, another justice of the court. The duel was held in the state of Mississippi, across the

Mississippi River from Helena, Arkansas, because dueling was illegal in Arkansas.[2]

During the election campaign of 1824, Secretary of the Treasury William Crawford (1772–1834), a Democratic Republican, former secretary of war, and former senator from Georgia, suffered from a string of attacks. Among these were a charge that he had engaged in the illegal sale of slaves, while secretary of war had treated Cherokee Indians too fairly in upholding their treaty rights—white settlers in Tennessee burned him in effigy for this favoritism—and had mismanaged federal funds at the Treasury Department. The latter allegations were included in a series of fifteen letters published in a Washington, D.C., newspaper, signed only with the initials "A.B." Crawford successfully defended himself against these charges, which were politically motivated, but lost the election to John Quincy Adams. During this era, letters published in newspapers—often unsigned or signed with fictitious nicknames—were a favorite method for political attacks.[3]

James Monroe

President James Monroe (1758–1831) was the object of three investigations by Congress into his expenditures for furniture. Following the burning of the White House in 1814 and Monroe's inauguration in 1817, the official presidential residence had not been fully restored nor its furnishings replaced. An agreement was reached between Congress and Monroe, allowing the new president to use his own furniture, which would be purchased with government funds and sold back to him after he left office, with the transactions of the "Furniture Fund" monitored by two government appointees, William Lee and Samuel Lane, both friends of Monroe. When Lane died, a large sum of government money was unaccounted for, and questions were raised regarding the president's potential profits from the furniture deal. The investigations turned up no evidence of improper conduct on the part of Monroe but the affair did generate negative publicity.[4]

In 1826, John Randolph (1773–1833), U.S. senator from Virginia, and Secretary of State Henry Clay (1777–1852) fought a bloodless duel, firing several rounds at each other before shaking hands. Both men were Republicans. The duel resulted from statements Randolph made during a debate in the Senate over an amendment to the Constitution that would provide for the direct election of the president and vice president. In his argument, Randolph had compared Clay and President Adams to two disreputable characters in the novel *Tom Jones*.[5]

John Randolph

1820 1839

Sam Houston (1793–1863), unaffiliated representative from Tennessee (and later Democratic senator and governor of Texas), was a supporter of General Andrew Jackson (then a Democratic Republican from Tennessee) and quarreled with General William White, who was politically opposed to Jackson. Houston and White fought a duel triggered by their political differences on September 21, 1826, while standing on the border between Kentucky and Tennessee. White was wounded in the exchange of fire but Houston escaped injury. Although he was known to have been challenged several other

Sam Houston

times in his life, Houston never again gave or accepted a dueling challenge.[6]

Robert Brank Vance (1793–1827), U.S. representative from North Carolina, was mortally wounded during a duel in 1827 with Samuel Price Carson (1798–1838), who had beaten him in his campaign for reelection. The duel took place in Saluda Gap, North Carolina, and was triggered by a comment made by Vance during the election campaign, in which he stated that Carson's father had "turned Tory" during the Revolution.[7]

In 1827, Henry Conway (1793–1827), a delegate from the Arkansas Territory, dueled with Robert Crittenden (1797–1834), the territorial secretary of state. The two men had a falling out when Crittenden switched his political support from Conway to an opponent.

Crittenden challenged Conway to a duel, which was held across the Mississippi River in Mississippi because dueling was illegal in Arkansas. Wounded in the duel, Conway died eleven days later, on November 9.[8]

During the presidential election campaign of 1828, Democratic candidate Andrew Jackson (1767–1845) was politically attacked from several fronts. One rival published a pamphlet titled "The Indiscretions of Andrew Jackson," in which the author listed 103 violent encounters and unethical activities the hot-tempered candidate had reportedly been guilty of. Several of these were duels, one of them resulting in a fatality. In that encounter, in 1806, Jackson shot and killed a man in a dispute over the payment of a gambling debt involving Jackson's best racing horse. Opponents also singled out Jackson for "living in sin" with his wife, Rachel, because she had reportedly married Jackson before she had been legally divorced from her first husband. A newspaper editorial at the time stated, "Ought a convicted adulteress and her paramour husband be placed in the highest offices of this free and Christian land?" In response, Jackson scheduled a second marriage ceremony. On the opposing side of the race, Federalist candidate John Quincy Adams was accused of having had premarital sex with his wife, not to mention she had been born an illegitimate child.[9]

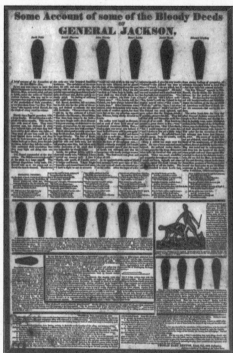

An early form of attack ad was the political poster. This 1828 poster exposes candidate Andrew Jackson's past. Among his alleged misdeeds are the deaths of six militiamen who were executed on his orders during the Creek War.

　The Petticoat War

President Andrew Jackson (1767–1845), already smarting from campaign attacks charging he had not been lawfully married to his wife, ran afoul of new scandals just after he was elected. One of the messiest became known as the "Petticoat War." It was initiated by John Eaton, a close friend of the president, after he was appointed secretary of war. Eaton was romantically linked to Margaret Timberlake, an attractive widow who had a somewhat dubious reputation—not deserved, by most accounts—among Washington's elite. After she married Eaton, the wives of the other members of the cabinet refused, because of Mrs. Eaton's reputation, to call on or receive her socially, a major breach of protocol. The affair esca-

lated over the course of a few years—despite a strong defense of Eaton and his wife from the president—culminating in a mass resignation of the cabinet in 1831, after Jackson attempted to force a resolution. Although major partisan politics were at play at the time, the public and many Washington politicians concluded the issue was mostly about social standards. According to some contemporary accounts, a popular toast was "To the next cabinet—may they all be bachelors—or leave their wives at home."[10]

A political cartoon about the mass resignation of President Jackson's cabinet in 1831. The title: "The Rats Leaving a Falling House."

"Carrying the *War* into Africa."

Jinnoowine
JOHNSON TICKET.

This election ticket for the campaign of 1836 makes a racist appeal against Richard Johnson because of his nonwhite mistress. The caption reads: "Let ebery good dimicrat vote for my husband, and den he shall hab his sheer ub de surplum rebbenu wat is in my bag."

During the 1828 election campaign in Kentucky, Senate candidate Richard Mentor Johnson (1780–1850) lost the support of his party, the Democratic Republicans. Although he had already served several terms in Congress, Johnson became a political liability due to his openly living with, though not being married to, Julia Chin, a slave he had inherited. Johnson fathered two children with Chin, who died in 1833. He was later successful in a bid for a seat in the House, and in 1837 was elected vice president of the United States despite lingering political ill effects related to publicity about his private life. While serving in this office, he stirred up more scandal and embarrassment for the president. Deeply in debt, the vice president opened a hotel and tavern in White Sulphur Spring, Kentucky, where it was reported he was living with "a young Delilah of about the complexion of Shakespears swarthy Othello."[11]

1820 1839

In 1829, Dr. Tobias Watkins, former auditor with the treasury department, was convicted and sent to prison for embezzling more than $7,000 ($151,000 in today's dollars) while he was serving in the administration of President Adams. His public trial was an embarrassment to the former president, but did not implicate him. Watkins stole the money on his own in order to cover gambling debts.[12]

On April 24, 1830, James Hawkins Peck (1790–1836), U.S. district court judge in Missouri, was impeached by the House and tried on a charge of "usurpation and exercise of arbitrary power." The judge was accused of imprisoning a lawyer for twenty-four hours and suspending his license for eighteen months after the lawyer had published an article criticizing one of Peck's legal opinions. The Senate found him not guilty the following year.[13]

Spencer Darwin Pettis (1802–1831), recently elected Jacksonian U.S. representative from Missouri, was killed in a duel on August 26, 1831, in the aftermath of a bitter election campaign. His opponent was Major Thomas Biddle, who also died from wounds suffered in the duel. According to contemporary accounts, the men were only five feet apart when they drew their pistols, and the barrels of the guns overlapped as they fired. Their violent encounter took place on "Bloody Island" on the Mississippi River, across from St. Louis. The instigation was an article written by Biddle, in which he opposed Pettis' election using terms that Pettis felt were designed to "render him contemptible in the eyes of his constituents." Pettis was the challenger, giving to Biddle, by custom, the choice of weapon. He selected flintlock pistols that had previously been owned by Aaron Burr and had been used in his fatal duel with Alexander Hamilton.[14]

1820 1839

Governor William Marcy was depicted in political cartoons with a prominent patch on his trousers.

In the election of 1832, the governor's race in New York was between Francis Granger (1792–1868), a state assemblyman, and William Learned Marcy (1786–1857), a U.S. senator. The former was backed by the National Republicans and the latter by the Jacksonian Democrats. The campaign was marked by mudslinging and a variety of charges. In one, Marcy was accused of requesting official reimbursement for fifty cents he had spent on having his trousers mended, resulting in a taunting nickname, "Marcy pantaloons." Nevertheless, he managed to withstand the personal attacks and won the election.[15]

On January 30, 1835, Richard Lawrence, an unemployed housepainter, attacked President Andrew Jackson inside the House of Representatives during a funeral service. Lawrence had two pistols, but both of them misfired. Following this event, the president instigated an investigation into George Poindexter (1779–1853), Republican senator from Mississippi and a noted political foe of the president.

Jackson and others, including some newspapers, accused Poindexter of organizing the assassination attempt, the first in the history of the presidency. A Senate committee concluded there was no evidence that implicated Poindexter in the event; two witnesses who testified against him were found not believable. But the senator, reportedly an "irascible" man, was not reelected and never served in public office again.[16]

Jonathan Cilley (1802–1838), U.S. representative from Maine, was killed in a duel with William J. Graves (1805–1848), U.S. representative from Kentucky, on February 24, 1838. Cilley, a Democrat, and Graves, a Whig, had political disagreements, but the challenge for the duel was personal and instigated by Graves. It began when Cilley criticized James Watson Webb, a newspaper editor and Whig supporter, for publishing an article linking Cilley with corruption. The editor wrote a note requesting that Cilley detail his complaints. Graves was selected to deliver the note, but it was refused by Cilley, who commented that it would not be accepted because it came from "a person of disputed respectability." Although Cilley was referring to Webb, Graves took it as a personal insult, believing it was intended for him as well as the editor. Their duel took place on the Marlboro Pike just outside of Washington, D.C. The loss of a prominent politician generated wide-

1820
1839

Public sympathy was high for Congressman Jonathan Cilley after he died in a duel in 1838. Political allies and many citizens believed that the killing was provoked by James Webb, a well-known newspaper editor and political rabble-rouser. Following the duel, various threats were made against Webb, prompting this cartoon, which shows the editor parading brazenly in public, daring retaliation. The caption reads: "I'm a small Army in Myself: I am afraid there is not much danger here after all."

PROFILE   Robert Potter

1820 1839

One of the few politicians to leave a legacy in more than one state, Robert Potter (c.1800–1842) had a remarkable history. A native of North Carolina, he was a midshipman in the U.S. Navy and then a lawyer in Halifax County. In 1826 and 1828, Potter was elected to the North Carolina State House of Commons, but not without a fight. Literally. After his first attempt at election in 1824 led to a defeat at the polls, he charged his opponent, the incumbent, with fraud and challenged him to a duel. Refusing to fight, the incumbent and his supporters were then attacked by Potter—well known for his reckless temperament—and a group of his friends, leading to one death and

several injuries. The event, which occurred in Potter's hometown, was labeled "The Hell in Halifax." Because of the threat of continued violence, the election in 1825 was canceled, but Potter finally succeeded in ousting his opponent in the election of 1826. During his term in office, Potter was involved in a number of political issues that attracted contention, chief among them a bill he sponsored to create a free college for poor young men. Attacking his adversaries in rhyme, Potter called one "a squinting, skipping, squatting, squalling elf ..." but not only did he fail to gather enough support to pass the bill, he failed to convince voters to return him to office in the next election. He then ran for and was elected as a state representative to the U.S. Congress (Sixth District), where he served beginning in 1829. But in 1831 in his home state, he was involved in a violent attack on two men—one a

Methodist preacher and the other a cousin by marriage—because he suspected both of being "too familiar" with his wife. Potter hog-tied the preacher and castrated him and then repeated his actions on the other suspected paramour. A widely reported event at the time, the term "potterize" was quickly adopted to refer to castration; it is still in limited use today in some parts of the South. Potter was tried and convicted of his crime and spent six months in jail, meanwhile resigning his seat in Congress. But he was hardly through with politics. While incarcerated, he ran a successful campaign to return to the state house of commons; his new term of service began in 1834. The following year, however, he was expelled, allegedly for "cheating at cards," but more likely because of his notoriety and ongoing political rivalry. Whether or not his future in politics in North Carolina was doomed, Potter responded to his situation by moving to Texas to join in the fight for independence. There, he was an official delegate from Nacogdoches in 1835 and 1836 and was one of the original signers of the Texas Declaration of Independence. He also fought in at least one battle against the Mexican Army and, because of his previous experience at sea, accepted an appointment as the secretary of the Texas navy. He landed in political hot water once again when he started a campaign to remove the popular hero Sam Houston as head of the Texas army. By then divorced from his first wife, Potter married a woman he befriended during the Texas revolution, even though she was already married. While serving as a representative to the Texas congress, he was assassinated in 1842 during the violent feud in east Texas known as the Regulator-Modulator War. Back in North Carolina, one final legacy of his infamous attack came from the state government, which passed "An Act to Amend the Law Relative to Malicious and Unlawful Maiming and Wounding." This legislation upgraded the crime of castration from a misdemeanor to a hanging offense.[17]

1820 1839

spread protests against dueling. On February 20, 1839, a congressional act was passed prohibiting duels in the District of Columbia.[18]

In 1838, Alexander McNutt (1802–1848), Democratic governor of Mississippi, and Seargent Smith Prentiss (1808–1850), a Whig, campaigned against each other for a seat in the U.S. House. McNutt attacked Prentiss by calling him a habitual drunk, prompting Prentiss, a lengendary orator, to reply: "My fellow-citizens, you have heard the charge against my morals, sagely, and, I had almost said, soberly made by the gentleman...had I said this, it would have been what the lawyers term a misnomer. It would be impossible for him to do or say anything soberly, for he has been drunk ten years; not yesterday, or last week, in a frolic, or, socially, with the good fellows, his friends, at the genial and generous board—but at home, and by himself and demijohn; not upon the rich wines of the Rhine or the Rhone, the Saone or the Guadalquivir; not with high-spirited or high-witted men, whose souls, when mellowed with glorious wine, leap from their lips sublimated in words swollen with wit, or thought brilliant and dazzling as the blood of the grape inspiring them—no; but by himself: selfish and apart from witty men, or ennobling spirits, in the secret seclusion of a dirty little back-room, and on corn-whiskey! Why, fellow-citizens, as the Governor of the State, he refused to sign the gallon-law until he had tested, by experiment, that a gallon would do him all day!"[19]

The state election in Pennsylvania in 1838 featured a confrontation between the Whig party, supporting Joseph Ritner (1780–1869), the governor, and David Rittenhouse Porter (1788–1867), the Democratic candidate. Porter appeared to be the winner with an edge of about 5,500 votes, but Ritner and his backers claimed election fraud and refused to acknowledge defeat. The confrontation escalated to a physical showdown when armed crowds congregated at the state house. Ritner issued a call to defend his office, suggesting supporters arm themselves with shotguns, which gave the incident its name, the "Buckshot War." A newspaper article at the time reported "Of all the state elections, that in the Key Stone [sic] rages most violently." In the end, the election results validated Porter.[20]

In 1838, Samuel Swartwout (1738–1856), in charge of customs collections for the Port of New York, left the country for England and was accused of embezzling $1,225,705.69 in federal funds ($26.5 million in today's dollars). Swartwout's position—and that of other port collectors—was a highly prized patronage job because of the kickbacks, as well as its prestige. When he lobbied for the job, Swartwout wrote in a letter, "Whether or not I shall get anything in the general scramble for plunder remains to be seen." Swartwout's theft was a major scandal for the administration of President Van Buren, although he had originally been appointed by President Jackson. Jesse Hoyt, the collector appointed to replace Swartwout—and the recipient of the letter quoted above—was later accused of embezzlement as well.[21]

An 1838 political cartoon showing Samuel Swartwout arriving in London. He is shown greeting William Price, a federal district attorney, who had also fled the United States after embezzling a similar amount.

1820 1839

Augustus Alston (1805–1839), former member of the Georgia house and aspiring politician in the territory of Florida, challenged Leigh Read (1809–1841), a political foe, to a duel on December 12, 1839, following an election defeat. Alston, known as "The Bulldog of the Party"—the Whigs—was an experienced duelist. Read, a Democrat, initially ignored the challenge, but Alston persisted, sending one of his slaves to post a public notice stating that Read was a "Coward and a Scoundrel," an act that convinced him to fight. The weapons were large-caliber rifles at fifteen paces. During the event, Alston's rifle misfired as he was turning and he missed his opponent. Read's shot hit its mark, killing Alston. Read was killed a few years later in a revenge attack by one of Alston's brothers.[2]

1840–1859

This period witnessed the first large-scale abuses of government funds, many triggered by land grants associated with the development of the national railroad system. Along with the rapid growth of companies that preyed on investors eager to cash in on this expansion of the transportation system, some politicians were just as enticed by the opportunities. One contemporary observer noted of a particularly bold speculator, "As he trailed his garments across the country, the members of twenty legislatures rustled like dry leaves in a winter's wind." One state in particular, New Jersey, was known to be so thoroughly in the clutches of railroad influence that it was sometimes called the Camden & Amboy State, after the largest regional railroad company. In 1841, a member of the U.S. House of Representatives was convicted of forgery and sent to the infamous Sing Sing Prison (he was later pardoned due to poor health), the first nationally elected official to be found guilty of this crime. Although many more accusations and indictments were to follow, few nationally elected politicians ended up behind bars for their misdeeds.

In the 1840 presidential campaign, Democrats attacked their Whig opponents by ridiculing their noted emphasis on alcohol to woo voters. Alcohol was widely used by both parties—a practice referred to as "treating"— but at the time it was popularly associated with the Whigs. The Whig candidate for president was William Henry Harrison, known as "Old Tippecanoe," but his nickname was sometimes altered to "Old

A political illustration entitled "Hard cider triumphant."

Tip-ler." One election song included the lyrics:
> Hush-a-bye baby;
> Daddy's a Whig.
> Before he comes home,
> Hard cider he'll swig;
> Then he'll be Tipsy and over he'll fall;
> Down will come Daddy,
> Tip, Tyler, and all.[1]

A month after he left office in March 1841, Charles Franklin Mitchell (1808–1865), Whig representative from New York, was convicted of forgery, the first elected national official to be found guilty of this offense. Mitchell was accused of writing forged checks in the amount of $1,400 ($32,000 in today's dollars) and cashing them in New York City. He fled the city, leaving behind a letter in which he stated "I have been accused by my enemies of being a great intriguer, of being a great schemer in politics, and I suppose, now that I have schemed in other matters, they will take upon themselves, no doubt, great credit for their sagacity in thus characterising [*sic*] me." He was captured, tried, convicted, and sentenced to three years at Sing Sing Prison, a notorious state penitentiary, but was pardoned by Governor Bouck and released before he completed his sentence, because of poor health.[2]

James Shields

Abraham Lincoln (1809–1865), state legislator from Illinois and the future president of the United States, was challenged to a duel by James Shields (1810–1879), the state auditor for Illinois, in September 1842. Shields, a Democrat, had been ridiculed in a satirical letter that Lincoln had published in the *Sangamon Journal* (Springfield, Illinois) on August 27, suggesting he was deficient in his job and should return to his home country, Ireland. Although he used an assumed name, Lincoln's identity was revealed to the irate Shields by the paper's editor, after which Shields challenged Lincoln to a duel. To avoid the illegality of dueling in Illinois, the pair and an accompanying party rowed across the Mississippi River to Missouri to fulfill their mission, which was to be fought with "cavalry broadswords of the largest size"—the choice of weapon was Lincoln's, according to tradition. Before the fight could begin, an acceptable accommodation was reached, with Lincoln offering an apology. Shields went on to become the only U.S. senator to be elected from three states—Illinois, Minnesota, and Missouri—was appointed governor of the Oregon Territory, and served as an officer in both the Mexican War and Civil War. Lincoln rarely mentioned this incident.[3]

1840 1859

On June 25, 1842, Thomas Francis Marshall (1801–1864), Whig representative from Kentucky, fought a duel with James Watson Webb, the editor of the *Courier and Examiner,* a newspaper in New York City. Noted for his strong political views, Webb was not only a Whig, but some sources give him the credit for giving the party its name (he borrowed it from the British political scene); it had previously been called the Republican Democrat party. In 1842, Webb trig-

James Webb

gered Marshall's anger through personal attacks in newspaper articles covering Marshall's action as a defense attorney in the trial of a swindler. In one article he wrote "...we are quite certain that there is not a female in the city who will read the speech of Mr. Marshall...but will agree with all those who heard it that he is 'as harmless as a sucking dove.'" The disagreement turned personal and Marshall challenged Webb to the duel. The event, which ended with the editor wounded in the leg, was witnessed by an estimated 150 people. Webb was convicted in New York of the crime of dueling and was briefly jailed before receiving a pardon from the governor. He was later appointed ambassador to Brazil by President Lincoln. Marshall was not cited.[4]

In December 1843, Felix Grundy McConnell (1809–1846), a Democratic representative from Alabama, generated a minor scandal when he was thrown out of a theater for "rioting and disturbance." This was not the first or the last time McConnell created a public scene. He was noted for brawling and drunkenness both in his home state and in Washington, D.C. One episode that provoked a public outrage occurred during a concert by the famed classical violinist Ole Bull. In the middle of Bull's performance, McConnell shouted from the audience, "None of your high-falutin, but give us 'Hail Columbia,' and bear hard on the treble!" It took the efforts of several policemen, and their clubs, to overpower the congressman and remove him from the concert hall. Although McConnell was credited with some useful work in Congress, he managed to stir things up there as well. In December 1845, he presented a resolution proposing that the United States annex Ireland. On September 10, 1846, he created a final splash. According to a newspaper report at the time, "Felix G. McConnell, member of Congress from Alabama, terminated his life of mixed good and ill, on Thursday, by stabbing himself with a knife at Washington City. No doubt can be entertained that Mr. McConnell committed the act in a state of mental hallucination—most probably under the influence of delirium tremens, brought on by his intemperate course of life. It appears that he inflicted two wounds upon his throat, and five upon his body with a jack-knife, producing almost instantaneous death."[5]

1840 / 1859

George Augustus Waggaman (1782–1843), former anti-Jacksonian U.S. senator from Louisiana, died on March 31, 1843, from injuries received in a duel held on March 10 in New Orleans. Waggaman's antagonist was Denis Prieur (1791–1857), former mayor of the city. According to some reports, the two men had a long-standing disagreement involved with "family affairs."[6]

Benjamin Tappan

On May 16, 1844, the Senate voted to censure Benjamin Tappan (1773–1857 for violating confidentiality rules. Tappan, a Democrat from Ohio, admitted sending a copy of a secret document to a newspaper, knowing it would be published. The document was a proposal from President Tyler defining an annexation agreement for Texas, a topic that was strongly tied to the hot political issue of slavery. Although censured, Tappan escaped a more serious punishment, expulsion.[7]

On May 16, 1844, the Senate voted to allow one of its members, John M. Niles (1787–1856), Democrat from Connecticut, to be seated as a legitimate member after first questioning his qualifications. Niles had been reelected by the Connecticut legislature in 1843 but delayed beginning his term for more than a year. He spent most of this time ill—according to rumors, mentally as well as physically—and finally showed up for work on the advice of his doctor, who believed it would do him some good. A Senate committee investigation was launched by the opposing Whig party, mostly on the grounds that Niles suffered "an alienation of the mind," but ultimately skirted the question of mental competency, voting only on the legitimacy of his election.[8]

On April 23, 1844, in the House of Representatives, a debate was held on the merits of charges that had previously been made against Henry Clay, including corruption and "intrigue." Defending Clay was the Speaker of the House, John White, a Whig from Kentucky; attacking him was George Oscar Rathbun (1803–1870), Democratic representative from New York. The debate escalated to a heated argument and White and Rathbun began striking each other, causing dozens of their colleagues to rush to pull them apart. During this disturbance, a visitor unknown to any of the congressmen jumped into the fray. Pulling a pistol before he could be seized, he fired a shot into the crowd, wounding a police officer assigned to the Capitol. White and Rathbun subsequently apologized for their behavior and were censured by the House.[9]

In the presidential campaign of 1844, one of the first known political dirty tricks played a major role in the election. A false story was published in Whig newspapers describing a man named Roorback, a slaveholder, who had discovered a group of slaves formerly owned by Democratic candidate James Polk (1795–1849). These slaves were de-

scribed as branded with Polk's initials, an indictment of slave ownership—already becoming onerous at the national political level—as
well as callousness, since the circumstances suggested that Polk had
sold them in order to raise money for his campaign. The letter was attacked as a forgery—headlines read "Infamous Forgery!" "A Most
Dastardly Cheat!" and "Fruitless attempt to deceive the People!"—with
Polk going on the defensive to deny his involvement. The publicity
may have lost him some votes, but the response also gained him some
sympathy for being the target of such a dirty trick. Since then, any false
document created to undermine a political campaign has been called
a "roorback."[10]

In 1845, Daniel Webster (1782–1852) was reelected as a U.S. senator
from Massachusetts. He had previously served terms as a U.S. representative from that state as well as New Hampshire, had been secretary
of state in two different presidential administrations, and was an unsuccessful candidate for president in 1836. After the 1845 election,
Webster was investigated by a congressional committee for "malfeasance" while he had been secretary of state, a charge that was not
proven, but other disclosures involving his personal finances developed into a scandal. During the campaign, his wealthy backers had

Daniel Webster and James Polk square off over the issue of the Mexican War and the
annexation of Texas. A political print from 1846.

created a fund for him to use to pay personal debts; he was also given an annuity from a life insurance company. According to a political critic writing at the time, "He is a prostitute in morals and something worse in politics....Loose in money matters, tainted with fraud, fixed in profligacy, he is a living ulcer and infection." Webster's issues with finances did not stop him from being elected, but hampered his opportunities for appointments and higher offices. Webster, a prominent Whig leader, was also opposed to the war with Mexico, a conflict that seemed intended primarily to allow the annexation of Texas. This made him a frequent target of political and personal attacks from Democrats and the Democratic administration of President Polk.[11]

Daniel Webster

On January 15, 1845, a duel was fought near Beltsville, Maryland, by Thomas Lanier Clingman (1812–1897), Whig representative from North Carolina, and William Lowndes Yancey (1814–1863), a Democratic representative from Alabama. The event was precipitated by Yancey's first speech on the floor of the House, in which he belittled Clingman's honesty. The larger context was political and involved the question of slavery and its place in the annexation of Texas, but it was the personal attack that prompted the duel. The two men exchanged one round of shots, neither was hit, and they mutually agreed their honor had been upheld. Clingman, who was later elected as a Democratic senator, was expelled from Congress in 1861 for supporting secession. Yancey was a member of the first Confederate States senate and was no stranger to violence; in 1838, he killed his wife's uncle.[12]

After he was elected vice president of the United States in 1845, George Mifflin Dallas (1792–1864), an attorney by profession, continued to practice law to supplement his income. At the time, there was not a clear set of rules governing this apparent conflict of interest. In one of his cases, he was retained as part of a prominent legal team to represent a wealthy client in Philadelphia in a widely publicized di-

George Dallas

vorce case. The man was Pierce Butler, a grandson of a U.S. senator from South Carolina, and he was married to a popular stage actress, Fanny Kemble, a somewhat scandalous relationship at the time because of the seedy status associated with the theater. Dallas's involvement in the heavily publicized case attracted significant criticism, some of it politically motivated. His response was that such complaints were nothing more than the "hissing and gobbling" of "snakes and geese."[13]

During the presidential election of 1848, a forged letter was circulated undermining the candidacy of Zachary Taylor (1784–1850), a Whig. The letter stated that Taylor would not oppose the Wilmot Proviso, an amendment to a bill authorizing a payment to end the Mexican War. The add-on, sponsored by Congressman David Wilmot, stated that all of the territory to be acquired from Mexico under the terms of the bill was not to be open to slavery, a key campaign issue. Candidates for president—as well as other national positions—were closely watched to determine if they were pro- or anti-slavery, and the letter, which was published in many newspapers, falsely skewed Taylor's position. It read: "Gentlemen:—I received yours of the 5th inst., and in reply say, that I will not veto any bill that Congress may see fit to pass on internal policy, unless I deem it unconstitutional; and when the action of Congress and the Executive have ruled a question to be constitutional, I will take it as such. Yours, &c., Z. TAYLOR." The bogus letter may have lost Taylor votes, but a strong and public denial by his backers helped counter the effect. He won the election.[14]

In 1848, Samuel W. Inge (1817–1868), Democratic senator from Alabama, was challenged to a duel by Edward Stanly (1810–1872), Whig representative from North Carolina. In the confrontation, both participants were slightly wounded. The location was Bladensburg, Maryland, a favored dueling site near Washington, D.C.[15]

Francis Preston Blair Jr. (1821–1875), who served Missouri as both a Republican U.S. representative and senator, had a violent political encounter before beginning his career in Congress. In 1849, he and a political rival in Missouri wrote opposing newspaper articles about noted local politician Thomas Hart Benton. The editorial clash caused Blair to challenge his rival to a duel. Following the custom of the dueling code, the challenged party selected the weapons and location, in this case to be bowie knives at a prominent street corner in St. Louis. Blair considered this choice frivolous and an attempt to avoid a fight. He

An editorial cartoon of Francis Blair, dramatizing his reaction to the defeat of a favored bill.

did not respond. When the two men later ran into each other on a city sidewalk, however, Blair attacked the other man with his umbrella. He was arrested, pleaded guilty, and was sentenced to a fine of one dollar and a minute behind bars.[16]

On February 27, 1850, Jefferson Davis (1808–1889), Democratic senator from Mississippi, challenged William Harrison Bissell (1811–1860), Democratic representative from Illinois, to a duel. Davis was incensed at the content of a speech Bissell, a colonel during the Mexican War, delivered in Congress. In it, he suggested that Davis, while a colonel at the Battle of Buena Vista in the same war, had actually played a less important role than officially described. The duel was set for the following day—muskets at fifteen paces—but both parties withdrew after intervention by General Zachary Taylor. He was Jefferson Davis' father-in-law and a national hero for his role in the Mexican conflict.[17]

In 1850, two national politicians were involved in a heated debate that got out of hand. Henry Stuart Foote (1804–1880), Democratic senator from Mississippi, and Thomas Hart Benton (1782–1858), Democratic senator from Missouri, had feuded verbally for days. They were divided on the contentious issue of slavery—Foote pro-slavery and Benton anti—with Foote, according to most sources, the primary antagonist. At various times, Foote accused Benton of being a traitor, and at one point even maligned the "nasality" of Benton's speaking voice. On April 17, the animosity escalated to a confrontation on the floor of the Senate. Benton strode toward Foote in an apparent rage, and Foote, in response, drew a pistol. The action enraged Benton further. According to

Henry Foote

witnesses, he shouted, "Let him fire!" At that point, other members of the Senate intervened, restraining both men and disarming Foote. A subsequent committee hearing chastised both parties for their actions—although neither was censured or otherwise penalized—but blamed the Senate itself for lax attention to its own rules, which should have prevented such an event.[18]

John Anthony Quitman (1799–1858), Democratic governor of Mississippi and a former army general, was indicted in federal court in 1850. The charge was violation of the Neutrality Act, "by beginning, setting on foot and furnishing the means for a military expedition

A dramatized illustration of the confrontation between Sentators Benton and Foote.

against the Island of Cuba." Quitman was a supporter of the independence movement in Cuba, then ruled by Spain. In 1851, Quitman
resigned from office and was tried in federal court, but the case was
dismissed. The governor later was elected to the House, apparently
suffering little from the political scandal.[19]

On January 8, 1850, Joseph Barker (1806–1862) was elected mayor of
Pittsburgh. He was in prison at the time, serving a year's sentence for
causing a riot and using "indecent, lewd, and immoral language calculated to deprave the morals of the community." Barker was a nativist,
part of an anti-immigration movement that had wide support in major
cities and part of the "Know-Nothing" movement. A street preacher
and reportedly illiterate, Barker directed most of his rhetoric at
Catholics, but he also attracted large audiences speaking out against
Masons, politicians, the upper class, and foreigners in general. At the

PROFILE   Galphin Claim Scandal

In the spring of 1850, the "Galphin Claim Scandal" disrupted the administration of President Taylor. The claim in question was a plot of land in Georgia,
claimed in 1773 when the area was ceded from local Creek Indians. George
Galphin, a trader, pursued what he thought was his right to the property with
the British government. When the claim was rejected, he took it to the

Georgia provincial government, which also rejected it,
and then to the first U.S. Congress. Denied again, the
claim was presented to every session of Congress
until 1848—through six decades and several genera-
tions of Galphin heirs. For much of this time, the agent
representing Galphin was George Walker Crawford
(1798–1872), a Whig, who was a lawyer before he became a politician. He was a member of the Georgia
house, a U.S. senator, and governor. In 1849,
Crawford finally succeeded, with the help of other
Whig congressmen, in having the claim accepted by

George Crawford

same time, he was opposed to slavery and alcohol. His arrest occurred while delivering a rabble-rousing speech on a city street. After he was elected, he was pardoned by the governor and released from jail. The judge who administered the mayor's oath of office was the same one who had sent him to prison. While serving as mayor, Barker had a local Catholic bishop arrested for "maintaining a public nuisance" and then arrested him a second time, along with the mother superior of a Catholic hospital, for illegally tapping into a sewer. Following his nativist sentiments in another case, he ruled that a calliope on a boat should be allowed to play, even though accused of drowning out the music of a German American band on a nearby boat, stating "The calliope is an American institution...and I am for America all the time." In that period in the city, the mayor was also the chief of police, a job Barker took to with enthusiasm—at times making arrests himself—

the secretary of the treasury, who authorized payment of the original $43,500 in question ($1.1 million in today's dollars). Crawford then upped the ante with a further claim for interest from 1773 to 1849, an amount totaling about $191,000 ($5 million), from which he was owed about $95,000 as a fee ($2.5 million). After President Taylor, also a Whig, began his term, he appointed Crawford to be his secretary of war, and shortly thereafter granted the request. A public uproar resulted, from Whigs—who had campaigned for honesty in government—as well as Democrats. A local paper at the time editorialized, "Now if our readers do not look upon this as a most corrupt and wicked piece of business, we much mistake their character.... No other term but 'robbery' can properly characterize this transaction." For a time, the word "Galphinism" was used to refer to government corruption. Crawford was not penalized for his bonanza nor were the cabinet members who helped him— he did not tell them nor did they know that he would be benefiting from their action. President Polk, however, was censured by the House for being in charge while the scandal took place.[20]

while fighting with the city council over the department's control. At one point in his one-year term, there were two competing police forces, which sometimes fought each other. All this while he continued street preaching. He was also arrested himself more than once during his term—for assault and for causing a riot—and was back in jail shortly after his term ended on another charge of inciting a riot. Unsuccessful in his attempts to be reelected, Barker continued to speak out and get into trouble. In 1862, while returning home from a meeting, he was struck by a train and decapitated.[21]

Edward Gilbert (1819–1852), a Democratic representative from California, was involved in a duel on August 2, 1852. Gilbert had recently ended his term in Congress and was working as the editor of a newspaper in Sacramento when he challenged General James W. Denver, a state senator, to a duel. The cause of their dispute was a letter to the editor from Denver, in which Denver made disparaging remarks about Gilbert's character, a response to an article in Gilbert's paper making negative comments about the state's governor. During the duel, a first round of rifle shots did not result in any hits; Denver deliberately aimed to the side and Gilbert's shot missed its target. The fight continued to a second round, reportedly because Gilbert believed that duels were not decisive unless they resulted in bloodshed. In the second exchange, he was struck in the abdomen and died a few minutes later.[22]

In October 1854, John Meiggs, the comptroller of San Francisco, California, secretly fled the city. He was accompanied by his brother Henry, known as "Honest Harry," a city alderman, their families, and thousands of dollars of city money. Henry was later indicted for fraud, but he avoided prosecution from the safe haven of Chile.[23]

In New Orleans, Louisiana, John L. Lewis (1800–1886), a Democrat, became mayor in 1854 in an election marked by unusual violence, even by New Orleans standards. The Know-Nothing party, with a strong anti-foreign, anti-Catholic philosophy, battled with Democrats and others for control of polling places. One policeman and two voters

PROFILE Know Nothing Politics

By the 1840s, the Democratic party established strong support for immigration, a policy that paid off in large cities and major ports of entry. Newly arrived adults provided a plentiful supply of new voters, and local political organizations developed quick and effective methods of recruiting these foreigners during elections. The practice fueled already simmering resentment over immigration and helped trigger a reform political movement that opposed it while upholding traditional "American" values. The concept became known as the Know-Nothing movement because local political groups and societies that supported it were often secretive. If asked about their politics, members would say they "knew nothing." The American Republican party and the Native American party were two public forms. Know Nothing politics was anti-slavery, anti-Catholic, and anti-alcohol, along with an opposition to

foreigners. The Native American party was noted more for its racism than a rational argument about immigration. In some cities, Know-Nothing gangs routinely attacked Irish and Chinese residents, their favorite targets. Relatively few politicians were elected with this nativist backing, but popular support for the movement played a role in many elections. Before it faded away—many members drifted into the newly formed Republican party before the start of the Civil War—Know Nothing politics was a noted element in extreme violence in several major cities.[24]

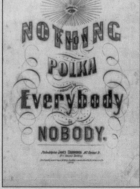

The editorial cartoon at the top illustrates New York City aldermen refusing to give jobs to noncitizens. The sheet music to the right put lyrics to the Know-Nothing philosophy opposing "foreign influence."

PATRONAGE POLITICS

From local to national offices, patronage was one of the major rewards of election. Politicians in power controlled jobs at many levels, making them a prime target for job-seekers. This illustration from the mid-1800s depicts one result, a frantic scramble for positions after an election. In some cases, patronage jobs were given out in payment for work or contributions made in support of a politican during a campaign. In other instances, positions were meted out in exchange for hard cash, a lucrative bonus for those elected to office.

1840 1859

were killed—one voter was shot when he entered a polling place holding his naturalization papers and a gun. The police chief was shot and wounded as well. Local newspapers heightened tensions, using inflammatory terms to describe the Know-Nothings: "murderers, thieves, thugs, orphan killers, brass knuckles, midnight assassins, widow makers, rowdies, bullies, plug uglies, house burners, dark-lantern ballot box breakers." The new mayor's term, otherwise uneventful, ended two years later, when election violence resulted in even more deaths.[25]

On October 11, 1854, election day in Baltimore, the Know-Nothing party scored a victory by electing their party's first mayor. Samuel Hinks (1815–1887), a local merchant, had been selected as the Know-Nothing candidate only a few weeks before the election, and the party helped him beat his Democratic opponent by deliberately printing their ballots in the same color and design as those of the Democrats in order to gain votes through confusion. In that era, ballots were often officially produced by separate parties instead of a neutral source. In office, Hinks lost the support of the Know-Nothings when he selected the best candidates to fill about five hundred city positions rather than following the party's intended patronage plan.[26]

Levi Day Boone (1808–1882), the grand-nephew of Daniel Boone, was a member of the anti-immigrant Know Nothing party, which backed him in a successful campaign for mayor of Chicago. Boone was credited with several beneficial accomplishments during a one-year term in office, but he was also responsible for engineering a large increase in licensing fees for bars, part of a campaign against alcohol consumption, a major element of the Know-Nothing philosophy. A public protest against this fee increase in 1855 turned into a riot when police shot and killed one of the protesters. After the Lager Beer Riot, Boone's name was tarnished by association and he never ran for office again.[27]

James Cross (1819–1876) was the Democratic mayor of Milwaukee from 1855 to 1858. During his three terms as mayor (in those days, a term lasted only one year), Cross was linked to political corruption in the Democratic party's control of the city. One scandal tied directly to him was an expensive lease for an entire floor of a building he owned, the tenant being the city council.[28]

In June 1856, California state supreme court justice David Terry (1823–1889) was arrested for murder. Terry had attempted to defend a naval officer from arrest by a vigilante group after the officer witnessed the hijack of arms by the vigilantes from a naval vessel in San Francisco Bay. In the scuffle, Terry stabbed a man in the neck with a bowie knife. The judge was arrested for murder because the stabbing was thought to be fatal, but he ended up on trial on a lesser charge when the victim failed to die. He was convicted and sentenced to banishment, an order he ignored. Several years later, in 1859, Terry once again got into trouble, this time killing Senator David Broderick in a duel precipitated by a harsh argument over slavery. In 1889, attacking a judge who had ruled against him in a civil case, Terry was himself shot and killed by a U.S. marshal.[29]

On June 2, 1856, Charles Waterman (1809–1860) was elected mayor of New Orleans. A member of the local Know-Nothing party, Waterman's election was marked by violence and at least one death; this was not unusual in the city's turbulent political history. He served only two years, during which time three large armed forces competed for control: the Know-Nothings, a private army, and a vigilance committee. At the height of the escalating conflict, the Board of Aldermen voted to impeach Waterman for refusing to appear at a meeting to deal with the issue, and he was expelled from office. On July 14, 1860, his hat was found on a ferry on the Mississippi River. It was presumed he had committed suicide, but his body was never found.[30]

At half past one on May 22, 1856, Preston Smith Brooks (1819–1857), Democratic representative from South Carolina, walked up to Charles Sumner (1811–1874), Free Soil senator from Massachusetts, as he was sitting in his chair on the floor of the Senate. According to contemporary accounts, Brooks stated, "Mr. Sumner, I have read your speech against South Carolina, and have read it carefully, deliberately, and dispassionately, in which you have libeled my state and slandered my white-haired old relative, Senator Butler, who is absent, and I have come to punish you for it." At that point, he raised his cane and began

The attack on Senator Charles Sumner by Senator Preston Brooks in 1856 was noted for its violence. It was also widely seen as symbolic of the deepening divide between North and South. This editorial cartoon depicts the event from a northern perspective. The caption reads: "The symbol of the North is the pen; the symbol of the South is the bludgeon."

striking Sumner vigorously on the head, smashing the inch-thick cane to splinters and driving Sumner to the ground. Bleeding profusely, Sumner cried out, "I am almost dead, almost dead." Other congressmen restrained Brooks from further violence. A Senate hearing failed to muster enough votes to expel Brooks, but he resigned on July 15 and was promptly reelected to fill his own vacancy. Sumner, whose "Crime Against Kansas" speech had instigated the attack by Brooks, could not return to the Senate until December 1859 because of his injuries. In the interim, he won reelection after shifting to the newly reformed Republican party.[31]

A recurring theme in the history of political mudslinging is illegitimacy. In debates and popular conversations, many politicians have

been accused of being "bastards," born out of wedlock and therefore debased in society. One of the few candidates to actually be a bastard was John C. Frémont (1813–1890), who was born to unmarried parents. This fact did not turn out to produce much of a scandal in the election of 1856, however, nor did charges that he was a crook, a slaveholder, and a drunkard—all proven false. On the other hand, his religion did create an issue. Frémont, the first presidential candidate of the newly reformed Republican party, was an Episcopalian, but the rival Know Nothing party circulated rumors—as well as several pamphlets—that he was a "Romanist," or Catholic, and would harm the country by supporting Catholic causes if he were elected.[32]

John Frémont, in an 1856 political cartoon.

In the state election in Wisconsin in 1856, Governor William Augustus Barstow (1813–1865), a Democrat, claimed reelection victory by a narrow margin—175 votes—and was sworn into office. His opponent, Republican Coles Bashford (1816–1878), also claimed victory. The state supreme court took Bashford's side, and swore him into office as well. Votes from the election were immediately the target of scrutiny, and there was clear evidence of fraud. In one town, 612 votes were cast by a population of about two hundred; votes were recorded from towns that did not exist and were "inhabited solely by wolves"; and polls were never opened nor votes counted in at least one location where Bashford had heavy support. The deciding factor: all of the state's election canvassers were Democrats. With legal support from the supreme court and the state legislature, Barstow faced mounting opposition. He resigned on March 21, yielding the governorship to Bashford.[33]

Coles Bashford

In the early 1850s, Benjamin Gratz Brown (1826–1885), Democratic member of the Missouri house of representatives (later a U.S. senator, governor, and candidate for vice president), became more and more antagonistic toward Thomas C. Reynolds, U.S. district attorney for

Benjamin Brown

Missouri. It was a political dispute mostly aligned with the escalating battle between pro- and anti-slavery issues. The dispute grew into personal animosity and eventually led to a duel on August 26, 1856. The two men faced off on a sandbar in the Mississippi River about forty miles south of St. Louis. A single exchange of pistol shots ended with Brown wounded in the knee.[34]

In June 1857, John Wentworth (1815–1888), mayor of Chicago, was arrested for stealing mail. It turned out to be a politically motivated ploy; the mayor was absolved when it became clear the mail bags in question were old and used not for mail, but to hold seeds and documents on his farm. One was noted to smell strongly of fish. A local paper stated, "This is the great fizzle of the year."[35]

On February 27, 1857, Orsamus Benajah Matteson (1805–1889), U.S. representative from New York, resigned his seat. Matteson was originally a Whig—he switched to the Republican party for the last of his four terms in Congress—and resigned to protest a House investigation into corrupt practices by several of its members, one of them being him. The probe looked into a claim that Matteson and others attempted to bribe various claimants who had asked for large sums of money for dispensing the politicians' influence with certain land claims. Matteson's defense was that, although he did not ask for this kind of payment, such bribes were necessary because of the corrupt nature of other politicians. He was not confessing, as it turned out, but being sarcastic. In a public letter the congressman sent to the committee investigating him, he stated, "If men, in public or private life, are to be subjected to censure, or even suspicion, upon evidence of trifles like this, there is not one who is safe, especially in Washington, where the father of lies seems to have surrounded himself with most numerous and most industrious progeny." Matteson was never charged in the matter and was quickly reelected.[36]

Francis Smith Edwards (1817–1899), American party representative from New York, resigned on February 28, 1857, in the wake of a House committee investigation that recommended he be expelled. He had been accused of offering a bribe of $1,500 ($34,700 in today's dollars) to another congressman to procure his vote on a bill involving railroad construction in the Minnesota territory.[37]

William Augustus Gilbert (1815–1875), Whig representative from New York, was the target of a House investigation into bribery. Gilbert was accused of receiving $14,500 ($335,800 in today's dollars), stock certificates, and land as a bribe for his help in passing the Iowa Railroad bill. Although he claimed innocence, Gilbert resigned on February 27, 1857, stating he wished to avoid further public scandal.[38]

On February 27, 1857, a "levee"—or gala reception—at the White House turned ugly. One guest, Doddridge Lee, a clerk in the Pension Office, accosted another guest, David Hume, a Virginia businessman, and accused him of being a pickpocket. On the following day, Hume went to the Pension Office to discuss with the offended party what he

PROFILE | Vigilante Politics

California fortunes, and politics, changed dramatically in 1848 when gold was discovered in the foothills of the Sierra Nevadas. The population and economy of San Francisco boomed as a result, even while law and order lagged behind. Criminal activity, prostitution, and gambling thrived, with local elected officials benefiting from the action. In 1851, a Committee of Vigilance was formed in response to the mayhem and corruption. This citizen's group was also a response to growing resentment and fear of the rapidly expanding population of Chinese, as well as the existing groups of local Indians and Mexicans. The vigilantes policed the streets, arrested criminals, tried and lynched suspected criminals, and harassed Chinese and other nonwhite residents. Targeting municipal reform, they also intimidated elected officials and attempted to clean up a notably corrupt political system, but were accused of illegal acts themselves. When the committee was disbanded after a short period of activity, the business and politics of corruption expanded anew. In 1853, a San Francisco newspaper wrote, "The city is full of the

Honorable, the members-elect of the legislature, and politicians and political gamblers are to be met with at every corner, ready to pounce on the State Treasury so soon as the wires can be arranged." In 1856, James King, the editor of another reform-minded newspaper, published an article about James Casey, an elected member of the Board of Supervisors, who had served time in Sing Sing Prison in New York and was renowned for his skill at ballot-stuffing. The supervisor took offense at the article and killed the editor, an act that helped fuel the momentum to create a second Committee of Vigilance. As soon as it was formed, this committee began a new round of arrests, trials, and hangings. In a final act before dissolving, the group encouraged civic-minded individuals to run for office and organized crews to ensure a fair, untainted election. But after this temporary success, corruption

1840 & 1859

soon returned to the city and infected state government as well. By 1877, a local historian noted, "Corruption had crept into every department of government; nepotism had been reduced to a system, official peculation to a science."[39]

James King, a banker and newspaper owner in the city, led the citizen's movement against corruption. He was killed by James Casey, a city supervisor, after King denounced him in print.

believed was a case of mistaken identity. With him was Colonel James Walker, the House reading clerk, a colleague who could attest to Hume's good character. Rejecting Hume's plea of innocence, Lee reiterated his belief that he had stolen his wallet. Hume hit him with his cane and Lee then pulled a pistol and shot Hume, killing him. The clerk was fired from his government position, but a jury acquitted him of a charge of first-degree murder.[40]

Continuing a tradition of political violence, New Orleans witnessed a major riot in 1858 during municipal elections. The local Know-Nothing party had escalated tensions by increasing assaults—in print and in person—on nonwhites, triggering the creation of a Vigilance Committee comprised mostly of Creoles, and Irish and German immigrants. A few days before the election on June 7, the city government had largely ceased to function amid this atmosphere of tension and violence. At the climax, about one thousand members of the Vigilance Committee seized an arsenal in the center of the city. After negotiations with the city council failed, the militia was called up and an opposing mob of citizens armed themselves in preparation for an attack on the vigilantes. Despite a few skirmishes—and accidents, one of which resulted in the vigilantes firing on their own men—an election was held, although with a very small turnout. By some reports, this election was one of the "most orderly" in the city's disorderly history.[41]

David Broderick

David C. Broderick, U.S. senator from California, was shot by David Terry, the former chief justice of the state supreme court, during a duel on September 13, 1859, near Lake Merced, California. Broderick died three days later, stating "They killed me because I was opposed to the extension of slavery and the corruption of justice." The duel was triggered by a negative personal comment aimed at Terry from Broderick, but the underlying animosity

1840/1859

revolved around a major split in the Democratic party, with Terry pro-slavery and Broderick pro-union. Terry was himself shot in 1889 during a different altercation.[42]

On February 27, 1859, Daniel Edgar Sickles (1819–1914), Democratic representative from New York, shot and killed Philip Barton Key, U.S. attorney for the District of Columbia and the son of Francis Scott Key, famous for writing "The Star-Spangled Banner." Key was shot three times at close range by Sickles, who was incensed after discovering Key was having an affair with Sickles' wife. As he confronted Key, Sickles stated, "You have dishonored my bed and family, you scoundrel—prepare to die!" He was found not guilty after a public trial. His defense rested on the argument that he had been temporarily insane at the time of the murder, which, in any case, had been justified by a code of personal honor.[43]

Representative Daniel Sickles shot and killed Philip Barton Key, the son of Francis Scott Key, but was acquitted at trial.

1860–1879

T he politics of segregation dominated the early 1860s. The Civil War, largely instigated by segregation, provided another political focal point. Abraham Lincoln, the winner of the election of 1860, was a major target for abuse in the South, where he was heartily smeared in the media. An editorial in the *Charleston Mercury* stated, "A horrid looking wretch he is, sooty and scoundrelly in aspect, a cross between the nutmeg dealer, the horse swapper, and the night man, a creature fit evidently for petty treason, small stratagems, and all sorts of spoils." It was worse during the 1864 campaign, when personal slurs were compounded by public disclosure of corruption in federal agencies. Following the end of the Civil War, corruption shifted from war contracts to the activities of the Reconstruction era in the South, with a lot of inadvertent help from the weak leadership of President Ulysses S. Grant. In 1868, the impeachment of President Andrew Johnson was a landmark event, although the president was not removed from office. In 1871, the governor of North Carolina fared less well, becoming the first elected head of a state to be expelled by impeachment. During this tumultuous decade, the widely publicized Credit Mobilier scandal was front-page news throughout the country, and in New York City, the exploits of the legendary "Boss Tweed" became a focus of conversation.

George William Brown (1812–1890), a Democrat, was elected mayor of Baltimore in 1860. After less than a year in office, Brown was arrested and jailed by federal officials as the scapegoat for a riot that occurred in the city in April 1861. Locals had attacked a troop of Union soldiers marching through town, and Brown was held responsible. He was kept in a federal prison until the end of his term, in 1862.[1]

In 1860, a long-running debate on the floor of the U.S. House escalated from name-calling to violence. The debate dealt with the issue of admitting Kansas to the union as either a "free" or pro-slavery state, a contentious issue. During one messy brawl, John Fox Potter (1817–1899), Republican U.S. representative from Wisconsin, grappled with William Barksdale (1821–1863), Democratic U.S. representative from Mississippi, in the process yanking off his wig. In response, Potter yelled out, "I've scalped him," ending the melee as widespread laughter engulfed the floor. Potter was reportedly capable of worse. He was known as "Bowie Knife" Potter for his favorite weapon, and in

A contemporary magazine illustration of the Barksdale–Potter fight.

April of the same year, he challenged Roger Atkinson Pryor (1828–1919), Democratic U.S. representative from Virginia, to a duel using this formidable weapon. The challenge was not accepted.[2]

William Augustus Lake (1808–1861) was a former U.S. congressman as well as a former state representative in Mississippi when he campaigned for a seat in the newly formed Confederate Congress in 1861. In Memphis, Tennessee, during the run-up to the election, he argued with Colonel Chambers, also from Mississippi, who was opposing him in the race. The argument escalated to a personal feud and then a duel. Outside of Memphis, on October 15, 1861, Lake was killed in this confrontation.[3]

In 1862, the Kansas legislature debated impeachment charges against Governor Charles Robinson (1818–1894). Robinson, a Republican, was linked to a fraud scheme, along with the state auditor and secretary of state. According to the charges, the group had sold state bonds at less than the rate set by the legislature in order to profit from the resale. The defense rested on a case of necessity, the bonds being sold below value because there was no market for them at the stated rate; plus, the parties involved did not profit from the transaction. The Senate voted to acquit the governor, and the two others were convicted on a technicality but not punished.[4]

During the Civil War, West Hughes Humphreys (1806–1882), a federal district judge in Tennessee, was accused of supporting the cause of secession. He was impeached by the House on June 26, 1862, because he

ELECTION DAY VIOLENCE

Election day in major cities was often accompanied by confrontations, last-minute political campaigning, and violence. This illustration depicts an election scene in a poor neighborhood in New York in 1864.

GOVERNMENT CONTRACT FRAUD

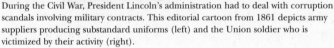

During the Civil War, President Lincoln's administration had to deal with corruption scandals involving military contracts. This editorial cartoon from 1861 depicts army suppliers producing substandard uniforms (left) and the Union soldier who is victimized by their activity (right).

1860 1879

had been appointed to the same post under the auspices of the Confederate States of America. However, he was acquitted of an additional charge, that he permitted the confiscation of property belonging to two prominent state residents who were allied with the Union cause, Andrew Johnson—then military governor of Tennessee—and John Catron, a justice of the U.S. Supreme Court.[5]

In 1862, a Senate investigation found James Fowler Simmons (1795–1864), Republican senator from Rhode Island, guilty of receiving promissory notes in exchange for influencing a large government contract. The deal involved firearms from a Rhode Island arms manufacturer. However, the Senate did not expel Simmons because they had only recently passed a law intended to stop such corrupt practices and his actions predated the new rule. On August 15, 1862, Simmons resigned his seat rather than face further trouble.[6]

On December 1, 1864, William Lewis Dayton (1807–1864), the U.S. minister to France, died suddenly in the apartment of a woman friend in Paris. According to a statement at the time: "After some pleasantries upon entering the apartment, [Dayton] called upon his hostess to give

Andrew Johnson (1808–1875) was vice president during the second term of President Abraham Lincoln. He assumed the presidency when Lincoln was assassinated in 1865 and was an easy target for criticism during the contentious political period following the end of the Civil War. Although a Democrat, he was out of favor with both major parties. Lincoln, who was a Republican, selected him in order to attract Democratic votes. The Republicans, who supported extreme restrictions on the South as punishment for the war, disliked his more lenient approach to post-war control of the former Confederacy. Johnson also

Andrew Johnson

attracted animosity because he vetoed bills that established civil rights for freed slaves in the South. On the other hand, he opposed the Fourteenth Amendment, which bestowed equal rights on all citizens. It was ratified despite his opposition. At odds with a majority in Congress, Johnson triggered an impeachment action in the House—eleven counts were adopted on February 24, 1868—when he suspended and

then replaced Edwin Stanton, the secretary of war. Members of Congress believed Johnson did not have the right to do so with-out their approval, a dispute re-lating to the Tenure of Office Act, which had only recently been passed. In addition, he was charged with being contemptu-ous of Congress and making it

In the office of the secretary of the Senate, the summons for the court of impeachment is prepared.

Representative Thaddeus Stevens makes the last speech in the House before the vote for impeachment is taken.

1860 1879

the object of "disgrace, ridicule, hatred," a response to public speeches he made critical of the legislative branch. Although both houses of Congress had majorities that opposed Johnson, the impeachment tally failed to gain the two-thirds majority necessary for conviction. The Senate lacked only one vote of achieving this threshold on its final vote on May 26. If the conviction had been achieved, some politicians believed a precedent would have been set for using the impeachment process for politically motivated attacks rather than its intended use, to remove publicly elected officials for "high crimes and misdemeanors." Although victorious, Johnson was unable to do much in his remaining months in office because of the effects of the impeachment scandal. Unlike other disgraced officials, however, he did have a future in politics. In 1874, he was elected to the Senate as a Democrat from Tennessee, the only former president to serve in Congress.[7]

three cheers for Abraham Lincoln, the news of whose reelection had just recently reached Paris." He then reported he felt ill, and died soon after. Details of Dayton's death were officially suppressed by the U.S. government, possibly because the woman in question was suspected of being a spy for the Confederates. On a more personal note, she was also believed to be the mistress of Dayton's personal secretary. Dayton had been the Republican candidate for vice president in the election of 1856 and was a former U.S. senator from New Jersey.[8]

On March 4, 1865, an assembly of congressmen, their families, and the press—not to mention President Abraham Lincoln—witnessed the in-auguration ceremony of Vice President–Elect Andrew Johnson (1808–1875). In ill health from a bout of typhoid fever, Johnson con-sumed three servings of whisky before the ceremony, and the combi-nation triggered an emotional harangue that shocked and embarrassed the audience. One senator wrote of the spectacle: "The inauguration went off very well except that the Vice President Elect was too drunk to perform his duties & disgraced himself & the Senate by making a drunken foolish speech."[9]

In 1866, James Blackmore (1821–1875), a Democrat, campaigned for mayor of Pittsburgh, but lost. On the morning of the election, rivals charged that during the Civil War he had been treasonous to the Union, a bit of dirty politics that was instrumental in swinging votes

NEGRO SUFFRAGE

Elections in both northern and southern states after the Civil War reflected the fears associated with the pending ratification of the Fifteenth Amendment, which guaranteed the right to vote for former slaves. This political illustration from 1866 was part of a racist attack on Republican candidates in Pennsylvania, who supported the amendment. The text states, "They are rich, and want to make the Negro the Equal of the Poor White Man, and then rule them both."

against him at the last minute. The story turned out to be false, however, and he ran again in 1868 as the Workingmen's party candidate. This time he won the race. His two-year term was marked by violence among competing political parties; at one point, Blackmore himself was attacked and beaten by a hostile mob.[10]

In 1868, Abraham Oakey Hall (1826–1898), a Democrat, was elected mayor of New York City. His election marked the beginning of the Boss Tweed era. Hall, known as "Elegant Oakey," and his partners systematically looted the city by creating legislation that allowed the mayor's office to control all city finances. Indicted three times for malfeasance while in office, Hall was never found guilty because there was not enough evidence to link him to criminal activity. At one trial, he admitted to nothing more than an "ineradicable aversion to details."[11]

On January 20, 1868, Damien Marchessault (1821–1868), former Democratic mayor of Los Angeles, shot and killed himself in the city council chamber, which was empty at the time. Marchessault, born in French Canada, had been a professional gambler before he began a political career. He was elected mayor three times (1859, 1861, and 1867) and also owned a restaurant, ice house, and "ice cream saloon." While in office, he oversaw an ambitious program to install the city's first piped water system, a scheme that ended up involving several companies that went bankrupt, and relied on wooden pipes that leaked, producing a major scandal. His suicide was linked to pressure from personal debt.[12]

On March 22, 1869, Virginia provisional governor Henry H. Wells (1823–1890) was arrested along with an official of the state Republican party. The charge was stealing a letter from the post office. Wells had been appointed provisional governor while the state was under Reconstruction, and rival political factions were vying for control of an upcoming election, a factor behind the arrest. The charges were later dropped, but Wells received a bigger blow, literally, on April 27, 1870. During a political meeting at the state capitol in Richmond, an extra-large crowd overstressed a balcony, which collapsed onto the delegates gathered on the courtroom floor. This floor in turn collapsed, falling into the hall of the house of delegates below. Sixty-two people were killed and 251 injured, with Wells among the dead.[13]

In 1870, Joel Turner (c. 1820–1888), Democratic mayor of Los Angeles, was charged with graft, tried, and sentenced to prison. In specific, the mayor and his council were accused of making and selling fake bonds for city projects, then pocketing the revenue. The verdict was later overturned on appeal.[14]

Benjamin Franklin Whittemore (1824–1894), Republican U.S. representative from South Carolina, was charged with accepting money to influence an appointment to West Point. The House voted to expel **1860** Whittemore on February 24, 1870, and he resigned the same day. In **1879** June, he was reelected to Congress but the House refused to certify his credentials. Before his political career, Whittemore served as a chap-

John Deweese

lain with the Union Army during the Civil War. John Thomas Deweese (1835–1906), Republican representative from North Carolina, was also charged with selling an appointment to West Point, and the House voted to censure him for this activity on March 1, 1870, one day after he resigned. The same investigation singled out Jacob Shall Golladay (1819–1887), Democratic representative from Kentucky, who re-

signed from the House on February 28, 1870, and Roderick Randum Butler (1827–1902), Republican representative from Tennessee, who was censured by the House on March 16, 1870. The House attempted to expel Butler, but could not muster enough votes. In the following election, Butler lost. Some politicians routinely made appointments to the military academies for compensation in this era, not believing it was a violation of law or ethics, but negative publicity stemming from the House cases in 1870 helped ensure the process became more democratic. There were, however, additional scandals to come.[15]

PROFILE Voter Intimidation

Politicians and political parties have used both "carrots" and "sticks" to produce votes. Carrots can be rewards or other encouragements, such as cash, liquor, or the promise of patronage jobs. Violence, or the threat of it, comprises the sticks. Intimidation dates to the earliest elections and may still be practiced today in some precincts. In the Reconstruction era in the South following the Civil War, it was widely used to deal with the real and imagined threat of black voters. The entrenched Democratic party considered the black vote dangerous to their cause as it was generally tilted toward the Republicans, providing motivation to keep blacks away from the polls. The Ku Klux Klan provided an organized and effective tool in this effort. In many cases, public gatherings by the Klan were enough to remind black voters that there could be a price to pay for the act of voting. But the

1860 1879

threats were often deemed ineffective, and violence was the end result, playing a frequent role up to and on election days. Sticks, whips, knives, and firearms were used to stop voters from reaching polling places, and injuries and deaths were common.[16]

A magazine illustration (left) depicts men gathering for a Ku Klux Klan raid. Above is an 1876 editorial cartoon, showing a Republican bribing a black witness to give false testimony during a trial of Democrats accused of voter intimidation.

On April 9, 1870, M. E. Susisky, city treasurer of St. Louis, was arrested for misuse of city funds. An investigation revealed that up to $120,000 ($1.9 million in today's dollars) was missing from city accounts, and the treasurer was found to be behind the loss. He had made large loans to friends and invested money in speculative ventures himself. Susisky had earlier been linked to the discovery of counterfeit warrants from the city, with his name attached.[17]

On May 21, 1870, in Yanceyville, North Carolina, John Walter Stephens (1834–1870), a state senator, was killed at the Caswell County courthouse. Stephens, a Republican, was present at a meeting of local Democrats when he was taken into a different room, bound, and had his throat cut. The murder was committed by local members of the Ku Klux Klan who were opposed to Stephens' well-known support of Reconstruction and issues involving civil rights for former slaves. In response to the crime, military forces led by Colonel George Kirk were ordered to the area by Governor William Woods Holden (1818–1892), leading to a tense standoff. The event became known as the "Kirk–Holden War." Holden declared martial law and suspended the writ of habeas corpus as well in an effort to curtail further violence. Subsequently, the state legislature impeached him for illegal use of martial law, denying the right of habeas corpus, suppressing the actions of the Ku Klux Klan, and other activities related to insurrections in the state. On March 22, 1871, Holden, a Republican, was found guilty on eight articles of impeachment by the state senate and expelled from office, the first governor in the history of the country to be impeached. Although Holden had supported his native state and the South during the Civil War, he was a critic of the Confederate government and later a willing participant in Reconstruction. The actions that resulted in his impeachment were an attempt to control the lawless disorder that was disrupting elections, but they caused resentment among some politicians and residents. In his memoirs, Holden stated, "...all I did in that movement was done with a purpose to protect the weak and unoffending of both races, to maintain and restore the majesty of the civil law, and not to gratify personal feeling on my part,

1860
1879

or to promote party interest or party ascendancy.... there is truth in the old adage, 'Desperate diseases require desperate remedies.' "[18]

On October 30, 1871, Rufus Brown Bullock (1834–1907), Republican governor of Georgia, resigned from office. He faced charges of selling pardons, bribing newspapers, and ransacking the finances of the state prison. His resignation came in anticipation of impeachment, which he believed was the result of political pressure. In his resignation letter, he wrote he would leave office to "defeat this nefarious scheme of these desperate political conspirators." After he resigned, Bullock, who had moved to Georgia from New York after the Civil War, returned to his home state, where he was arrested in 1876 on charges of embezzlement during his Georgia administration. At trial, he was acquitted because of a lack of evidence.[19]

In 1871, the state legislature in South Carolina brought impeachment charges against Governor Robert Kingston Scott (1826–1900). Scott, a Republican, was the first governor of the state following the Civil War. He and other officials were suspected of issuing state bonds in excessive amounts. There were insufficient numbers to carry an impeachment vote and Scott remained in office, although he did bring a lawsuit for libel against a New York newspaper that had printed an article stating that his financial activities with the state were fraudulent. In 1880, retired from office for several years, the former governor was in the news again when he shot and killed a friend of his son. His defense was that the pistol he was carrying went off accidentally. At trial, he was acquitted.[20]

In 1871, the state legislature in Nebraska brought articles of impeachment against Governor David C. Butler (1829–1891). Butler was charged with corruption in the use of his powers, deception in the use of federal funds, reckless loans using state funds, appropriating profits for personal use from the sale of state land, and other fraud. One charge involved a sum of about $17,000 ($281,000 in today's dollars) missing from a school construction fund. An investigation determined that Butler had received the money from the U.S. government sale of

PROFILE   Boss Tweed

William Marcy Tweed (1823–1878) was not
the first political boss in an American city
and may not have been the most extreme.
But as "boss" of a major city, his name has
become synonymous with the corruption
and excesses associated with local machine
politics. A native of New York City, Tweed
worked a variety of jobs before entering politics in 1852, when he was elected as an al-

Boss Tweed tobacco label.

derman. At the time, the Board of Aldermen was dominated by a core

An 1871 editorial version of Tweed.

of notably corrupt politicians known
as the "Forty Thieves." Also in 1852,
he was elected as a U.S. representative from New York, serving one term
before settling on local politics back in
New York City, where he rapidly expanded his influence, particularly
within the powerful political organization that ran Democratic politics in the
region, the Tammany Society. In
1868, he became the leader of this
group and extended its power in local,
state, and national elections. At the
height of his power, he exerted control over the mayor, several key local
judges, the majority of the Board of Aldermen, the school board, the
street department, the city and county treasurer, the city comptroller,
and the city attorney, as well as the state's governor and an influential
group of state legislators. Tweed used his control of the local machine
for bribery, extortion, kickbacks, and other forms of municipal corruption, taking a large cut of many of the city's transactions, at one point

pulling in an estimated $18 million (about $275 million in today's dollars). Much of this was shared with his collaborators. Among the notable items targeted in this graft were a set of thermometers installed in the city courthouse for $7,500 ($116,000) and a two-day plaster job on a city building billed at $138,187 ($2.1 million). At the same time, Tweed exercised almost complete control over the ballot boxes, police department, and justice system. In one case, a Tweed operative who was found guilty of four murders was fined six cents (about $1) and later, after he was convicted of killing a police officer, served only one year in prison before being pardoned by a Tweed-controlled governor. This level of corruption attracted the attention of both reformers and the

media, including the *New York Times*, which ran a series of articles exposing the mess. In 1871, Tweed was arrested and convicted on 204 counts and sentenced to twelve years in prison and a fine of $12,750 ($210,000). An alarmed state legislature created new laws to deal with Tweed's deeds, and their attention resulted in an additional civil trial, where the boss was found guilty and re-

In this 1871 editorial cartoon, Boss Tweed lectures the city comptroller in his brand of math. The caption reads: "Never mind the public. Mind me. I will make a rich man of you. 12 years ago I was poor, now I am rich by this new arithmetic."

quired to repay the state $6,537,117 ($108 million). In the midst of these legal developments, he escaped from a city jail and fled to Cuba, but was discovered and returned to the United States. He died in prison in 1878. His last words were reported to be "I have tried to do some good, if I have not had good luck."[21]

territorial land but had not deposited it with the state treasury, making personal use of it instead. Butler was also attacked for his actions in the location of the state capitol and the construction of the state university, among other questionable activities. Votes in both House and Senate found him guilty, and he was expelled from office.[22]

In 1871, Governor Powell Clayton (1833–1914) of Arkansas was the target of an impeachment move. On February 20, the state senate assembled to proceed with this issue, but only seven senators were present. The rest had deliberately left the city in order to prevent a quorum and thus deter just such an action. But those senators who did

show up voted on impeachment anyway. The action was triggered when Clayton certified the election results for U.S. Representative John Edwards, even though Edwards' opponent had received more votes. The state supreme court overturned the impeachment on the grounds that Clayton had correctly invalidated fraudulent votes. In any case, Clayton, a Republican, resigned the same year in order to take up his new duties in Washington as a U.S. senator

Powell Clayton

from the state, the result of the same contested election. The election of Congressman Edwards, also a Republican, was challenged in the U.S. Senate and overturned in favor of his opponent in 1872.[23]

On April 15, 1874, a year after state elections in Arkansas, Governor Elect Elisha Baxter (1827–1899) was physically thrown out of office by his opponent, Joseph Brooks. Brooks, who challenged the results of the election, had unsuccessfully appealed to various courts and the state legislature and finally used a questionable decision from a state circuit court to declare himself the victor. Different factions in the state's Republican party supported Baxter or Brooks, and their internal squabbles escalated to violence. The state capital turned into a "fortified camp," and as many as thirty-eight men were killed before the violence ended, brought about by the arrival of federal troops. The event came to be known as the "Brooks–Baxter War." Months later, President Grant, acting on the advice of the U.S. attorney general, declared Baxter the true winner, but a year later Grant confounded the issue when he made a public statement supporting Brooks' claim. Making things even more confusing, the lieutenant governor, the acting head of the state during the long-running confrontation, attempted to keep his position rather than turning it over to the returning Baxter, because in the interim the state had adopted a new constitution, reducing the governor's term from four years to two.[24]

Harvey Doolittle Colvin (1815–1892) was elected mayor of Chicago in 1873. He was a Democrat after a short previous affiliation as a Republican. According to the laws then in effect, Colvin believed that his term should run through 1877, but a new, conflicting state law shortened this term, making it end in 1876. In April 1876, a new mayor, Thomas Hoyne, was selected in a special election despite Colvin's objections, and for several months the city had two men who claimed the right to be in charge. A court decision eventually upheld Colvin's position, and the challenger was unseated until yet another election was held later in the year.[25]

In 1872, Florida governor Harrison Reed (1813–1899) was impeached for the second time. In this action, the Florida house found him guilty

REPEAT VOTERS

Politicians and parties often relied on "repeaters" to push up the vote count on election day. Repeaters were voters hired to make multiple votes, either in the same place with different names or by moving from one polling place to another. This illustration depicts repeaters just off the train from New York, brought in to vote in Philadelphia in 1872.

PROFILE Credit Mobilier Scandal

In September 1872, the *New York Sun* published an article about a questionable relationship between Oakes Ames (1804–1873), Republican representative from Massachusetts, other elected officials, and the Credit Mobilier Corporation. Credit Mobilier, although a real company, was a front set up as a financial scam to provide construction contracts to the Union Pacific Railroad. The same set of owners secretly controlled both companies, giving them the ability to rig contracts with the government for inflated figures—the final tab was $2 million higher than actual costs—and reap extra benefit from stock sales. Credit Mobilier stock was also used as bribes to influence members of Congress to ignore the illegal corporate transactions as well as to pro-

duce dividends for the Union Pacific and the members of Congress who owned shares. On February 27, 1873, after a major investigation, the House censured Ames for "seeking to procure congressional attention to the affairs of a corporation in which he was interested." His defense was that he had done nothing more than sell stock to colleagues and had no intent to bribe. He remained in office but died the same year. James Brooks

Oakes Ames

(1810–1873), Democratic representative from Maine, was also implicated and was censured on the same date. He was a ripe target because he had formerly been a Republican, attracting the distrust of Democrats in Congress. Coincidentally, like Ames, he died in 1873, also while still in office. More than a dozen other senators and representatives—mostly Republicans—were ultimately investigated by a select committee of the Senate, although most escaped with nothing more than the embarrassment of public exposure. Vice President

Schuyler Colfax (1823–1885) was the highest-ranking official tied to the scandal and suffered more than others, particularly because of public statements he made disavowing any connection to the mess just

before evidence was disclosed proving otherwise. The House introduced a resolution calling for his impeachment, but it was rejected in committee. His term ended before further action could be taken, but the loss of credibility kept him from being renominated. Vice President Henry Wilson (1812–1875), who replaced him, was discovered to have briefly owned Credit Mobilier stock in his wife's name. Other politicians made the headlines

Schuyler Colfax

as well. James Harlan (1820–1899), Republican senator from Iowa, had his term expire before action could be taken. James Willis Patterson (1823–1893), Republican senator from New Hampshire, was accused of giving false testimony to the committee about his ownership of stock in both companies and was recommended for expulsion. Henry Wilson (1812–1875), Republican senator from Massachusetts, was reprimanded although he had not benefited financially. James Asheton Bayard Jr. (1799–1880), Democratic senator from Delaware, was a notable exception to other politicians implicated in the scandal. In 1868, when offered the tainted stock, he replied, "I take it for granted that the corporation has no application to make to Congress on which I should be called upon to act officially, as I could not, consistently with my views of duty, vote upon a question in which I had a pecuniary interest." John Alexander Logan (1826–1886), Republican senator from Illinois, likewise recognized the scheme for what it was, albeit belatedly. When presented with a $329 dividend check ($4,700 in today's dollars), he returned it two days later with an additional $2 ($29) to cover interest.[26]

of misapplication of public funds as well as having received unlawful compensation while in office. Reed interpreted the impeachment as a dismissal from office, but a later action by the Florida supreme court ruled that he was officially still in charge. A subsequent special session of the legislature resulted in the dismissal of all charges. In an earlier event in 1868, he was impeached for lying, incompetency, embezzlement, bribery, corruption, and misuse of power, but the impeachment proceeding was dismissed by the state supreme court because a quorum had not been present during the impeachment vote.[27]

In 1873, Henry Clay Warmouth (1842–1931), governor of Louisiana, was impeached by the state legislature. The charges involved his role in an election in 1872 in which fraud was prevalent. Warmouth was a

1860 1879

Republican politician in Louisiana during the Reconstruction era, a period noted for its corruption, and he was no stranger to this activity. Among his unethical activities were the ownership of a newspaper that

was granted the state printing contract, and personal speculation in state bonds. What got him impeached, however, was a political struggle fought for control of election returns between rival factions of the Republican party in the state, one opposing him as well as the election of Ulysses Grant, and another favoring him. Before the impeachment process came to a vote, his term ended.[28]

Henry Warmouth

The U.S. Senate held hearings in 1873 to investigate allegations that one of its members, Samuel Clark Pomeroy (1816–1891), Republican from Kansas, used bribery to get elected. In Kansas, he was known as "Subsidy Pom," an indication that this activity was not a secret. Witnesses reported a locked valise filled with cash, a $2,000 down payment ($34,000 in to-

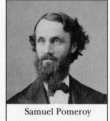

Samuel Pomeroy

day's dollars) to secure the vote of a state legislator, and a midnight meeting in a hotel that involved a backroom vote deal. Before the Senate could decide what to do, Pomeroy's term in office expired, ending the impeachment process. Back in Kansas, a state trial on bribery charges dragged on for years before the case was finally dropped by prosecutors. A fictionalized version of Pomeroy's exploits appeared in *The Gilded Age*, a novel about political corruption, by Mark Twain and Charles Dudley Warner, published in 1873.[29]

A U.S. Senate committee issued an official report in 1873 stating that one of its members, Alexander Caldwell (1830–1917), Republican from Kansas, was guilty of fraud, having bribed Kansas state legislators to vote for him. Initially defiant, Caldwell resigned his seat on March 24, 1873, anticipating a move by the full Senate to expel him. Back in Kansas, he began a new career as the president of a bank.[30]

In 1874, an investigation focused attention on Alexander Robey Shepherd (1835–1902), the governor of the territory of the District of Columbia, because of alleged corruption in the awarding of pavement contracts in Washington. His career had been lauded up to that point—he was credited with being the person "who lifted Washington out of the mud," referring to the beautification of the city, not its political mire—but the paving contract scandal and overspending in the city budget tarnished his image. His term ended in 1874 when Congress removed the role of territorial governor.[31]

PRESIDENT ARRESTED!

President Grant was fond of driving himself around Washington in a horse and buggy. On one occasion, while driving a little too fast on city streets, he was stopped for speeding by a policeman, at least according to some published accounts. Upon recognizing the president, the officer apologized, but Grant demanded that he do his duty and give him a ticket. One version of this story reports that the officer was one of the first African Americans to serve on the Washington police force. Another version adds an additional twist. Recognizing that Grant was driving while intoxicated, the officer confiscated the buggy and made the president walk back to the White House.[32]

The administration of President Grant was adversely affected in 1874 when an investigation disclosed irregularities with the collection of delinquent federal tax. Known as the "Sanborn contracts scandal," the issue involved a lapsed provision that permitted outside contractors to provide this service for the government in exchange for a percentage of the amount recovered. Even though the practice had been officially discontinued, Sanborn and a few other companies were exempted and continued to benefit from large bonuses—up to half of the income they generated. The scandal involved cases where the contractors went after taxes that were not considered unrecoverable by the government, padding their income at the expense of the Treasury Department. The secretary of the treasury, William Richardson, was targeted for the most blame and was expected to be censured by Congress for his role. He resigned before this action was taken.[33]

An editorial cartoon shows President Grant struggling with the weight of various political scandals that involved his administration. Although not personally implicated, negative publicity hampered his effectiveness in office.

The "Mississippi plan" was a loosely organized attempt to gain black votes in the South through a combination of promises and intimidation. It was put into effect in various states during the elections of 1875. The promises included offers of jobs, political positions, and investment to win votes. The intimidation to scare off voters was in the form of violence, including beatings, whippings, murders, and mass attacks. In many cases, the threat of such activity was all that was needed. A few years later, in 1877, Lucius Quintus Cincinnatus Lamar (1825–1893),

Democratic senator from Mississippi, had his election to Congress challenged on the grounds of voter intimidation and other issues related to the violent election season in 1875. Although not personally implicated, Lamar, who had served in the Confederate Army, was linked by association. But by the time he was singled out, Congress had been overwhelmed with similar charges, and over time the issue faded in importance. Ultimately, Lamar kept his seat, even winning the vote of a black Republican from Mississippi, who sided with the majority in voting to acknowledge Lamar's election.[34]

Lucius Lamar

William Smith King (1828–1900), Republican U.S. representative from Minnesota, was accused of accepting a payment in exchange for supporting a bill that provided a federal subsidy for the Pacific Mail Steamship Company. During a congressional investigation, evidence was shown that the company had paid $275,000 ($5 million in today's dollars) to a lobbyist to secure votes. Despite witnesses who tied King to this source, no charges were filed against him by either the House or a subsequent committee in the Minnesota legislature.[35]

Following the Civil War, the first black politicians were elected in the South, but not without difficulty. Republican John Adams Hyman (1840–1891) of North Carolina was one of the first. A former slave, Hyman was elected to the state senate for several terms before moving up to the U.S. House in 1874, where he served a single term. During this career, he was a constant target for attack, from politicians, newspaper editors, and residents of both North Carolina and other southern states. In addition to the standard political treatment by white politicians unwilling to accept the change in their status quo, Hyman battled personal accusations of frauds and payoffs, but was never charged with a crime. According to the *Georgia Weekly Telegraph*, a white-owned newspaper, he had "during the session been seized with a desire to get possession of other people's wealth without rendering an equivalent therefor [*sic*]. John Adams will now probably retire from Congress and become a candidate for the North Carolina penitentiary." In 1889, another southern paper, the *Charlotte News*, commented that Hyman's election "was one of those disagreeable results that in politics will occur when incapacity and ignorance, or worse, under the upheaval of the waters that are solely disturbed, are spawned and the people suffer."[36]

William Worth Belknap (1829–1890), secretary of war in the administration of President Grant, was charged with various unscrupulous activities. One charge was that he violated the neutrality of the United States in 1870 during the Franco-Prussian War by selling arms and ammunition to the French. A congressional committee concluded that such a deal had occurred, with Belknap's involvement, but he was not charged with any wrongdoing. More seriously, he was tied to the award

William Belknap

of a trading post position in Indian territory in exchange for a substantial cash payment. In the original deal, cash was paid to his wife; when she died in 1870, ongoing payments were made to her sister, who ended up marrying Belknap, keeping the money in the family. Belknap resigned his position just before an impeachment vote in Congress acquitted him. The vote did not reflect innocence, but an acknowledgment that as an ex-official, he was no longer impeachable. A parallel deal for trading posts involved a brother of President Grant, but no congressional or legal action was taken in that case.[37]

William Pitt Kellogg (1830–1918) had a long, full career as a politician, serving as governor, U.S. senator, and U.S. representative, all for the state of Louisiana. Although originally from Illinois, Kellogg went south at the end of the Civil War, seeking political opportunities in the Reconstruction period. The misadventures that followed included a contested election in which both Kellogg, a Republican, and his opposition declared victory and were sworn into office on the same day,

William Kellogg

January 14, 1873, by competing state legislatures. A military intervention by President Grant was required to restore order; the president declared Kellogg to be the legitimate head of the state. While in office, Kellogg was impeached by the state house—but not convicted by the senate—on the grounds he misappropriated state funds.[38]

The administration of President Grant was tied to another scandal in 1876, this one involving George Maxwell Robeson (1829–1897), the secretary of the navy. Robeson's personal income and assets increased significantly after his appointment, arousing suspicion and eventually triggering a congressional inquiry. The investigation disclosed that A. G. Cattell & Company, a grain company, received large government contracts that were tied to Robeson's influence, even though there was no "paper trail" that showed he received compensation from them. Nevertheless, between 1872 and 1876, his income grew by $320,000 ($6 million in today's dollars), and there were other clues that linked Cattell to him, including gifts of real estate. Just as impeachment momentum increased, Grant's term as president ended, as did Robeson's position in the cabinet, and no further action was taken. The former head of the navy later served two terms as a Republican representative from New Jersey.[39]

Adelbert Ames

On March 29, 1876, Governor Adelbert Ames (1835–1933) of Mississippi resigned from office. Ames, a Republican, was impeached following charges he had misused state funds in the construction of a prison, improperly took over the duties of the state treasurer, used prisoners for personal benefit, and purposely neglected to fill a political vacancy. Following his resignation, all charges were dismissed. Ames, a career military officer—he was awarded the Congressional Medal of Honor for gallantry at the Battle of Bull Run—had been appointed provisional governor

PROFILE   Whisky Ring Scandal

President Grant's two terms as president were marred by a continual string of scandals tied to various cabinet departments and political appointments. One of the largest of these—in terms of scope as well as publicity—was a widespread pattern of corruption within the liquor industry. Alcohol, one of the first commodities to be targeted for federal licensing and tax, was also wide open to corruption because of the size of the market and the quick profits to be made by avoiding the payment of taxes. The "Whisky Frauds" of the Grant administration focused mainly on Missouri, but ended up implicating individuals, businesses, and officials in other states as well. Suppliers, retailers, and officials were involved, but the main ploys occurred at distilleries. There, government reports were falsified, undercounting production, and government tax collectors were bribed to support the undercount. The less alcohol reported on paper, the smaller the taxes. Because many of those involved were part of an organized, if informal, group, the scandal was also referred to as the "Whisky Ring." An investigation funded by Congress and led by Secretary of the Treasury Benjamin Helm Bristow, a political foe of Grant, found corruption at all levels—even Grant's private secretary, son, and brother were implicated—and about 350 arrests resulted. Grant himself was not accused of involvement, but his prestige suffered. The highest-ranking official to be convicted was General John McDonald, who had been appointed by

Grant to be the supervisor of internal revenue for seven western states, including Missouri.[40]

Scene from the Whisky Ring trial in St. Louis in 1876.

during Reconstruction. As a Republican, Ames represented unwanted change for the entrenched Democrats in the state. Following a particularly violent election in 1873, he attempted to have the results, which heavily favored the Democrats, thrown out, the act that triggered the political move to have him impeached.[41]

James Blaine defends himself in Congress.

On June 5, 1876, James Gillespie Blaine (1830–1893), Republican U.S. representative from Maine and minority leader of the House, defended himself against charges he had received a $64,000 loan ($1.2 million in today's dollars) from a railroad—using bonds of little or no value as collateral—in exchange for legislative favors. The proof for these charges was alleged to be in several letters written by Blaine and discovered by James Mulligan, a bookkeeper. The scandalous documents were referred to at the time as the "Mulligan Letters." Blaine subsequently recovered them from Mulligan before they could be given to investigators. Instead of turning over the potentially incriminating documents to the Judiciary Committee, which was investigating the charge, Blaine read from them during a June 5 speech in Congress. In this closely watched address, he used selected quotes to prove his innocence, but the full contents were not read aloud. During the same event, he dramatically disclosed a copy of a telegram from an executive at the railroad company in question, absolving him of blame. The telegram had been previously sent to the chairman of the

1860 1879

A political cartoon shows candidate James Blaine suffering under the weight of the Mulligan Letters. Although Blaine appeared to have an adequate defense, many voters got the impression that he was not being honest.

Judiciary Committee, a Democrat and a political opponent of Blaine, but had not been made public. By revealing this "ace card" at the same

PROFILE   The Great Election Fraud of 1876

The presidential election of 1876 is considered to be one of the most fraudulent in U.S. history. Election misconduct was widespread, which was a common occurrence in the political climate of the era, but it also was particularly intense in several key states. Unlike most previous elections, the results were so close that the fraud appeared to affect the outcome, attracting more scrutiny than usual. Rutherford Birchard Hayes (1822–1893), Republican governor of Ohio, was eventually declared the winner over Samuel Jones Tilden (1814–1886), Democratic governor of New York. The results of the popular vote gave Tilden about 265,000 more votes than Hayes, but there were wide-

Samuel Tilden

Rutherford Hayes

spread reports of ballot stuffing, repeat voting, voter intimidation, and other forms of election fraud, especially from some southern states and the machine-controlled cities in the North. The key electoral vote tally also initially gave a majority to Tilden—184, to 166 for Hayes—but the total was one short of the threshold required for victory, triggering a political battle over the legitimacy of the electoral votes from several states, particularly Florida, Louisiana, and South Carolina. Here, Hayes supporters attempted to use the argument of fraud to have enough Tilden votes invalidated to swing the final tally to their side. The argument ended up in Congress, which established a bipartisan commission of selected members and five judges from the Supreme Court. The latter included two Democrats and two Republicans, with the final judge appointed by deliberation of the first four. This was carefully designed to reduce the chance of partisan bias, but it only made matters worse. The final tie-breaking choice was a Republican, and because both the congressional panel and

1860
1879

the original four judges were evenly split along party lines, the decision was made by a Republican, who selected Hayes as the winner. The decision, which did not come until February 28, produced widespread animosity and criticism. Jeremiah Black, the former secretary of state, summed up the feelings of many in a statement after the event: "If you want to know who will be president by a future election, do not inquire how the people of the states are going to vote. You need only to know what kind of scoundrels constitute the returning boards, and how much it will take to buy them." In office, Hayes was often referred to as "His Fraudulency" or "Rutherfraud" because it appeared to many that Tilden had been robbed of his rightful victory. However, some modern historians believe that the disputed electoral vote count was too unstable to determine a "correct" result, no matter how it was tallied, because of the widespread fraud that was practiced on both sides.[42]

The country watched and waited while Congress dealt with the contested election results in 1876. Here, Representative David D. Field, Democrat from New York, is shown objecting to the electoral votes from Florida.

time he appeared to be discounting the value of the Mulligan letters, Blaine turned the tables on his opponents. He was cheered for his successful defense, which was a major political event that occurred while he was in the running for the Republican nomination for president. Neverthess, he lost the spot to Rutherford Hayes.[43]

The contentious presidential election of 1876 was closely tied to several key state elections, including Oregon. In that state, Democrats striving to help elect Samuel Tilden were led by Governor La Fayette Grover (1823–1911). Grover used his power to disqualify a Republican member of the Oregon election commission, replacing him with a Democrat. In addition, illegal voting lists were generated and other election frauds were claimed, leading to an investigation, which resulted in all of Oregon's presidential electoral votes being given to Hayes. In the same election, Grover was elected to the U.S. Senate, which looked into charges of electoral misconduct, lying under oath, bribery, and corruption. Despite the charges, he was seated. After more than a year of investigation, a Senate committee concluded there was no evidence to support the accusations.[44]

1860
1879

Robert Smalls

In 1877, Robert Smalls (1839–1915), Republican representative from South Carolina, was convicted of accepting a bribe. The evidence in his trial was a check for $5,000 ($96,000 in today's dollars), made out to cash. It was intended to buy a vote from the congressman, according to a single witness. That witness, a local printer, used handwritten notes to detail the bribe; the notes were written in pencil and encrypted so that only he could interpret them. Contemporary accounts suggested that Smalls had been singled out for persecution because he was a Republican in a primarily Democratic district, but he suffered as well from notoriety that dated to his activity in the Civil War. A slave in Charleston during the war, he escaped, stole a Confederate boat loaded with arms and ammunition, and delivered it to the Union naval forces. His actions were widely publicized, and he was made the first black captain of a U.S. Navy ship. In the North, he was widely hailed as a hero for this action, but in the South and his hometown, his deeds generated a less beneficial response. When he returned after the war and entered politics, he was a marked man. After his trial, Smalls appealed his conviction and the verdict was eventually dropped, not so much because of the trumped-up charges, but as a result of a political deal with state Democrats, who in return were absolved of their involvement with fraud in a state election.[45]

In November 1878, a new scandal relating to the already fraud-ridden presidential election of 1876 was made public. A large collection of secret messages dubbed the "Cipher Telegrams" was discovered and decoded. These revealed plans and negotiations for bribing electors in Florida in favor of the Democrats. There was no evidence that Samuel Tilden, the Democratic candidate, had any involvement in the telegrams' content, but his nephew, Colonel William T. Penton, and

One of the cipher telegrams that linked the Tilden campaign to election fraud in the presidential campaign in Florida in 1876.

other political colleagues were directly implicated. The disclosure kept Tilden from being renominated.[46]

President Rutherford Birchard Hayes (1822–1893) was an easy target for his Democratic rivals after his disputed election. Among the more trivial attacks, he was accused of wasting six dollars of taxpayers' money to purchase a special set of croquet balls. His wife, Lucy—a strict teetotaler, she was ridiculed with the nickname "Lemonade Lucy"—had to fight a running battle with State Department officials who insisted on serving wine and other traditional alcoholic beverages at the White House when foreign dignitaries were being entertained. Lucy believed she was the winner in this battle, not

A White House servant serves oranges spiked with liquor. The practice was hidden from the first lady, a teetotaler.

knowing that a special rum punch was available, concealed in whole oranges. According to a contemporary newspaper editorial, "...common gossip has it that more than one Christian Statesman and many bright lights of the total abstinence cause were hauled away by night from the Executive mansion in a hilarious if not a maudlin condition."[47]

On December 2, 1879, a nominating convention in a Democratic ward in Philadelphia got out of hand. Disputes between factions attempting to control the selection of candidates escalated from shouting to violence. A local paper reported: "At this juncture another small army of men, who think it is a stigma on the record of the party for a Democratic Convention to get through without the firing off of a single shot, arrived on the scene." Another newspaper account summed up the action: "The result may be summarized as follows: One man killed, one man's face split open, one man (the notorious Jimmy Kane, recently out of prison after serving seven years) with a bullet through his hand, Squire McMullen pretty well beaten by a mob and an indiscriminate mangling of noses."[48]

In 1879, Isaac Kalloch (1834–1887) ran for mayor of San Francisco as a member of the Workingmen's party, whose motto was "The Chinese Must Go." The Workingmen's party was part of a grassroots movement in California that was vehemently—and often violently—against immigrants. Charles de Young, the publisher of the *San Francisco Chronicle* and a political rival, printed a story about Kalloch a few weeks before the election. The main disclosure was that Kalloch had been tried in court for adultery in 1857 (the trial ended in a hung jury). In the editorial style of the era, his character and personality were attacked as well; the headline compared him to an "unclean leper." Kalloch, who was the head of a large Baptist church, used his pulpit to denounce de Young—in front of a large audience—calling Charles and his brother

Workers in San Francisco gather in an empty lot to protest against foreign residents in California, particularly the Chinese. The heated nature of this protest developed into a local political movement that contributed to the death of the publisher of the *San Francisco Chronicle*.

"bastards of progeny of a whore born in the slums and nursed in the lap of prostitution." Suitably angered at the insult to his mother, de Young then shot Kalloch twice with a pistol. Wounded but not dead, Kalloch received a large sympathy vote and won the election for mayor on September 3. While leading the city, he was subject to several impeachment attempts led by the political opposition, but these were all unsuccessful. In 1880, before de Young went on trial for his attack on Kalloch, Kalloch's son took his own justice, shooting and killing the publisher. He was later acquitted on the grounds of self defense.[49]

1880–1899

Forged letters, bought votes, and pressure on federal employees played a role in the election of President James Garfield in 1880, not to mention leftover dirt from a previous issue, the "Star Route" scandal. In office only 199 days, Garfield was assassinated by a deranged voter who was disappointed at not being appointed to a federal position. Vice President Chester Arthur took over both the office and several lingering scandals; he had to dismiss two key appointees implicated in improper activities. But Arthur, credited with being a fair and honest leader, had little opportunity to start a trend. The subsequent election of Benjamin Harrison in 1888 was marked by excesses of electioneering that set new records. In one contested state, Indiana, the price of a vote escalated to $20 (about $400 today). This period was marked by the recognition that wealth had a strong connection with congressional seats, and in the 1890s, the U.S. Senate was first dubbed the Millionaire's Club. One contemporary journalist observed that the Senate was an "eager, resourceful, indefatigable agent of interest as hostile to the American people as any invading army."

Joseph A. Shakespeare (1837–1896) was elected mayor of New Orleans, Louisiana, in 1880, serving a term before being reelected in 1888. Campaigning as a reformer, he fought against the Democratic-controlled political machine and achieved some notable improvements, despite running his own form of graft. He created the "Shakspeare Plan [sic]," in which illegal gambling operations were required to make regular payments to the city instead of individual politicians or police officials. This solution was chosen because the mayor believed gambling was best controlled by making it legal, even though the state constitution prohibited licensing it.[1]

From an article in the *National Police Gazette* (1880): "The prevalence of immoral men in public life in Washington has always been a subject of comment. The recent statement in the *Evening Critic* that a well-known Southern Senator had accomplished the ruin of a young girl at an assignation house, which is the scene of frequent orgies of men in high station, was not therefore calculated to startle the public mind, except as it promised an exposure.... The Southern Senator alluded to has had a very unsavory reputation in this regard for a few years past, and on one or two occasions, it is related, very narrowly missed what would have been not only an exposure, but bodily harm."[2]

On January 16, 1880, Leonard A. Harris (1824–1890), former mayor of Cincinnati, Ohio, shot and wounded his brother-in-law in a saloon. Harris reported that his brother-in-law, whom he had been supporting financially for twenty years, demanded money in "an offensive and profane manner." Refusing the demand, Harris called the man "an un-

1880
1899

grateful scoundrel," prompting his brother-in-law to hit him with a heavy cane, an assault which precipitated the shooting.[3]

Individual politicians have a long history of serious antagonism with their brethren, not counting traditional party rivalry. In the early 1800s, animosity was obvious—and public—between Roscoe Conkling (1829–1888) and James Blaine (1830–1893), both Republican representatives, Conkling from New York and Blaine from

James Blaine and Roscoe Conkling embrace while wrapped in a ribbon of "patronage." From an 1881 editorial cartoon in *Puck* magazine.

Maine. In one speech Blaine delivered in the House, he called Conkling "haughty," likened him to a "dunghill," a "singed cat," and a "whining puppy," not to mention ridiculing his exaggerated stride, which Blaine called a "turkey-gobbler strut." Politics being more important than personalities, however, Conkling ended up supporting Blaine during his 1884 run for the presidency.[4]

PROFILE Franklin Moses

Franklin J. Moses Jr. (1838–1906) was born into wealth and power in South Carolina. His father was the chief justice of the state supreme court. Moses became a Republican after the Civil War and energetically involved himself with Reconstruction politics. He was elected to the state legislature and became the Speaker of the House, then was elected governor in 1872. About that time, col-

Franklin Moses

1880 1899

leagues noted he began using the power of office to increase his personal cash flow, which was spent on a lavish lifestyle. While governor, he was indicted by a grand jury on charges that he set up a local black resident as a county treasurer so that he could steer funds to Moses. Prosecution, however, was blocked on the technicality that as governor, he would have to be tried

in an impeachment process first. Before this could happen, his term in office expired. His next move was to use his legislative connections to have himself appointed judge, but the new governor blocked the appointment. From then on, Moses appeared in a variety of cities, from New York to Chicago to Boston, and perpetrated a string of swindles along the way. In a typical event, he was arrested for fraud in New York City on March 29, 1882. According to the victim, a piano manufacturer, Moses, using an assumed name, cashed a check from a nonexistent bank for $175 ($3,500 in today's dollars), after ordering one of his instruments. A police investigation revealed that several other local businessmen had been cheated in the same manner, each time with Moses using a different alias. A similar charge from South Carolina resulted in an extradition order, but Moses escaped before it was served. At various times he was sentenced to a few months to a few years in prison, and during one stint behind bars in Massachusetts in 1887, he was pardoned by the governor. A few years later, still in Boston, he was arrested for defrauding a local resident of $5; in 1902, he was arrested for stealing an overcoat. Drug addiction was reportedly an issue in his decline.[5]

On March 23, 1882, E. St. Julien Cox, a judge in the Ninth Judicial District in Minnesota, was impeached and removed from office by a vote of the state senate. He was charged with seventeen counts of individual drunkenness, one of habitual drunkenness, a specific act of lewdness—driving to a brothel in a carriage with a "notorious" woman—and general lewdness of conduct. The last two charges were dismissed. The defense claimed that drunkenness was not an impeachable offense in general and in this case had to be directly related to activity on the bench or it was not applicable. Unfortunately for Cox, witnesses were able to describe just such a situation. At the hearing, witnesses testified he was "drunk in the court-room, unwashed, bleareyed [*sic*], thick of spech [*sic*], and muddy of thought." Others told of regular proceedings in which the judge, the jury, the lawyers, and the spectators would all get drunk together.[6]

Philip Thompson

On April 27, 1883, Philip "Phil" Burton Thompson Jr. (1845–1909), Democratic representative from Kentucky, encountered Walter Davis, a Kentucky business owner, on a passenger train in that state. Pulling a pistol, Thompson shot and killed Davis, then turned himself in. In his statement to a judge, the congressman explained, "The deceased took my wife and, having plied her with drink until she was utterly besotted, well knowing her infirmity in that regard, debauched her and made her the victim, in her unfortunate condition, of his degraded lust.... This has broken up and destroyed my domestic relations.... My daughter, dearer to me than all else on earth, is in exile from home, an outcast from society. She has sobbed herself to sleep on my bosom under this great calamity. This blood is but a feeble atonement for her tears, and if Davis had a hundred lives, all of them would not atone for this great wrong." According to a contemporary newspaper account, "If ever the slaying of a man was justifiable it was so in this case." The congressman was acquitted.[7]

In late January 1883, Isaac Vincent, state treasurer of Alabama, disappeared with $212,687 of state money ($4.3 million in today's dollars). Vincent, a Democrat, was serving his third term in office and was believed to be speculating on cotton futures using state funds.[8]

Citizens of Long Island City, New York, won a court victory against their former mayor on April 13, 1883. They had filed a civil suit against Mayor Henry S. De Bevoise the previous year, charging him with misappropriating city bonds in the amount of $108,000 ($2.2 million in today's dollars). When he was first arrested on the charge, the mayor reportedly asked the sheriff if he could use additional city bonds as collateral for bail.[9]

William Behan (1840–1928), mayor of New Orleans, lost his bid for re-election in 1884 by alienating the local Democratic party leaders who had supported him when first elected in 1882. In an election marked by ballot fraud and vote buying, the party successfully supported another candidate, dumping Behan, who had behaved honorably while in office, using objective decisions to make political appointments instead of selecting party favorites, and had reformed a corrupt system of payment used to compensate city employees.[10]

J. Valsin Guillotte (1850–1917), a favorite of the "Ring" (officially, the People's Democratic Association), the ruling political machine in New Orleans, was elected mayor to replace William Behan, the unreliable former mayor who had failed to support their corrupt endeavors. The machine took almost complete control of the election, using policemen to control ballot boxes and campaign workers to alter ballots. According to a local newspaper, "The election was a mockery...The people cast the ballots but the ring counted them." True to form, Guillotte allowed the machine to have its way, which included appointing its members as policemen. A subsequent increase in crime included the murder of two city officials.[11]

James Gillespie Blaine (1830–1893), former Republican senator from Maine and a former secretary of state, campaigned to be the Republican nominee for president in 1876 and 1880—he was unsuc-

James Blaine (left) and Grover Cleveland (right) represented the opposing parties in the presidential election of 1884. Both had to deal with major negative campaign issues. Blaine was represented as a liar and Cleveland a man of loose morals. Cleveland's problem prompted humorist Mark Twain to quip, "This present campaign is too delicious for anything. To see grown men, apparently in their right mind, seriously arguing against a bachelor's fitness for President because he had private intercourse with a consenting widow!"

cessful—but made another run in the election of 1884, finally getting on the ballot. Blaine had weathered previous scandals involving allegations of corruption but was the target of even more attacks in the glare of the presidential campaign. Focusing on his previous troubles, Democrats attacked his character and ties to big money with the negative campaign chant "Blaine, Blaine, James G. Blaine, the Continental Liar from the State of Maine." Republicans countered with attacks on the character of the Democratic candidate, Grover Cleveland, the governor

An editorial cartoon shows Grover Cleveland reacting to a baby who cries out, "I want my pa."

THE CAMPAIGN PIG

Political campaigns in earlier eras were accompanied by buttons, banners, trinkets, and other promotional items, just as today. Starting with President Grant and running through President McKinley, one of the more unusual concepts was a small gold- or silver-colored pig charm. A candidate's portrait in miniature could be seen through a small hole. Making a cynical statement about politics, this hole was on the pig's rear end.[12]

Side and rear view of a Cleveland campaign pig, actual size.

PROFILE Tammany Hall

Tammany Hall was the long-running center of politics in New York City, both as an actual building and an organization. The site was in several locations, the last in Union Square, where it is currently part of New York University. Its roots date to the late 1700s, when it was founded as the Society of Saint Tammany, a political and social organization partly based on Native American tribal customs; the name came from a Delaware

1880
1899

Tammany Hall in the early 1900s.

Tammany "workers" prepare for violence at the Pell Street polls, New York City, 1889.

Indian chief named Tammanend. By the early 1800s, the Tammany Society was a Democratic stronghold and had mastered a city-wide approach to politics based on the large number of immigrants who arrived from Europe, especially Ireland. The first major success for

of New York, who was publicly accused of having an illegitimate child. The anti-Cleveland chant was "Ma, Ma, where's my pa?" Cleveland acknowledged responsibility for the child even though it was not certain that he was the father, and he gained public support when he was able to show he had paid child support from the beginning as well as making sure the child was raised by a respectable family (the boy's mother had become an alcoholic and had been committed to a mental institution). Meanwhile, zealous Democratic campaign workers dug up a little parentage dirt on Blaine. It turned out his first child was born only

the Tammany machine was the election of Fernando Wood as mayor in 1854, simultaneously marking the ascent of William "Boss" Tweed, one of the most notorious of the Tammany leaders. Tweed was never mayor, but he ran the organization as the chairman of the Democratic party of New York County and the Grand Sachem (leader) of the Tammany Club, both centers of corruption, and when he was appointed commissioner of public works, he used his position to milk the city of millions. The Tammany organization backed a string of machine-controlled leaders that lasted through the mid-1950s, a continuity broken occasionally by opposition candidates and reform movements. Notable Tammany-supported mayors included Richard Croker, Alfred Smith, Robert Wagner, James Walker, and Carmine De Sapio, although these and other Tammany politicians were not uniformly corrupt; during the Tammany reign, major improvements were achieved, and several Tammany mayors were noted for running efficient, beneficial administrations. Because of the large population in New York City, the votes that Tammany controlled were highly coveted, and many state and national leaders sought the backing of the organization.[13]

"Boss Croker," one of many powerful mayors backed by Tammany Hall.

1880
1899

three months after his marriage, prompting a quick attempt at damage control. His official response: the public marriage was not the "real" marriage. He and his wife had actually been married a year earlier, but they kept the affair secret because of family opposition, and finally held a new marriage ceremony because they feared the original event may not have been legal. The biggest negative issue for Blaine in 1884, however, turned out to be a speech in New York that he attended, at which a Protestant minister lambasted the Democrats as the party of "Rum, Romanism, and Rebellion," a catchphrase that was quickly linked to Blaine and widely repeated, alienating many Catholics, who ended up voting against the Republican candidate.[14]

On October 31, 1885, Michael Delehanty, justice of the peace of Long Island City, New York, was found guilty of malfeasance. He had been accused of collecting fines and keeping them for his own use, failure to file appropriate records, and other charges. In one instance, it was reported he had led a raid on an illegal cockfight in which nine men were apprehended. Each was fined $10, which Delehanty pocketed. While he was awaiting judgment in this case, the lawman was involved in another incident. In attendance at an illegal prizefight in Brooklyn, he was captured along with a handful of other spectators.[15]

In April of 1885, Charles William Jones (1834–1897), second-term Democratic senator from Florida, arrived in Detroit, Michigan, for a visit with former Detroit mayor William Thompson. While in the city, he met Clotilde Palms, the young and attractive daughter of a local millionaire. According to public accounts at the time, he was smitten with her, although she did not return his affections. In any case, he neglected to return to Washington—or to his home state, where he left a wife and four children—and missed the next two sessions of Congress completely, leading to his defeat in the following election. Whether or not the young lady was involved in his defection, others noted a decline in his mental health. A political colleague commented at the time, "Jones is crazy on several subjects—on religion, on women, on liquor, and the Constitution." Without a job or income, he became a vagrant, believed he was being persecuted, and was ultimately committed to an insane asylum, where he died in 1897.[16]

On November 13, 1885, former Senator William Sharon (1821–1885) died. A Republican from Nevada, Sharon's political career ended in 1881, a year after meeting Sarah Althea Hill, who became his mistress. Hill, who was in her twenties, and Sharon, in his sixties, split up a few years later, prompting Hill to sue the ex-senator for divorce, claiming they had a common-law marriage and flaunting a note Sharon had written to that effect as evidence. The divorce case—and the corre-

PROFILE   Star Route Scandal

President Garfield's administration was hit by a major scandal in 1881, involving corruption in the postal system for assigning star routes. Star routes were those where mail was carried by conveyance other than railroad, including wagon and steamship—about 10,000 routes altogether—with the routes won by bids. Such routes were marked with an asterisk on printed documents, hence the term. Because the cost of supplying mail service varied consider-

ably from one route to another and costs could be billed as expenses, the area was a prime target for corruption. In response to growing reports about the system, Garfield stated, "I direct you not only to probe this ulcer to the bottom, but to cut it out." He was assassinated, however, before the scandal peaked, and his successor, President Arthur, was stuck with most of the consequences. The assistant postmaster generals got most of the blame, as they managed the star routes. The second assistant postmaster general, Thomas J.

Chester Arthur

Brady, was directly involved, helping create a "ring" to expedite bribes and kickbacks; he resigned on April 20, 1881. Although not personally implicated in the mess, James N. Tyner (1826–1904), first assistant postmaster general, also resigned, on October 26, 1881.

Others implicated included Stephen Dorsey, Republican senator from Arkansas, and several key post office clerks. Estimated loss over a five-year period: $4 million ($79 million in today's dollars). Dozens of people were indicted during the investigation, but all the trials ended with hung juries or acquittals. On the plus side, important reforms were implemented to prevent the same opportunities for

James N. Tyner

corruption from occurring in the future. Because several Republican administrations in a row were involved, the scandal contributed to major Democratic victories in the election of 1884.[17]

1880
1899

sponding lawsuit for fraud filed by Sharon, who claimed the note was a forgery— spawned several trials, with one judge awarding Ms. Hill alimony in 1884 and another issuing a guilty verdict on the fraud charge in 1885. Unfortunately, the fraud verdict came on the same day that Sharon died, but the aftershocks continued. The senator's heirs appealed the divorce decree and won a reversal a few years later. In the interim Hill appealed her fraud verdict, which ended up in the U.S. Supreme Court in 1889 in favor of the original decision. Meanwhile, Hill married her attorney, David Terry, a former chief justice of the state supreme court with a reputation for a violent temper (in 1859, he had a duel with David Broderick, a U.S. senator, killing him).

William Sharon

Both parties were loud and combative in their various courtroom appearances, and at one point, Hill's new husband attacked a federal marshal with a knife, prompting judge Stephen J. Field to throw him in jail for contempt. In 1889, while the last legal stage of the case was still unfolding, Terry ran into the same judge on a train and attacked him. A bodyguard assigned to the judge intervened, shooting and killing the lawyer. In 1892, his widow, the original jilted lover, was committed to an insane asylum, where she lived until her death in 1947.[18]

In 1888, elections in some parts of the country were still associated with the free flow of alcohol to encourage votes. But temperance was also a rising issue and had an increasing influence on political platforms as well as election campaigns. In the governor's race in New York that year, David Bennett Hill (1843–1910), the incumbent governor and a Democrat, had a close match with Warner Miller (1838–1918), the Republican candidate. Hill was backed by major business interests—including the influential State Liquor Dealers' Association, which helped support his campaign—and had recently vetoed a bill

PROFILE Cartoon Politics

The second half of the 1800s was a prime time for political humor. Magazines and newspapers provided a platform for the best satirists, cartoonists, and illustrators to attack candidates, parties, corruption, scandals, and politics in general. Among the magazines that were known for their political humor were *The Century*, *Harper's Weekly*, *Judge,* and *Puck*. Among these, *Judge* and *Puck* were primarily political; *Judge* was editorially Republican; and *Puck* backed the Democrats. *Judge* debuted in 1881 and ran through the 1930s. *Puck* started in 1876 and lasted until 1918. Both specialized in harsh, stinging caricatures of the opposing side and were also often radically antagonistic toward various changes in the election systems, including suffrage for blacks, Asians, and other minorities, not to mention women. At the same time, any politician "outed" for corruption was a ripe target for abuse.[19]

OUT IN THE COLD.

that would have greatly increased license fees for beer and liquor dealers. On October 16, members of the Dealers' Association were active participants in a parade held in the candidate's honor in Kingston, New York, supplying wagons representing brewers, liquor dealers, and saloons. On one wagon, a group of men were seated, playing cards and drinking beer. Elsewhere in the parade, a group of men carried a banner saying "We Want Free Whisky." A public outcry ensued—mostly from Republicans—and almost cost Hill the election, which he won by a narrow margin. At the time, the Democratic party was backed by large numbers of Irish and German immigrants who opposed temperance legislation, while the Republican party was quickly becoming identified with the movement to legislate against alcohol consumption.[20]

James Williams Tate (1831–1889?), state treasurer of Kentucky, embezzled an estimated $150,000 ($3 million in today's dollars) from state funds, a deficit uncovered after he disappeared on March 16, 1888. Anecdotal evidence—a few letters and comments from friends—originally suggested Tate, known as "Honest Dick," ended up in China or Japan, where he supposedly died. In 1887, he was "discovered" in Brazil, where he supposedly owned a coffee plantation. One newspaper report at the time his embezzlement was discovered stated, "Moral: Short terms for state treasurers."[21]

A few days before the November election in Nyack, New York, in 1888, a fire alarm caused a brief moment of political unrest. Simultaneous rallies by local Democrats and Republicans were under way when the town's fire alarm was sounded. According to local reports, the first response from some of the Democrats was suspicion, thinking it a Republican dirty trick to disrupt their event. At the same time, some of the Republicans had the same reaction, believing the alarm was set off by Democrats to interfere with their own get-together. Both sides ended up eventually responding to a real house fire.[22]

During the 1888 presidential campaign, President Cleveland, running for reelection, was the victim of a dirty trick engineered by his

Republican opponents. A letter from the British ambassador, Sir Lionel Sackville-West, was solicited by a Republican in California, George Osgoodby, posing as a British expatriate named Murchison. In the letter, Murchison asked for advice on whom to vote for in the coming election. Sackville-West suggested that Cleveland was the better choice for British interests, a pronouncement that was undiplomatic—it was later described as the action of a "foolish man"—and

Lionel Sackville-West

resulted in the Sackville-West's dismissal. After it was first published on October 21 in the *Los Angeles Times*, the "Murchison Letter" was widely covered by other papers, stirring resentment among Irish Americans, who shifted their vote to Benjamin Harrison, a senator from Indiana and the Republican candidate. Other voters also suspected Cleveland of an inappropriate alliance with England, as he had recently championed a new trade treaty with Canada (which had been defeated by Republicans in Congress). Appearing a few weeks before the election, it arrived at just the right time to trigger Cleveland's defeat. Some political analysts believe this may be the first political dirty trick to actually swing a presidential election.[23]

1880
1899

On February 28, 1890, William Preston Taulbee (1851–1890), former Democratic representative from Kentucky and son of a Kentucky senator, was shot in the Capitol and died a week later, on March 11. The killer was Charles Kincaid, a reporter for the *Louisville Times*, who had broken a story the previous year that Taulbee had engaged in illicit sexual relations with women of ill

William Taulbee (left) and Charles Kincaid (right) had a fatal clash inside the Capitol Building in Washington, D.C., in 1890. The bloodstains remain on the marble steps leading to the restaurant in the basement.

repute, sometimes in the hallways of the Capitol. The story triggered
the breakup of the congressman's marriage and ended his run for reelection. In February 1890, Taulbee, working as a lobbyist in the capital, accidentally ran into Kincaid, attacked him, and threatened him
with further harm. Reportedly in fear of his life, when Kincaid returned to work he carried a pistol, and when he ran into the former
congressman on the marble steps leading to the basement restaurant,
he fired. He was acquitted on the grounds that it was a justifiable act of
self-defense.[24]

In 1890, Stevenson Archer (1827–1898), state treasurer of Maryland,
chairman of the state Democratic party, and former Democratic representative (both his father and grandfather were also representatives
from the state), was charged with embezzlement after $132,000 was
found missing from state funds ($2.9 million in today's dollars).
Archer apparently used this money to replace deficiencies from trusts
he managed. He then attempted to generate enough to replace what
he took through speculation on risky ventures, a failed effort. He
pleaded guilty and was sentenced to five years in prison, serving most
of the sentence before being pardoned by the governor due to poor
health.[25]

On December 11, 1890, South Carolina attorney general Young J.
Pope, a Democrat, was arrested for improperly firing one of his clerks.
Pope's stated reason was the clerk's known support for the opposing
party. Lawyers supporting the clerk pointed out that the state constitution prohibited discrimination against any state residents because of
their political beliefs; Pope defended his action, claiming the statute in
question only applied to "colored Republicans and negroes."[26]

In 1891, the state senate of Kansas voted to impeach Judge Theodosius
Botkin, a Republican. It was the first impeachment action in that state.
The judge was tried on charges of gambling, being drunk while at trial,
throwing innocent citizens into jail because they were personal or political enemies, and releasing from jail citizens who were personal or
political friends.[27]

After the presidential election of 1892, political opponents of President Grover Cleveland published reports that the president beat his wife. It was also rumored that he beat his mother-in-law. Other rumors suggested that Frances, Cleveland's young wife, was having an affair with Henry Watterson (1840–1921), a prominent newspaper editor who had previously served as a Democratic U.S. representative from Kentucky. The president entered the White House as a bachelor and married the much younger

Frances Folsum Cleveland

woman—he was twenty-seven years older—there in a highly publicized ceremony on June 2, 1886. Both the first lady and her mother issued formal statements denying the rumors.[28]

John Patrick Hopkins (1858–1918) was appointed mayor of Chicago in 1893 to fill the vacancy created by the assassination of Mayor Carter Harrison. Hopkins, a machine Democrat, benefited financially while in office by collaborating with political colleagues to receive payoffs from lucrative city contracts and leases. The greatest windfall came from helping create the Ogden Gas Company to compete with the People's Gas Company, then the exclusive supplier of gas to the city. As it was established in a subsequent investigation, the Ogden deal was a scheme designed by the founders to threaten the existing gas company with competition; to remove the threat, the gas company was obliged to purchase stock.[29]

William Campbell Preston Breckinridge (1837–1904), Democratic representative from Kentucky, was served with legal papers from the supreme court of the District of Columbia on August 12, 1893. The case involved a breach-of-promise suit filed by Madeline Pollard, who had met the congressman in 1884, when she was seventeen years old and sat next to him on a train. Known as the "silver-tongued orator of the Blue Grass," Breckinridge seduced the young woman, who ended up being his mistress and bearing several of his children. Waiting through two marriages (his) for him to marry her, she finally decided on a legal course of action. A public trial and a high-powered defense team failed to convince the jury that Pollard was lying, despite the renown and established reputation of her political paramour. She was awarded $15,000 in damages ($336,000 in today's dollars), and Breckinridge, who had a well-known speaking career supporting the concept of chastity for young, unmarried women, became the object of a major voter backlash despite a public apology. He lost his next election and never held office again.[30]

Court reporter's sketches from the breach-of-promise lawsuit trial of Congressman William Breckinridge and Miss Madeline Pollard. March 31, 1894.

In 1893, William Nathaniel Roach (1840–1902), Democratic senator from North Dakota, was the focus of a short-lived scandal in Washington, D.C. The Senate held several debates before deciding not to pursue an official investigation of his alleged illegal activity during a prior career as a bank cashier in Washington. Newspaper reports that surfaced after his election suggested he had embezzled money while working in that capacity twenty years before. The attack on Roach was partisan, led by Republicans hoping to have him unseated. The charges were likely true, but they did not result in a vote of censure. However, the publicity may have contributed to his loss in the following election back in North Dakota.[31]

After a state election in Kansas in 1893, the Kansas house was closely balanced between two opposing parties, Republicans and Populists, with only a four-seat difference. Each side elected a presiding officer, and both attempted to rule the assembly, sending opposing messages to the state senate and the governor that each had control. The senate, with a Populist majority, and the governor opted to back the Populist claim, triggering a rush by the house's Populists to arm themselves and seize physical control of the assembly room. In response, the state militia was called out, but its appointed leader, a Republican, would not follow the governor's order to remove his fellow party members, prompting the governor to replace him with a leader with Populist credentials. The ensuing standoff lasted weeks until a decision by the Kansas supreme court awarded the control of the house to the Republicans.[32]

In September 1894, the district attorney in New Orleans initiated impeachment action against the mayor, John Fitzpatrick (1844–1919), head of the locally powerful Democratic machine. Fitzpatrick was accused of corruption, favoritism, and gross misconduct, as well as both malfeasance and misfeasance. Among other questionable activities, he engineered a long-running exclusive franchise for the Illinois Central Railroad to build a loop around New Orleans, an agreement that required no payments to the city. During his term, twelve members of the city council were indicted for accepting bribes—several of them refused to perform city duties unless they were paid large sums of money—and a contract to install plumbing in a new courthouse was awarded to a company owned by the mayor's wife. Despite such activity, the impeachment attempt floundered because of a lack of evidence. Nevertheless, public sentiment ran against Fitzpatrick, and a local newspaper wrote that it was unable to "look on the decision as otherwise than a public calamity."[33]

On May 13, 1895, four aldermen in Haverhill, Massachusetts, were sentenced to fifteen months each in prison. The elected officials, along with several local businessmen, had been charged with accepting bribes to influence the assignment of permits to sell alcohol.[34]

An investigation by the legislature in New Jersey in 1895 disclosed widespread graft and corruption in state offices. Democrats were the party in power in New Jersey since 1869 and took most of the blame,

PROFILE Attacking a Candidate

At the 1896 Democratic National Convention, William Jennings Bryan (1860–1925) rose to national prominence with his "Cross of Gold" speech, promoting the concept of a silver-based dollar. It convinced delegates to nominate him as their presidential candidate. He was already a celebrated personality, however, and an easy target for political opponents, who often portrayed him as clownish, if not an actual clown. But after his speech,

rivals wasted no time in targeting Bryan as a potential threat to the economy, and rumors were circulated about his fitness to be president. In September, a report from an anonymous alienist (psychiatrist) was published in the *New York Times*, citing various negative characteristics in Bryan's per-

1880
1899

even when not directly involved. George Theodore Werts (1846–1910), the Democratic governor, was implicated. He and the Democratic majority in the state legislature were replaced by Republicans in the following election. One of the triggers was a law enacted in 1893—heavily supported by the Democrats—that legalized racetrack gambling, a politically motivated scheme to increase income potential for businesses backing some of the incumbent politicians.[36]

On February 21, 1895, the citywide convention for local Republicans in Chicago got out of control. In the process of nominating a candidate to run for mayor in the next election, the delegates escalated from verbal arguments to physical assaults; at one point chairs were used as weapons. Police were called in to quash the disturbance.[37]

sonality. The report stated he had "a life of restlessness and mental vagabondage; an intense, overmastering and growing egotism; grandiose ideas that are almost, if not quite, delusional, a morbid querulousness and sensitiveness to criticism," and "a confused and illogical mental state." In addition, "His judgment is false, his actions foolish, egotistic, and extravagant," and the candidate had "a bad hereditary history." The *New York Times* followed up with a survey of local psychiatrists on the subject of this analysis. Of the nine doctors contacted, two withheld comment, three considered Bryan sane, and four agreed with the previously published diagnosis.[35]

1880 1899

On April 7, 1896, riots broke out at several polling places in Chicago. According to a contemporary account, the "First Ward provided its usual quota of brawls, with fists, rocks, and clubs as weapons, and whisky as the accessory in every case." Violence was also reported in the Second, Eighteenth, Nineteenth, and Twenty-second wards. At various places, the violence included gunshots, and several people were wounded. Although election violence was not unknown in Chicago, in this case it was particularly intense because of a drive to reform the notorious machine politics of the city. In the 1896 election, the reform was successful—although not permanent or effective—with twenty-six of thirty-four aldermen being replaced by the "respectable element of the community."[38]

PROFILE War of the Copper Millionaires

The young state of Montana finally elected William Andrews Clark (1839–1925) as U.S. senator in 1899. He spent more than a decade attempting to gain this office. Clark, wealthy from copper mining profits, also spent large sums in his quest, and his expenditures were matched by his chief rival, Marcus Daly, another mining millionaire. Shortly after Clark's arrival in Washington, a Senate committee investigated charges that the election involved bribery and electoral misconduct. During several months of testimony, witnesses and evidence showed that the Clark campaign had spent hundreds of thousands of dollars despite a Montana law limiting election expenditures to $2,000 ($49,000 in today's dollars). Spending included direct cash gifts to electors, debts and mortgages paid in exchange for votes, and financial backing for business ventures, all to influence the state electoral votes needed to win the election. Up to this period, U.S. senators were selected by state

Statue of Marcus Daly.

electors, not a direct popular vote. Some of the recipients of Clark's largesse included the eleven Republican legislators who helped provide the winning margin. At the same time, the investigation reported similar activity coming from the Daly organization. On May 15, 1900, facing certain expulsion from the Senate, Clark resigned, but his political career was hardly over. Four days later, the acting governor of Montana appointed Clark to fill the seat he had just vacated by resigning, taking advantage of the regular governor's absence from the state. A few days thereafter, when the governor returned, he negated this action and appointed another person in Clark's place. The Montana senate responded by refusing to ratify either appointment, but in January, the legislature revisited the issue by

holding another vote. Once again, it voted to appoint Clark to the Senate post, a task made easier because in the interim, Daly, Clark's political rival, had died. With the competition gone and the majority of the new Montana legislature voted into office with the benefit of Clark's financial support, he had little trouble winning. In March 1901, William Clark finally began his career as an elected representative from his home state, this time without complaint from Congress. He served only one term, but left a much larger legacy. Partly because of the well-publicized bribery issues associated with his run for office, and the corruption traditionally associated with the electoral vote system for senators, Congress finally debated, then accepted

William Clark (above) and the mansion his copper fortune financed.

a proposal to adopt the popular vote for senators in 1911. The House followed shortly thereafter. The Seventeenth Amendment to the U.S. Constitution, establishing this voting method, was ratified on April 8, 1913.[39]

The Democratic political convention in St. Louis, Missouri, assembled to select a candidate for mayor in 1897. Dissension between factions escalated to a violent confrontation, resulting in a riot call to the police department and the arrests of several key instigators. When one arrested delegate was released on bail, he returned to the meeting and continued the fracas. Eventually, the group split in two and held separate meetings.[40]

In 1898, Robert Anderson Van Wyck (1847–1918), a Democrat and judge in the city court, was elected mayor of New York City. He was an active representative of the Tammany Hall political machine during a period of prolific corruption. Among the noted issues that were tied to his term in office was the "Ice Trust Scandal," in which the city allowed one company to have a monopoly on ice supplies in exchange for shares of stock owned by city leaders, including the mayor. Another scandal was the "Ramapo water steal," a sweetheart city contract awarded to a dummy corporation. And there were others as well. At one point, Governor Roosevelt was involved in an attempt at the state level to have Van Wyck removed from office—an effort that did not succeed, although he only managed to serve one term in the face of mounting reform pressure. According to rumors, the mayor reportedly left office having amassed a personal fortune of $3 million ($39 million in today's dollars). After he died, his obituary in the *New York Times* stated that

Robert Van Wyck, one of the noted Tammany Hall politicians, was involved with several major corruption schemes while he was mayor of New York City. One was the "Ice Trust Scandal." Here, the mayor is depicted floating amid chunks of ice in an editorial cartoon from the period.

he "became involved in probably more administrative scandals than any Mayor in the city's history."[41]

Marcus Hanna

Marcus Hanna (1837–1904), Republican senator from Ohio, survived an investigation by a Senate committee looking into charges of bribery during his election in 1898. Bribery charges were increasingly common among elected leaders at the time, and in the Senate, significant evidence was necessary to convict a member. Following precedent, it was necessary to show evidence to connect an accused member directly to the bribery; if it happened without their knowledge or involvement, they were clean enough to serve. In Hanna's case, connection was not proven, letting him off the hook, despite evidence that bribery had occurred. However, the investigation did turn up a telling detail. The transcript of a telephone conversation implicated one of those involved in the bribery talking directly to a member of Hanna's campaign staff. At this time, when telephones were still a relatively new technology, there was no law against eavesdropping, a fact that Hanna's opponents used to their advantage by employing a stenographer to write down the overheard conversation.[42]

1880 1899

On July 19, 1899, Secretary of War General Russell A. Alger resigned. Alger was in charge of the War Department during the Spanish American War, when various scandals involving its activities emerged. He ended up being the McKinley administration's scapegoat even though he was not personally implicated. One of the scandals that made the newspapers was the purchase of tainted canned meat intended as food for the soldiers in Cuba. Rumors spread among the troops that the smelly meat was left over from the Civil War, and it was widely believed that hundreds or thousands of them died after eating it. Their nickname for the meat was "embalmed beef."[43]

Russell Alger

Samuel H. Ashbridge (1849–1906), a Republican, was elected mayor of Philadelphia in 1899, beginning an era of conspicuous corruption. Lincoln Steffens, famous muckraking author, paid sarcastic tribute to Ashbridge, a coroner before his municipal career, for establishing a new benchmark for graft, as he had "broken through all the principles of moderate grafting." In Steffens' view, Philadelphia was "the most corrupt city in America" and its citizens "corrupt and contented." A report issued by the Municipal League of Philadelphia at the time referred to the mayor's cronies as a "crew of pirates." Known both as

PROFILE   Kentucky Election Violence

1880 1899

William Goebel (1856–1900), Democratic governor of Kentucky, served a very short term after the state election in 1899. The hotly contested election results ended up in the hands of the Board of Election Commissioners, which decided the election should be awarded to Goebel's opponent, William S. Taylor, the Republican candidate and former governor. This decision was overturned by a special panel of the state legislature in January 1900, but

Governor William Taylor

in the interim Taylor remained in his office, literally, and called out the state militia to protect him. On January 30, before the legislature's decision was put into effect, Goebel was shot by an assassin hiding in a state office building; the man blamed for the shooting was a rural resident of Taylor's home county. Gravely wounded, Goebel was sworn into office and died a few days later. The governor's post then reverted to John Crepps Wickliffe

Governor William Goebel

Beckham (1869–1940), the lieutenant governor, which precipitated a lawsuit by the former governor Taylor, who insisted that as the original—and rightful—winner of the election, the job should go to him.

"Stars and Stripes Sam" and the "Boodle Mayor," Ashbridge was reportedly $40,000 ($972,000 in today's dollars) in debt when he was nominated for the office. When his term was up, he left office a rich man. Among the practices noted during his term were a water plant loan inflated from $3.7 million to $14 million ($90 to $340 million in today's dollars), inflated payments to favored contractors, and the appointment—for free—of a lucrative streetcar franchise to a well-connected supporter. A quote attributed to him: "I mean to get out of this office everything there is in it for Samuel H. Ashbridge."[44]

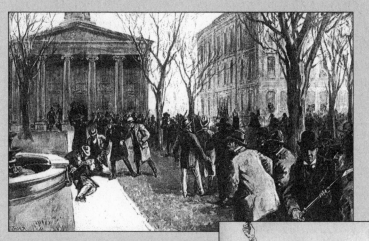

Several months later, the issue was settled by the U.S. Supreme Court, with Taylor losing. Criminal cases were prosecuted against several men implicated in Goebel's murder, including the former secretary of state. All were convicted.[45]

Above, a contemporary illustration of the Goebel assassination scene near the state capitol. At right, a political cartoon from the *Pittsburgh Dispatch*. The caption: "In Kentucky the Cruel War Is Over."

1900–1919

The arrival of a new century coincided with the birth of a new movement in journalism, muckraking. Ida Tarbell, Upton Sinclair, Lincoln Steffens, and others discovered a rich new source for their journalism: corrupt businessmen and politicians. The term was coined by President Theodore Roosevelt, who used it in a 1906 speech encouraging the exposure of "every evil practice." The "Rough Rider" president, however, was known to use a few questionable tactics himself, including switching political parties, and—according to reports that were never substantiated—accepting large amounts of money from major companies during his reelection campaign in 1904. But he established himself as a maverick, unwilling to play along with the unethical practices of the time. According to Henry Frick, a major industrialist, "We bought the son of a bitch and then he did not stay bought." Congress passed election reform legislation in 1907, but laws then and now merely changed the methods used to support candidates, not the amount of money involved or the pressure to influence the outcome.

On April 9, 1901, in Denver, the first woman was arrested for voter fraud in U.S. history. The charge against Mrs. M.A. Ratcliffe was that she had "willfully, knowingly, and unlawfully" voted in a precinct in which she was not registered. Ratcliffe, a Democrat active in local politics, was targeted by local Republicans who were engaged in a campaign to combat election fraud in the city. After a short trial, a judge dismissed the charge against her because of insufficient evidence.[1]

Mrs. M.A. Ratcliffe

Benjamin Tillman

On the floor of the Senate on February 22, 1902, a routine debate over a pending bill erupted into a fistfight between two senators, both Democrats from South Carolina. Benjamin Tillman (1847–1918) physically attacked John McLaurin (1860–1934) after the two exchanged heated remarks over McLaurin's apparent willingness to side with Republican positions. The Senate voted to censure both for actions that were "derogatory to its high character"— Tillman for initiating violence and McLaurin for using inappropriate language—and, within a few months, changed its rules to reflect a heightened sense of decorum. The new language governing conduct in the Senate: "No Senator in debate shall, directly or indirectly, by any form of words impute to another Senator or to other Senators any conduct or motive unworthy or unbecoming a Senator." Meanwhile, newspapers reported that the two men armed themselves in anticipation of further action.[2]

One in a long line of colorful politicians in San Francisco, Eugene Schmitz (1864–1928) was elected in 1902 on a Union Labor ticket. A professional musician and orchestra leader, "Handsome Gene" ruled for three successful terms. He was linked to local political leader Abe Ruef, a noted machine boss who controlled a city heavily infested with corruption and graft. During Schmitz's time in office, a city official disappeared with more than $39,000 in city tax revenues, businesses were required to make under-the-counter payments to politicians and local crime figures, two police commissioners were forced to resign following allegations of "whisky grafting," the mayor himself was arrested on an indictment charging him with extorting payments from a French restaurant, and a grand jury disclosed he received more than $550,000 from "boodling" operations. Schmitz was formally removed from office after he was found guilty of extortion on June 18, 1907, but the verdict was overturned on appeal. The mayor then returned to his former role as the leader of a local orchestra, and he was later elected to two

PROFILE Bathhouse John

In 1892, John J. Coughlin (1860–1938) began a long career as an alder-man in Chicago. Coughlin, widely known as "Bathhouse John," had an earlier career as a "rubber," or masseur, at a Turkish bathhouse, hence his nickname. He used his earnings to open his own establishment and even-tually branched out into other endeavors, including saloons, banking, and insurance. As an alderman in the heavily Democratic First Ward, he had a firm grip on party politics, beginning with the choice of candidates, and made decisions about ballot counters, poll watchers, city judges, and even state offices. Coughlin supporters had access to city revenue, official contracts, and patronage jobs, a significant power that he wielded for

decades. Anything that was done politically in Chicago had to meet with his approval. His control included criminal racketeers such as Al Capone, who maintained a close relationship with Coughlin. He also had power over the appointment of policemen—even police captains—and in his ward, any illegal activity had to factor in the cost of police protection, in-cluding a cut for the ward bosses. When reform movements first arose at the close of the 1800s, Coughlin's ward was the target of periodic investi-gations and cleanup campaigns. In fact, some historians believe that the modern urban reform movement arose in the First Ward because it was the prime destination for observers eager to see how the "old school" of politics worked. Until 1923, Coughlin worked in tandem with a second al-

terms on the city's Board of Supervisors. Although increasingly dis-liked in the city because of the specter of corruption tied to him, Mayor Schmitz gained widespread credibility for his leadership during the historic earthquake and fire in 1906.[3]

In 1902, a grand jury in St. Louis issued a report exposing widespread corruption in the city. Ex-mayor Henry Ziegenhein (1845–1910) was charged with depositing city funds in his own bank and transferring in-terest on the account to himself. Other past and present members of

"Hinky Dink" and "Bathhouse John"

derman in the ward, Michael Kenna—known as "Hinky Dink" because of his short stature—before a change in the city's charter mandated there could only be one elected official from each ward. After that, their arrangement was for Bathhouse John to handle the public side while Hinky ran the behind-the-scenes business. Bathhouse John was notably more than a political power, he was well-known and recognized for his appearance. His clothes were once charitably described as "vociferous." He favored pants that came in shades such as "gas-house blue" and "startled fawn" and shirts and vests in various shades of green. At one point, he shifted to "menagerie" shirts—hand-embroidered shirts with images of up to forty different kinds of zoo animals—to help publicize one of his out-of-state business ventures, a zoo and amusement park in Colorado Springs, Colorado. He also attracted publicity through his occasional stabs at songwriting—"Dear Midnight of Love" and "Ode to a Bowl of Soup" were two examples. Bathhouse John served for forty-five successive years as alderman, dying in office in 1938 at the age of seventy-eight.[4]

1900 1919

the city assembly were charged with bribery, extortion, and kickbacks. The report stated, "Members of the Municipal Assembly have come before our body and brazenly admitted that they sought seats in the Assembly for the money they could make selling their votes...and no bill of consequence has passed unless money has been paid to secure favorable action."[5]

In July 1902, things went from bad to worse in city politics in Minneapolis. Mayor Albert Alonzo Ames (1842–1911) left town in a hurry, leaving the city in charge of his private secretary, Thomas Brown. The mayor's brother, the chief of police, also left in a hurry. These two and others were indicted by a grand jury, which found numerous cases of illegal activity tied to their activities.

In what was called the "Big Mitt Game," travelers were swindled by confidence men and then quickly escorted out of the city by officers before they could raise an alarm. Overall, the police department used a variety of practices to extort money from legal and illegal enterprises; some officers stood guard during crime capers. A contemporary newspaper report stated, "In Minneapolis every form of vice has been rampant for months and has plainly been winked at by those in authority. Frequently there have emanated from the Mayor's office orders to the effect that certain resorts must close. They have closed only to open again within a day or two. Robberies have been occurrences of every night—robberies of the most daring kind, and yet the police have made but few arrests of importance." Mayor Ames—often called "Doc" because of his previous career as a local doctor—had been prominent in local and state politics for years. At various times either a Democrat or a Republican, he was first elected mayor in 1876 and served a total of four terms. During his third term, allegations of corruption increased, and one local paper characterized his administration as "a stench, an offence against honesty, decency, and even the ordinary safety of the common citizen." After Ames left town in 1902, he was eventually tracked to New Hampshire and arrested. His defense to a charge of bribery rested primarily on his claim that health problems affected his sanity. In addition, his brother had once been committed to an insane asylum, indicating a hereditary condition of mental problems. Found guilty at trial, he was sentenced to six years hard labor, but before he began serving time, the state supreme court reversed the original indictment. He was tried a few more times on the original charges, but each trial resulted in a hung jury.[6]

Mayor Ames, pictured in a magazine exposé in 1903. The author Lincoln Steffens called him a "moral leper."

1900 1919

On January 15, 1903, James H. Tillman, Democratic lieutenant governor of South Carolina and nephew of a U.S. senator, pulled a pistol and shot Narciso Gonzales on a public street in Columbia, South Carolina. Gonzales, the editor of a local newspaper, had previously written strongly worded editorials against Tillman's unsuccessful campaign for governor, calling him, among other things, a "criminal candidate," "blackguard," and "proved liar." Gonzales died a few days later. At his murder trial, Tillman claimed self-defense, reporting that he saw Gonzales reaching into his pocket, supposedly for a gun. He was acquitted.[7]

Edmund Hope Driggs (1865–1946), former Democratic representative from New York, was indicted by a federal grand jury in 1903 for accepting money to influence the awarding of a federal contract while he was in office. The case involved the Edward J. Brandt-Dent Company and the sale of 250 cash registers to the U.S. Post Office. For his help in arranging the sale, Driggs received $12,500. At trial, Driggs defended himself by arguing he had not known he was doing anything illegal. Throughout the investigation and trial, he willingly answered all questions, impressing both the judge and jury. Although found guilty, he was sentenced to only one day in prison.[8]

George Bruce Cortelyou (1862–1940), secretary of commerce in the administration of President Theodore Roosevelt, became the campaign manager for the president in his reelection campaign in 1904. Although not personally attacked as unethical, Cortelyou became the target of reformers because he was also the chairman of the National Republican Committee and had led a major effort to collect large contributions from corporations. This kind of fund-raising activity had only recently begun to be regulated by the Commerce Department. An editorial in the *New York Times* lashed out at this arrangement, calling it a "public scandal" and a "national disgrace." For a time, the

George Cortelyou

concept of attracting financial support from large companies in exchange for real or implied government favors was known as
"Cortelyouism." Roosevelt's campaign, a successful one, was tarnished
by the allegations of large corporate contributions. A few days before
the election, Roosevelt addressed the issue, stating that charges of misconduct were false and contributions from large businesses had been
made to both parties, a practice that was legal and ethical. He also declared, "If elected, I shall go into the presidency unhampered by any
pledge, promise, or understanding of any kind, sort, or description."
Over the next few years, however, the allegations surfaced again and
the president was forced to defend himself several more times, especially after letters appeared providing evidence of some inappropriate
fund-raising. In one case, Roosevelt was called to testify in an investigation involving Standard Oil and a large contribution they made to his
campaign in 1904. Not only was no link made between this money and
Roosevelt himself, the oil company—and other large companies that
had backed his candidacy—complained that they had suffered during
his adminstration because of new government restrictions he championed. If he had accepted contributions in exchange for favors, the favors had not been delivered.[9]

President Teddy Roosevelt leaving a congressional investigation of campaign contributions.

John Shafroth

On February 15, 1904, John Franklin Shafroth (1854–1922), Democratic representative from Colorado, resigned his seat in Congress. In a public speech on the floor of the House, Shafroth declared that reports that surfaced after his election suggested that fraud had been commonplace in the polls, making his victory unethical. Although he had nothing to do with the fraud, he believed his opponent, Republican Robert W. Bonynge, should replace him. He was thereafter referred to as "Honest John" and was widely applauded for his action, which was a novelty in Congress. His reaction went even further. Some published reports suggested that the vote fraud that led to his decision involved women—in Colorado, women had been voting in state elections since 1893—but the ex-congressman did not support this conclusion. He stated, "Of the persons implicated very few were women—not more than one in ten at the outside.... Everybody knows there are bad women as well as bad men; but what would any good man think if it were proposed to take his vote away from him because a few bad men somewhere had cheated at an election?" Shafroth had been a Republican himself for four terms before switching parties. In 1908, he was elected governor of Colorado and returned to Congress as a senator in 1913.[10]

Martin Behrman (1864–1926), Democrat, began his first term as mayor of New Orleans in 1904. He served until 1920 and was elected again in 1925, serving until his death the following year, a total of almost seventeen years in office, the longest in New Orleans history. Behrman's reign was noted for the presence of the Democratic-backed Choctaw Club, a political machine that controlled most city activities. One example of its control was its success in stalling efforts by civic reformers and the U.S. Navy to terminate a notorious zone of prostitution in the city known as Storeyville. It was finally closed down in 1917, during World War I, at which point Behrman stated, "You can make it illegal, but you can't make it unpopular." The club also severely restricted political participation by black citizens and blocked other movements associated with progressive government. Behrman and his machine, however, were credited with some improvements, including building schools, hospitals, sewer systems, and water works, the development of the Public Belt Railroad, and expanding the city's port.[11]

On September 25, 1904, Alonzo J. Whiteman, former mayor of Duluth, Minnesota, was arrested in St. Louis on a charge of fraud. Whiteman was the son of a millionaire and had inherited a sizable estate before he became addicted to gambling. After burning through his own money, he shifted to crime to raise cash. The ex-mayor—also ex–state legislator and ex-chairman of the Minnesota Democratic Central Committee—had been hunted by Pinkerton agents on behalf of the American Bankers Association due to his success in forging checks. Although he originally worked alone, Whiteman eventually organized a gang and, according to police records, established elaborate schemes to provide alibis and keep himself from being caught, but not always successfully. A newspaper report stated he had been arrested twenty-three times and sentenced to a total of sixteen years. After his arrest in 1904, Whiteman escaped from detectives and was not caught again until 1905.[12]

The election in 1904 in Colorado resulted in an apparent victory for Democrat Alva Adams for governor. However, evidence of widespread election fraud caused his Republican opponents to challenge the outcome and claim victory for their candidate, James Peabody. The election involved so much illegal activity that the state supreme court took control of ninety-nine precincts in Denver. A judge eventually ordered a grand jury to investigate this activity, stating "...the grossest frauds were committed on election day, May 15 last; that a bold and brazen attempt was made to steal the election, and on the face of the

Alva Adams

returns succeeded, by debauching of the ballot boxes and the corruption of public officials, in stealing valuable assets of the community; that public officials charged with the ferreting out of crime and the punishment of criminals were either parties to this outrage or were so negligent in the discharge of their duties as to make the particepes criminis." Significant ongoing acrimony in the state legislature over the contested returns eventually forced them to void both the Democratic and Republican candidacies—each claimed victory—and the lieutenant governor, Jesse McDonald, a Republican, was placed in office as a compromise. The grand jury investigation resulted in a number of people indicted, tried, and convicted of activities that altered the vote, particularly the use of "repeaters" to bolster the count. On December 10, 1904, four election officers received sentences ranging from three to nine months in prison and fines of up to $500 each; additional arrests and trials ensued.[13]

In 1905, John Newton Williamson (1855–1943), two-term Republican representative from Oregon, was convicted of conspiracy to defraud the U.S. government and conspiring to commit perjury. The case involved Williamson, U.S. Senator John Mitchell, a former judge, an Oregon land commissioner, and others. All were alleged to be connected to a land fraud scheme in which up to one hundred people were enticed to apply for plots carved from government land. A private company owned by some of the defendants was to be the actual beneficiary. Williamson's conviction was overturned on appeal, and he was tried twice more, both cases ending up with hung juries.[14]

John Green Brady (1847–1918), three-term governor of the Alaska territory, was implicated in unfair practices activity in 1905. The Reynolds Alaska Development Company, a mining company, employed Brady as its director, a fact they advertised to help influence business and boost the sale of the stock. Responding to criticism, the company dropped Brady from his position, but the governor initially refused requests to resign from office. Complaints from other companies, politicians, and even the White House, however, finally forced him to leave office, effective February 14, 1906.[15]

Charles Henry Swayne (1842–1907), U.S. district court judge in Florida, was impeached by the U.S. House on December 13, 1904, the first impeachment of a government official since 1876. He was charged with misconduct in office related to "maladministration" of a bankruptcy matter before him, as well as illegally purchasing land that was involved in a case he was trying. On February 27, 1905, the Senate voted for acquittal.[16]

On June 4, 1906, Joseph Ralph Burton (1852–1923), Republican senator from Kansas, resigned his seat, anticipating congressional action to expel him. He had been convicted in Missouri for illegally accepting $2,500 from a St. Louis grain company in exchange for his influence in a mail fraud investigation against the company. Although found guilty—he ultimately served five months in prison—Burton delayed the inevitable by twice appealing his case to the U.S. Supreme Court. The first time, the Court ruled in his favor and forced a federal grand jury in Missouri to retry the case, but this also resulted in a conviction. The second appeal sealed his fate.[17]

Sherburn Becker

Sherburn Becker (1876–1949), Republican mayor of Milwaukee, was elected to office in 1906. A flamboyant campaigner and a colorful mayor, the youthful Becker was elected when he was twenty-nine years old. Called the "boy mayor," he promoted the city by driving through the eastern states in a bright red automobile dubbed the "Red Devil," even dropping in on President Roosevelt at his home in New York. Becker's term was marked by a scandal involving retail signs on city streets and the city's signature "tower clocks," up to fifty at the turn of the century. There were ordinances banning some of the clocks and many retail signs because they obstructed traffic, but nothing had been done to fix the problem. The mayor's solution was a sneak attack, removing the offending units under cover of darkness. Public outcry resulted, along with lawsuits against the city, cutting short Becker's political career.[18]

In 1906, William A. Martin, a member of the city council of Pittsburgh, Pennsylvania, was arrested for participating in a graft scheme. Martin and the president of a local railroad company conspired to bribe other members of the council to vote in favor of awarding this company a franchise. A fund of $70,000 was used and allegedly stashed in a safety deposit box in a local bank, to be drawn upon by council members willing to participate. When several of them went to claim their share, however, they discovered a bundle of newspaper comics instead of the promised cash. They promptly blew the whistle on the affair and fingered Martin, who took the blame and was convicted. In a statement, he said that officials were elected with honest motives, but only the strongest ones could resist the temptations offered by corporations seeking their votes for or against various issues.[19]

1900 1919

In his first term in office, Mayor John Francis Fitzgerald (1863–1950) of Boston, Massachusetts, created a new job in order to employ a friend. The position: tea warmer. Reformers began to put more pressure on cities at this time to clean up obvious sources of corruption, but patronage jobs remained one of the major elements that city leaders relied on to reward supporters. And Fitzgerald had a lot of supporters to reward. He was a two-term mayor and head of a strong political machine—and also the maternal grandfather of future political brothers John, Robert, and Edward Kennedy. "Honey Fitz" had served three terms as a Democratic representative from Massachusetts before being elected mayor. He was noted for running successful campaigns that relied on heavy expenditures and a trademark style. He became a target of both reformers and rival politicians, however, and finally left office in 1914 as another noted local machine leader, James Curley, jockeyed for power. Curley used an intimidation ploy to force Fitzgerald to drop his bid for

John Fitzgerald
(left of center)

a third term. A newspaper ad was placed reporting that Curley would have several speeches ready to deliver if necessary. The title of one was "Great Lovers: From Cleopatra to Toodles." Most readers may have missed the meaning of the second name, but not Fitzgerald. "Toodles" was the nickname of a blond cigarette girl who was rumored to be his girlfriend. The threat of public disclosure was enough to prompt his exit from the race.[20]

Arthur Brown

On December 9, 1906, Arthur Brown (1843–1906), former Republican senator from Utah (1896–1897), was shot in Washington, D.C., and died a few days later. Mrs. Anna Bradley, arrested for the shooting, stated that Brown, an attorney, had fathered two of her children during a long-running illicit affair. He was in Washington to argue a case before the Supreme Court when she shot him. The ex-senator was not a stranger to violence from women. His first wife also shot at him, reportedly after she caught him paying too much attention to a newsstand clerk, but that shot missed its target. Remarried after a divorce, his second wife also caught him straying— with Anna Bradley—after intercepting their encoded love letters. Successfully decoding them, she used the contents to have her husband and Bradley arrested. After his second wife died of cancer and Bradley's husband divorced her, Brown refused to "do the right thing," prompting Mrs. Bradley's extreme action. After a lurid public trial, she was acquitted on the grounds of temporary insanity.[21]

In Philadelphia, John Edgar Reyburn (1845–1914) was elected mayor in 1907 after serving three terms as a U.S. representative. During his four-year mayoral term, the former congressman led a well-organized Republican machine that was implicated or charged in several cases of graft and corruption. The mayor himself was charged with receiving $400,000 or more from corporations, politicians, contractors, and public officers. His defense was that his name had been forged. Several public officials and private contractors were eventually convicted, but Reyburn was never indicted or tried. Near the end of his term, a noted minister of an Episcopal Church announced in a public address that Reyburn was "disreputable and degenerate and unfit to hold office." A local Methodist preacher joined the attack, stating "The entire city is disgraced by the rotten gang in authority." He went on to chastise the mayor's wife for holding bridge parties, which he equated with gambling. A newspaper article at the time stated, "Every four years Philadelphia elects a Mayor, who is a pooh-bah and a czar... Nothing is valid without the Mayor's signature. Common rumor declares that no man need be Mayor of Philadelphia and be poor at the end of his term unless he wishes." Although Reyburn survived legal attacks while he was in office, he also had a close call that was more physical. In 1910, a man walked into the mayor's office and, after drawing a crude sketch of Reyburn on a piece of paper, stated, "... that's the mayor, and I came here to kill him." He stabbed a pencil through the drawing and was arrested before any violence was attempted.[22]

In July 1907, Charles Boxton (1860–1927), a dentist, was appointed to take the place of San Francisco mayor Eugene Schmitz, who had been deposed after being convicted of extortion. Boxton had also been involved in the extortion scheme but had not been charged because he had agreed to provide evidence to help convict Schmitz. San Francisco

THE ART OF MUDSLINGING

Politicians have attacked one another since the first election. When attacks become personal or negative, they are called mudslinging. In the presidential election of 1908, mudslinging was common among the major candidates. This political cartoon from that campaign shows Roosevelt, Bryan, Hearst, and other politicians blaming one another for the practice. The caption reads: " 'He began it, teacher.' The National Schoolteacher is somewhat indignant at the prevalence of mudslinging."

voters, upon learning that the newly appointed mayor represented "business as usual," raised a ruckus, forcing Boxton to resign after eight days in office. This set the record for the shortest term for any mayor in the city's history.[23]

In 1907, Governor James H. Higgins (1876–1927) of Rhode Island, a Democrat, made an attempt to control corruption in the state. Higgins believed that General Charles Brayton, the leader of the state Republican party, was conducting personal and political business in a local sheriff's office, which was state property, and he attempted to have him physically removed. The sheriff defied the governor's request. The matter escalated until Brayton resigned his position with the state Republicans, ending a long reign in control of local politics. He was known as "The Blind Boss" because he had lost most of his vision a few years earlier. Higgins, the youngest governor in state history when elected—and the youngest in the country—had campaigned on a platform combating corruption in state government.[24]

Los Angeles was the setting for a recall election for mayor in 1909, the first recall election for mayor in any U.S. city. The sitting mayor, A. C. Harper, had been increasingly linked to corrupt activities, which became a major public issue when exposed by a local newspaper. The mayor and his chief of police were accused of involvement in a protection racket for a local red light district, run by a character known as the "Tenderloin King." On March 12, 1909, just before the recall election, the mayor resigned, stating that the editor of the newspaper "had the dope on me, and the only thing I could do was to get down and out." His chief of police resigned as well.[25]

On September 3, 1909, President William Howard Taft was stopped for speeding while being driven through the town of Newbury, Massachusetts. The stop came from a speed trap set up by local constables. Upon recognizing the president—who apologized for traveling faster than the speed limit—they let him continue on his way. Taft was known for his support of the automobile industry and was the first president to own a car, a 48-horsepower Pierce Arrow.[26]

In 1910, Mayor William P. White of Lawrence, Massachusetts, and three colleagues were convicted of bribing city aldermen in order to influence their vote to remove the fire chief. While in jail, he contended he had the authority to perform his duties, but on the outside, the president of the Board of Aldermen, who had taken over the mayor's duties when he was imprisoned, insisted he had the same authority, giving the city two apparent mayors. Eventually, White conceded and, on July 22, 1910, resigned from office. In his resignation he stated, "It is manifest that I cannot now perform the duties which my office would require of me, and I cannot suffer the interest of the city to be jeopardized or embarrassed."[27]

On November 16, 1907, Oklahoma became the forty-sixth state, and Charles Nathaniel Haskell (1860–1933) was appointed governor. A

few years later, Haskell decided that the state capital in Guthrie should be moved a few miles away, to the rapidly growing town of Oklahoma City. Although the move had some practical value, one of the underlying motivations was politics. In Guthrie, the Republican party was dominant and provided little support for Haskell, who was a Democrat. He preferred the atmosphere in Oklahoma City, a Democratic stronghold. Initially, the decision to move was tackled through normal political channels, starting with a debate in the state legislature. Rather than wait for the outcome, however, the governor packed up the state seal and key papers and moved his office himself early on the morning of June 12, 1910, creating a minor scandal.[28]

Charles Haskell

In Portland, Maine, on May 2, 1910, Frederick Hale (1874–1963), Republican candidate for U.S. representative, attacked the editor of a local newspaper and beat him with a horse whip, stating "Take that, you cur." The editor had published an article in which he wrote that Hale's mother deserved scorn

Frederick Hale

for supporting her son's ambitions, because in doing so "she lays aside the garments of modesty which in New England protect womanhood from political asperities, and stands forth in all the hideousness of open corruption." When questioned about the whipping, the editor replied, "It was a manly thing to do. A man who won't stand up for his mother doesn't amount to much." Hale lost the election but in 1916 was elected to the U.S. Senate. His father was Eugene Hale, also a U.S. senator.[29]

Isaac Stephenson (1829–1918), Republican senator from Wisconsin, barely escaped losing his seat in Congress following allegations of campaign corruption during the 1909 election. An investigation in the state found that he had spent $107,000 during the race even though Wisconsin had recently passed a law that limited expenditures to $7,500. His defense was that the law was not yet in effect. In addition, the state had adopted a primary election process in which the popular vote was used to indicate voter preference for senatorial candidates, although the results were not binding. Only a year later, the Seventeenth Amendment was ratified, making popular election of senators a national standard. Still, the Senate voted to keep Stephenson in office, partly because of the realization that the campaign "traditions" of the past were about to become history and partly in deference to his advanced age. He was eighty-three at the time.[30]

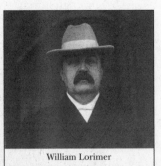

William Lorimer

On July 13, 1912, William Lorimer (1861–1934), Republican senator from Illinois, became the last U.S. senator to be expelled from office for corrupt electoral practices. Lorimer, an English immigrant, served two terms in the House before his ill-fated run for the Senate in 1909. Nicknamed "The Blond Boss," Lorimer used his wealth—he made a fortune in brick manufacturing and real estate—to entertain voters and influence legislators at the tail end of the era when senators were elected by electoral votes. In the 1909 election, he bribed legislators, several of whom had been found with "unusual sums of money in bills of large denominations." Two Senate investigations were held following accusations of misconduct. The first ended with a slim majority voting in his favor, the second found his election fraudulent and he was expelled.[31]

In July 1912, thirteen aldermen in Detroit, Michigan, were caught taking bribes to influence the outcome of a vote on the expansion of local railroad property. The aldermen were trapped using a detective imported from Los Angeles and a newfangled invention, the dictagraph, a machine that recorded human voices. The leader of the group was Thomas "Honest Tom" Glinnan, a candidate in an upcoming election for mayor.[32]

William Sulzer

On October 17, 1913, William Sulzer (1863–1941), governor of New York, was removed from office after being impeached. Sulzer, a Democrat, was found guilty of diverting campaign contributions for personal use and being "contemptuous" of the power of the state assembly. The impeachment was also politically motivated, a reaction to his campaign to end the patronage practiced by Tammany Hall politicians. The Tammany Democrats—based in New York City but strong enough to influence state politics—controlled enough votes in the assembly to remove any impediment to their activities, including a reform-minded governor. At the time of his impeachment, Sulzer had been in office for only ten months. Later the same year, he won election to the state house while running as an Independent.[33]

In 1913, Robert Woodrow Archbald (1848–1926), associate judge of the U.S. commerce court, was accused of illegally collaborating with officials in mining and railroad companies. The U.S. House impeached him in 1913 after a recommendation from its Judiciary Committee, which stated, "Your committee is of the opinion that

Judge Archbald's sense of moral responsibility has become deadened. He has prostituted his high office for personal profit. He has attempted by various transactions to commercialize his potentiality as Judge." On January 13, 1913, the U.S. Senate found Archbald guilty on five of thirteen articles of impeachment and voted he be removed from office.[34]

William Forte Willett Jr. (1869–1938), former Democratic representative from New York, was charged with bribery. The congressman, whose second term ended in 1911, was tried along with two other politicians for attempting to obtain a nomination to the state supreme court. Willett was found guilty and sentenced to twelve to eighteen months in prison.[35]

In Los Angeles in 1915, Mayor Charles Sebastian was publicly embarrassed by a court case during his election campaign. He was charged

PROFILE   Ohio Voter Fraud

The simplest method of election fraud is buying votes. One of the most spectacular cases of vote buying occurred in 1910 in Adams County, Ohio. Following a local election, 1,679 voters were arrested, tried, and convicted of selling their votes, more than 25 percent of the total number of voters in the county. The legal action put so much pressure on the local court system that the first night session in Ohio history was held to accommodate the traffic. Death threats were made against Judge A. Z. Blair, who presided over the activity—he also admitted to being a vote buyer earlier in his career, before he reformed—as well as the members of the grand jury who issued the indictments. Among the defendants were farmers, lawyers, doctors, business owners, and three pastors. Each of the names was on a list along with the amount needed for their vote. Prices ranged from a shot of whisky to $25 each, with the average being $8. Running for office here was so expensive that according to some residents, more than one prospective candidate bribed his political party not to have his name listed for office because of the high cost of running.[36]

with having sex with his girlfriend in front of her underage sister. Although acquitted by the jury, a local citizen angry at the outcome shot at him several times after the trial. The bullets missed their mark, but publicity about his brush with death produced a sympathy vote that propelled Sebastian into office. He resigned a year later.[37]

In 1916, a federal grand jury indicted one hundred beer-making companies in Pennsylvania for illegal political activity. The United States Brewers' Association was included in the indictment. Specifically, these entities were charged with "unlawfully, willfully, knowingly, fraudulently, and feloniously" contributing to the campaigns of several U.S. congressmen and a senator during the 1914 election. The case was one of the first applications of a new campaign law that restricted contributions from corporations in presidential and congressional elections. All of the defendants pleaded "nolo contendre" and paid a fine.[38]

The Adams County grand jury, with seven Democrats, seven Republicans, and one Prohibitionist selected to try the case. Photographed for *McClure's Magazine,* November 1911. In the same issue, an article by Judge Blair covered the background and story of the vote-buying extravaganza in Ohio.

Thomas B. Smith (1869–1949), mayor of Philadelphia, was indicted in 1917 on charges of conspiracy in the killing of a city policeman. The murder was part of an election-related fraud, which included a riot in one of the city's wards. A local judge stated that the mayor was "the chief and primal factor in this great disgrace, for which I personally feel ashamed of my city." The mayor, a Republican and head of the local party machine, was acquitted of the charges.[39]

James Edward Ferguson (1871–1944), Democratic governor of Texas, resigned from office on August 25, 1917. Ferguson, who was known as "Farmer Jim," faced impeachment at the beginning of his second term. The charges included embezzlement, diversion of a special state fund, and misapplication of other state funds. The state senate found him guilty on ten counts. Ferguson had originally been accused of irregularities in 1916, but a legislative investigation at the time did not find enough evidence to pursue a case. A year later, probably because of his involvement in political wrangling over funding for the University of Texas, the new charges were brought forward, forcing his resignation. Ferguson's wife, Miriam, popularly known as "Ma Ferguson," was elected governor of the state in 1925, and while in office tried unsuccessfully to clear her husband's name.[40]

In February 1919, Victor Luitpold Berger (1860–1929), U.S. representative from Wisconsin, was sentenced in federal court to twenty years in the penitentiary after a conviction for treason. He had vocally opposed the involvement of the United States in World War I. Berger was one of the few Socialists ever elected to a national office but had his seat blocked in the House by a resolution based on the treason charge. The federal court sentence was reversed in 1921 by the U.S. Supreme Court. Despite several subsequent campaigns in which he was again elected to the House, Berger was always blocked from serving by the House and was never officially seated as a congressman.[41]

PROFILE   The Model T Candidate

The election for the U.S. Senate in Michigan in 1918 was not the first or the last to involve a major industrialist, but it created a national stir at the time because of who was involved. Henry Ford (1863–1947), wealthy automobile manufacturer and Democrat, challenged Truman Newberry (1864–1945), Republican and a wealthy industrialist himself. He was president of

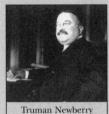

Truman Newberry

Detroit Steel & Spring Company. Despite newly enacted legislation that limited campaign expenditures, both candidates spent lavishly. Ford hedged his bets by entering both the Democratic and Republican primaries, but in the end came up short in both, with Newberry the winner. Ford contested the election results, claiming unlawful expenditures and voter intimidation. Newberry and others involved in his

1900 1919

Henry Ford

campaign were indicted and found guilty after a wide-ranging investigation funded in part by Henry Ford. The U.S. Supreme Court later reversed Newberry's conviction on technical grounds and the Senate exonerated him in its own inquiry, although it did condemn the large sums spent during the campaign.[42]

Above, workers burn Ford–Newberry ballots at the order of a federal judge. Right, Ford's telegram contesting the election.

1920–1939

Teapot Dome, a scandal that emerged in the early 1920s, became a major showcase for the misuse of government contracts. Chapters of this story dominated headlines from 1922 to 1931 and involved speculators, the secretary of the interior, the Senate, and President Warren Harding. Even before news of the scandal broke, the eminent journalist H. L. Mencken summarized his feelings on Harding: "No other such complete and dreadful nitwit is to be found in the pages of American history." Although Harding escaped direct accusations of misdoings, he was responsible for appointing enough perpetrators of fraudulent activity to set the record for the most abusive administration to date. Under his reign, the Justice Department was known as the "Department of Easy Virtue." This atmosphere, along with the lingering effects of Prohibition and the arrival of the Great Depression, provided a ripe opportunity for the election of a reform politician, Franklin Delano Roosevelt, with a "New Deal" promising relief to millions. Although popular, FDR was not untouched by political problems. His administration suffered from scandals tied to the huge piles of "funny money" coming from the new government programs, and his wife—a precedent-setting first lady—attracted criticism as well.

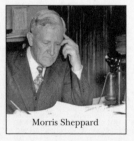

Morris Sheppard

On September 6, 1920, an illegal still was discovered north of Austin, Texas, on a farm owned by U.S. Senator Morris Sheppard (1875–1941). Sheppard, a Democrat, was the principal author of the Eighteenth Amendment, which created Prohibition. The federal agents who raided the farm reported the still had the capacity of 130 gallons a day. Along with the still, they seized 400 gallons of whisky and seven barrels of sour mash. The operators of the still escaped, and Sheppard was not implicated in its operation. In 1930, Senator Sheppard was quoted as saying "There's as much chance of repealing the 18th Amendment as there is for a humming bird [*sic*] to fly to Mars with the Washington Monument tied to its tail."[1]

On August 16, 1920, a chauffeured car carrying Governor James M. Cox (1870–1957) of Ohio was stopped for speeding on a state highway. At the time of the incident, members of the governor's staff stated they

James Cox

thought local Republican officials had created a speed trap just to catch the governor, who was a Democrat and a candidate for president of the United States. Cox previously served two terms as U.S. representative from the state. The motorcycle policemen who stopped his car asked him to return to the station—a standard request—but the governor, in a hurry, ordered his driver to move on.[2]

1920
1939

Fred Kohler (1864–1934), Republican, was elected mayor of Cleveland despite a spotty record in public service. In 1913, while he was chief of police for the city, he was removed from office on charges of "gross immorality, conduct unbecoming a gentleman and an officer, and conduct subversive to good order and discipline in the department." The latter issue related to allegations he had improper relations with the wife of a traveling salesman. Previous charges included intoxication and insubordination. Known as "The Golden Rule Chief," Kohler continued to be controversial while mayor and was also accused of accepting unethical campaign contributions. In 1926, prisoners in the municipal jail rioted, complaining of a "starvation diet," reportedly the result of an emaciated budget that had been deflated by profiteering. The publicity generated by this revelation disclosed that while the prisoners got "bread and water" meals, they were offered pies for a fee.[3]

In 1921, the former governor of Florida, Sidney Johnston Catts (1863–1936), was indicted on charges he had accepted bribes to grant pardons. Another charge, on peonage (using enforced or involuntary labor), ended up with his arrest in public at a railroad station in Albany, Georgia. In 1928, a further indictment charged he had "aided and abetted" a gang of counterfeiters. In the first two cases, the charges were dismissed, but the final case ended up at trial, where a jury dead-locked on a decision. Before he went into politics, Catts was a Baptist minister.[4]

In 1921, voters in North Dakota held a recall election and voted to re-move Governor Lynn Joseph Frazier (1874–1947) from office. This was the first statewide recall election in the United States. Frazier had

1920 1939

been backed politically by the state's Non-Partisan League, and the recall was sponsored by the Anti-Non-Partisan League. The Non-Partisan move-ment in the state primarily represented a faction of the Republican party; the "anti-" faction was organ-ized to oppose them. The issue that precipitated the recall was a crisis involving the Bank of North Dakota, in which the State Industrial Commission was blamed for burdening small private banks with demands for payments for outstanding loans. The

Lynn Frazier

commission's members included the governor, the attorney general and the commissioner of agriculture, both targeted for recall as well. After his ouster, Frazier was elected to the U.S. Senate in 1922 as a Republican and served successive terms until 1941.[5]

J. B. A. Robertson

In 1921, the legislature in Oklahoma at-tempted to impeach Democratic Governor J. B. A. Robertson (1871–1938). The attempt ended with a tie vote, leaving him in office. The tie resulted from a decisive vote by a sick Democratic legislator who was carried from his hospital bed to the capitol so that he could vote against the resolution. The impeachment was precipitated by charges of corruption in Robertson's administra-tion, partly motivated by partisan politics. In the legislature's report on the matter, they concluded: "Governor Robertson's administration of office has been characterized by waste and incompetency so great that it is beyond the time and facility of this committee to present concrete instance in full." Specifics included excessive and questionable granting of clemency to convicted criminals, illegal transfers of state funds to the governor's private bank account, and hiring state employees to lobby for initiatives, among other charges. During the drawn-out political confrontations in the wake of the failed impeachment, an Oklahoma businessman refused to shake hands with Robertson in a public venue in 1922, resulting in a physical attack by the governor. The same month, the governor and the state bank commissioner were indicted on a charge of accepting a bribe. Robertson's indictment was later dismissed by the state supreme court.[6]

1920 1939

Thomas J. O'Dally, a cashier in the city treasurer's office in Boston, was arrested on April 20, 1921, on charges he embezzled up to $40,000 in city funds. O'Dally's theft was discovered during an audit conducted just after he had been promoted to city treasurer. The cashier, whose nickname was "Honest Tom," had been employed by the city for thirty-five years and admitted to illegally withdrawing funds for ten of them.[7]

On August 9, 1921, Governor Lennington Small (1862–1936) of Illinois was arrested and charged with embezzlement of state funds. The governor, a Republican, was accused of conspiring with the lieutenant governor and another man to profit from interest on official state investments—he benefited by an estimated $700,000—while in his previous position as state treasurer. This was the first time in Illinois history that a sitting governor was arrested on a criminal charge. When first informed of a pending indictment, the governor claimed immunity, sparking a heated legal debate. In the end, all charges except for conspiracy were dropped because of technicalities. For the embezzlement charge, for instance, the foreman of the grand jury had signed his name in the wrong place on a court document, making it invalid. On June 24, 1922, the governor's trial concluded

Lennington Small
AP Images

PROFILE | Teapot Dome Scandal

Teapot Dome, Wyoming, is not on most maps. It is a more or less teapot-shaped sandstone formation about twenty-five miles north of Casper, Wyoming. Near this spot is the site of U.S. Naval Oil Reserve Number Three, 9,481 acres that encompass a large underground deposit of oil set aside in 1915 for strategic use. After the reserve was transferred to the control of the Interior Department through the Oil Land Leasing Act of 1920, Albert Fall, the secretary of the interior, secretly leased lucrative drilling rights to the reserve—and a similar one in Elk Hills, California—to two oil companies, a fact that became public in 1922.

The teapot dome rock formation north of Casper, Wyoming.

Although the leasing itself did not violate any laws, other issues turned this into a major scandal. An investigation disclosed that the owners of

Albert Fall

the two companies had loaned large sums to Fall without charging interest and, in addition, the leases had been awarded without competitive bidding. The two executives were cleared of bribery charges in a federal trial, but their companies were forced to give up the leases, forfeit their investment in drilling, and pay back more than $47 million they had profited from the federal deal. Harry Daugherty, the attorney general, took heat —publicly and politically—for not pursuing the case with enough vigor, and Edwin Denby, the secretary of the navy, was blamed for allowing the Interior Department to take over the administration of the reserves.

Both resigned. On October 25, 1929, after lengthy court battles, Fall was convicted of accepting a bribe, sentenced to a year in prison, and fined $100,000, roughly the same amount he had accepted from one of

Harry Daugherty questioned by reporters during the investigation.

the oil men, who, as noted, was acquitted of providing the bribe. Teapot Dome is the event most often associated with the scandal-ridden Harding administration, but the story did not become public until after he died in office, dragging the mess into the presidency of Calvin Coolidge. Secretary of the Interior Albert Fall resigned before the scandal broke and before his involvement became public. He didn't leave to avoid scrutiny, but to spend time expanding and fixing up his Wyoming ranch with the income he made from the deals.[8]

1920 1939

The Senate committee in the process of investigating the oil leases at Teapot Dome.

PROFILE   Big Bill Thompson

William Hale Thompson (1867–1944) was first elected mayor of Chicago on April 6, 1915. "Big Bill" was in office until 1923, when he was defeated during a strong reform movement, but was reelected in 1927 and remained in office until 1931. In his two stints as mayor, Thompson, a Republican, presided over one of the most corrupt periods in Chicago history, an era that included Prohibition and organized gang activity. City jobs were tightly controlled as patronage positions, city employees at all levels were expected to con-

William Thompson

tribute—cash and votes—to the local party, and contracts for city business required bribes and kickbacks (as with many other political machines). At the same time, police and prosecutors allowed gambling, prostitution, and alcohol sales to flourish, getting a cut of the action for their permissiveness. In 1927, Thompson estimated that citywide police payoffs from criminal activities totaled $30 million. One of Thompson's major supporters was Al Capone, who directly benefited from Big Bill's administration. Capone not only contributed to cam-

with an acquittal. In a subsequent civil trial brought by the state to recover funds allegedly diverted by Small when he was treasurer, the governor lost and agreed to a settlement of $650,000.[9]

On November 7, 1922, Earle Bradford Mayfield (1881–1964) was elected as a Democratic senator from Texas. The 1922 election was marked by numerous irregularities, both on Mayfield's side and from his opponent, George Peddy, a prominent attorney who was forced to run as a write-in candidate after the Democrats succeeded in keeping his name off the ballot. During a Senate investigation, a recount of the ballots found "thousands" of improper votes, as well as illegal campaigns, members of his crime syndicate helped determine the outcome of some elections. Apart from the rampant corruption, the mayor was also noted for his eccentricities. At one time, he made a public proclamation that he would like to punch the king of England in the mouth, stating "If King George comes to Chicago, I'll crack him on the snoot." Big Bill had a large base of support among German American voters, angered other politicians by courting black voters and supporting causes beneficial to them, campaigned to replace the history textbooks then in use in the schools, and once led a burro on a halter during a reelection campaign, shouting "If you want a mayor... who cannot be bought, bluffed, or bribed, vote to reelect Bill Thompson." When he died in 1944, Thompson's estate

""Big Bill" works a parade.

*1920
1939*

was estimated to be worth about $150,000, but the contents of several safety deposit boxes, including cash, checks, and securities, quickly inflated the total to more than $1.5 million. Witnesses described wads of cash springing out of deposit boxes "like a jack-in-the-box."[10]

paign expenditures. In addition, it was disclosed that the Ku Klux Klan actively supported Mayfield (at the time, the KKK was heavily involved in the state Democratic party). The Senate concluded, however, that none of these irregularities would have altered the outcome of the election, and Mayfield was allowed to keep his seat. In 1948, Peddy made another try for the Senate seat. This time, he was defeated by a young Lyndon Johnson.[11]

On August 6, 1922, the mayor of Ansonia, Connecticut, was arrested for allowing a baseball game with paid admission to be played on a Sunday. John Mead, the mayor, was charged with violating state statutes that banned such activity. The game had been organized to raise money for a local high school.[12]

Jack C. Walton (1881–1949), Democratic governor of Oklahoma, was impeached and expelled from office on November 19, 1923. Walton was at odds with his own party and opposed by many powerful groups in the state, especially the Ku Klux Klan. He was accused of misuse of martial law (he called out the state militia in response to public floggings linked to the Klan); the appointment of a "radical" to run a state college; issuing pardons for criminals, including a man who had killed a police officer; as well as commuting the death sentences of six prisoners to life imprisonment. Before he was governor, Walton, an engineer, designed the state's electric chair. His impeachment, however, was on other charges: obstruction of a special election organized to amend the state constitution to change the rules for impeachment; collecting excess campaign funds; padding the state payroll; and "general incompetence."[13]

On February 28, 1923, Colonel Charles Robert Forbes, director of the Veterans' Bureau, resigned his office. A friend of President Harding, Forbes was under increasing criticism for presiding over a department that was mismanaged and inefficient. His official reason for resigning was poor health, and at the time of his resignation, he had to use a cane to help him walk. A few weeks later, the general counsel for the Veterans' Bureau also resigned, then committed suicide. Before the

Charles Forbes

end of the year, a special Senate committee opened an investigation into the affairs of the organization, during which they uncovered cases of bribery and kickbacks to Forbes and others from private firms with department contracts, as well as evidence of extravagance and mismanagement. In one example of reported malfeasance, Forbes asked a contractor to help him "dispose" of 67,000 bottles of liquor and $5 million in medical drugs that were assigned to one veterans' hospital.

In February 1925, Forbes and one of the contractors implicated were found guilty of conspiracy to defraud the federal government and sentenced to two years in prison and fined $10,000. Forbes completed his sentence in November 1927 and reported he was healthier coming out than when he went in.[14]

Smith Brookhart

In a senatorial election in Iowa in 1924, incumbent Republican Smith Wildman Brookhart (1869–1944) won a narrow victory over Democratic challenger Daniel Steck (1881–1950), or did he? At the opening of Congress in 1925, Brookhart's win was contested by claims of illegal election activity and an erroneous vote count. The Democratic-led challenge was also supported by many Republicans—those in Iowa and from other states—due to Brookhart's progressive leanings. He was not considered a "reliable" Republican because in the presidential election, he had refused to support Coolidge, the Republican candidate. In his own Iowa campaign, the Republican party had resorted to publicly supporting Brookhart's Democratic opponent and at one point distributed sample ballots to registered party members with Steck marked as the candidate of choice, not Brookhart. A Senate investigation included a ballot recount and ended by reversing the outcome, as the majority of votes now favored Steck. Despite protests over irregularities in the recount process, including questions about how individual voters intended their votes to register, the full Senate voted forty-five to forty-one to replace Brookhart with Steck. The following year, Brookhart, still a registered Republican, ran for the other senatorial seat from Iowa, and won again. The results were not contested.[15]

1920 1939

Indiana governor Warren Terry McCray (1865–1938) resigned from office on April 29, 1924. For most of the preceding year, a scandal had been building, with the governor at the center. A slump in the state economy caused him heavy financial losses and forced a tough financial battle to save his personal assets, which included his family farm. When it was disclosed that forged loan notes were involved with his personal finances, legal problems ensued. McCray, a Republican, was indicted for embezzlement and other charges relating to income of $225,000 from the state Board of Agriculture and other organizations. The embezzlement charge was later dropped. He resigned his office one day after being convicted at trial, which resulted in a sentence of ten years in prison. He was paroled after serving three. President Hoover granted him a full pardon in 1930.[16]

1920 1939

Frederick Zihlman

In 1924, a grand jury indicted Frederick Nicholas Zihlman (1879–1935), seven-term Republican U.S. representative from Maryland, and John Wesley Langley (1868–1932), nine-term Republican U.S. representative from Kentucky. They were charged with bribery in a case involving cases of whisky removed from a government warehouse. Specifically, they accepted money to help facilitate a transfer of the illicit goods. Zihlman, a noted "dry" politician, was quickly exonerated by a grand jury and later by a House committee, which reported, "The evidence is conflicting and sharply contradictory and the question of the credibility of the individual witnesses has frequently arisen." Langley did not fare as well. In addition to the

bribery charge, he was indicted for conspiracy and influence peddling, was found guilty, and was sentenced to two years in federal prison. While waiting for a verdict on his appeal, he was reelected, but not before being arrested for drunkenness and jailed for four hours for contempt of court because he used profanity in his court hearing. In 1926, his appeal rejected, Langley began his prison term; his

John Langley

wife was elected in his place. While serving in Congress, she convinced President Coolidge to pardon her husband, making him eligible for public office again, although Langley did not take advantage of this opportunity. He maintained his innocence all the while. When he got out of prison, he wrote his autobiography, which was entitled *They Tried to Crucify Me.*[17]

William Freeland Kendrick (1874–1953), Republican, was elected mayor of Philadelphia in 1924. Generally considered a sound, honest leader (a Mason, Kendrick is credited with creating the concept of Shriner's

hospitals for crippled children), his troubles began when he tried to bring reform to a sinful city. At that point during Prohibition, *Time* magazine described Philadelphia thusly: "In addition to being the upkeeper of its own 13,000 saloons and speakeasies, Philadelphia appeared as a spigot from which alcohol poured out to all parts of the country with a source of supply dwarfing even Chicago's." Kendrick appointed noted Marine general Smedley Butler to clean up the city, a task that Butler—also known as "Old Gimlet Eye," the "Fighting Quaker," and in Philly, "The Dry Tsar"—pursued with zeal, raiding more than one thousand speakeasies, hotels, dance

1920
1939

William Kendrick meets boxing champion Jack Dempsey.

halls, and gambling dens. He also attempted to clean up the police department, expelling crooked cops and hiring new officers. At one point, he had the roofs of police cars removed so that officers would be less inclined to sleep on duty. Despite having earned two Medals of Honor for action in battle (he is the most decorated Marine in history), Butler ran afoul of many citizens, rich and poor, who felt victimized by his single-minded approach to the law. He ended up being a liability to the mayor, who fired him. The general summed up his experience by stating, "Cleaning up Philadelphia was worse than any battle I was ever in." The mayor was bruised further while presiding over the city's Sesquicentennial International Exposition in 1926 because the event turned out to be a major financial failure. He did not run for another term.[18]

Smedley Butler

George Washington English (1866–1941), federal judge in Illinois, resigned his position on November 4, 1926, while awaiting the opening of an impeachment hearing against him in the U.S. House. He was charged with "usurption of powers and other high misdemeanors" for allegedly manipulating funds held in bankruptcy cases, threats used against juries and counsels, misuse of judicial power, and swearing while on the bench. His resignation ended the purpose of an impeachment—to remove an official from office—and the hearing was canceled.[19]

In 1926, Pennsylvania created one of the more contested election outcomes in U.S. history. Battling for a senatorial seat, two wealthy candidates, William Wilson (1862–1934), Republican, and William Vare (1867–1934), Democrat, spent a combined $2 to $5 million on the primary race alone. Both candidates were experienced campaigners, each had been a U.S. representative, and both had large and established political forces behind them. Alarmed by reports of excessive campaign spending and vote fraud in the primary—phantom voters, voter intimidation, votes from unregistered voters, repeat voters, etc.—the Senate began an investigation before the general election and expanded its inquiry after the outcome determined Vare the winner. The Senate committee studying the events declared, "The fraud pervading the actual count by the division election officers is appalling." Their conclusion: a legitimate voter in Philadelphia only had

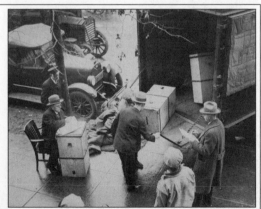

A congressional investigation required a close look at the ballots from the Pennsylvania election battle between William Vare and William Wilson. In this photograph, workers unload the ballot boxes at the U.S. Capitol under the close supervision of authorities.

William Vare

a one in eight chance of having his ballot correctly counted. However, political and legal maneuvering kept the investigation and subsequent Senate vote hanging for many months. The final outcome was not decided for three years, with two Supreme Court rulings pertaining to the case issued along the way. On December 6, 1929, the full Senate, by a large majority, voted to reject William Vare as the apparent winner—even though a majority of the nonfraudulent votes had likely been in his favor—because of the general unsavory nature of the election and the massive amount of money spent. At the same time, Vare's opponent, William Wilson, was also rejected, on the grounds that he had actually lost the election, fraud or no fraud. The governor of Pennsylvania ended up appointing a third man, Joseph Grundy, to fill the vacant seat. This, too, generated turmoil, although Grundy eventually was sworn into office.[20]

PROHIBITION POLITICS

Politicians in Washington, D.C., shared the same difficulties as the rest of the country during Prohibition. The city provided many opportunities to obtain alcohol, but law enforcement could make access a problem. This photograph shows Prohibition officers raiding a lunchroom on Pennsylvania Avenue, about seven blocks from the White House.

Frank Leslie Smith (1867–1950), Republican from Illinois, won the general election in 1926 for U.S. senator. Smith had previously been a member of the U.S. House and was well connected in state politics. But before Smith began his term, he faced allegations of campaign corruption tied to the 1926 primary. In that race, some sources charged he had made excessive expenditures, exceeding the maximum allowed. More important, he was accused of accepting $125,000 from the owner of a public utility while he was the chairman of the Illinois Commerce Commission, the state agency that regulated such utilities. After a lengthy inquiry, the Senate voted on January 19, 1928, to disqualify Smith from serving, stating that his credentials were "tainted with fraud and corruption." A few weeks later, the governor appointed Smith to his own vacant Senate seat, but Smith did not follow through by accepting. The governor then scheduled a special election to decide the issue, in which the voters were asked to decide both the outcome of the Senate vacancy and the fate of the governor himself. Both men lost to a third candidate.[21]

Malcolm E. Nichols (1876–1951) was elected mayor of Boston in 1926, one of the few Republicans to hold that office. A one-term mayor, Nichols was heavily tied to local Republican party boss Charles Innes and handicapped by following in the footsteps of notorious Boston Democratic boss James Curley. Problems during his term included the discovery of serious shortages in the accounts of the City Collecting Department, the delay of subway construction—a dodge to allow time for business colleagues to acquire land along the proposed route—as well as general vice and corruption. A widely publicized article in *Plain Talk Magazine* in 1929, entitled "Bawdy Boston," listed other specifics, including the operation of a "white slave ring" that provided prostitutes throughout the city, a large "dope racket," blackmail schemes, and bootlegging. While it was not all directly tied to the mayor, he was tainted enough to have his career cut short.[22]

On December 6, 1926, Alabama governor William Woodward Brandon (1868–1934) went on trial for possession of illegal alcohol. The Democratic governor, eight of this friends, and a black servant

William Brandon

were arrested at a fishing camp when a raid uncovered thirteen quarts of "rare old liquor." They were playing poker at the time. With no knowledge of the alcohol, Brandon was found innocent and Henry Hudson, his black servant, took the blame. Claiming ownership in court, Hudson was promised a pardon by the governor. Brandon was a former judge popularly known as "Plain Bill" and was an outspoken supporter of Prohibition.[23]

In 1927, the county attorney of Hennepin County, Minnesota, issued a legal injunction against a Minneapolis newspaper, the *Saturday Press*. The charge was the paper had violated a state law prohibiting any "malicious, scandalous, and defamatory newspaper, magazine, or other periodical." In specific, the injunction stated the paper had defamed the city's mayor, chief of police, members of a county grand jury, two other city newspapers, and "the Jewish race" by stating that Minneapolis and its leaders allowed the city to be controlled by a Jewish gangster involved in gambling, racketeering, and bootlegging. The case ended up in the U.S. Supreme Court, where the injunction was voided because the state law on which it was based was found to be unconstitutional.[24]

1920 1939

In March 1927, Thomas Woodnutt Miller (1886–1973) was sentenced to eighteen months in federal prison for defrauding the U.S. government. Miller, a former Republican representative from Delaware and son of a Delaware governor, was the Alien Property Custodian in 1921, serving under Attorney General Harry M. Daugherty (1860–1941). The government charge was that Miller and Daugherty had failed to use appropriate diligence in their approval of a claim for $7 million in assets for a company that had been seized during the war because of its partial ownership by German nationals. Another party in the original indictment killed himself during the subsequent investigation. The prosecution also claimed that both Daughterty and Miller had accepted bribes in the form of Liberty bonds for their role in expediting claims, although this was never proven. A jury found Miller guilty but it could not agree on a verdict for Daugherty, who went free. The Miller conviction came at the end of a second trial, because the first ended in a hung jury. It also set a record for the longest jury deliberation to date in a federal trial, more than sixty-five hours. Miller served a partial sentence before being paroled, and was later pardoned by President Hoover.[25]

In 1927, the mayor of Indianapolis, John Duvall, was charged with violation of the Corrupt Practices Act. Details of the case included failure to list campaign contributions and the promise of patronage jobs in exchange for political support. Duvall's political backers included the state's Ku Klux Klan and its leader, Grand Dragon D. C. Stephenson. Prosecutors revealed a written promise from Duvall, who stated, "I promise not to appoint any person as member of the Board of Public Works without they first have the endorsement of D. C. Stephenson." On another charge, accepting an illegal payment of $12,000, Duvall defended himself by claiming he did it to protect the public. On September 22, 1927, he was found guilty. Anticipating he would soon be out of a job, Duvall appointed his wife city controller, which would make her next in line to be mayor. He was sentenced to thirty days in jail and a fine of $1,000, and while appealing his conviction, he refused to resign. In the interim, the city council rejected his wife's appointment and named their own acting mayor, but this man was unable to take office, because Duvall barricaded himself inside the mayor's office suite, protected by a cordon of policemen. When he finally accepted the inevitable and left, things got even more complicated. His wife, questionable appointment or not, had appointed a re-

Ku Klux Klan parades were large public events in the 1920s. This is one was held in 1926 in the nation's capital.

placement to serve for her, creating a confusing collection of potential heads of the city. A court eventually intervened, placing yet another person in the position.[26]

Edward L. Jackson (1873–1954), Republican governor of Indiana, was a defendant in a lawsuit filed by the former wife of D. C. Stephenson, the state leader of the Ku Klux Klan. Stephenson had played a promi-

Edward Jackson

nent role in state politics before being convicted of murder, and at the time was behind bars. Stephenson's ex-wife sought financial support for her daughter, and she included Governor Jackson in her legal quest for Stephenson's property, including cash and automobiles, because the Klan had previously supported Jackson in both political and material ways. More serious for Jackson was the jailed Ku Klux Klan leader's testimony

that he wrote thirty-one checks to state politicians as campaign contributions and participated in a scheme to bribe the former governor. Jackson was acquitted in this case because the statute of limitations had expired, but the scandal effectively ended his career in politics.[27]

Hobart E. Pillsbury, secretary of state of New Hampshire and chairman of the Republican City Committee in Manchester, resigned his position on November 4, 1928, after an arrest warrant for him had been issued on charges of improper disbursement of state funds. Pillsbury was suspected of funneling money to his wife after up to $1,000 was found missing from the budget he controlled. A local newspaper disclosed that Pillsbury's wife had also been paid $134 for work on the primary campaign. At the time, she was a county commissioner noted for leading an anti-corruption campaign. In addition, the newspaper running the story reported it had been the target of several attempts at bribery to keep it from publishing this material. Pillsbury claimed innocence but resigned his position a few days later. His wife was defeated in her election. The following year, after a trial and conviction on a charge of misuse of state funds, Pillsbury was sentenced to one to three years in state prison.[28]

During the national election campaign of 1928, the Republican National Committee was attacked by Democrats working for presidential candidate Al Smith, the governor of New York. The Democrats accused the Republicans of stirring up religious hatred by circulating

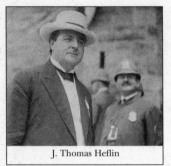

J. Thomas Heflin

malicious publications about the Catholic Church. Smith, a Catholic, was the target, not the first or the last Catholic politician to receive this treatment. In one incident, George Moses, a U.S. senator from New Hampshire, was found to have signed a letter urging recipients to help publicize anti-Catholic material; enclosed with the letter was an anti-Catholic pamphlet. The letter was intended for an address in Lexington, Kentucky, but was mistakenly delivered to Lexington, North Carolina, uncovering its existence and triggering the Democratic protest. In another incident in 1928,

Senator J. Thomas Heflin of Alabama took the attack on Catholics to the floor of the Senate. In a speech on May 17, he proclaimed, "They've not only put their colors in the president's room [a room in the Capitol that had red drapes], but they're flying the Roman cross on our battleships, and they've got the cross and rosary on our dollar bills."[29]

Al Smith

In 1928, just after he was paroled from federal prison, Warren McCray, a former Republican governor of Indiana, testified at the trial of the current Republican governor, Ed Jackson. Jackson had been charged with conspiracy and bribery in actions that dated back to McCray's administration. According to evidence presented at the trial, Jackson, while serving as secretary of state, had promised $10,000 to then-governor McCray if he would name a Jackson friend as a county prosecutor. Jackson promised he would also intercede in McCray's financial problems, preventing what eventually happened, a conviction that sent McCray to prison. McCray testified he refused to accept the bribe. The case was compounded by other attempts to bribe McCray, including one from D. C. Stephenson, the "grand dragon" of the Ku Klux Klan in Indiana. Stephenson and the Klan were heavily involved in state politics in this era. Stephenson was quoted as saying "I am the law in Indiana." But although there was clear evidence that Jackson had done wrong, the judge directed that he be acquitted because the statute of limitations in the case had expired.[30]

In Philadelphia in 1928, a grand jury turned up evidence of extensive fraud in the municipal government, including ties to criminal gangs and cases of "police liquor graft." The Republican mayor, Harry A. Mackey (1873–1938), successfully distanced himself from the fray—at one point a bodyguard was assigned to protect him after his life was threatened—but the city's director of public safety was forced to resign. Mackey took more heat in 1930 when a police raid on a local American Legion hall turned up a thriving speakeasy. Prosecution was hampered by the fact that the raiding officers drank most of the evidence.[31]

Charles A. Bowles (1884–1957) was elected mayor of Detroit in 1929, reportedly with the support of the Ku Klux Klan, but was kicked out of office eight months later in a recall election. During his brief stint in office, the city was beset with a number of murders, other violence, and general corruption related to a war between rival gangs fighting for control of the underground liquor trade. In the midst of an epidemic of gang-related murders, Mayor Bowles stated, "It is just as well to let these gangsters kill each other off, if they are so minded. You have the scientists employ one set of parasites to destroy another. May not that be the plan of Providence in these killings among the bandits?" In a climactic event, "Jerry" Buckley, a major radio personality, anti-corruption crusader, and outspoken critic of Mayor Bowles, was himself murdered. This crime occurred on the same day as the mayor's recall election, sealing his fate. However, despite the implication that Bowles and his political backers were involved, he was never tied to the crime.[32]

In 1929, Magne Alfred Michaelson (1878–1949), Republican representative from Illinois, was indicted for a violation of the Prohibition Act. Michaelson, who had voted for Prohibition, was charged with the importation, transportation, and possession of illegal alcohol—specifically, smuggling eleven quarts of whisky and one ten-gallon keg of rum into Florida from Cuba. In his defense, the congressman claimed that the alcohol was found in several trunks that were part of his baggage, but did not belong to him. The owner of the liquor-laden bags turned out to be his brother-in-law, along for the trip. The trial resulted in acquittal. Later in the year, the Justice Department reported it was opening a new investigation, but this was not pursued. The following year, Congress amended a tariff bill to remove the exemption for themselves and other federal officials. Federal law at the time allowed congressmen to bring luggage into the country without being searched.[33]

On November 4, 1929, the U.S. Senate voted to censure Hiram Bingham (1875–1956) for hiring an adviser who was an official of a trade organization. Bingham was a Republican senator from Connecticut. The censure statement described the act as inappropriate but not corrupt, because the senator had not intended to influence legislation with this choice of employee. Previously, Bingham had been the lieutenant governor of Connecticut and was elected governor in 1923. He only served for one day, however, because between the election and the inauguration in 1924, he was also elected to the Senate in a special election to fill a vacancy.[34]

Hiram Bingham

On November 19, 1929, Edward E. Denison (1873–1953), Republican representative from Illinois, was charged with a violation of the Prohibition Act. Denison, a "dry" politician who voted for Prohibition, was charged with possession of six bottles of gin, eighteen bottles of Scotch, and six bottles of other miscellaneous liquor. The alcohol was discovered in Denison's offices in the U.S. House Office Building in January of 1929. A railway express employee had called Prohibition agents, stating "There's a leaking suitcase in this place and it smells like liquor." Denison's defense rested on his insistence that the case was not his and had been delivered to him by mistake. However, prosecutors noted that the bag had Denison's name and address on it and that a second, unknown name had been painted on—an apparent attempt to support the misdelivery claim—after they had first followed it to the congressman's office. Nevertheless, he was acquitted.[35]

In 1929, the Oklahoma house of representatives began impeachment proceedings against Governor Henry Simpson Johnston (1870–1965). The charges included a wrongful pardon for a convicted murderer, unlawful issuance of financial certificates, unlawful interference with a previous legislative session using the state militia—the purpose of the

session had been to impeach the governor, but he was acquitted—and general incompetence. During the affair, the Democratic governor stated that the proceedings were "an example of Mexican politics by a legislature not quite brave enough to commit physical assassination to get me." In March, he was found guilty of a single charge, "general incompetence," and removed from office. In 1932, the former governor was elected to the state senate.[36]

Henry Johnston
AP Images

Asa Keyes, district attorney for Los Angeles, was convicted of bribery on February 8, 1929. Keyes, a veteran of twenty-five years as a prosecutor, was found guilty of multiple charges of accepting money in exchange for allegedly "fixing" cases. He served nineteen months of a five-year sentence, before being released to begin a new career as a car salesman.[37]

Flamboyant governor Huey Pierce Long (1893–1935) of Louisiana was brought before the state legislature for impeachment in 1929. The articles of impeachment stated that the Democratic governor was guilty of intimidation, bribing state legislators, interfering with a state training school, use of state money for personal use, approving state payments to contractors for substandard work, inappropriate firing of state officials, insults to citizens, an "unfit temperament," misuse of state funds, and incompetence. Found guilty in the house, debate in the state senate ended with the dismissal of all charges. Known as the "Kingfish," Long served a single term as governor before moving on to the U.S. Senate. While governor, he waged a running battle with an entrenched political

Huey Long

machine and succeeded in passing numerous bills that replaced legislative control of state agencies, funds, and processes with his own, progressive changes. At the same time, his methods alienated other politicians—friends and foes—and disenfranchised many of the voters who had supported him. When he went to the U.S. Senate in 1932, he left behind a hand-picked crew of state officials he hoped to use to continue his control over the state.[38]

On December 6, 1929, William Scott Vare (1867–1934), Republican senator from Pennsylvania and a former U.S. representative, was denied a seat in Congress. He had been voted into office in 1926, but a long-running congressional investigation concluded that his election had involved corruption and fraud.[39]

In 1930, a close election marked the race for governor of Kansas. Both the Democratic and Republican candidates were supported by the American Legion, and neither smoked, gambled, or drank alcohol. Harry Hines Woodring (1890–1967), the Democrat, ended up eking out a victory, but he and his major opponent were almost upset by a dark horse, write-in candidate John Brinkley. Brinkley was a multimillionaire doctor who made his fortune—and attained international fame—as the head of a Kansas clinic famous for promising to restore men's sexual drive by implanting them with goat testicles. The "Goat Gland" doctor had his license revoked by the Kansas medical board—for obvious reasons—only a few days before entering the race, which he wanted to win in order to reform the medical licensing regulations of the state. According to some political analysts, Brinkley might have won if organized, widespread election fraud had not eliminated many ballots intended for him. In any case, he ran again in 1934, by which time his political foes found ways to attack his populist campaign by dredging up unethical escapades from his past. A loser once again, his two campaigns were noted for the pioneering use of radio. In the tiny town of Milford, the site of his clinic, the doctor ran one of the most powerful radio stations in the country, which he used to promote his medical and political messages.[40]

*1920
1939*

John Brinkley

John H. Bankhead II (1872–1946), Democrat, won the Alabama election in 1930 to become a U.S. senator, defeating Thomas Heflin (1869–1951), the Democratic incumbent. His brother William was a U.S. representative from Alabama from 1917 through 1940 and was also the father of famous actress Tallulah Bankhead. Following a protest by Heflin, the Senate investigated the election and found that voting irregularities were so widespread that a majority committee report recommended issuing a declaration that no election had taken place. Following debate in the full Senate, however, Bankhead retained his seat.[41]

During Prohibition, American consumers were not the only ones who flouted the law. In Congress, politicians had a special room in the basement of the Capitol building where they could relax, play cards, and consume alcoholic drinks. The room was unofficially called the Bureau of Education.[42]

On March 2, 1930, a grand jury in Atlanta indicted eleven officials in the city following an investigation into graft and corruption. The charges included perjury, larceny, and bribery, with the city clerk, Walter Taylor, and a councilman named as the heads of a "grafting ring." Taylor's trial resulted in a conviction on a single count. Soon after this, a grand jury indicted five additional people on charges of jury-tampering in Taylor's trial. In that case, it was disclosed that one juror had held out for the single guilty count and demanded that none of the other jurors reveal what had happened in the jury room.[43]

In 1931, the New York state legislature created a special committee to investigate charges of corruption in New York City. The Seabury Committee—referred to after its head, Judge Samuel Seabury—uncovered widespread fraud in the city. It also implicated popular Mayor James John Walker (1881–1946) after uncovering irregularities in his bank account. Walker, first elected in 1926 with the backing of the Democratic political machine, was unable to adequately defend certain business transactions or deposits, implying illegal activity. In all, fifteen charges were filed, including suspect financial activities, neglect of duty, and a lack of truthfulness in his testimony. On September 1, 1932, Mayor Walker resigned rather than face further hearings—especially because they involved Franklin D. Roosevelt, then governor of the state, and a political enemy—professing his innocence and protesting his treatment as politically motivated.[44]

James Walker

Harry Emerson Rowbottom (1884–1934), three-term Republican representative from Indiana, was indicted by a federal grand jury on February 13, 1931. He was charged with taking money to recommend applicants for positions as postmasters in the state. Rowbottom, a tailor before he entered politics, was convicted in part through a ploy involving a wad of $100 bills that had been marked with pinpricks to track their use. He was sentenced to one year and a day in federal prison and a fine of $2,000. A few years before his indictment, Rowbottom had been linked to the former head of the state Ku Klux Klan, but the scandal faded when allegations in the case could not be proven.[45]

In Tennessee, the state legislature moved to impeach Governor Henry Hollis Horton (1866–1934) on the grounds of criminal conspiracy. Horton, along with other politicians and businessmen, was accused of diverting state funds to private banks, including institutions that collapsed during the Depression. In one case, the result was a loss of $6 million in highway funds. During the initial investigation of the loss, the governor stated, "Every man guilty of a betrayal of trust, however exalted his position, should be exposed, condemned and removed from office." The state legislature produced seven articles of impeachment against Horton, including one that found him guilty of "great moral delinquency and gross breach of decorum," because he voted against spending state money on a piano for the executive mansion, then acquired it anyway. The state house of representatives voted against impeachment. Meanwhile, several businessmen involved in the questionable bank transactions were tried and convicted of fraud and sent to the state penitentiary. Horton did not run for governor in the following election, stating "I have made mistakes, but they were mistakes of the head, not of the heart."[46]

Edwin Broussard

Flamboyant Senator Huey Long (1893–1935), Democrat from Louisiana, used his strong political organization to help John Holmes Overton (1875–1948), another Democrat from Louisiana, get elected to a second senatorial seat in the 1932 election. Even while in Washington, Long attempted to control politics in the state, just as he had when he was governor. A Senate investigation was instigated after incumbent senator Edwin Broussard, the loser in the election, claimed that Long had used illegal tactics to gain the advantage for Overton. The charges included using state employees as campaign workers, coercing financial support from state workers, promising families of prisoners leniency or early release in exchange for campaign support, and other questionable activities. Despite the evidence supporting these claims, Overton was seated because he had not been involved with Long's machinations. The conclusion: the results of the election were likely to have been in his favor even without the "irregularities."[47]

In December 1932 and again in January 1933, the U.S. House of Representatives voted on a resolution to impeach President Hoover. Among the grounds stated for this action: he had "dissipated the financial resources of the United States," prevented receipt of money due the United States from foreign countries, and held secret negotiations with the German government on the issue of monetary policy. The resolution was voted down by a substantial majority.[48]

 In Indiana, incumbent senator Frederick Van Nuys (1874–1944), a Democrat, won reelection with the help of the Two Percent Club (formally known as the "Hoosier Democratic Club"). This organization, on the verge of being illegal because of new legislation, required all appointed and elected state officials to pay 2 percent of their salaries into a fund used by the reigning Democrats to support election campaigns for themselves and other party members. Van Nuys, anticipating a ban on such campaign funding, made a public announcement disavowing support from this source. A lawsuit was filed in the state in 1940 by Republicans attempting to squash the practice, stating the club engaged in "various pernicious and unlawful and corrupt practices and activities." Eventually, both state and federal laws were passed banning the practice.[49]

Harold Louderback (1881–1941), U.S. district court judge in California, was charged with favoritism in the assignment of lucrative receiverships and was investigated by a committee of the U.S. House. The charges included "tyranny and oppression, favoritism, and conspiracy." On February 24, 1933, the House voted to impeach him on five counts, but a vote in the Senate acquitted him of all charges.[50]

On February 7, 1933, the U.S. Senate voted to dismiss their sergeant-at-arms, David Barry. Barry had written an article entitled "Over the Hill for Demagoguery" for *The New Outlook* magazine, in which he stated that some congressmen sold their votes for money, a charge that he later explained was not based on personal knowledge or observation. In reality, according to his defense, he had stated that "only a few senators" were so guilty, which he meant as support for the majority of the Senate who were "clean." He commented, "I have for a great many years heard these charges against members of Congress being crooks. It is taught in the school here and in the universities."[51]

On March 27, 1933, Charles Kline (1870–1933) two-term Republican mayor of Pittsburgh, was removed from office by a court order. In 1931, a grand jury had charged Kline and one of his colleagues with forty-three counts of graft. The charges related to specific activities in the city's Department of Supplies. In one case, Kline reportedly advanced $5,000 to a car dealer in exchange for used trucks worth less than that amount. Although originally sentenced to prison, Kline's punishment was suspended in exchange for his exit from office and payment of a fine. Ill health was a contributing factor in this deal. He died a few months later.[52]

1920 1939

On April 11, 1933, a federal court in New York found James McCormick, deputy city clerk and chief of the Marriage License Bureau, guilty of

Charles Kline

not reporting income tax, particularly $69,000 in "tips" received from couples he married. It was estimated he may have taken in up to $250,000 over many years of practicing this extortion tactic. McCormick was a major member of the Tammany Hall machine and the political leader of an assembly district for twenty-two years. His punishment was four months in prison and a $15,000 fine.[53]

In November 1933, James Rolph Jr. (1869–1934), Republican governor of California, got into hot water by publicly approving a lynching.

PROFILE   Huey Long Bathroom Medal

On August 26, 1933, Huey Pierce Long (1893–1935), Democratic senator from Louisiana, was involved in yet another scandalous event. While attending a fund-raiser at the Sands Point Bath and Country Club on Long Island, New York, Long, known as the "Kingfish," emerged from the men's

room with a cut on his forehead and a black eye. He avoided questions about the shiner for a few days before admitting that he had been jumped by thugs while in the restroom, stating he "was lucky to have escaped." Newspapers across the country ran the headline "Who Hit Huey?" and a conflicting report soon emerged. According to several witnesses, while impatiently waiting his turn to use a urinal, the senator had attempted to relieve himself between the legs of the man in front of him. He missed, prompting retaliation from the unfortunate target. One of the men in the restroom, navy pilot Alford Williams, denied being the one who struck Long but was observed with notably swollen and discolored knuckles on his right hand the next week. Another man known to be in the room at the time was the police chief of a nearby community; he, too, was seen with bruised knuckles and also denied striking Long. *Collier's* magazine, not a fan of Long or his politics, raised money to have

1920 1939

The lynching, a public event witnessed by up to ten thousand people, was of two men in San Jose who had been arrested for kidnapping and killing the son of a well-liked local merchant. After the impromptu hanging, the governor was quoted as saying "If anyone is arrested for this good job, I'll pardon them all." His statement echoed the sentiments of many of his constituents and paralleled public attitudes from earlier in the century, when San Francisco was briefly ruled by vigilantism. Rolph, known as "Sunny Jim," was widely condemned for his reaction, which implied approval of an illegal act. A public lynching of a black teenager in Missouri was reportedly encouraged by public supa commemorative medal created to mark the event and celebrate the anonymous hero. The one-of-a-kind gold medal turned out to be so popular that copies were made for sale to the public. The engraving on the medal is that of a rampant fist rising from a toilet lid, striking a "kingfish" and dislodging a crown from its head. The Latin inscription reads: *Publico Consilio Pro Re In Camera Gesta* (by public acclaim for a deed done in private). The original medal was presented to the American Numismatic Society in a ceremony on September 20, 1933, during which the society's president stated, "I appreciate the honor of accepting this medal commemorating the act of this noble but unknown hero. I feel sure it will find its place in history along with the medals presented at Marathon. Some day it may hang side by side with the medal presented by the Emperor Honorium to the general who defeated Alaric, the Goth, the inscription on which reads: 'Triumphator barbarorum,' which means, 'The conqueror of the Barbarians.'" The senator was shot by an assassin on September 8, 1935, and died on September 10.[54]

1920 1939

Front of the washroom medal.

port following the San Jose event, and the following year, photographs of the event showed up in a Nazi propaganda film. In that case, the victim was the son of a mixed marriage between a Jew and a Catholic, favorite targets of the Nazis.[55]

On July 17, 1933, President Roosevelt's son Elliott and daughter-in-law were granted a divorce after less than two years of marriage, creating a minor scandal. Two of the president's children were divorced while he was in office, but the issue did not become a major campaign problem even though divorce was not a "respectable" concept in that era.[56]

Before he first ran for president, Alf Mossman Landon (1887–1987), Republican governor of Kansas, faced a scandal in his home state. An audit of the state treasury disclosed that school bonds had been forged—$426,000 in total value at final count—and used as collateral on private loans. Several state politicians were implicated—the attorney general, state treasurer, and state auditor among them, as well as Ronald Finney, the son of a major businessman who had contributed a large sum to Landon's political campaign. The governor turned out to be blameless, but the businessman's son was charged, found guilty, and sentenced to thirty to six hundred years—he ended up serving twelve—while the state treasurer received four to ten years. The attorney general and state auditor were impeached but found not guilty.[57]

In July 1933, Louis Kotecki, city comptroller of Milwaukee, shot an assistant and then killed himself. Kotecki had been indicted by a grand jury that had uncovered an embezzlement of $500,000 in city funds. Other Kotecki associates were also under indictment, and Mayor Daniel Webster Hoan, one of the few Socialists ever elected to a major office in the United States, was subject to a recall partly instigated by the discovery of the embezzlement. The mayor survived the recall vote.[58]

The governor's race in California in 1934 was a battle between Republican Frank Merriam (1865–1955) and the author Upton Sinclair (1878–1968). Sinclair had run for other offices previously—and unsuccessfully. In 1934, his campaign, as before, revolved around his support for socialist concepts, a political stance that attracted much grassroots support as well as mainstream antagonism. Sinclair proclaimed that he would radically alter the tax system, redistribute land, and guarantee income for the homeless.

Upton Sinclair

Unlike his earlier attempts, this time he bolstered his political accept-
ability by switching affiliation, abandoning the Socialists—at least in
public—in favor of the Democrats. He managed to capture the top
spot on the Democratic slate in the primary, running as a dark-horse
candidate. Alarmed at the threat his candidacy posed, activists in both
major parties worked against him. At one point, Louis B. Mayer, the
head of MGM as well as the chairman of the state Republican party,
produced a series of bogus newsreels carefully slanted to undermine
the Sinclair campaign. In the newsreels, large numbers of umem-
ployed people were seen flocking to California to take advantage of his
egalitarian politics. Another ploy was the production of a pamphlet
that reported Sinclair was endorsed by Communists. This effort
helped reverse Sinclair's momentum, and his Republican opponent
was elected governor.[59]

William N. McNair (1880–1948), Democrat, was elected mayor of
Pittsburgh in 1934, ending a run of Republican city control that
stretched back to 1905. Known as a colorful character, McNair once
wore a large cowboy hat and a lasso while he rode a steer through
downtown streets, acted in a local play, and passed out apples to support a tax bill. More controversial was a two-hour stint in jail, the result
of his refusing to refund a fine that was claimed to have been improperly collected. Another arrest was on charges of "halting the machin-
ery of the law." He was also often at odds with his own party. At one
point a bill was introduced into the state legislature by the Democrats
to replace the mayoral system of government in Pittsburgh with one
run by a city manager, a scheme intended solely to get rid of McNair,
who did not support the patronage activities of the party. In 1936, reacting to a city council that refused to support one of his appointments—during a single year he appointed and fired four different
safety directors—he resigned from office, only to change his mind two
weeks later. Unfortunately, his resignation was ruled legal by a Board
of Judges and he was unable to regain his position.[60]

George Ernest Foulkes (1878–1960), a first-term Democratic U.S. representative from Michigan, was charged with receiving illegal political

contributions from postmasters. He was convicted at trial and sentenced to eighteen months in federal prison and a fine of $1,000. Before his election, Foulkes was an attorney and special agent with the Treasury Department. Two others were indicted along with Foulkes in this case, including Dan Gerow, who worked for the Michigan Democratic State Central Committee.[61]

Kansas City, Missouri, was the site of a bloody election day political battle on March 27, 1934. Thomas Pendergast and his political machine, the controlling force in local politics, confronted the opposition—candidates and voters supporting a newly formed local reform movement—using a variety of violent tactics. More than two hundred cases of assault were tallied during the election, with attacks by fists and sticks as well as firearms, including pistols, shotguns, and machine guns. Four deaths were recorded and about a dozen serious injuries. But Pendergast's methods produced results. The candidates he backed received 59,000 more votes than their opponents. Between 1932 and 1938, Pendergast was reportedly behind the election of every state official in Missouri, as well as those in Kansas City and the surrounding counties. His offices on the second story of a Kansas City building were referred to as the "Capitol of Missouri," as well as "Uncle Tom's Cabin." One local politician supported by the Pendergast machine was Harry Truman, who began his political career as a county judge (manager), selected and backed by the organization in 1922 from his former occupation as a haberdasher. Truman went on to be supported by Pendergast in a successful election for U.S. senator in 1934.[62]

Harry Truman signing checks at his Jackson County desk in 1927.

Marion Anthony Zioncheck (1901–1936), Democratic representative from Washington, was arrested in the U.S. Capitol on April 23, 1936, after he attempted to avoid dealing with a traffic citation. A few months earlier, he was arrested for disorderly conduct for commandeering the telephone switchboard at his apartment building. In another incident, he threw a roommate's household belongings out his apartment window. In response to his erratic behavior, he was sent to a mental hospital for observation, but he escaped. Later, while on his honeymoon in the Virgin Islands, he was thrown out of a hotel dining room because he "lapped his soup" with his tongue. Also during his honeymoon, he was arrested twice more for speeding and, when not behind the wheel, bit his driver on the neck. The congressman's well-known affinity for alcohol was a factor, but he was known as eccentric and hotheaded even while sober. On one occasion on the floor of the House, he yelled at a fellow representative, "The gentleman from Texas once said I was doped, and I shall put it into the record that the gentleman from Texas is a son of a Texan. On second thought I'll revise my remark and leave a blank for the final word." The congressman in question lunged at him but was restrained by colleagues; the remark was later expunged from the official record. In another bizarre episode, Zioncheck showed up at the White House and left a present for President Roosevelt, a black bag containing empty beer bottles, an empty container of mothballs, and a box of Ping-Pong balls. In July 1936, Zioncheck announced he was not going to run for reelection, then changed his mind after talking to his mother, who wanted him to demonstrate that he was "neither crazy nor foolish." On August 7, 1936, in his reelection headquarters in Seattle, Zioncheck jumped to his death from a fifth-story window. According to one newspaper account, the congressman had recently been diagnosed with "depressive melancholia."[63]

In 1935, the *Miami Beach Tribune* published a series of articles about graft and corruption associated with gambling in the area. The articles prompted a local judge to formally charge several editors and reporters with making false and malicious statements about him, specifically pertaining to the trial of state senator Hays Lewis on gambling charges. According to the newspaper's report, this trial had been presided over by the same judge, a key element in the news stories but, as it turned out, an error. After losing an appeal, one reporter,

Shannon Cormack, paid a fine of $50 and served one day in jail for contempt of court. Just before this, he was shot and wounded by a local lawyer who had also been mentioned in the newspaper series as having links to corrupt activities.[64]

In North Dakota, Thomas H. Moodie (1878–1948) was elected governor in 1935, setting off a politically charged debate over whether he was eligible to hold this position. The attorney general charged that Moodie, a Democrat, was not a legal resident. According to the state constitution, this was an appropriate interpretation because Moodie was born in Canada and had not been naturalized after immigrating to the United States. The real issue, however, was that Moodie could not prove he had been a resident of the state for at least five years, a requirement for the office. Since he took office knowing this to be true, he should be impeached, according to his opponents. On January 18, 1935, twelve days after Moodie was sworn into office, the North Dakota house of representatives voted for impeachment. Within a month, the state supreme court ruled that Moodie was indeed unqualified, nevertheless stating "He violated no law and did no wrong." He was expelled from office on February 2, twenty-seven days after he began his term. Political reporters in the state believed the move to oust Moodie was motivated and driven by former governor William Langer, who left office a year earlier after being convicted of a federal crime; he was out on bond at the time and appealing his conviction.[65]

John Henry Hoeppel (1881–1976), two-term Democratic representative from California, was charged with influence peddling in 1936 in a case involving the sale of an appointment to West Point. The prospective applicant, James Ives, who had competed at the Olympic Games, gave Hoeppel's son a promissory note for $1,000 in anticipation of an appointment. Ives passed the entrance requirements but declined to pursue it in the wake of the scandal. There were allegations by the prosecution that Ives had been selected in order to improve the quality of the football team at the academy. Hoeppel was charged along with his son, and both were convicted. They were sentenced to four months to one year in federal prison on January 10, 1936, but neither man—free on bond at the time—showed up to begin serving their sentences, prompting a manhunt by the FBI. They were captured about a month later.[66]

Halstead Lockwood Ritter (1868–1951), U.S. district court judge in Florida, was impeached for accepting money from a former law partner in order to influence his appointment in managing a receivership, for practicing law while on the bench in government service, and for attempting to influence the activities of the court. He was convicted on April 17, 1936. Technically, the impeachment verdict found him guilty of "high crimes and misdemeanors in office." As a result of the verdict, Ritter was removed from office and taken off the federal payroll.[67]

During the primary election season in New York City in 1938, the race for a Democratic congressional seat turned ugly. The campaign of John J. O'Connor was tied to the publication of a circular that appeared to be from the Communist party. The publication endorsed O'Connor's opponent, James H. Fay. An official with the Communist party in the region made an official statement claiming the circulars were a fraud. Fay survived the attack and won the election.[68]

Richard W. Reading (1882–1952) was elected mayor of Detroit in 1938 and served a single term. While in office, he and twenty-four others were charged with taking thousands of dollars in bribes to protect organized gambling operations in the city. Convicted, he served three years of a longer sentence before he was paroled because of illness. At the trial, the judge stated: "As mayor you were responsible for good government. You violated a public trust and became part and parcel of a scheme or corruption." An article in *Time* magazine covering the trial reported, "Every time Judge Ferguson got a new witness to talk, it was like turning up a rotten log; the bugs swarmed out and he had to work fast before they got away." The article repeated the judge's philosophy: "People say it's no use trying to clean up a city because graft is bound to spring up again. Sure it is. That's why you have to keep after it all the time." Altogether, 216 people were indicted, and trials were held for the sheriff, a county prosecutor, political aides, ten police lieutenants,

PROFILE	Target FDR

President Roosevelt's politics were a prominent target for Republicans and even conservative Democrats, who labeled them economically dangerous—even communistic—in refererence to the New Deal's theme of redistribution of wealth. Paranoia about war caused concern as well, from isolationist politicians, at least until the attack on Pearl Harbor. Eleanor Roosevelt also presented a visible target as the most active and public first lady in history, often engaged in progressive social issues. In various of the president's campaigns, buttons suggested Eleanor be replaced as well as her husband. Elliott Roosevelt, one of the president's sons, also attracted criticism. He was inducted into

**1920
1939**

thirty-four police sergeants, six detectives, thirty-seven patrolmen, various gamblers, and the mayor's son. The initial investigation was sparked by the suicide note of a numbers operator who had been jilted by her lover, a policeman involved in the corruption.[69]

Republican mayor Frank L. Shaw (1877–1958), former police captain Earle Kynette, and several other high-ranking police officials were accused of conspiring to kill a private investigator in Los Angeles in 1938. This investigator had been working for a group probing corruption in the city government, particularly links to gambling and other vice activities. Kynette was the only one convicted of the charge. However, in the face of negative publicity, Mayor Shaw was voted out of office in a recall election the following year.[70]

George J. Zimmerman (1882–1938), former Democratic mayor of Buffalo, New York, was indicted for bribery in 1938. Only a year out of office, the mayor was charged with nine counts of bribery connected to a $15 million sewer construction project. Other city officials were also charged along with the former mayor, but some of the indict-

the Army Air Corps Reserve in 1940 as a captain, without military training. This action initiated criticism from friends and foes and inspired anti-Roosevelt campaign buttons that stated "I want to be a captain too." Making things even stickier, Elliott was divorced in 1933—just after FDR's first term began—not considered a decent thing for proper people to do in that era. During the final campaign, in 1944, a rumor circulated that the president had assigned a navy ship to carry his dog, Fala, back to the continent after it had been accidentally left behind on an official trip to Alaska. FDR addressed this in one of his speeches, stating "The Republican leaders have not been content to make personal attacks upon me, or my wife, or my sons...they now include my little dog, Fala....I am accustomed to hearing malicious falsehoods about myself, but I think I have a right to object to libelous statements about my dog."[71]

1920
1939

ments were later dropped. Zimmerman pleaded innocent to the charges and died before the case went to trial.[72]

Secretary of the Commonwealth of Pennsylvania David Leo Lawrence (1889–1966) was indicted on January 7, 1939, for blackmail, conspiracy, and several election law violations. Lawrence, who was also the chairman of the Democratic State Committee, was charged with illegally issuing state contracts to a gravel company that had fixed prices for gravel, which turned out to be of poor quality as well as overpriced. Local Democrats complained that the investigation into the so-called "Erie Gravel Scandal" was triggered by Republican opponents of Lawrence. In any case, he was acquitted of the charges. In 1940, he was indicted and tried again, on charges that he and other officials required state workers to pay kickbacks to support political campaigns. This trial resulted in another acquittal. In both trials, the jury members were mostly Republicans. These cases and related legal action occurred during the administration of Governor George Earle and disrupted his term in office.[73]

"Business as usual" continued in Louisiana in 1939, beginning with the indictment of ex-governor Richard W. Leche (1898–1965) on charges that he violated the federal "hot oil" act (barring shipments of unlicensed petroleum) and illegally profited from state construction projects. The Leche investigation ended up snaring other officials as well. Facing impeachment, Leche, a Democrat and a close ally of Huey Long, resigned from office on June 26, 1939. He was convicted in 1940 and sentenced to ten years in federal prison. Paroled in five years, he received a pardon from President Truman in 1953.[74]

On May 22, 1939, political boss Thomas Pendergast was found guilty of evading federal income tax, a significant blow to his long-running reign in Kansas City, Missouri. He was given a fifteen-month prison sentence and fined $10,000, effectively ending his rule. At the sentencing, the judge stated: "If the crime charged is, as here, tax evasion, the punishment should be for tax evasion. Not a jot or tittle should be added to the punishment because it is judicially noticed that the defendant has been a political 'boss,' nor because it is judicially noticed that the city and county which he has dominated have been governed with indescribable corruption and dishonesty."[75]

On August 21, 1939, in Waterbury, Connecticut, Mayor T. Frank Hayes was found guilty of conspiracy to defraud the city of more than $1 million over a period of eight years. He was sentenced to a ten-year prison term. The same trial resulted in sentences for twenty additional defendants, which included the city controller, city banker, superintendent of Streets and Water Department, the city purchasing agent, city assessor, and the chairman of the Board of Police Commissioners.[76]

On October 16, 1939, Maury Maverick Sr., the mayor of San Antonio, Texas (and a former U.S. representative), was indicted for "improper payment of poll taxes." He had used his own money to pay the poll tax for poor voters to allow them to vote, a violation of the law. The charges were the result of ongoing attacks by political rivals who were incensed by the liberal mayor's defense of free speech rights, not to mention his support of President Roosevelt, an unpopular leader in

PROFILE   Hitler *v.* Cranston

Before Alan Cranston began a second career as a U.S. senator from California (1968–1992), he was a foreign correspondent for the International News Service prior to World War II. Back in the United States, Cranston was shocked to find that the authorized American version of *Mein Kampf*, Hitler's best-selling autobiography, had been edited, removing the German dictator's most extreme statements, especially those concerning his anti-Semitism and plans for military action in Europe. In response, Cranston produced

his own translation of the book in 1939, including its damning content and illustrated with editorial cartoons. His version was distributed through newsstands and priced at ten cents. In response, Cranston and his partners were sued by Hitler's attorney and sales were halted by court order, but not before thousands of copies had been sold. Later, near the end of his political career, Cranston's reputation was marred by the "Keating Five" savings and loan scandal. For his part in this scheme, he was reprimanded for improper conduct by the U.S. Senate Select Committee on Ethics.[77]

Alan Cranston

the region. When he granted a per-
mit for a meeting of local
Communists on city property, his decision triggered a riot. Maverick, who
was once described to be "as subtle as
a brass band"—at one point in his political career, he rode his horse into
the U.S. House—was acquitted of the
poll tax charge. Maverick's grandfather was credited with spawning the
term "maverick," used on the range

Maury Maverick

before Maury Maverick inspired its use in politics. His great-great-
great-grandfather Charles Lynch was thought to be responsible for the
verb "lynching." Maverick Jr., a noted social reformer and liberal,
coined his own notable term while in office: "gobbledygook."[78]

In 1939 in Albany, New York, the state senate held impeachment hearings for George W. Martin. Martin, a county judge, was accused of various indiscretions, including use of his office to make appointments to
the state Lunacy Commission. Doctors who served in this capacity were
paid for sanity evaluations. An official report in Brooklyn, Martin's ju-
risdiction, disclosed that six doctors received about 25 percent of all
such fees in the preceding seven years, suggesting improper behavior.
Martin was also accused of taking bribes. He had been tried and acquitted by a jury on the same charges previously, and the senate failed
to muster the votes required to oust him once again. In 1941, however,
local Democratic leaders dropped their support for him because of the
negative publicity.[79]

Following the primary elections in New York City in 1939, District
Attorney Thomas E. Dewey opened an investigation into reports of
voter fraud. The probe revealed that in four districts, out of a total of
476 voter signatures, 262 were forged. In one Republican district
where a candidate was running unopposed, eighteen forgeries were
also discovered. According to newspaper reports at the time, the ex-
planation was that this was likely just for practice.[80]

On February 7, 1939, New York Circuit Court Judge Martin Thomas Manton (1880–1946) resigned after twenty-three years in that position. Manton, who had once been considered as a candidate for the U.S. Supreme Court, was targeted by Thomas E. Dewey, the district attorney for New York City, because of evidence Manton was receiving large amounts of cash and had released convicted criminals for unusually low amounts of bail. In the investigation, the judge was found to have received at least $235,000 and as much as $600,000 between 1932 and 1938. Manton was tried in a federal court in April 1939. After two weeks of testimony, he was found guilty and sentenced to two years in prison. He was the first federal appellate court judge to be tried for bribery and the first convicted.[81]

John Warren Davis (1867–1945), a circuit court judge in New York, was implicated in 1939 in illegal judicial activity uncovered by the investigation of his fellow judge, Martin Manton, who resigned the previous month. There was no prosecution of Davis until 1941, when he was indicted for accepting bribes—specifically, receiving up to $27,500 in unsecured loans from a former movie producer, William Fox, in exchange for the beneficial outcome of a bankruptcy case, and taking payoffs to influence the outcome of a patent case. Two trials resulted in hung juries, after which the case was dropped. The judge then agreed to retire in exchange for the U.S. House Judiciary Committee dropping its own proceedings for impeachment. Davis left the bench on November 24, 1941.[82]

Eugene L. McGarry, municipal judge in Cook County, Illinois, was indicted in 1939 for malfeasance in office. He was charged with fixing a case, obstructing justice, and allowing false references on bail bonds. In several cases, he accepted the same building lot as collateral for bonds even though it was valued at only $97 and the bonds were valued at much more. McGarry's case was the first time in the history of that municipal court that a grand jury targeted a sitting judge.[83]

1940–1959

Worl War II did not so much diminish political corruption and scandal as divert it from the public eye. One of the few politicians active in uncovering political misdeeds during this period of national unity was Harry Truman, Roosevelt's vice president. Dogged and ruthless, Truman used congressional investigations to uncover fraud, waste, mismanagement, profiteering, and other irregular activity. As he stated to the U.S. Senate, "I have had considerable experience in letting public contracts, and I have never yet found a contractor who, if not watched, would not leave the Government holding the bag." As president, Truman was also a conspicuous target for investigation, from scandals attached to his administration to past association with the notorious Pendergast machine in his home state. One politician who got nailed along with the contractors was James Curley, Democratic representative from Massachusetts, who was sent to prison in 1947 for defrauding companies. From 1940 to 1959, at least half a dozen other congressmen were indicted and imprisoned on charges ranging from bribery to income tax invasion. Preshadowing his later brush with dishonor, candidate Richard Nixon—first as a gubernatorial prospect, then as Eisenhower's selection for vice president—became a lightning rod for political attacks.

Benjamin Frank Whelchel (1895–1954), three-term Democratic representative from Georgia, was charged in 1940 with being part of a conspiracy to "buy, sell, and barter appointive offices of the government," specifically a position as postmaster in his home state. Whelchel proclaimed his innocence and stated the charges were politically motivated. He was acquitted of all charges and won reelection to two more terms.[1]

Democrat Franklin Roosevelt (1882–1945), a popular president, was willing to use dirty politics if necessary. During his reelection campaign in 1940, Roosevelt's staff discovered that his Republican opponent, Wendell Willkie, was having an extramarital affair with a book reviewer. The president began using a tape recording in 1940 to archive conversations in the Oval Office, and was taped discussing with his aides how to

Henry Wallace

benefit politically from Willkie's indiscretion. "We can spread it as a word-of-mouth thing, or by some people, way, way down the line. We can't have any of our principal speakers refer to it, but the people down the line can get it out.... Now, now, if they want to play dirty politics in the end, we've got our own people." This kind of mudslinging turned out to be unnecessary because of the Democratic lead in the campaign, but it also played a part in a secret "backroom" bargain between the two opposing camps. In return for the Democrats' suppressing information about Willkie's behavior, the Republicans promised not to reveal potentially dangerous material they held about the Democratic vice presidential candidate, Henry Wallace. The dirt on Wallace turned out to be a series of letters in which he made frank, un-

1940
1959

flattering comments about some political leaders and his own religious beliefs, including his support of a Russian spiritual leader named Nicholas Roerish. The correspondence, dubbed the "Guru Letters," suggested the candidate believed in "mystical fiddle-faddle." Not to mention sympathy for the Soviet Union, which suggested he was pro-communist.[2]

Wendell Willkie

In Philadelphia, Pennsylvania, the president of the city council, Bernard Samuel (1880–1954), automatically became mayor upon the death in office of Robert Lamberton. Samuel, loyal to the local Republican party machine, was unable to solve major problems in the city, partly because of intense opposition from Democratic factions

PROFILE	Wild Bill Langer

"Wild Bill" Langer (1886–1959) earned his nickname. Born and raised in North Dakota, he was a lawyer, country attorney, state attorney general, governor, and U.S. senator. Originally an Independent and later a Republican, he was considered by both friends and enemies to be unorthodox, personally leading raids against illegal liquor stores and brothels and censuring hundreds of public schools for failing to fly the U.S. flag. Some blamed him for pushing a former attorney general to commit suicide. In July 1934, the North Dakota supreme court ordered him to be removed from his position as governor because of a conviction for soliciting political contributions from government employees. In response, Langer called out the National Guard and declared martial law. A special session of the state legislature confused matters more in an attempt to validate Langer's position; it ended by placing the lieutenant governor in charge. The federal charges were dropped after an appeal, and in 1937 Langer was reelected as governor. After being elected to the U.S. Senate in 1940, a Senate committee investigating his fitness to be a member recommended he be expelled because of his "moral turpitude," stat-

1940
1959

and partly because of entrenched corruption. A challenger in 1946 claimed that Samuel allowed gambling in city hall, accepted expensive presents, tolerated graft in the police department, and had been responsible for other officeholders protecting speakeasies during Prohibition. He lost the election to Samuel. According to a *Time* magazine description of the city in 1948, "In Philadelphia, civic corruption is like the pigeons that swarm in City Hall courtyard. Both are nourishing, messy and endemic." The mayor, responding to pressure to increase city salaries, created a commission—known as the "Committee of Fifteen"—to recommend how much, and how, to fund such a request. As an unintended consequence of their labor, the commission discovered that there was less a need to raise additional funds than to recover the funds that city employees were stealing. Further consequences: a minor functionary in the office of receiver of taxes hanged

William Langer

ing that he had "never permitted the law to stand between himself and his personal desires, ambitions, and greed," and that his behavior represented "a continuous, contemptuous, and shameful disregard for the high concepts of public duty." A debate by the full Senate, however, considered that the events and activities that happened before his election should not keep him from being seated and were beyond the scope of judgment for that body. The subsequent vote failed to gain the two-thirds majority needed to deny him his seat. While in office, he was known for frequently switching his vote; one report found that during the Republican-led Eisenhower administration, he voted against the majority more often than with it. He also occasionally got into trouble for his sense of humor. With the country anticipating a visit from Winston Churchill in 1951, he telegraphed the Old North Church in Boston and requested they hang two lanterns from the belfry. Nevertheless, North Dakota voters reelected him term after term. He died in office in 1959.[3]

himself, and a box with $16,400 in cash and bonds was found in his basement; a purchase inspector was found to have issued fake bills and collected up to $16,000 in response; large quantities of city supplies were missing; and fire inspectors charged payments in exchange for permits. The original committee's work ended up with a grand jury investigation as well as an inquiry from the state. By 1951, convictions and firings had given way to the creation of a new city charter, changing the way the city did business in order to end, or at least limit, similar corruption in the future.[4]

In 1941, an investigation in Detroit, Michigan, disclosed that several elected officials had accepted bribes for helping approve a construction contract for a city-sponsored housing project. Three city councilmen were among those implicated and convicted.[5]

On October 2, 1941, Daniel H. Coakley, a member of the governor's council in Massachusetts, was impeached for accepting payments to obtain pardons for convicted criminals. Coakley, the executive councilor for the state, was convicted on ten of fourteen counts of misconduct and "maladministration." He was also barred from holding any other positions of trust in the future. In 1921, while a practicing attorney in Boston, he had been disbarred for accepting payments to influence the outcome of criminal prosecutions. The impeachment by the Massachusetts Senate was the first in more than one hundred years.[6]

Lyndon Johnson, a Democratic member of the U.S. House from Texas, began active military service on December 9, 1941, the first person in Congress to serve in World War II. As a navy lieutenant commander, Johnson was sent by President Roosevelt on an inspection tour of the Pacific theater in 1942, during which he tagged along on a bombing mission over Japanese-held territory in New Guinea. After the flight, General Douglas MacArthur awarded him the third-highest decoration in the military, the Silver Star, for "gallantry in action," because of an attack by Japanese fighters during the mission. Although unchallenged at the time—or for years after—the combat action either did not happen at all or was greatly exaggerated; Johnson's role as an observer certainly did not support the award.[7]

Lyndon Johnson

1940 1959

On January 22, 1946, DeLesseps Story Morrison (1912–1964) was elected mayor of New Orleans, marking the beginning of a run in office that lasted until 1961. Initially known as "The Boy Mayor"—he was thirty-four years old at the time—Morrison was a reformer credited with significant improvements to the city, including a new civic center, a new recreation department, a new passenger train terminal, and an upgraded drainage system. At the same time, he was head of a powerful local political machine, the Crescent City Democratic Association.

PROFILE Ballot Theft

In 1946, President Harry Truman dropped his support for a fellow Missouri Democrat, Congressman Roger Caldwell Slaughter (1905–1974), because Slaughter had voted against a key bill the president supported. In the primary election in Missouri in August, the incumbent Slaughter was heavily—and unexpectedly—defeated by an alternate Democratic candidate supported by both Truman and the machine politics of Kansas City. Within days, charges of fraud arose, and several investigations quickly disclosed that "there had been a deliberate and calculated plan to miscount votes and otherwise steal the election." A federal report concluded this was not the case—the U.S. attorney who headed the probe was given a promotion—but a local grand jury found otherwise and indicted seventy-one election workers. The grand jury also had all the ballots and election forms collected for further review and stored in the vault at the Jackson County courthouse in Kansas City. Before they could be examined, the vault was blown open with nitroglycerin and all of the ballots and records were stolen, ending the investigation. Truman, who happened to be in Kansas City when the ballot theft occurred, was never implicated, but questions about his past associations with the Pendergast machine dogged his career in Washington.[8]

Tom Pendergast and his family at the inauguration of President Truman in 1949.

Although linked to various racketeers and vice activities in the city, the main activity of this group was obtaining city jobs for its members. The mayor himself was accused of accepting large campaign contributions from known racketeers and brothel operators, and he was blamed for not supporting actions to integrate the city in a period when this activity was just beginning to attract wider public interest. Although generally well liked, Morrison had his political detractors, even within his own party. In 1947, there was a short-lived movement to oust him from office, led by his father-in-law.[9]

PROFILE Theodore Bilbo

1940 1959

Theodore Gilmore Bilbo (1877–1947), also known as "The Man," incumbent Democratic senator from Mississippi and a former governor of that state, was reelected in 1946. Black voters, however, were blocked in large numbers from participating in the election; they instigated a Senate investigation, charging Bilbo with intimidation, corruption, and campaign irregularities. The action was postponed when Bilbo was diagnosed with cancer of the mouth and returned to Mississippi for surgery. From his first term in office, Bilbo was

Theodore Bilbo

noted for his vocal support of white supremacy and segregation; his book, entitled *Take Your Choice, Separation or Mongrelization,* actively supported segregation. In his home state, he was known for his outspoken policy about blacks and voting, and in one election he called on every "red-blooded Anglo-Saxon man in Mississippi to resort to any means to keep hundreds of Negroes from the polls …And if you don't know what that means, you are just not up on your persuasive measures." In a later interview, Bilbo stated, "Although I am honestly against the social intermingling of Negroes and whites, I hold nothing personal against the Negroes as a race. God made them as they are, and they should be proud of their God-given heritage, just as I am proud of mine." During a term as state senator, Bilbo was the subject of an impeachment vote, but he came out on top by a

During the Democratic primary campaign in Montana in 1946, Burton Kendall Wheeler (1882–1975), U.S. senator from the state and a former unsuccessful candidate for vice president, was attacked with a book his opponents created to discredit him. The text of this book described Wheeler as a Nazi and someone who liked communism and pornography. Wheeler, a Republican, had been accused of being a "Nazi lover" as early as 1941, because of statements he made about the inevitable triumph of the Nazis in Germany. Other Democrats and even President Roosevelt—whose politics were often at odds with

A political cartoon from 1946 titled "Something Has Happened to the Halo."

1940 1959

single vote. A resolution by the Mississippi senate stated he was "unfit to sit with honest, upright men in a respectable legislative body," a statement later removed from the record after he was elected lieutenant governor. Public hearings revealed that the congressman was a member of the Ku Klux Klan, and a Senate minority report stated that he had violated the "Constitution, the Federal Criminal Code, and the Hatch Act." However, the majority report found that the senator was guilty only of "crude and tasteless campaign oratory." A separate investigation by the Senate, however, uncovered widespread issues from World War II when Bilbo had received improper contributions and gifts from companies in exchange for federal contracts. Among these: a swimming pool, the excavation of a lake around one of his homes (creating an island for the house), a new Cadillac, and paint and furnishings for two of his residences, "Dream House Number 1" and "Dream House Number 2." Before any of these committee findings could be acted on by the Senate, Bilbo's cancer killed him.[10]

Burton Wheeler

Wheeler—were damaged by these allegations as well. Wheeler was not pro-Nazi but an isolationist before the war. Like others who shared his position, he supported the war after the country entered it following the attack at Pearl Harbor. The accusations dogged him throughout his political career, however, and his position in Congress ended in 1947. After the war, documents found in Germany listed Wheeler and other politicians as potentially helpful if the Nazis won, but Wheeler was an unknowing partner to this inclusion.[11]

Andrew Jackson May (1875–1959), eight-term Democratic representative from Kentucky and chairman of the House Military Affairs Committee, was convicted in federal court of bribery and conspiracy in July 1947. The charges involved influencing government contracts during World War II; May reportedly received up to $53,000 from businesses for awarding contracts in their favor. Sentenced to serve eight to twenty-four months, he was paroled for good behavior after serving a little more than nine months; his poor health contributed to the decision. While behind bars, the congressman was assigned work in the library and was responsible for tending the prison's flock of poultry. In 1952, President Truman granted him a full pardon. Leading up to and during the war, May authorized an investigation into the illegal influencing of military contracts, and then-senator Truman gained national recognition chairing a Senate committee investigating wasteful and illegal defense expenditures.[12]

Frank Hague (1876–1956), eight-term mayor of Jersey City, New Jersey, resigned two years before his last term expired. The boss of a machine well entrenched in the city, Hague had been in power since 1918—he was frequently quoted as saying "I am the law"—and oversaw decades of patronage, graft, election fraud, and general corruption. Although his maximum salary as mayor was only $8,500, he amassed personal assets worth more than $2 million, including four homes. The administration that followed Hague sued him for $15 million, a sum that represented the amount of bribes and kickbacks taken from city workers over the period of his rule. This suit was later dismissed. During Hague's reign, city employees and anyone doing business with the city were expected to give back a set percentage of whatever they were paid. At one point in his career, he publicly stated, "I think 3 percent—the rate for city employees and contractors—is a bargain for getting good service." According to *Time* magazine, which covered his funeral, one mourner held up a hand-lettered sign that read "God have mercy on his sinful, greedy soul."[13]

Frank Hague and his wife.

On March 24, 1947, Albert Williams Johnson (1872–1957), former U.S. district court judge in Pennsylvania, was acquitted of charges of fraud and conspiring to obstruct justice. Johnson had retired in 1945 but was tried in connection with alleged activities associated with criminal, bankruptcy, and receivership cases he had presided over during his term on the bench. In 1944, a U.S. House judiciary subcommittee had stated that Judge Johnson was "wicked and malicious" and used his court for a "black market operation of the most despicable, malicious and degrading sort." The judge would have been impeached but resigned and voluntarily waived his pension in exchange for an end to the impeachment action. Johnson had been on the federal court since 1925. At his federal trial, the judge's three sons and two others were also included in the charges. Two of the sons and the other men were found guilty and sent to prison, but they refused to testify against the judge. Johnson was subsequently acquitted for lack of evidence. Johnson later was elected president of his local bar association and sued the government to restore his pension, a claim that was rejected.[14]

1940
1959

In the early 1940s, Edward Fretwell Prichard Jr. (1915–1984) was a young lawyer who worked as an adviser to President Roosevelt and was a law clerk for Supreme Court Justice Felix Frankfurter. According to those who knew him, he was a young man with a future. He returned

PROFILE	James Curley

A noted leader of the Democratic machine in Boston, Massachusetts, James Michael Curley (1874–1958) was a career politician who served terms as a state legislator, governor, alderman, and U.S. representative to Congress, and multiple stints as mayor of Boston. While a U.S. congressman in 1943,

1940
1959

James Curley

Curley was charged and convicted of mail fraud and conspiracy, but the conviction was voided the same year; in 1944, he was recharged on the same grounds and once again convicted. He was sentenced to six to eighteen months in federal prison, but appealed, stating "I have never begged for mercy in my life…I don't do it now. But I do ask for justice." In the interim, his job shifted from Washington back to Boston, where he was in power as mayor when the sentence was upheld. He served five months behind bars before the sentence was commuted (in 1950, President Truman, also a Democrat, issued him a pardon, allowing him to run for office again, which he did, unsuccessfully), all the

to his home state of Kentucky in 1945 and began working in local politics with a plan of someday running for governor. But following the presidential election in 1948, his future potential withered after he was tried and convicted of forging voter signatures as part of an election fraud scandal. Prichard, known as "The Philosopher," was sentenced to two years in prison and served 161 days before being pardoned by President Truman.[15]

Lyndon Baines Johnson (1908–1973), Democratic representative from Texas, ran for an open seat in the Senate in 1948. In a runoff primary election with his Democratic opponent, Coke Stevenson, the former governor of Texas, Johnson initially appeared to lose by 112 votes, before an uncounted box of ballots was unexpectedly discovered in the

while retaining his position as mayor. Curley was no stranger to legal problems. In 1904, he was sent to prison for the first time after taking a civil service examination using another person's name. He came from a poor Irish
Catholic background, and much of his later success in politics came from a
well-organized base of immigrant support due to the projects and funds he
funneled into immigrant neighborhoods. Curley relied heavily on patronage
to keep his machine running but was rarely implicated in the scandals and
corruption associated with this practice. In 1938, he was sued in a civil case

by the city of Boston to recover $35,000 he had
received to help settle a claim against the city,
but he was not prosecuted for the criminal involvement or for perjury he committed during
the trial. Colorful and outspoken, Curley was
the subject of several books, including his own
autobiography, and was reportedly the inspira-
tion for the main character in the Hollywood
movie *The Last Hurrah*, starring Spencer
Tracy.[16]

1940
1959

James Curley (left), campaigning with
New York governor Franklin Roosevelt
in 1932. *AP Images*

west Texas town of Alice. This region had long been politically controlled by George Parr, one of Johnson's major backers. Johnson
ended up the winner after this episode—dubbed the "Miracle of Box
13," as the missing votes were from the Thirteenth Precinct—because
the missing ballots included 201 votes for him and only 2 for
Stevenson. Stevenson supporters immediately contested the results,
leading to verbal and physical threats—at one point, there was an
armed standoff between Texas
Rangers and local law officers outside
the bank where the disputed ballots
were stored. Johnson ultimately pre-
vailed by using a ruling from a U.S.

Johnson campaiging in 1948.

PROFILE   The Red Snapper

Edward Hull Crump (1874–1954) practiced an old-fashioned style of political bossing in Memphis, Tennessee, his home base. A Democrat, Crump ruled state politics for several decades because of his ability to guarantee a large block of votes, from a heavy population base in the city. The large concentration of voters in Memphis—more than one-fourth of the state's total—could guarantee election outcomes in the county and state. In his own political career, Crump had been both fire and police commissioner in Memphis, mayor, and county treasurer, and served two terms as a U.S. representative in Congress. His first political position was election officer in 1901, where he earned the nickname "Red Snapper" for his red hair and aggressive personality. Unlike other southern politicians, who avoided black voters, Crump had a popular—and obedient—black following. He was also

Ed Crump   *AP Images*

known for his colorful prose, once suggesting that an opponent "lies by nature and tells the truth by accident." Early in his career, in 1909, he hired a little-known local songwriter named W. C. Handy to write him a campaign song, which today—with new lyrics—is widely known as "Memphis Blues." In the private sector, he owned a prosperous insurance company and farmland throughout the state. Crump also had political enemies, some because of his strong opposition to the Ku Klux Klan and others who could not buck his overriding control of the political environment. In a local newspaper editorial in 1946, it was reported: "Memphis seems to have good government if one overlooks the fact that the very essence of good government is missing... the right of the citizens to choose their candidates for public office rather than to be told by a political machine who those candidates will be."[17]

1940
1959

Supreme Court justice to prevent a federal court in Texas from examining the case. This appeal to the court was handled by Abe Fortas, an attorney who ended up serving on the Court when Johnson became president. In the interim, the contents of Box 13 disappeared before they could be verified, with only a single outside glimpse of the first seventeen votes. Of those, observers noted that the voters' names were all in the same handwriting, and they appeared to have voted in alphabetical order.[18]

During the general election in 1950, controversial senator Joseph McCarthy, although from Wisconsin, got involved in a Senate race in Maryland. McCarthy supported the campaign of fellow Republican John Butler in Butler's effort to unseat incumbent Democrat Millard Tydings, an outspoken political foe of McCarthy. Among other questionable activities, McCarthy and campaign organizers distributed 300,000 copies of a tabloid publication designed to smear Tydings. The publication falsely claimed that Tydings was responsible for instigating the Korean War and had deliberately weakened U.S. military defenses, among other allegations. Also included was a doctored photograph that made Tydings look like he was talking with the head of the American Communist party. Butler won the race, but a subsequent investigation in the Senate reported it had been a "despicable 'back street' campaign" and was at least partly the fault of the senator from Wisconsin.[19]

On January 2, 1950, John Parnell Thomas (1895–1970), Republican representative from New Jersey and chairman of the House Committee on Un-American Activities, resigned from office. A six-term congressman, Thomas stepped down after being charged and convicted of salary fraud. In this scheme, he added fake employees to his payroll—with the assistance of his secretary, who was also implicated—and pocketed the salaries for himself. Facing a maximum penalty of thirty-two years in prison, he was fined and sentenced to do six to eighteen months. He served nine months before he was paroled for good behavior and because he was in poor health. In 1953, he was given a pardon by President Truman.[20]

On June 12, 1951, Walter Ellsworth Brehm (1892–1971), five-term Republican representative from Ohio, was sentenced to five to fifteen months in prison and fined $5,000 after being found guilty of accepting illegal campaign contributions, a violation of the Corrupt Practices Act. The prison sentence was suspended. Specifically, the congressman was charged with taking involuntary "contributions" from federal employees—two clerks in his Ohio office—by deducting amounts from their federal paychecks, up to half of one clerk's total salary. When the charges were first made public, Brehm insisted he was the target of a political plot, then denied knowing the activity had occurred, then defended himself by declaring he did not know such activity was illegal. Following the court decision, which Brehm unsuccessfully appealed, he did not run for office again, returning to his former career as a dentist.[21]

William Casey Marland (1918–1965) was elected governor of West Virginia in 1952. Marland was the first Republican governor in twenty years—and the youngest in state history—and served a single term in office that was marked by political brawls and a notable drinking habit. He had increasing problems with alcohol after leaving office, his marriage ended, and he lost various jobs before being "discovered" in Chicago, Illinois, in 1965, where he lived as a recovering alcoholic driving a cab.[22]

In 1952, in Boston, John Derham, a district court judge, was tried on charges he used unethical means—a cash payment—to settle a lawsuit against the commonwealth. He was disbarred for his activity, but the person alleged to have received the payment—the state attorney general, Francis E. Kelley—was cleared because of a lack of evidence. Later, Alfred Cenedella, the district attorney who originally brought charges in the case, ended up going to federal prison because he was found to have evaded paying income tax.[23]

During the presidential campaign of 1952, rumors and speculation circulated regarding an affair that Dwight Eisenhower, the Republican candidate, allegedly carried on during the war in Europe with his at-

Dwight Eisenhower

tractive British driver. The potential for a scandal escalated during the election year when the woman in question, Kay Summersby, published a book entitled *Eisenhower Was My Boss*, which was eagerly anticipated and then a disappointment to those expecting it to reveal a romance—it didn't. Other rumors spread, however, pointing to a scheme to have the book suppressed by wealthy Republican businessmen, and in 1976, after Summersby died, her second autobiography was published posthumously, entitled *Past Forgetting, My Love Affair with Dwight D. Eisenhower*, which claimed the original rumors were true, although the affair had been less physical than emotional.[24]

1940
1959

In September 1952, Senator Richard Nixon, Republican candidate for vice president, visited Maine on a political excursion. At the time, a scandal was unfolding in the administration of Republican Governor Frederick G. Payne, who was running for the U.S. Senate in the same election. The chairman of the state liquor commission was indicted after an investigation disclosed illegal political contributions and rumors circulated that other officials might be involved as well. At one campaign stop, Nixon remarked, "Here we find a grand jury, given the facts, moving swiftly to remove possible corruption, whereas, in Washington, it is condoned and covered up."[25]

On September 18, 1952, a newspaper report revealed that Republican vice presidential candidate Richard Nixon's campaign was supported by a secret fund. The fund—totaling $18,000—came from a "millionaire's club" set up by wealthy business owners in California in order to help Nixon finance his campaign. Because the use of such funds could have been illegal, Nixon was under heavy pressure to resign in order to spare Dwight Eisenhower,

Nixon gives his "Checkers speech" on national TV in 1952.

AP Images

PROFILE	Presidential Gifts

As president, Eisenhower was a generally well-liked ruler who coasted on his unassailable record as the general who won World War II in Europe, but mismanagement, questionable appointments, and charges of inappropriate gifts also attracted negative press during his administration. In 1955,

1940 1959

a magazine article raised questions about the overall volume of gifts he accepted as president. *Newsweek*, in a December issue, reported that since he had been elected, up to $40,000 in products had been given to the president and his family by individuals, organizations, and corporations, some of it landing at Eisenhower's farm in Gettysburg, Pennsylvania. A few years later, columnist Drew Pearson reported the total value of gifts for the farm was at least $300,000. This in-

Mamie Eisenhower

cluded a tractor, farm implements, forty-eight spruce trees, eighteen Aberdeen Angus beef cows, a wicker cart and a pony to pull it, a greenhouse, an electric cart (with a cattle-call horn), a putting green valued at $3,000, and other things that were put to use on the property. All such gifts were not considered income by the IRS and were not taxed. Other officials in the Eisenhower administration who received gifts were not treated the

his running mate, embarassment and political damage. On September 23, Nixon addressed the issue during a live television broadcast. He adamantly refuted the notion that such money was being used to support his family or lifestyle, which would have been unethical and illegal, although he did not deny such a fund existed. He did admit accepting one personal gift, a cocker spaniel puppy his daughter Tricia named Checkers. Public reaction was very positive, and pro-Nixon appeals convinced Eisenhower to keep Nixon on the Republican ticket.[26]

Following national elections in 1952, there were reports of fraud in several states, including Tennessee. One radio news program stated,

President Eisenhower admiring his new gift tractor on his farm in December 1955. *AP Images*

same way; a few were forced to resign because of the implication of influence attached to this kind of generosity. While the issue was explored by the media, it was mostly ignored by the president, although he did make a few public statements regarding the policy of accepting things for free while in office. On one occasion he stated, "...I need no gifts and I never accept gifts that I believe have any personal motive whatsoever behind them, I mean any selfish motive of any kind." Mamie Eisenhower was also exposed in newspaper articles covering the issue. She accepted the gift of a diamond necklace from King Saud, a gold purse from Emperor Haile Selassie, an antique Indian carpet, and various pieces of expensive furniture. Like Ike's, her image survived the suggestion of scandal. A congressional act helped Ike solve another problem, more than $1 million in royalties from a book he wrote about the war in Europe. He was granted a large discount from the regular tax rate on capital gains for this income.[27]

1940 1959

"Election in the state of Tennessee always presents an example of fraud. Threats and coercion in the state have become a recognized thing." The report singled out Edward Crump as the political boss who was responsible for controlling the state's election, someone so firmly in power that he "does not conceal the fact that it is he who appoints and dismisses the state's governors and city mayors." This was hardly news in Tennessee, but the report was broadcast from the U.S.S.R. on Radio Moscow.[28]

In 1953, Ernest King Bramblett (1901–1966), Republican representative from California, was charged with perjury. His indictment related to an investigation of kickbacks from employees on his staff. Although it was proven he had at least one person listed on his payroll who did no work—his only function was to draw a salary that was requisitioned by Bramblett—the representative was not charged with this act, only the fact that he had lied about it. His conviction was the first for a congressman under the "false statements" statute (U.S. Code, Title 18: Section 1001), enacted in 1948 and intended to hold government officials—in the executive as well as the legislative branch—liable for what they said, even when not under oath. His trial resulted in a conviction on February 9, 1954, with a suspended sentence of four months to one year in prison; a fine of $5,000 was also assessed. Bramblett filed two appeals, both of which were denied.[29]

Harold Giles Hoffman (1896–1954), former Republican representative from New Jersey and an ex-governor of the state, died on June 4, 1954. He left a sealed envelope for his daughter in which he disclosed a lifetime of government theft. Hoffman was elected governor when

Harold Hoffman (right)
AP Images

he was thirty-nine years old, in 1935, and served until 1938. Before that, he had been state commissioner of motor vehicles, a position he exploited to embezzle up to $50,000 a month to support a lavish lifestyle; while governor, he stole tens of thousands more. The letter also revealed an embezzlement of $300,000 from a New Jersey bank and the fact that he had been blackmailed at one point for $150,000 by another politician. While he was head of the state Unemployment Compensation Commission from 1938 to his death—with time out for military service during World War II—he used his control over millions in state funds to manipulate accounts and cover up his embezzlements, all while drawing a salary of $13,500 a year.[30]

On December 2, 1954, the Senate voted on charges levied against Joseph Raymond McCarthy (1908–1957), Republican senator from Wisconsin. Five categories of charges were initially involved, ranging

Political cartoon of Joseph McCarthy following his first election victory.

from receipt of a classified document to "abuse of Senate colleagues." The latter involved a pattern of intimidation and poor conduct he exhibited during numerous hearings involved with his partisan hunt for communists within the U.S. military. He was ultimately censured for two: "non-cooperation with and abuse of the Subcommittee on Privileges and Elections" and "abuse of the Select Committee to Study Censure." The senator was questioned by the Senate about collecting donations and other funds to support the fight against communism and then diverting the money to other purposes. He was also suspected of conflict of interest in accepting income from major corporations in return for promoting his anticommunist work as a Senator. A few years after his censure, he attended a rally in Wisconsin.

1940 1959

Campaign workers requested he leave the stage in order that he not cause political embarrassment to the other politician present, Vice President Richard Nixon.[31]

Francis Higbee Case (1896–1962), Republican senator from South Dakota, created a stir on February 3, 1956, when he delivered an unexpected speech on the floor of Congress. Case disclosed he had been approached by an attorney who offered him $2,500 as a campaign contribution if he would vote to support an upcoming bill favoring natural gas companies. Case, who had previously supported this bill, announced he

Francis Case

would now vote against it because of the implications of unethical behavior, although he did not divulge the name of the lawyer. Lyndon Johnson, majority leader of the Senate, responded, "The Senate of the U.S. can ill afford to prostrate itself before phantoms. This is no time for hesitation." A vote was pushed through and the bill passed, but it was vetoed by President Eisenhower, who had also supported the bill before Case made his revelation. After the "arrogant" lobbying effort, the president changed his mind. Shortly thereafter, Senator Johnson led an effort to reform unethical lobbying and election practices, announcing "You better saddle your horses and put on your spurs if you're going to keep up with Johnson on the flag, mother, and corruption." The subsequent committee investigation concluded, "Lobbying is proper; contributions are proper—but they must not be combined for an ulterior purpose. This is a case of irresponsibility run riot."[32]

In 1956, Thomas Joseph Lane (1898–1994), Democratic representative from Massachusetts, was convicted of income tax evasion. He was sentenced to four months in federal prison for evading $38,542 in taxes and was fined $10,000. Elected to the same position continuously since 1942, Lane ran for election after he served his time and was voted back into office, serving until 1963.[33]

Orville Hodge, the auditor of public accountants for the state of Illinois, resigned in 1956 when an investigation revealed up to $2 million was unaccounted for. It was subsequently found that Hodge had embezzled it. Personally wealthy, Hodge confided, "I don't know why I did it. I didn't need the money." He was sentenced to twelve to fifteen years in federal prison.[34]

Robert Tripp Ross (1903–1981), the assistant secretary of defense in the administration of President Eisenhower, was the target of a congressional inquiry in 1957. Ross's wife, Claire, was the president of a company in Tennessee—Ross himself had previously been vice president—that manufactured clothing and had a contract from the army for 249,000 pairs of trousers, triggering concerns about conflict of interest. Ross took an indefinite leave of absence while the matter was under investigation, then resigned, although he was never charged and the Senate ended up dropping its investigation. Ross had previously been elected to the U.S. House as a Republican in 1946 and 1952.[35]

On July 30, 1957, George Berham Parr (1901–1975), owner of a large ranch in western Texas, was sentenced to ten years in prison for fraud, one of eight people found guilty of misusing tax funds designated for a school district. Parr was also fined as part of his sentence, but the verdict was later overturned by the U.S. Supreme Court because the indictment, based on the use of the mails to defraud, had not been properly proven. Parr, known as

George Parr (left) at his trial in New Braunfels, Texas, in 1957. He was charged with stealing money from a local school district. *AP Images*

the "Duke of Duval," was the well-known head of Democratic party politics in several western Texas counties, and his support was considered a necessary part of local and statewide Democratic campaigns. It was Parr who was behind the "Miracle of Box 13," which elected Lyndon Johnson to the U.S. Senate in 1948. In 1954, Parr faced an earlier charge of income tax evasion, but the case was later dismissed. In 1945, he was sent to prison for assault while on probation after being convicted of yet another income tax evasion charge, but the sentence was cut short when he was pardoned by President Truman, also a Democrat. In 1973, he was reelected to the school board in Duval County, one of his long-held political positions, while facing yet another round of charges involving income tax, which resulted in a conviction in 1974. He was sentenced to prison for ten years, but appealed. On April 1, 1975, shortly after his appeal was turned down, he shot and killed himself on his ranch.[36]

On March 28, 1957, Mayor Terry Schrunk of Portland, Oregon, was arrested on charges of accepting a bribe while employed in his previous position as sheriff. The bribe was reportedly from the owner of a local gambling establishment who hoped to avoid a raid. The mayor defended himself by declaring the charge a "frame-up," organized by local racketeers hoping to keep him—entered in an upcoming election for mayor—from getting elected. A jury acquitted Schrunk on the bribery charge, and additional charges, which included perjury, copying a wiretap, and conspiracy, were later dismissed.[37]

In 1958, Adam Clayton Powell Jr. (1908–1972), Democratic representative from New York, was charged with evading income tax, contempt of court, and failure to appear in court. In 1960, after a lengthy sequence of hearings and motions, two of the three counts were dismissed. A trial on the third count ended up in mistrial. In 1965, he was the loser in a defamation suit brought by a widow whom Powell claimed—on live television—was a "bag woman" involved in illegal gambling. Powell was noted for championing civil rights legislation while in office, but an allegation that he had misused federal funds and ongoing issues involved with court orders in his home state ended up putting him at odds with colleagues. At one point he was legally prevented from entering New York except on Sundays because of ongoing legal action. In 1967, he was asked to "stand aside" by a full vote of the House, which in the terminology of Congress meant to exempt himself from voting pending the results of a committee investigation. The congressman was the first in the history of Congress to fight this order by filing suit in federal court. Meanwhile, in response to the technical vacancy created by the exclusion order, his con-

1940 1959

Adam Clayton Powell (left) during a press conference with Rev. Martin Luther King Jr. in 1965. *AP Images*

stituents voted him back into office in a special election. The House honored this election and accepted him back, and in a Supreme Court ruling in 1969, his previous exclusion order was voided. But by this point, the congressman was absent most of the time from Washington, D.C. Instead, he favored extended stays in the Bahamas, where he lived openly with the winner of a beauty pageant, a young woman originally hired to serve on his staff. At the same time, his estranged wife was also a paid staff member, although living in Puerto Rico. While under a growing threat of another attack in the House, Powell lost his next election.[38]

In 1958, the administration of President Eisenhower was rocked by a scandal involving Sherman Adams (1899–1986), assistant to the president. Adams, the former governor of New Hampshire and a former Republican U.S. representative from that state, had been appointed to his position by Eisenhower in 1953. Not counting a few minor political issues, he did not get into serious trouble until midyear 1958, when a congressional investigation implied he had been improperly involved in a regulatory case

Sherman Adams (right) with Ike in 1954. *AP Images*

against Bernard Goldfine, a textile company owner in New England. The impropriety blamed on Adams involved gifts he received from Goldfine, including the payment of a hotel bill, an Oriental rug, and a vicuña coat for Adams' wife. With an eye to the upcoming election and negative publicity building against the incumbent Republicans, Adams resigned on September 22, 1958, while proclaiming his innocence.[39]

Earl Kemp Long (1895–1960), Democratic governor of Louisiana, had a running battle with political foes. At one point in 1959, he was forcibly committed to a mental institution, supposedly the victim of a vendetta led by his wife, Blanche, and a coalition of political opponents. Their plan was to strip him of power in order to control the state. Long thwarted the takeover by filing for separation from his wife and discharged both the head of the mental hospital and the state director of hospitals—while still imprisoned—and appointed a new hospital director, who promptly declared the governor sane, allowing his release. Long ruled Louisiana with a flamboyant hand, and was related to other notorious state politi-

Blaze Starr arrives in New Orleans in 1959. *AP Images*

cians, most notably Huey "Kingfish" Long. After his mental health escapade, Long was estranged from his wife and spent his leisure time with Blaze Starr, a famous New Orleans stripper, an affair fictionalized in the 1989 movie *Blaze*, starring Paul Newman as Earl Long.[40]

1960–1979

Following a pattern set in the previous two decades, 1960 to 1979 was marked by a seemingly never-ending series of hearings, trials, and appeals for politicians accused—if not eventually found guilty—of conspiracy to defraud the government, conflict of interest, income tax evasion, using campaign funds for personal use, extortion, bribery, perjury, and other charges. John F. Kennedy had a tough time following in Ike's footsteps. His administration was embarrassed by its secret support for the botched Bay of Pigs attack in Cuba in 1961, which forced the president to authorize a ransom payment for the invaders captured and held by Fidel Castro. Contemporary accounts make much of Kennedy's sexual escapades in office, but this was not public information at the time. Lyndon Johnson succeeded JFK with a different menu of problems, some related to the escalating war in Vietnam. Pressures about this conflict contributed to LBJ's withdrawal from the 1968 presidential race. In 1971, the mishandling of the war—as well as information released to the public about it— embarrassed the Nixon administration after the unauthorized publication of the Pentagon Papers. But by 1972, even this major story was diluted as the saga of Watergate—the mother of all political corruption events—began to unfold.

During the 1960 presidential election campaign, John F. Kennedy and Lyndon Johnson (presidential and vice-presidential candidates, respectively) made a campaign stop in Amarillo, Texas. According to observers, they ran into some turbulence during an appearance at the local airport. Johnson's speech was drowned out deliberately by pilots—presumably Republicans—who revved the engines of planes parked on the tarmac while the Texan was speaking.[1]

In Chicago on January 29, 1960, indictments were issued for three municipal court judges, a clerk at the municipal court, and four referees of the city's traffic court. All were charged with participating in a scheme to "fix" traffic tickets, with $500,000 in profits reportedly involved. Five years later, an investigation turned up further charges, this time allegations that between 100 and 300 tickets were voided every day in Chicago traffic court in return for bribes of up to $1,800 per ticket. In 1964, it was estimated that this illegal activity generated about $1 million for the clerks involved.[2]

In Chicago in 1960, the administration of Mayor Richard Daley was rocked by a major police scandal. More than a dozen officers were charged with conspiracy in an ongoing scheme to steal property from homes and businesses. The officers involved relied on a professional safecracker for some of their illicit missions. The thief got to keep the cash and the policeman pawned whatever else was pilfered, sometimes retreiving it in their police cars. Seventeen officers were suspended, six officers were convicted and sent to prison, and the police commissioner resigned in the wake of the disclosure. The scandal also triggered a war of words between the mayor, a Democrat, and Governor William Stratton, a Republican. The governor pressured the mayor to clean up the city, and the mayor responding by accusing Stratton of "cheap politics."[3]

Richard Daley

Mayor Richardson Dilworth (1898–1974) of Philadelphia resigned from office in 1961 to run for governor. Dilworth, a Democrat, was a well-known reformer and had campaigned against local Republican-led corruption as early as 1947. He was first elected mayor in 1957 and while in office spearheaded successful urban renewal projects as well as starting a major public transit program. But in 1961, he found himself enmeshed in a municipal scandal, crippling his political career. He received much of the heat after an investigation turned up a "payola" scheme in which a contractor reportedly paid at least $75,000 in bribes to city officials; the city treasurer and others received bottles of whisky at Christmas, wrapped in $100 bills. Another scheme involved a car dealer who sold new cars to the city and bought them back after they had been "reevaluated." Although not personally involved, Dilworth lost the race for governor and did not hold elected office again.[4]

John Kennedy

John Fitzgerald Kennedy (1917–1963), Democratic president of the United States, was the object of many rumors, both before and during his presidency, relating to his extramarital sexual activities. Though by most accounts varied and frequent, none of these were reported in the media. Not so for a minor scandal involving an alleged secret first marriage. Before Kennedy's wedding to Jacqueline Bouvier—according to several accounts as well as a self-published book on genealogy—he was married briefly to a woman named Durie Malcolm. Rumors about the alleged event escalated to political attacks and items printed in gossip columns and the mainstream media, prompting a denial by the White House. The woman in question, whom the president did admit dating, made a flat denial.[5]

1960 1979

The administration of President Kennedy was shaken in 1962 by a scandal triggered by an entrepreneur in Pecos, Texas. Billie Sol Estes, a fertilizer dealer and investor, used connections at the Department of Agriculture and political clout from Vice President Lyndon Johnson, a former Texas congressman, to take advantage of federal subsidies on cotton production, eventually generating millions in profits. A low-ranking Department of Agriculture employee triggered an investigation, however, when he refused to accept a bribe for allowing illegal transfers of cotton allotments. When this employee turned up dead—followed shortly by an accountant working for Estes—the case attracted the scrutiny of a grand jury. In time, allegations of bribery associated with Estes reached as high as the secretary of agriculture, Orville Freeman, and two additional deaths were linked to the scandal. A congressional investigation cleared Freeman—and reduced the negative effects on the Kennedy administration—but other politicians got

Orville Freeman

caught in the crossfire between investigators and the media. H. Carl Andersen, Republican U.S. representative from Minnesota, was one. Columnist Drew Pearson tied him to the Estes mess in a column, causing the congressman to refer Pearson as "this polecat...this vile, corrupt creature...this damnable skunk." Estes ended up convicted in federal court of fraud and other charges and was sentenced to fifteen years in prison. A Supreme Court decision freed him, however, declaring his trial to be unfair because of television coverage.[6]

In 1962, legendary political trickster Dick Tuck found an unusual way to needle California gubernatorial candidate Richard Nixon about a questionable loan to his brother from Howard Hughes. Nixon was running for governor following two terms as vice president and the Republican nomination for president in 1960; he lost the election to Kennedy. During a campaign stop in Chinatown, San Francisco, protestors held up signs in Chinese, reading "What about that Hughes loan?" The loan in question—for $205,000—had been obtained by Donald Nixon from Hughes in order to prop up his failing business, a drive-in restaurant. The restaurant went bankrupt shortly after the money was received, and the loan was never paid back.[7]

1960 1979

In 1962, congressmen Frank William Boykin (1885–1969) and Thomas Francis Johnson (1909–1988), both U.S. representatives, from Alabama and Maryland, respectively, were indicted along with two other co-defendants on a charge of influence-peddling and conspiracy to defraud the U.S. government. The case involved an attempt to use congressional influence to have mail fraud charges dropped against one of the codefendants as well as using political pressure to support the rights of independent savings and loan associations in Florida. The latter involved speeches made on the floor of the House. In 1963, the trial ended with a guilty verdict for Boykin, who had been in Congress for twenty-

Frank Boykin (left) with Rev. Billy Graham in 1958. *AP Images*

eight years. He was fined $40,000 and placed on probation. Johnson
was also found guilty, sentenced to six months in federal prison, and
fined $5,000. Boykin's lighter sentence was because of the congress-
man's poor health, which may also have contributed to a decision by
President Johnson to grant him a pardon in 1965. The two co-defendants, a business promoter and a lawyer, were also found guilty and
sent to prison. Boykins and Johnson, both Democrats, were defeated
in election campaigns in 1962. Decades earlier, in 1924, during
Prohibition, Boykin was convicted of bribing a federal agent and sentenced to two years in prison, but the conviction was later overturned.
As for Johnson, his problems continued. After he won an appeals case
on the conspiracy charge, a retrial ended with a second conviction and
he spent six months in prison. In a related episode, two high-ranking
officials in the Justice Department—John Mitchell and Richard
Kleindienst—were accused of pressuring the U.S. Board of Parole to
release Johnson (no relation to the president), a charge denied by the
Justice Department.[8]

In New Jersey in 1962, twenty-one police officers and municipal officials pleaded guilty to charges they fixed traffic tickets. Fixing tickets, a
long-running theme in municipal graft in many states, was the target
of a New Jersey supreme court action in 1948, which set rules for lower
courts to make fixing tickets a greater criminal offense.[9]

In 1963, the Massachusetts Crime Commission made its first report after being created a year earlier by the state legislature. Among the findings, the commission found "corrupt payments are often made to men
in low income brackets, who act as conduits and who receive and pay
taxes on payments under the guise of fees," and these "conduits" are
used to "distribute the cash after taxes to the members of the controlling group." In general, the report concluded that the state's corruption "is not sporadic or haphazard but is controlled by a group of
powerful politicians in which both parties are represented."[10]

During the presidential campaign of 1964, *Fact Magazine* published the
results of a poll of psychiatrists regarding the mental fitness of Barry

Goldwater, the Republican candidate. The magazine received 2,417 replies to a questionnaire sent
to all of the psychiatrists listed with the American
Medical Association (more than 12,000 total). Of
the replies, 1,189 stated Goldwater was unfit to be
president. A similar journalistic ploy was run by the
New York Times in 1896. Then the target was
William Jennings Bryan, the Democratic presidential candidate, who was also declared to be unstable presidential material.[11]

Barry Goldwater was the
target of a large variety of
"anti-" campaign buttons.

President Johnson found himself in a tough spot in 1964. On the
grounds of the White House during a public event, he was pho-

tographed lifting one of the White
House beagles by the ears. The Johnson
family had two beagles named "Him"
and "Her." The flap occurred on May 4
as Johnson explained, "It's good for
them. It does them good to let them
bark." The event created a minor scandal for a few days, with some harsh responses from animal lovers. The ASPCA
stated, "If somebody picked you up by
the ears, you'd yelp too."[12]

President Johnson lifts Him by his ears.

On October 7, 1964, Walter Wilson Jenkins (1918–1985), special assistant to President Lyndon Johnson, was arrested in a restroom at a
YMCA a few blocks away from the White House. He was charged with
disorderly conduct, a generic charge that covered Jenkins' specific illegal act, a homosexual liason that was observed by two police officers
through a peephole. In 1959, Jenkins was charged with the same crime
in the same restroom, but the previous arrest had not been publicized.
On the verge of becoming a national story with the potential to cause
political damage—the event occured only weeks before the presidential election—Jenkins quickly resigned.[13]

William Stratton, former Republican governor of Illinois, was indicted on charges of income tax evasion in 1965. Stratton, who left office in 1960 after two terms, was the first politician to be targeted with a "net worth" approach to income. With this method, the government's case rested on a comparison of assets over a period of time. If there is more at the end than can be accounted for by reported sources, something is considered amiss; they do not attempt to prove where the excess income might come from. In Stratton's case, he was charged with not reporting $86,000 of income between 1957 and 1960. After a trial, he was acquitted.[14]

On June 23, 1967, a majority of senators voted to censure Thomas Joseph Dodd (1907–1971), Democratic senator from Connecticut. Originally spurred by press reports of improper activity, Dodd was found guilty of using his office to gain public funds for personal benefit. Specifically, he was reported to hold testimonials or fund-raising events in order to generate money used to pay personal income tax and home improvement projects, and to pass on to

Thomas Dodd

family members. Dodd, who had been a U.S. representative before entering the Senate, was first elected to Congress in 1953. In the election following his censure, he lost.[15]

Cornelius Edward Gallagher (1921–), Democratic representative from New Jersey, was targeted by an article in *Life* magazine (August 9, 1968) entitled "The Congressman and the Hoodlum," claiming collaboration between him and a noted New Jersey member of the mob. According to Gallagher, the article was the result of false information given to the magazine by the FBI in a ploy to force him from office. The congressman stated he was also the target of FBI politics because he opposed Director J. Edgar Hoover's push for expanded wiretapping authority. In public comments made after the article was published, Gallagher remarked that *Life*'s "entire batch of charges adds up to one monstrous lie." Gallagher held office for fourteen years before losing an election in 1972. On October 9, 1973, he pleaded guilty to income tax evasion and was sentenced to two years in federal prison, of which he served sixteen months.[16]

Daniel Baugh Brewster (1923–), former Democratic senator from Maryland and a former U.S. representative, was indicted in 1969, a year after he left office, on a charge that he had accepted a bribe while a senator. The bribe was from a mail order catalog company and related to an upcoming vote on postal rates. Brewster denied any involvement. In 1975, after a trial, conviction, and reversal on appeal, Brewster agreed to plead no contest to a new charge of accepting an illegal gratuity of $4,500. He was fined $10,000.[17]

In September 1969, Joseph Alioto (1916–1998), mayor of San Francisco, was accused of having links to the Mafia. An article in *Look* magazine entitled "The Web That Links San Francisco's Mayor Alioto and the Mafia" made this a national topic, but the claim was never substantiated. In 1972, Alioto won a major libel suit against the magazine. Meanwhile, in 1970, in the state of Washington, eight public utilities and other parties combined in a civil suit against him, charging price-fixing. This case also resulted in a victory for Alioto. In yet another attack, in 1971, the federal government indicted him and several of his colleagues for bribery after linking them to a payment scheme in the same price-fixing case. Alioto once again was successful in defending himself; the federal judge in charge of the case ordered an acquittal even before the defense had presented their side. The notoriety of these legal battles, however, had a major effect on Alioto's political career. He withdrew from a race for governor of California and instead ran for reelection as mayor, winning in 1971.[18]

Abe Fortas (1910–1982), associate justice of the U.S. Supreme Court since October 1965, resigned on May 14, 1969. He had been targeted for an ethics issue, an apparent conflict of interest that arose between his role on the Court and his involvement in a nonprofit group, the Wolfson Family Foundation, which had been charged with securities fraud. Their case had been appealed to the Supreme Court but had

Abe Fortas

**1960
1979**

been rejected. At the time, Fortas recused himself. It was revealed in an article in *Life* magazine that the foundation had given Fortas $20,000, reportedly as a consulting fee. He returned the money, but there remained questions about his involvement with the organization. After the story was published, an investigation by the Justice Department discovered a contract between Wolfson and Fortas, agreeing to pay him $20,000 a year for life. Fortas subsequently claimed he had withdrawn from the contract. No legal actions or charges were filed against him, but he resigned nevertheless in the face of the negative publicity.[19]

In 1969, Hugh J. Addonizio (1914–1981), mayor of Newark and former Democratic U.S. representative from New Jersey, was charged with conspiracy, extortion, and evading income tax payments. On June 16, 1970, he went on trial. The mayor was convicted and received a sentence of ten years in federal prison and a fine of $25,000. His corruption case involved $1.4 million in kickbacks and allegations of links to organized crime. While Addonizio was in prison, a judge on the federal district court issued an order releasing him, but the U.S. Parole Commission rescinded the order and he was back behind bars ten days later. Addonizio had spent a total of twenty-two years in office, fourteen years in the state legislature. During World War II, before his political career, he was in the first wave of troops assaulting Omaha Beach on D-Day.[20]

Hugh Addonizio outside of federal court in New Jersey in 1970. *AP Images*

On July 18, 1969, Senator Edward Moore Kennedy (1932–), Democrat from Massachusetts, was driving a car on the island of

Chappaquiddick, near Martha's Vineyard, when it careered off a wooden bridge and plunged into the water. A passenger in the car, Mary Jo Kopechne, drowned, but Kennedy swam to safety. A scandal erupted not only because the senator had left the scene of the accident, but he did not report it or mention it to his friends, suggesting he was hiding something. His defense for this action was based on being in a state of shock. At the time of the accident, Kennedy was on vacation on the island, and Kopechne, who had worked as a staff member for Robert Kennedy, Edward's brother, was there with friends who were also connected with the Kennedy brothers' staffs. An official inquest determined that the plunge off the bridge had been an accident. Kennedy was only charged for leaving the scene of an accident; the verdict came with a suspended sentence. However, he was the target of significant media and public speculation for months, much of it dealing with the unanswered questions posed by the incident. In the following election, he was voted back into office.[21]

Mary Jo Kopechne AP Images

In the hotly contested race for governor of Alabama in 1970, current governor Albert Brewer (1928–) faced former governor George Wallace (1919–1998) in the Democratic primary. As lieutenant governor in 1968, Brewer had succeeded Lurleen Wallace, George's wife, after she died in office. Brewer, even though he was a Democrat, was improbably backed by support—financial as well as political—from the national Republican party, which was concerned about the growing national influence of Wallace and his potential to be a third-party candidate for president, a threat to President Nixon's reelection campaign. With this support, Brewer pulled ahead, triggering a heavy response from Wallace and the state Democratic party. Some election analysts believe the result was one of the dirtiest campaigns in state history. Wallace, who had lost an earlier state race to a noted segregationist by taking a moderate approach to the topic of race, reportedly

stated after that loss, "I will never be outniggered again." In the 1970
race and his subsequent presidential campaigns, he used race as a key

tactic. One example was the publication of a
leaflet illustrated with a faked photograph of
Brewer's daughter holding hands with a black
teenager. With integration tentative at best in
the traditional culture of the state, Brewer lost
votes from a large proportion of the white public that were afraid of interracial contact.
Wallace was elected.[22]

Governor Wallace (center)
blocks integration efforts at the
University of Alabama in 1963.

Alfonso Cervantes (1920–1983) was elected mayor of St. Louis in 1965,
after being a well-known and respected member of the city council for
years. Cervantes championed the city, was responsible for important
improvements, and was well regarded by voters. But he lost a bid for reelection in 1973 after *Life* magazine published an article entitled "The
Mayor, the Mob and the Lawyer," alleging Cervantes had business and
personal ties to organized crime.[23]

Paul Powell (1902–1970), Illinois secretary
of state and a former member of the state
legislature, died in a hotel room in
Rochester, Illinois, on October 10, 1970.
Sharing a room with him was his personal
secretary, Mrs. Margaret Hensey. Initially,
publicity about the death was limited to
speculation about Mrs. Hensey's relationship with the high-ranking politician, but
within a few months the story took a more
dramatic turn. Hundreds of thousands of
dollars in cash were discovered in Powell's
belongings, stuffed into shoe boxes, bowling

Paul Powell *AP Images*

bags, and an office safe. During a political career that spanned thirty-
six years, Powell, a Democrat, was quoted as saying "There's only one
thing worse than a defeated politician, and that's a broke politician."
Some sources for this money included inside dealing on racetrack

stock, kickbacks and bribes from lobbyists, and a special "flower fund," a traditional kickback system in which patronage workers made cash "contributions" in exchange for their jobs. Powell controlled up to five thousand positions. According to one report, he also collected up to $20,000 in a five-year period by confiscating the change from vending machines in the capitol building. Powell's estate was ultimately valued at more than $3 million, but after several years of legal wrangling, most of it was divvied up by the IRS and the state of Illinois.[24]

Martin B. McKneally (1914–1992), Republican U.S. representative from New York, was indicted on December 16, 1970, for failure to file federal income tax returns. McKneally, a one-term congressman, had previously been a national commander of the American Legion. He was convicted, fined $5,000, and received a one-year suspended sentence.[25]

George Lloyd Murphy (1902–1992), one-term Republican senator from California, lost his bid for reelection in 1970. The first professional actor to become a U.S. senator (he starred with Shirley Temple, Fred Astaire, and Ronald Reagan, among others), Murphy was defeated primarily because of a campaign issue relating to his income. Although not illegal, he admitted receiving $20,000 a year as a consultant to the Technicolor Corporation, for which he had formerly been a vice president. This arrangement gave an unfavorable impression to voters—and ammunition to political opponents—because of the implication of conflict of interest.[26]

George Murphy

On July 6, 1971, Thomas J. Whelan (1922–2002), mayor of Jersey City, New Jersey, was found guilty of conspiring to collect kickbacks from businesses seeking contracts with the city. Over a period of about eight years, more than $3.3 million was generated from this tactic, illegal income that was shared by the mayor and seven others, including the chief of police, president of the city council, city purchasing agent, county treasurer, county Democratic chairman, and a commissioner of the Port Authority of New York. The sweeping scandal led to the defendants being called the "Hudson Eight" because the corruption occurred within Hudson County. Another defendant, John V. Kenny, a former mayor, was originally included, but his case was separated from the others because he became ill. Later in the year, Kenny was indicted for extorting a $20 million payment from a contractor involved in a $40 million federal construction project. Known as "The Little Guy" because of his short stature, Kenny was found guilty, fined $30,000, and sent to prison for eighteen months. He had been elected as a reform mayor in 1949 to replace long-running political boss Frank Hague. Whelan was elected in 1963, also with a reform image.[27]

John Vernard Dowdy (1912–1995), Democratic U.S. representative from Texas, was found guilty on eight counts of bribery and perjury on December 30, 1971. Dowdy, in office since 1952, appealed the verdict, which came with a sentence of eighteen months in prison and a $25,000 fine. The strongest evidence presented at the trial was tape recordings of conversations between Dowdy

John Dowdy at his office in 1970.
AP Images

and Nathan Cohen, a businessman who had cooperated with the FBI to entrap the congressman. Dowdy served on a House subcommittee investigating problems with a real estate development of Cohen's; the bribe was in exchange for Dowdy's help thwarting the investigation. The appeal resulted in a reversal of the bribery verdict but not the charge of perjury. Dowdy was sentenced to eighteen months in federal prison and served six months.[28]

On March 29, 1971, William Wallace Barron (1911–2002), former Democratic governor of West Virginia, pleaded guilty to a charge of bribery after a string of legal troubles. In 1968, he was charged with corruption in office, but a jury trial acquitted him. The case involved the establishment of out-of-state corporations to receive up to $200,000 in kickbacks from companies that did business with the state. Four additional defendants were involved, and all were found guilty. In another case a few years later, Governor Barron, State Finance Commissioner Truman Gore, State Senator W. Bernard Smith, Clerk of the Senate J. Howard Myers, and several other state officials were charged with bribery and conspiracy to take kickbacks. Once again, the governor was acquitted. In the 1971 bribery scandal, he admitted

he had bribed the foreman of the jury in the 1968 trial. Barron's attorney and wife were also involved in this unethical activity. The attorney was found guilty, but charges against Barron's wife were eventually dropped. During the original 1968 trial, testimony showed that Barron had $25,000 in cash in a brown paper bag delivered to the wife of the jury foreman on the day the trial went to deliberation.

William Barron (center) on the way to a federal trial for bribery in 1971.
AP Images

Barron was sentenced to a total of twelve years in federal prison and a fine of $50,000. The jury foreman received a similar sentence.[29]

In 1972, President Richard Nixon proposed Richard Kleindienst (1923–2000) as his choice for U.S. attorney general. A major scandal involving corporate giant I.T.T. almost scuttled the appointment, however. A syndicated newspaper column written by Jack Anderson disclosed that I.T.T. may have been involved in unethical dealings with the Republican party in order to influence a government case against it. Kleindienst, at the time a senior executive in the Justice

Department, had signed off on an agreement to settle a long-running antitrust case against the corporation, reversing an earlier government position. In return, the company had allegedly promised to donate hundreds of thousands of dollars to the GOP to defray expenses for the 1972 convention, to be held in San Diego, California. The "smoking gun" in the subsequent congressional hearings was an internal I.T.T. memo written by Dita Beard, a lobbyist working on the company's behalf, suggesting just such an

Richard Kleindienst resigns on April 30, 1973. *AP Images*

arrangement. Partisan debates over Kleindienst's nomination led Republican senators to accuse their Democratic colleagues of "jackassery" in their opposition, which was primarily based on the I.T.T. connection. Despite some evidence and testimony incriminating I.T.T.—not to mention numerous members of Nixon's staff, including several who would soon become infamous in the much larger Watergate scandal—Kleindienst was confirmed as attorney general. (He resigned in 1973 during the Watergate scandal.) The GOP convention was moved to Miami, Florida.[30]

John Lindsay making a speech in 1965.

In the 1972 presidential primary race, John Lindsay (1921–2000) was unsuccessful in his attempts to get his opponent, George Wallace (1919–1998), to hold a public debate. Both were Democrats (Lindsay switched parties in 1971). Frustrated, Lindsay's staff released eight chickens in a hall where Wallace was speaking in Florida. Attached to each hen was a sign reading "I'm George Wallace and I'm afraid to debate." In the 1992 presidential campaign, Bill Clinton's organization tried a variation of this ploy on George H.W. Bush, Clinton's opponent, when he was slow to respond to a request for a debate. Instead of live fowl, they opted for a volunteer dressed in a chicken suit, who appeared at several events where Vice President Bush was appearing.[31]

During the 1972 presidential campaign, the U.S. Democratic senator from Maine, candidate Edmund Muskie (1914–1996), was the target of repeated attacks from the Republican side, which backed his opponent, Richard Nixon. A conservative newspaper in New Hampshire, the *Manchester Union Leader*, published an article that reported Muskie's wife, Jane, had exhibited unprofessional behavior during the campaign, including the use of foul language and excessive drinking.

Muskie appeared on television with a public response to the article. The candidate's speech, broadcast live, showed him as angry, bitter, and tearful, "unpresidential" characteristics that hurt him in the campaign. A letter published in the same paper reported that Muskie was anti–French-Canadian—a major issue in a region so close to Quebec—but this was discovered to be a forgery, ginned up by the "dirty tricks" team working for the Nixon campaign.[32]

Thomas Francis Eagleton (1929–2007), U.S. senator from Missouri, was selected to be the vice presidential running mate for George McGovern in the Democrat race for the White House in 1972. Shortly after the announcement of his selection, reports surfaced that the candidate had been a patient in mental hospitals three times in previous years. It was also disclosed he had been given psychiatric counseling and twice received electric shock treatments, all to treat bouts of depression. At the time,

Thomas Eagleton

this condition was referred to as "nervous exhaustion." The resulting scramble for news coverage included a report by syndicated columnist

Jack Anderson, stating that Eagleton had been arrested eleven times for drunk driving. This revelation turned out to be completely erroneous, forced an apology from Anderson, and boosted sympathetic support for the senator, but it turned out to be the only unfactual content. It also wasn't enough to offset the revelation about Eagleton's hospitalization, and after seventeen days of intense press coverage, McGovern was forced to drop him from the ticket to avoid further damage.[33]

Mayor Ralph Perk (1914–1999) of Cleveland had a tough time in office in 1972. Holding a blowtorch intended to cut a ceremonial steel ribbon at the first day of a convention for the American Society of Metals, he set his own hair on fire. The same year, the mayor's wife caused some local embarrassment when she turned down an invitation from President Nixon for dinner at the White House. The excuse: it was her bowling night.[34]

On January 16, 1973, Fred Hubbard, a former alderman in Chicago, surrendered to federal agents in Los Angeles, California. He was sentenced to serve two years after pleading guilty to embezzlement. The theft was discovered a few years earlier when checks from a city program—a fund set up to expand the number of minority workers in construction jobs, which he directed—bounced. He hid from authorities for a year before his capture.[35]

Otto Kerner Jr. (1908–1976), a judge in the U.S. court of appeals (and the son of a federal judge), was convicted of bribery on February 19, 1973. On July 22, 1974, Kerner resigned his position. The conviction marked the first time an active judge on the federal court of appeals was convicted in a criminal trial, although the charge related to previous illegal activities when Kerner had been governor of Illinois. He was charged with accepting $300,000 in stock for a company involved in Thoroughbred racehorses in exchange for favors. Additional charges included

Otto Kerner *AP Images*

evading income tax, conspiracy, mail fraud, and perjury. The verdict produced a sentence of three years in federal prison and a fine of $50,000. Kerner, a Democrat, had previously achieved national prominence as the head of President Johnson's National Advisory Commission on Civil Disorders. A Chicago newspaper editor wrote, "At a time when political clay feet are almost standard equipment, Otto Kerner has never been touched even by a whisper of scandal, or political hanky-panky." Theodore Isaacs, the former director of the Department of Revenue in Illinois, was also convicted of bribery, conspiracy, and evading income tax. He was sentenced to three years in prison.[36]

On March 29, 1973, Casimir J. Staszcuk and Joseph Potempa, aldermen in Chicago, Illinois, were indicted by a federal grand jury for extortion and failure to pay income tax. They were accused of taking payments from clients who hoped to get favorable rulings for property rezoning issues. In the past, prosecutors had been criticized for picking on Democratic politicians, who represented a large proportion of the city's elected officials. In this case, the prosecutor, a Republican, stated, "There are three Republican aldermen currently in the city council and now two-thirds of them have been indicted."[37]

In 1973, John Irving Whalley (1902–1980), Democratic U.S. representative from Pennsylvania, was charged with mail fraud, payroll abuse, obstruction of justice, and threatening a witness. He pleaded guilty to all charges and received a sentence of three years probation and a fine of $11,000. His crime was taking kickbacks of 10 to 20 percent of the paychecks from his staff workers. Whalley was in the House for twelve years before this scandal surfaced.[38]

In 1973, Bertram L. Podell (1925–2005), three-term Democratic U.S. representative from New York, was charged with bribery, conspiracy, conflict of interest, and perjury. He pleaded guilty to two counts—conflict of interest and perjury—and was sentenced to six months in federal prison and a fine of $5,000. The case involved the congressman accepting a total payment of $41,350 from Florida Atlantic Airlines in exchange for his influence in having it assigned an air route from Miami to the Bahamas. The company did not get the route. Podell, a lawyer, lost his appeal bid and in 1980 was temporarily disbarred as a result of the conviction. He was also successfully sued by the U.S. government for the amount of income he received, the first such legal decision involving a congressman. In that case, the judge stated that a "member of Congress who is secretly compensated for advocating private interest as an attorney before government agencies and departments has clearly divided loyalties."[39]

Spiro Theodore Agnew (1918–1996), Republican vice president of the United States, resigned from office on October 10, 1973. He was only the second vice president in U.S. history to take this action, and the only one to do so because of pending legal action against him. Agnew was increasingly considered a burden to the administration of President Nixon because of a federal investigation that had begun earlier in the year. This probe related to questionable activities Agnew had engaged in during his previous position as governor of Maryland, including campaign fund-raising efforts that were linked to the awarding of state contracts, kickbacks, bribery, extortion, and conspiracy. The ongoing investigation also turned up evidence that as vice president, Agnew may have continued to receive money as compensation for past political favors. While waiting to see if he would be indicted or impeached, Agnew publicly denied any wrongdoing and promised to re-

main in office. But Nixon, facing growing problems of his own, pressured Agnew to resign in order to prevent unwanted disclosures that might arise in the impeachment process. At the same time, a grand jury in Baltimore had already begun to examine Agnew's activities. The president also supported a deal with the Justice Department that would reduce the threat of a criminal indictment for his vice president. As speculation rose about Agnew's fate, even some Democrats felt sorry for him. Edward Kennedy, for one, stated, "The White House and the Department of Justice have an obligation of fundamental fairness to the vice president to let the investigation take its course, free of the pervasive current atmosphere of a kangaroo trial.... He deserves the nation's respect for his demeanor in this unprecedented situation." In a compromise with a federal prosecutor, Agnew pleaded "no contest" to a single charge of income tax evasion in exchange for a suspended sentence, payment of back taxes, and a $10,000 fine. The rest of the charges were dropped. According

Spiro Agnew (center right) takes the oath of office for vice president in 1969.

to one of the federal attorneys assigned to the Agnew case, "I have never seen a stronger extortion case. If it had gone to trial, a conviction would have resulted. The man is a crook." Some of the cash to cover Agnew's fine came from a loan made by his friend Frank Sinatra.[40]

During the final days of the Watergate scandal in the summer of 1974, prominent local and national politicians increasingly called for President Richard Nixon to step down rather than deal with a messy— and nationally embarrassing—impeachment process in Congress. Bill Clinton, a professor of law at the University of Arkansas at the time, stated, "I think it's plain that the president should resign and spare the country the agony of this impeachment and removal proceeding...an admission of making false statements to government officials and interfering with the FBI and the CIA is an impeachable offense."[41]

Jerry Springer (1944–), a member of the city council in Cincinnati, Ohio, resigned his position in 1974 after an FBI raid on a massage parlor in Kentucky turned up a check he had written to a known prostitute. A few years later, Springer returned to politics, was reelected to the council, and was then elected mayor in 1977. He later abandoned politics for television.[42]

Jerry Springer *AP Images*

Thomas E. Keane (1906–1996), the Chicago alderman second in command behind Mayor Richard Daley, was convicted of mail fraud and conspiracy in a federal court on October 9, 1974. Keane and several colleagues were accused of purchasing tax-delinquent properties and reselling them to the city for a large profit, without obtaining official permission to reduce or remove the tax liens. A total of 218 parcels of land were involved over a period of time extending to 1966. The group made a profit of 126 percent. Keane, a veteran of twenty-nine years in his elected position, was sentenced to five years in federal prison. His wife, Adeline P. Keane, succeeded him in office.[43]

PROFILE   Watergate

The career and presidency of Richard Nixon began its downfall on June 17, 1972. Responding to a request from the president to use more "dirty tricks" like those of the legendary Democratic trickster Dick Tuck, the Committee to Re-Elect the President (CRP, or more popularly, CREEP) and several top Nixon aides conspired to break into the national headquarters of the Democratic party at the Watergate apartment complex in Washington, D.C., in order to plant a listening device. They broke in more than once and on June 17 returned to retrieve a bug that wasn't working. They were caught in the act. The caper was first dismissed as a "third-rate burglary attempt," but police, FBI, and media investigations—particularly one conducted by Carl Bernstein and Bob Woodward of the *Washington Post*—soon disclosed the involvement of the White House. In the interim, Nixon was reelected. Following the conclusion of the burglary trial in March 1973, a grand jury investigated allegations that linked the bur-

The Watergate Hotel

glary and its participants to John Mitchell, the former attorney general and head of CREEP; John Dean, Nixon's attorney; and others in major positions. By the end of April 1973, key members of the president's staff resigned—including John Ehrlichman, H. R. Haldeman, John Dean, and Attorney General Richard Kleindienst—although Nixon still denied he was personally involved or aware of any unethical or illegal activity by them or others working for him. The Senate opened its own investigation in May through the Select Committee on Presidential Campaign Activities (also known as the "Ervin Committee," after its chairman, Senator Sam Ervin). By July, testimony disclosed that Nixon's conversations in the White House had been captured on tape. However, the president's office refused to provide the tapes when subpoenaed, citing executive privilege. In October, Nixon fired the special prosecutor in the case as a last resort to prevent access to the tapes, which were expected to provide "smoking gun" evidence that would tie him to the crime. On December 8, the tapes were finally surrendered. Two of the reels requested were missing and there was a significant gap on one of those provided, prolonging the suspense. At this point, the support of many Republican politicians began to wane and even George H. W. Bush,

the chairman of the national Republican party, stated about the scandal, "It is grubby." On July 30, the Judiciary Committee of the U.S. House of Representatives voted to adopt articles of impeachment against the president. A few days later, the White House released several additional tapes that made it clear Nixon not only had knowledge of the break-in, he had issued an order to the FBI to end its probe of the event. On August 9, before the impeach-

John Ehrlichman (right) with President Nixon.

ment proceeding could move to a full hearing in Congress, Nixon resigned, the first and only U.S. president to do so. In September, Gerald Ford, who had replaced Nixon, issued a presidential pardon for him in order to end the long-running scandal. The pardon effectively removed the threat of a criminal trial for Nixon, but created a scandal for Ford, who was accused of conspiring to protect him. Aftereffects lingered until 1975, when John Ehrlichman, H. R. Haldeman, Robert Mardian, and John Mitchell, who participated in the planning and cover-up, were convicted and sentenced to prison. Evidence from testimony in the hearings and trials following the original break-in also uncovered additional unethical activities linked to CREEP and Nixon, including the use of secret slush funds, large cash donations from wealthy donors, and other burglaries.[44]

*1960
1979*

Frank J. Kuta, an alderman in Chicago, Illinois, was convicted of extortion and income tax evasion in 1974. Kuta was charged with accepting $1,500 from a Realtor in exchange for his vote on a zoning change that affected the Realtor's property. Kuta unsuccessfully appealed his conviction all the way to the U.S. Supreme Court, arguing that he had been wrongfully charged with a violation of interstate commerce law. He was sent to prison and lost his law license. In 1987, he was indicted again, along with eleven others, in a federal case involving the city's Licensing and Inspection departments. In 2000, after his law license was reinstated, he lost it a second time when he was accused of taking more than $100,000 from an escrow account he controlled for a client.[45]

Frank James Brasco (1932–1998), Democratic U.S. representative from New York, was convicted of conspiracy to accept bribes in 1974. The charges related to his influence in the awarding of a contract from the U.S. Post Office to a mob-controlled transportation company in New York City. The conviction came after a second trial in the case; the first resulted in a hung jury. Brasco appealed the verdict—which came with a sentence of five years in prison—and served three months in 1975 after the U.S. Supreme Court failed to reverse the outcome.[46]

At about 2 A.M. on October 7, 1974, Wilbur Daigh Mills (1909–1992),

Democratic U.S. representative from Arkansas and the chairman of the House Ways and Means Committee, was pulled over while in a speeding car with no lights on near the Tidal Basin in Washington, D.C. With Mills were another man and three women, one of whom, Annabell Battistella, ran from the car and jumped into the water. Mills was apparently intoxicated and was bleeding from scratches on his face. He explained at the time that he had been slightly injured when he attempted to restrain Battistella, who was described as "ill." It was subsequently reported that Battistella was an Argentine immi-

Wilbur Mills with Fanne Foxe in 1974, while she was performing in Boston.
AP Images

grant who worked as a stripper under the name of Fanne Foxe, aka the "Argentine Firecracker." Mills, who had been in Congress for nineteen consecutive terms, did not run for reelection.[47]

In April 1974, Edward John Gurney, Republican senator from Florida, was indicted by a county grand jury on charges he violated state election laws. The indictment was for a single misdemeanor charge related

Edward Gurney

to campaign contributions. The senator had accepted contributions before designating a campaign treasurer or setting up a bank account for the purpose, a violation of the rules governing this activity. The judge hearing the case dismissed it as "fatally defective." In July of the same year, a federal grand jury indicted Gurney—along with six others—for extortion and influence-peddling, which included requiring payments in advance from contractors

and others wishing to do business with the state. Gurney had been a member of the Senate committee investigating Watergate, and as a conservative Republican he defended Nixon before the president resigned. In his current predicament, he claimed the indictments were politically motivated. A jury exonerated the senator on five of the charges, and during a second trial, another jury exonerated him on the remaining two charges. Meanwhile, Gurney resigned his Senate seat, and in a subsequent election he was defeated in a bid to return to Congress.[48]

On July 27, 1974, Edwin Reinecke, lieutenant governor of California, was found guilty of perjury by a federal jury. He had been indicted on three counts relating to his statements in an official inquiry by the Senate Judiciary Committee. The committee was investigating the activities of the I.T.T. Corporation and its alleged involvement in the site selection for the Republican National Convention in 1972. The company was accused of promising a payment to the Republicans in exchange for a decision favoring San Diego, California. Reinecke was accused of lying about a discussion of the matter between himself and

I.T.T. After his conviction, he was sentenced to eighteen months in prison—the sentence was suspended—and resigned from his position. A year later, a federal appeals court overturned the verdict because the alleged lies had been made to a committee that was meeting without a specified quorum of members. The same scandal had cropped up during the confirmation hearing of Richard Kleindienst for U.S. attorney general in 1972.[49]

While he was governor of Texas in 1963, John Bowden Connally (1917–1993) was in the presidential motorcade in Dallas when John F. Kennedy was shot. Connally was himself severely wounded in the assassination attack. Almost a decade later, he was appointed sec-

retary of the treasury by President Nixon. In 1975, after he had left this post, Connally was charged with accepting a $10,000 bribe in return for using his political influence to push through a raise for the federal support level for milk. The beneficiaries of this increase were milk producers, and reportedly the source of the bribe. During his trial, the character witnesses for the defense included Reverend Billy Graham, the president of the World Bank, the secretary of state, and Lady Bird Johnson—the former first lady— among others. In her testimony, Lady Bird

John Connally

said of the defendant, "Some folks don't like him, but I don't think any of them doubt his integrity." Connally was acquitted. At the other end of the alleged bribery, the head of the largest milk cooperative in the country pleaded guilty in 1974 to a charge that he made a payment to the former secretary, even though the same payment had failed to prove guilt when it was disclosed during Connally's trial. Originally a Democrat, Connally switched to the Republican party in 1973, prompting one of his old Democratic colleagues to quip "It's the first time in recorded history that a rat has swum toward a sinking ship."[50]

David Hall (1930–), Democratic governor of Oklahoma, was indicted for racketeering, extortion, and perjury on January 13, 1975, a few days after leaving office at the end of his term. He had been elected in 1971 by the closest margin in the history of the state. One charge involved his acceptance of a $25,000 payment from a brokerage firm that was later recommended as the underwriter for bonds used to finance a large state construction project. The payment was classified as a kickback to the governor in a grand jury investigation because he was involved in implementing the company's recommendation. As it was disclosed during the inquiry, this kind of money was known in the region as "frog hair," because it was "as slippery and smooth" as the hair on a frog. Another charge was the illegal funneling of state employee retirement accounts to an out-of-state investment fund in exchange for additional kickbacks. Hall, who did not appear to personally benefit from any campaign-related income, was quoted as saying "If only the rich can run for office, we'll soon have nothing but government by a select group." On March 14, 1975, he was convicted and sentenced to three years in federal prison. He served nineteen months.[51]

Daniel Baugh Brewster (1923–), a former Democratic senator from Maryland, was charged with three counts of accepting an illegal gratuity while in office. The charge came in 1975 after a previous trial in 1969 in which he had been convicted in a similar case. The 1969 ruling was later reversed. In the 1975 case, Brewster pleaded "no contest" and received a sentence of eight months to two years in federal prison for each count, as well as a fine of $10,000 on each count.[52]

On April 18, 1975, George Vernon Hansen (1930–), Republican U.S. representative from Idaho, was sentenced to two months in prison by a federal court. Hansen was found guilty of violating campaign finance rules and paid a fine of $2,000. The prison sentence was dropped. At Hansen's sentencing, the judge stated, "If the people who make the laws can't obey them, who can be expected to obey them?" In a later case, in April 1984, Hansen was convicted of four felony charges for failure to disclose information that was required by the Ethics in Government Act. He stated, "It is no fun trying to be responsible in the irresponsible atmosphere of the nation's capital." While appealing this verdict, he ran for election and lost by seventy votes. A recount requested—and paid for—by Hansen revealed he had actually lost by 170 votes. The U.S. House voted to reprimand him on the ethics issue, and after losing an appeal in the court case, he served eleven months in prison and paid a fine of $40,000. In 1992, after he had retired from his political career, another federal trial found him guilty of bank fraud related to his involvement in a check-kiting scheme.[53]

In Chicago in 1975, Floyd T. Fulle, the chairman of the Cook County Republican party and a former county commissioner, was convicted of extortion, perjury, and nonpayment of income tax. Fulle was found to have received up to $69,000 from contractors and developers in exchange for not delaying or challenging requests for zoning changes. During his trial, it was disclosed that he kept up to $15,000 in cash in a cookie box in his home, for "family expenses." Fulle denied all charges, even after he was released from prison after serving half of a five-year sentence.[54]

James L. Oakey Jr. was dismissed from his position as associate judge on the Cook County, Illinois, circuit court on July 16, 1975. He was charged with a violation of judicial rules governing outside activity. In this case, it turned out Oakey was running a private investigation agency at the same time he was serving as a judge. He was convicted and sentenced to six years in prison.[55]

In 1975, Andrew Jackson Hinshaw (1923–), Republican U.S. representative from California, was charged with embezzlement, conspiracy, soliciting a bribe, bribery, and misappropriation of public funds. On October 2, 1976, another member of the U.S. House from California introduced a resolution to expel Hinshaw, but the measure was voted down by a voice vote. On December 4, 1976, he was convicted of petty theft, bribery, and misappropriation of public funds and sentenced to one year in federal prison. The charges were related to his activities while serving as the Orange County, California, assessor in 1972.[56]

Nelson Rockefeller

During a speech in Birmingham, New York, during campaign season in 1976, Vice President Nelson Rockefeller was continually interrupted by hecklers in the audience. At the time, Rockefeller was campaigning for Republican vice presidential candidate Bob Dole in the upcoming election. Unable to silence the interruptors, Rockefeller eventually responded by using his middle finger to make a rude gesture, which was captured by a news photographer and widely published.[57]

In 1976, Colleen Gardner, a secretary to John Andrew Young (1916–2002), Democratic U.S. representative from Texas, resigned her job and made a public statement implicating the congressman in sexual misconduct. According to Gardner, Young had sexual relations with her over a period of several years and, in fact, her primary duty was to accommodate his sexual needs rather than be a secretary. Her salary was increased to compensate for this activity even though she was otherwise assigned no meaningful work. An investigation by the Justice Department was unable to corroborate her story, which was denied by the congressman. His initial response was "Poppycock!" However, the negative publicity contributed to his defeat in the 1978 election.[58]

In 1976, Henry J. Helstoski (1925–1999), six-term Democratic U.S. representative from New Jersey, was charged with conspiracy, bribery, perjury, and obstructing justice. He was reportedly paid more than $8,000 in return for sponsoring legislation to help certain citizens of Chile immigrate to the United States. Following several years of legal maneuvering, all of the charges were dropped. In the interim, the congressman, who insisted he was a victim of a political frame-up, lost his race for reelection. He was quoted as saying "I got a dim view of politics, what people do to advance themselves. You certainly get a good perspective of what human nature is; the extent of greed, ambition, the standards and morality of the people." In 1976, the congressman's aide was convicted and sentenced to six years in prison on a related charge: accepting payments for the sponsorship of permanent residency bills for specific foreign nationals.[59]

In 1976, Joseph David Waggonner Jr. (1918–), Democratic U.S. representative from Louisiana, was arrested in Washington, D.C., for soliciting sex from an undercover policewoman. He was released without charge because of congressional immunity. Later in the year, the District of Columbia police reported they were ending the policy of immunity that they had followed for at least one hundred years. In the U.S. Constitution, Article I, Section 6 states that senators and representatives are "privileged from arrest" except for "treason, felony, and breach of the peace," but legal rulings—including a case in the Supreme Court in 1908—had established that this was not intended to protect legislators from criminal arrest, just political reprisals. The D.C. policy was grounded in courtesy, not law. In 1980, Congressman Waggonner retired, reporting he wanted to spend more time with his family.[60]

1960 1979

In June 1976, Allan Turner Howe (1927–2000), first-term Democratic U.S. representative from Utah, was arrested in Salt Lake City after he had solicited sex from two undercover city policewomen. He was convicted of a misdemeanor charge and appealed, professing his innocence. The conviction was upheld and he lost the next election.[61]

In 1976, Elizabeth Ray, who had formerly been a secretary for Wayne Levere Hays (1911–1989), Democratic U.S. representative from Ohio, charged that her employment had been a cover-up. In a public statement, she said she had been paid to provide sexual rather than secretarial services. In an exposé provided to the *Washington Post*, she admitted, "I can't type, I can't file, I can't even answer the phone." Ray also reported that while working for another

Elizabeth Ray promotes her book in 1976. *AP Images*

congressman, Kenneth James Gray (1924–), Democrat from Illinois, she was ordered to provide sexual favors to other politicians to help in Gray's quest for legislative votes. The allegations led to an investigation by the FBI and an escalating political scandal, but little came of it other than negative publicity. Ray detailed many of these activities in a novel titled *The Washington Fringe Benefit.* Hays retired shortly after the scandal peaked.[62]

In 1976, James Fred Hastings (1926–), Republican U.S. representative from New York, was charged with mail fraud and making false statements. The charges related to kickbacks paid to him by members of his congressional staff. He was also charged with filing false vouchers for office expenses. The congressman was convicted and sentenced to federal prison, where he served fourteen months. He resigned his seat in 1976 as a result of the scandal.[63]

During the 1976 election for the U.S. House in Georgia, incumbent John James Flynt Jr. (1914–), a Democrat, was opposed by Newt Leroy Gingrich (1943–), a university professor of history and geography and a Republican. Flynt was attacked on several issues, including the appearance of conflict of interest. He leased some land he owned to the Ford Motor Company, and as a congressman he had publicly opposed legislation requiring automobile companies to install certain kinds of pollution controls and was the target of criticism for supporting the car companies. He was also the chairman of the House Ethics Panel, making him an apt target for Gingrich in another questionable business deal in which Flynt switched the title of real estate he owned to a former aide, apparently to avoid paying an assessment. Despite the attacks, Flynt, who had held office since 1954, was reelected.[64]

In 1976, Robert Louis Leggett (1926–1997), six-term Democratic U.S. representative from California, was questioned by the Justice Department regarding his involvement in a Korean-based influence-peddling case. This scandal ended up implicating several congressmen, although Leggett was never officially charged. At the same time, however, the investigation turned up a personal relationship between

Leggett and a Korean American woman who was an aide to Congressman Carl Albert, the Speaker of the House. Although Leggett was married, it turned out he had been having an affair with the aide as well as a long-running affair with another woman, and the latter relationship resulted in the birth of two illegitimate children. Leggett divorced his wife and married the aide, and in the following election did not run for office.[65]

Robert Lee Fulton Sikes (1906–1994), Democratic U.S. representative from Florida, was ousted from his position as chairman of the House Appropriations Subcommittee on Military Construction on January 26, 1977. The move came in the wake of disclosures from the previous year. Then Sikes had received a reprimand from the House for misconduct related to financial transactions with several companies in his home state. He did not run for reelection in 1978.[66]

Less than a year after being appointed director of the Office of Management and Budget under President Carter in 1976, Thomas

Bert Lance (left) and Secretary of Defense Harold Brown.

Bertram Lance (1931–) was the target of a federal probe. The issue was that he had not sold his personal shares in a Georgia bank, as required by his new position, and he was accused of improper business deals during a previous stint as head of the bank. Plus, he was thought to have used his new political clout to influence his own finances—specifically, hundreds of thousands of dollars in personal loans. Although Lance defended his actions, the negative publicity affected his position. On September 21, 1977, he resigned. In a federal trial in 1980 based on some of the same charges, he was acquitted.[67]

Governor Marvin Mandel of Maryland (1920–) was impeached and removed from office after being convicted of corruption in 1977. On August 23, 1977, a jury in a federal trial found Marvin and five business colleagues guilty of eighteen counts each of racketeering and mail fraud. The charges were tied to activities in which cash, investments, jewelry, vacation trips, and other gifts were given to the governor in exchange for official favors. Marvin, a Democrat, was originally appointed to the post to replace the previous governor, Spiro Agnew, who had resigned to serve as vice president of the United States. Agnew resigned this position in the face of similar allegations. Mandel's case spanned two years and two trials; the first resulted in a mis-

Marvin Mandel and his wife on their way to federal court. *AP Images*

trial. The eventual verdict came with a sentence of four years, but the conviction was overturned on appeal in 1979, in time for him to return to office for the final two days of his term. Six months later, a federal court nullified the reversal and reinstated the original conviction. Mandel entered prison in 1980 and was released on parole in 1982 after President Reagan commuted his sentence. In 1987, five years after he completed his punishment, the original conviction was once again overturned, based on a Supreme Court ruling on improper application of the federal mail fraud law, clearing Mandel's record if not his reputation.[68]

Elected in 1976, Richard Alvin Tonry (1935–), Democratic U.S. representative from Louisiana, was in office less than six months when he resigned on May 4, 1977, while he faced congressional and criminal investigations into election fraud. Waiting for the legal outcome, he campaigned to be nominated for the special election called to fill his own vacancy, but lost. In 1978, he pleaded guilty in the case, which involved four violations of the federal campaign finance law. In 1986, he was charged with attempted bribery for trying to get an Indian reservation in the state to allow bingo games. He was convicted and sentenced to three years in federal prison and paid a fine of $15,000.[69]

Edward Alexander Garmatz (1903–1986), former Democratic U.S. representative from Maryland, was the target of a Justice Department investigation in 1977. The probe tied him to bribery and influence-peddling activities. The case was dropped in 1978 because federal prosecutors came to believe that a key witness's statements were false. If the government's case had been supportable, the congressman, who was the chairman of the Merchant Marine and Fisheries Committee in the House, would have been linked to $25,000 in payments from two shipping companies that were intended to support passage of legislation that benefited their businesses. In 1970, it was disclosed that Garmatz had hired Ralph Casey as special counsel to the House committee. Casey's former job had been as executive vice president and lobbyist for the American Institute of Merchant Shipping, where he bolstered support for federal aid for shipping lines. The first government allegations of "unlawful gratuities" and bribes linked to Garmatz surfaced shortly thereafter.[70]

In 1977, in Massachusetts, a federal investigation revealed a scheme to divert funds from state vocational education programs. Indictments and convictions of nineteen people resulted, including that of Patrick J. Weagraff, associate commissioner of education, and George Rogers, a state senator. The corruption, which was made public during the administration of Governor Michael Dukakis, was referred to as the Voke Ed Scandal and played a role in the state's gubernatorial election of 1982. Dukakis was not directly blamed for the affair, however, because the principal participant had been appointed during the previous governor's administration. Weagraff was linked to kickbacks on federal grants and grants funded to nonexistent people—in one instance, he authorized a payment to his dead mother—and phony institutions, with up to $500,000 wrongfully dispensed.[71]

Joshua Eilberg (1921–2004), Democratic U.S. representative from Pennsylvania, was charged with accepting illegal compensation in 1977. While the case was under way, he was also implicated in an effort to sidetrack the federal investigation probing it. This probe uncovered fraud by the administrators of a Philadelphia hospital and tied Eilberg to $34,900 in payments from the hospital in exchange for helping it get a federal grant of $14.5 million. In an earlier incident, in 1975, the congressman admitted to using his position to try to influence a parole hearing for a former Philadelphia city commissioner who had been convicted of corruption. In 1979, Eilberg reacted to the ongoing scrutiny of his activities from the local prosecutor—U.S. Attorney David Marston, a Republican—by telephoning President Carter, a Democrat, and complaining. Carter in turn called Attorney General Griffin Bell and—according to some accounts—reportedly pressured Bell to find a replacement for Marston. The naming of the replacement, a Democrat, coincided with the opening of Eilberg's trial. However, the trial was called off when the congressman agreed to a plea bargain, accepting a fine and five years probation in exchange for a guilty plea.[72]

Joshua Eilberg at a news conference in 1975. *AP Images*

In 1978, Otto Ernest Passman (1900–1988), former Democratic U.S. representative from Louisiana, was charged with bribery, conspiracy, and income tax evasion. He was tied to Tongsun Park, a political agent allegedly working on behalf of the South Korean government. Park paid Passman up to $98,000 in illegal bribes and gratuities for his help in political matters relating to South Korea. Passman's trial resulted in acquittal in 1979. Payments from Park were also traced to Charles Herbert Wilson (1917–1984), John Joseph McFall (1918–2006), and Edward Ross Roybal (1916–2005), Democratic representatives from California. The three men received reprimands from the House for their involvement in what was dubbed "Koreagate." Richard Thomas Hanna (1914–2001), a Democratic representative from California as well, did not get off so easy. He was charged with conspiracy to defraud the federal government, pleaded guilty, and was sentenced to prison. Passman was also implicated in another illegal payment scandal, this one tied to Dr. Murdock Head, the director of the Airlie Foundation. An investigation of Head's illegal payoffs found a payment of $12,000 to Hanna. He was also charged with funneling $28,000 to Daniel Flood (1903–1994), Democratic representative from Pennsylvania.[73]

In 1978, Frank Monroe Clark (1915–2003), Democratic U.S. representative from Pennsylvania, was charged with mail fraud, perjury, and income tax evasion. The charges related to employees Clark added to his federal payroll even though they were not working in his congressional office. A grand jury also investigated links between Clark's personal finances and his interactions with a large national union. Clark pleaded guilty to the charges of mail fraud and income tax evasion, and was sentenced to two years in federal prison and fined $11,000.[74]

Governor Leonard Ray Blanton (1930–1996) of Tennessee left office on January 17, 1979, three days before his term officially ended, because of an escalating scandal. He was accused of receiving money in exchange for pardoning three inmates and granting executive clemency to forty-nine others. The governor was never officially charged, but a grand jury indicted six others in the matter, including four of his former aides. One was acquitted and two others convicted, but these verdicts were overturned on a technicality. In 1981, Blanton, a Democrat, was in trouble again, this time charged with mail fraud and conspiring to sell liquor licenses while in office. He was convicted and served twenty-two months in prison. The mail fraud conviction was overturned on appeal while he was jailed. The former governor continually proclaimed his innocence. Years later, he stated, "I never took a dishonest dollar in my life. I was the only governor to ever leave office broke." In 1983, a book was published about the corruption during the Blanton administration. *Marie: A True Story*, by Peter Maas, was made into a movie in 1985— *Marie*, starring Sissy Spacek and Fred Thompson (who switched careers from

Ray Blanton (center) and his attorneys leave the grand jury in 1978. *AP Images*

acting to politics in 1994, when he was elected to the U.S. Senate from Tennessee). After leaving prison, Blanton made an unsuccessful run for the U.S. Senate before beginning a new career as a used car salesman.[75]

In 1979, Michael Joseph Myers (1943–), Democratic U.S. representative from Pennsylvania, was charged with disorderly conduct for his participation in a barroom brawl in Arlington, Virginia. He pleaded no contest.[76]

On October 11, 1979, Senator Herman Eugene Talmadge (1912–2002), Democrat from Georgia, was censured by the U.S. Senate. A Senate committee determined that the long-term senator was responsible for—if not aware of—various financial misdoings in his office, including excess reimbursements, inaccurate campaign finance reports, and the use of campaign funds for other purposes. Talmadge stated, "The ultimate ethics committee are the people of Georgia." In the following election, he lost. Before his career in Congress, Talmadge was the governor of Georgia.[77]

Herman Talmadge

In 1978, Anthony Claude Leach Jr. (1934–) was the winner by a narrow margin in an election for U.S. representative from Louisiana. He won the election by only 266 votes. The following year, Leach, a Democrat, was charged with buying 440 votes for $5 each. A trial resulted in an acquittal on all charges, but prosecutors were successful in convicting more than twenty other local citizens for similar illegal activity in the same campaign. Shortly after Leach's trial, he was prosecuted again, this time for buying votes in the primary stage of the same election, but in 1980, these federal charges were dropped. The same year, Leach lost the race for reelection.[78]

1980–1999

In the 1980s, Ronald Reagan dominated national politics. He was the first two-term president since Eisenhower, was well liked—even by many Democrats—and thought to be personally ethical, yet Reagan and his administration managed to top the previous champion—President Harding—for the greatest number of appointees indicted, accused, or implicated in criminal activity. One major political scandal involved the savings and loan industry, and taxpayers ended up covering as much as $500 billion in losses. The Iran-Contra affair, in scope and importance perhaps the next biggest presidential scandal after Watergate, damaged Republican politicians but had little effect on Reagan's popularity. The Abscam sting operation resulted in indictments and convictions for several in Congress and set a benchmark for law enforcement. The presidency of George H. W. Bush was marked by few scandals, but he generated significant press in his last days of office by issuing an official pardon for the officials previously convicted of wrongdoing in the Iran-Contra affair, thrusting them—and it—back into the public eye. Bill Clinton followed Bush with a much greater impact on public morals because of his now well-documented sexual shenanigans in the White House.

In 1980, ex-governor Marvin Mandel (1920–) of Maryland, previously evicted from office for corruption, was in trouble again. This time, the former Democratic head of the state was accused of removing a truckload of items from the state mansion when he was forced to move out. Among the items: champagne glasses, ashtrays, silverware, Chippendale wing chairs, a brass bed, a mahogany bed, the entire official supply of liquor and wine (750 bottles), cleaning supplies, groceries, and up to one hundred cases of dog food. The state of Maryland sued the ex-governor for the loss, and a settlement was reached in 1983. He agreed to pay $10,000 in restitution, but there was a delay of a few years while Mandel served time in prison on a political corruption charge.[1]

Charles Diggs (right) meets with tennis star Arthur Ashe in 1970. *AP Images*

Charles Coles Diggs Jr. (1922–1998) was first elected as a Democrat to the U.S. House from Michigan in 1954, a career move from his previous business as a mortician. He owned the House of Diggs, a funeral parlor in Detroit. He served successive terms until June 3, 1980, when he resigned after being censured by the House for his involvement in payroll kickbacks. He admitted to diverting more than $60,000 of funds designated for the salaries for employees in his congressional office, using it to pay personal and office bills. A federal trial on the same charges ended with a conviction. He served seven months out of a three-year sentence and then returned to his original profession.[2]

In October 1980, U.S. Representative Robert Edmund Bauman (1937–), a Republican from Maryland, pleaded not guilty to charges that he had solicited sex from a sixteen-year-old boy. The congressman—who was the chairman of the American Conservative Union, which promoted "family values" and an anti-homosexual philosophy—publicly admitted to having "homosexual tendencies" as well as drinking problems but refused to drop out of his campaign for reelection. The charges were later dropped in return for Bauman's agreeing to counseling. He was defeated in his reelection bid.[3]

William J. Scott, the attorney general for Illinois, was convicted of income tax fraud on March 19, 1980. Scott was accusing of taking $22,153 in campaign funds from the 1972 race and his conviction came because he underreported this income on his tax forms. He was sentenced to one year and one day in federal prison and served seven months. At the time of his trial, Scott, a Republican, had been in office for four terms and was running for the U.S. Senate. He lost the election, which was held one day before his conviction.[4]

In January 1980, Dan Quayle, Thomas Evans, and Tom Railsback—Republican congressmen, from Indiana, Delaware, and Illinois, respectively—roomed together during a weekend golf vacation in Atlantis City, Florida. An additional roommate was Paula Parkinson, an attractive lobbyist working to prevent passage of a proposed crop insurance bill. There were allegations of influence-peddling, not to mention inappropriate conduct, following media exposure of this event in early 1981. The Justice Department investigated rumors that the three Republicans exchanged their votes for money or sexual favors, but no charges were filed.

Dan Quayle

Parkinson later posed nude in *Playboy* magazine and stated she had slept with at least eight members of Congress, Quayle not included. When Quayle was selected to be George Bush's vice presidential running mate in the 1988 election campaign, the issue came up again, without raising much ruckus. His wife, for one, laughed off the allegations, stating that those who knew her husband would understand he would always choose golf over sex. All three politicians voted against the bill in question.[5]

Stanley Zydlo, 26th Ward alderman, Chicago, Illinois, was convicted in 1980 of accepting a bribe in order to change the results of entrance tests for the Chicago Fire Department. The tests were for two applicants who were relatives; he received $1,000 for his participation. Zydlo was sentenced to sixty days in jail, but this was reduced to probation because of his health problems.[6]

Daniel John Flood (1903–1994), Democratic U.S. representative from Pennsylvania, resigned on January 30, 1980. Known as "Dapper Dan"

Daniel Flood on his way to a competency hearing in 1980.

AP Images

because of his waxed moustache and fancy clothes, he served various terms in Congress since 1945 but now faced charges of conspiracy, bribery, and perjury. As the chairman of the House Appropriations Subcommittee, Flood was charged with using his influence in exchange for payments totaling $50,000 from businesses and lobbyists. In a first trial, a jury was unable to agree on a verdict—they voted eleven to one for conviction. Flood was declared incompetent to stand a second trial and agreed to enter a plea of guilty to one charge of conspiracy. He received a sentence of one year probation and was fined.[7]

On April 13, 1981, Jon Clifton Hinson (1942–1995), Republican representative from Mississippi, resigned his seat in the House. He was the target of increasing negative publicity following an arrest in February in Washington, D.C., on a sodomy charge. Hinson was nabbed by Capitol police officers in the men's room of the Longworth House Office Building while performing a sexual act with a male employee of the Library of Congress. He pleaded guilty to a reduced charge of attempted sodomy, a misdemeanor, but the event was compounded by earlier disclosures of other homosexual encounters, including a close brush with death at a gay movie theater that had burned down, killing nine men. Representative Hinson, a conservative and married, initially denied he was a homosexual, then became an advocate for gay rights. He died of AIDS in 1995.[8]

Democratic Congressman John Wilson Jenrette Jr. (1936–), from South Carolina, saw his political career come to an end in 1980 after being convicted of participation in the Abscam scandal. In 1981, his notoriety increased when his estranged wife, Rita, published a diary detailing her sex life with her husband while he was in office, including a sexual escapade performed one night on the steps of the U.S. Capitol. The revelations appeared first in *Playboy* magazine, where they

PROFILE   Abscam

The FBI and the Department of Justice carried out a twenty-three-month undercover investigation that ended in 1979. They called it the "Arab Scam," or Abscam for short. The object was to use agents disguised as wealthy Arabs to test the ethics of elected politicians in Washington as well as state legislators in New Jersey and others involved in official business. The agents used large amounts of cash to barter for political influence in their business investment in the United States. There was considerable outrage over the result, from politicians claiming entrapment to voters demanding justice. The evidence included video surveillance that graphically illustrated the willingness of the participants to benefit from the cash offered. Senator Harrison Williams was caught stating "You tell the sheik I'll do all I can. You tell him I'll deliver my end." Congressman Richard Kelly

1980 1999

was caught on camera stuffing thousands of dollars in bills into his suit as he commented, "If I told you how poor I am, you'd cry. I mean, the tears would roll down your eyes." Other politicans were taped picking up suitcases full of cash, arguing over the terms of illicit deals, and participating in other questionable

Surveillance video from the Abscam sting. *AP Images*

activities. Scenes of this activity were widely televised when the legal cases were prosecuted. Despite the evidence, some of the indicted politicians fought the charges by claiming innocence. John Jenrette, for one,

denied his guilt, claiming after his conviction "I can look at my two beauti-
ful children and my gorgeous wife and say, regardless of what those tapes
say, that I didn't take any money." Criminal trials and committee investigations in Congress meted out justice for those caught in the sting. Of those
politicians involved who attempted to continue their careers, all lost their
next elections. Dozens of officials were investigated and indicted as a result of the Abscam sting, and five nationally elected politicians were convicted for their involvement.   John Wilson Jenrette Jr. (1936–),
Democratic U.S. representative from South Carolina, was convicted on
October 7, 1980, and sentenced to two years in prison. He resigned his
seat in the House on December 10, 1980. Richard Kelly (1924–2005),
Republican U.S. representative from Florida, was convicted on January
26, 1981. He served thirteen months in prison; his term expired on January
3, 1981. Raymond F. Lederer (1938–), Democratic U.S. representative
from Pennsylvania, was convicted on January 9, 1981, and sentenced to
one year in prison. He was reelected after his indictment and resigned office on May 5, 1981. John Michael Murphy (1926–), Democratic U.S. representative from New York, was convicted on December 3, 1980, and
sentenced to three years in prison. His term ended on January 3, 1981.
Michael Joseph Myers (1943–), Democratic U.S. representative from
Pennsylvania, was convicted on August 31, 1980, and sentenced to three
years in prison. He was expelled by the House on October 2, 1980, the first
member of the House to be expelled in more than one hundred years.
Frank Thompson Jr. (1918–1989), Democratic U.S. representative from
New Jersey, was convicted on December 3, 1980, and sentenced to thirteen months in prison. He resigned on December 29, 1980. Harrison
Arlington Williams Jr. (1919–2001), Democratic senator from New Jersey,
was convicted on May 1, 1981, and sentenced to three years in prison. He
resigned on March 11, 1982.[9]

were accompanied by a pictorial spread of the author in various stages of undress. Jenrette, who resigned his seat in December 1980, did not have to worry about the effect on his next election.[10]

John and Rita Jenrette *AP Images*

On August 25, 1982, Frederick Richmond (1923–), Democratic U.S. representative from New York, resigned from office in the wake of a guilty plea to a federal charge of income tax evasion and possession of marijuana. Richmond was first elected in 1975 and was affected by a pre-

vious scandal in 1982. That year, he was accused of soliciting sex from a sixteen-year-old boy and then soliciting sex from an undercover officer. Other issues included a grand jury investigation that disclosed he used cocaine and accepted illegal payments from one of the businesses in which he had a controlling interest.[11]

On May 11, 1982, Mayor William V. Musto of Union City, New Jersey, was reelected to office. The previous day, he had been convicted of federal racketeering charges for illegal activities in his additional position as a state senator. He was found guilty of receiving kickbacks from contracts awarded for school construction. A court ruled that Musto, a convicted felon, was not eligible to hold his new mayoral position. His wife ran for the position in her husband's place, and won. Musto spent three years in prison. When he got out in 1987, the city held a large celebration in his honor, during which he stated, "Who can say they had as many friends—not acquaintances—friends!—as Billy Musto? If anybody got more letters in prison than Billy Musto, I can't believe it." In 1988, prosecutors billed him and six colleagues for damages in the case—a total of $728,640—because the kickback scheme had involved federal funds.[12]

In 1982, James A. Kelly Jr., a Democratic state senator in Massachusetts, was convicted of extortion and sentenced to two years in prison. The crime dated to the previous decade, when Kelly was the chairman of the Ways and Means Committee in the state senate and received $35,500 from an architecture business in exchange for granting them a state contract.[13]

On December 7, 1983, Louis P. Farina, alderman in Chicago, and Martin Tuchow, Cook County commissioner, were convicted of extortion. They were charged with conspiring to require contractors to make payments to them before permits would be issued for the rehabilitation of buildings in the city. The sentences were originally for four years in prison for Farina and eight years for Tuchow, but a judge later reduced Farina's term to three years. In his resentencing decision, the judge stated that Farina deserved "mercy" but Tuchow did not because the latter had continued to practice law after his conviction, despite the fact that his license had been revoked.[14]

1980 1999

In 1983, William B. Carothers, Democratic alderman in Chicago, was convicted of extortion for his part in the "shakedown" of a company constructing a local hospital. He was sentenced to three years in federal prison and required to pay $10,000 in restitution. While he was in prison, he, his two sons, and another man were ordered to pay damages in an unrelated case, a lawsuit stemming from a state election in 1982. The day before that event, the group had used physical violence and intimidation to attack the opponent of the Democratic candidate backed by Carothers. The victim was Arthur Turner, then a Republican state representative, who lost the election. He and others in his group were attacked twice on the same day, and one suffered severe injuries. Carothers had deputized his two sons before the attack, and both carried guns during the confrontations. Ozzie Hutchins, the Democratic candidate and winner of the election, was indicted and convicted along with Carothers in the hospital shakedown case.[15]

Weeks before the November 1982 gubernatorial election in Mississippi, a major scandal surfaced about the Democratic candidate, State Attorney General Bill Allain. Allegations from Leon Bramlett, the Republican candidate, and his supporters contended that Allain led a double life as a homosexual and had paid male prostitutes for sex. The story—including interviews with several of the prostitutes— came from an investigation by a private detective agency paid for by the Republicans. The attorney general strongly denied the story, calling it "damnable, vicious, malicious lies" and stated, "I'm no sexual deviate, and Leon Bramlett knows it." More decisively, he took an independent lie detector test that corroborated his claim, and in an apparent sympathy vote for the underhanded politics behind the allegations, he was elected. Shortly thereafter, three of the male prostitutes stated they had been paid to make their statements.[16]

Bill Allain at a public event in 2004. *AP Images*

1980 1999

Daniel Bever Crane (1936–), Republican U.S. representative from Illinois, was the focus of a public scandal in 1983. Crane, married and the father of six children, admitted that he had sexual relations in 1980 with a congressional page in the House, a seventeen-year-old girl. A few years earlier, Crane had led a fight against a bill that sought to change the penalties for sexual conduct in the District of Columbia. In his opposition, he stated, "When the Washington, D.C., council legalizes homosexual conduct and the seduction of children and decreases the penalty for forcible rape, we have lost sight of the moral codes for a God-fearing society." A House investigation resulted in a vote of censure for Crane, who apologized but did not resign. The House could have voted for a harsher sentence, but in the words of one congressman at the time, "We must punish them for misconduct...but let's not cannibalize them." Crane lost his bid for reelection.[17]

Dan Crane, with his wife and daughter, makes an emotional apology for his behavior on July 16, 1983. *AP Images*

In April 1983, Walter Kozubowski, city clerk in Chicago, resigned from office ten days after he entered a guilty plea to charges of bank fraud, mail fraud, and income tax evasion. Kozubowski had held his position for fourteen years and used it to create dozens of "ghost" employees on the city payroll, collecting the salaries for his personal gain. In other cases, he hired real people but only if they kicked back part of their salaries to his campaign fund. At least $476,000 was attributed to this activity. He pleaded guilty to the charges.[18]

In 1983, Gerry Eastman Studds (1937–), Republican U.S. representative from Massachusetts, came out of the closet and admitted that he

Gerry Studds speaks to reporters following his censure by the U.S. House in 1983. *AP Images*

had had sexual relations with a male House page in 1973 and made advances to two others. Although the page was only seventeen at the time, it was found to be consensual activity and Studds was not prosecuted. He was censured by the House for his actions but objected to the attention paid to what he defended as private, voluntary activities. Remaining in office, he was reelected repeatedly until he retired in 1996.[19]

1980 1999

Clarence McClain, aide to Chicago Mayor Harold Washington, resigned his position in 1983 because of negative publicity. Local newspapers had disclosed that McClain had a criminal record, including three convictions for running an establishment for prostitution. Later, in 1989, he was convicted of bribery after it was proven he had accepted a bribe of $35,000 to arrange a contract with the city involving collections from parking tickets. Sentenced to eight years in prison and fined $135,000, McClain appealed, without success.[20]

Tyrone T. Kenner, alderman in Chicago, was convicted in 1983 of accepting bribes from applicants seeking city jobs, as well as obstruction of justice, mail fraud, and conspiracy. Kenner appealed—unsuccessfully—on the grounds that this activity was associated with his role as a member of the local Democratic party committee and not as an elected official. His sentence: five years in federal prison.[21]

On June 6, 1984, Roger William Jepsen (1928–), Republican senator from Iowa, publicly admitted he had visited a house of prostitution. The event had been years earlier—in 1977, according to the senator— before he was elected, and had become an issue when it surfaced as a campaign-related story on radio stations in the state. His supporters questioned the timing of the release, which coincided with the opening of the primary campaign season. According to Jepsen's story about his escapade in 1977, he had mistakenly thought the enterprise he dropped in on was a health club. The news stories, however, disclosed he had signed a membership form that described it as a sex club. A born-again Christian and a politician noted for his conservative positions, Jepson was first elected to the Senate in 1978. Although nominated in the Iowa primary in 1984, the scandal contributed to his defeat the following November.[22]

In 1984, Attorney General Paul Douglas of Nebraska was impeached by the state legislature. He was charged with failing to disqualify himself during the investigation of a failed bank, failing to properly investigate the bank, and lying about what he had done. He was sentenced to three years probation and a fine of $25,000 but was later acquitted on these charges by the Nebraska supreme court. After a jury found him guilty of perjury in the same case, he resigned. The latter action was also overturned on appeal.[23]

During the presidential campaign in 1984, Democrat Walter Mondale was the target of a dirty trick before the primary election. Supporters of Gary Hart, the main Mondale competitor and also a Democrat, planted special fortune cookies during a fund-raising dinner for Mondale in Pennsylvania. The fortunes in the cookies read: "Hart Wins Pennsylvania." An earlier fortune cookie prank was engineered by the Democratic trickster Dick Tuck

Dick Tuck *AP Images*

while campaigning against Richard Nixon in 1960, when the Republican was running for governor of California. At a fund-raising dinner at a Chinese restaurant in San Francisco, the fortune cookies planted for the benefit of Nixon supporters, read, "What about the Hughes loan?" a message referring to a controversial loan made to Nixon's brother by Howard Hughes, suggesting a ploy for political favors.[24]

The court system in Cook County, Illinois, the largest system in the country, was the target of an undercover investigation in the early 1980s. Dubbed "Operation Greylord," the investigation led to dozens of indictments on charges of extortion, racketeering, bribery, mail fraud, and conspiracy. In the end, a total of sixty-seven officials pleaded guilty, including judges, lawyers, clerks, and others associated with the county courts. The final toll for judges was sixteen convictions. Judges and other officials caught were involved in everything from traffic cases to homicide trials, and their crimes included suppressing evidence, reducing bail for defendants, and altering the outcome of cases, all in exchange for money. Richard LeFevour, the chief of the traffic court, was convicted of accepting eight free cars and $400,000 in cash to dismiss drunk-driving and other traffic charges, as well as referring cases to specific attorneys for a kickback.[25]

In 1985 in Alaska, a grand jury implicated Governor William Jennings Sheffield (1928–) in an investigation involving inappropriate handling of lease specifications and misstating his involvement. A follow-up probe by the state senate did not end in a vote for impeachment, but a senate investigating committee reported they found "substantial, but not clear and convincing evidence" of wrongdoing that could be impeachable. The governor, a Democrat, had been targeted because of a $9.1 million lease for state business that had been recommended to an organization whose part owner had contributed to the governor's election campaign.[26]

In 1985, Lee Alexander (1927–1996), Democratic mayor of Syracuse, New York, was sentenced to ten years in prison for extortion, conspiracy to obstruct justice, and evasion of income taxes. An investigation by a grand jury uncovered his role as the head of a local scheme to extract payments for businesses in exchange for city contracts. After his arrest,

PROFILE Iran-Contra Scandal

During President Reagan's administration, behind-the-scenes activities involved with international politics took on new significance in late 1986. Illegal acts involved with the National Security Council (NSC), CIA, other branches of the government, and the White House surfaced in a scandal that came to be called the "Iran-Contra Affair." Before the media settled on this label, it was also referred to as "Irangate," "Armsgate," "Contragate," "Iranscam," and other twists on accepted scandal-naming conventions. The story began with secret negotiations with the government of Iran for the sale of arms—specifically, antitank and antiaircraft missiles. Iran was not an ally of the United States, which necessitated the secrecy. The strategy was to leverage the goodwill demonstrated by the sale to achieve the release of U.S. citizens held captive in Lebanon by allies of Iran. Money generated from the arms sales was sub-

Ronald Reagan

personal assets of \$1.2 million were forfeited to the government. Sentenced to ten years in federal prison, he served six. In 1977, he was the president of the U. S. Conference of Mayors and he also served for six years as the president of the National Conference of Democratic Mayors.[27]

Raymond Donovan, the secretary of labor in the administration of President Reagan, resigned in 1985. He had been indicted on 137 counts of conspiracy to defraud the New York City Transit Authority, illegal activity that dated to his previous position as head of the Schiavone

Raymond Donovan (left) and his attorney at court in 1987. *AP Images*

sequently used to fund pro-American rebels in Nicaragua—the Contras—who needed arms for their own activities. Although none of the participants who engineered this two-part deal did so for personal gain, their actions violated various federal laws and policies, including a specific ban on military support for the Contras. President Reagan was not held personally responsible for the breach of law, although there were indications the concept originated in the White House. As the scandal unfolded, he stated, "I watch every day like everybody else to find out what will come out. I'm as puzzled and interested as anybody." The mess triggered an investigation headed by former senator John Tower—the subsequent report was called the "Tower Commission Report" and was published in 1987. Two individuals who were heavily involved—Admiral Poindexter, head of the NSC, and Lt. Colonel Oliver North, NSC staff member—were punished for their leadership roles. Poindexter resigned, North was fired, and both were tried on various charges, including perjury, conspiracy, and destruction of government records. Each was found guilty, but their convictions were later overturned following appeals.[28]

Construction Company. Donovan was accused of conspiring to get contracts intended for minority businesses and submitting false claims for work done for subway construction in the city. In 1982, previous charges relating to the same activity were dismissed by a federal prosecutor. Donovan originally took a leave of absence from his cabinet position while the legal case was resolved but finally resigned on March 15, 1985. On May 25, 1987, a jury found him not guilty.[29]

On September 2, 1985, news reports disclosed that David J. Friedland, former state senator in New Jersey, was missing and presumed drowned in a scuba-diving accident in the Bahamas. Soon after, however, it turned out the ex-legislator had faked the event by hiding extra air tanks near the site of the dive. He used these to swim away undetected. In 1988, he surfaced in the Maldive Islands and was arrested and returned to the United States. In 1980, Friedland had been tried and convicted of taking kickbacks for his involvement in the illegal manipulation of funds from a Teamsters Union account; he was also implicated in the misuse of other Teamster investments. At the time of his disappearance, Friedland faced a seven-year sentence and had negotiated with federal prosecutors for a reduced sentence in exchange for becoming an informant. Following his capture, he was sentenced to fifteen years in federal prison, of which he served nine.[30]

On October 9, 1985, Roger Hedgecock, mayor of San Diego, was convicted of violating campaign finance laws during a second trial on the same charges. Hedgecock, a Republican, was first indicted in 1984 but the trial resulted in a hung jury (eleven to one for conviction) while he was serving his first term and running for his second. He was reelected after the indictment but before the trial. The charge involved $360,000 of campaign money that was improperly collected and perjury involving his statements about this fund. Following the verdict, he resigned, then changed his mind when he decided to challenge the validity of the second trial on the grounds of jury tampering. After being turned down on a request for a third trial, Hedgecock resigned for real on December 11. Five years later, in 1990, the California supreme court overturned all of the charges except one, for which Hedgecock was fined $5,000.[31]

In 1986, Henry Barbosa Gonzalez (1916–2000), Democratic U.S. representative from Texas, was charged with assault following a public incident in a restaurant in San Antonio, his hometown. Gonzalez shoved and hit a man after the man said to his face, "There's Henry B. Gonzalez, our number one biggest communist." In 1963, Gonzalez voted against increasing appropriations for the House Committee on Un-American Activities. The congressman, although seventy years old at the time, had been a boxer in college and stated, "If I wanted to coldcock him, I could have." The charges were dismissed the following year.[32]

Henry Gonzalez *AP Images*

On December 18, 1986, a judge declared a mistrial for Edwin Washington Edwards (1927–), Democratic governor of Louisiana, after jurors could not agree on a verdict. The governor and four colleagues had been charged with fraud and racketeering in a case involving profits gained from selling federal certificates for hospital construction. Edwards' defense was that the certificate income was legitimate as it came from work he did as a lawyer while not in office. He was reprosecuted on the same charges and acquitted after a second trial.[33]

Bess Myerson, commissioner of cultural affairs in New York City, was forced to resign in 1986 because of reports she used improper influence in a divorce case involving her boyfriend, Carl Capasso. Capasso's

case was tried by Hortense Gabel, a New York supreme court justice. Myerson, Capasso, and Gabel were tried on charges of bribery, conspiracy, and fraud; the judge was charged with abuse of power after allegedly reducing alimony payments for Myerson's boyfriend. In return, Gabel's daughter was given a job in the city department headed by Myerson. All the defendants were acquitted but not before tarnishing the image of Mayor Ed Koch in a scandal referred to locally as the "Bess Mess." Gabel resigned in 1987 in response to the scandal.[34]

1980
1999

Myerson had more troubles in 1988, when she was arrested for shoplifting. *AP Images*

Harry E. Claiborne, federal district judge in Las Vegas, was impeached by Congress in 1986. At the time, he was serving a sentence of two years in prison after being found guilty of evading income tax. This was the first such impeachment for a federal judge since 1936. The judge's problems began in 1982, when a grand jury investigated him for accepting a bribe from the owner of a brothel in the state. Evidence uncovered then led to the trial and conviction. In his defense, Claiborne denied accepting bribes—this charge was later dropped—and blamed his income tax problem on an accountant's error. At the same time, he accused the Justice Department of hostility toward him. One fact that cropped up during the investigation was that part of Claiborne's defense fund came from Frank Sinatra.[35]

On May 28, 1986, Joseph A. Bevilacqua, chief justice of the Rhode Island supreme court, resigned his position. The judge faced an impeachment hearing because of allegations involving his personal associations with reputed mob members. Another allegation involved free electrical work the judge reportedly accepted from a contractor who also handled work for the state's court system. In addition, the judge was accused of committing adultery in a motel that was owned by convicted felons. Escalating publicity and the threat of impeachment forced his decision.[36]

John Zaccaro, husband of Geraldine Anne Ferraro (1935–), Democratic U.S. representative from New York and former Democratic nominee for vice president of the United States, was indicted in 1986 on charges of attempted extortion and bribery. The case involved alleged coercion of bribes—up to $1 million—from a company attempting to gain a cable television franchise in the borough of Queens. In 1987, the same investigation produced indictments for twenty-six city staffers employed by the New York Board of Education, with the charges including bribery, conspiracy, and grand larceny. Zaccaro was acquitted in his

Geraldine Ferraro

trial. Previously, when Ferraro was running for vice president in 1984, her husband was targeted in a case involving fraud in a real estate financing deal. In 1985, Zaccaro pleaded guilty to a misdemeanor in that case. In 1988, yet another scandal dogged Ferraro; her son, John Zaccaro Jr., was convicted of selling cocaine. Ferraro ended her career in the House in 1985, and in two campaigns for the U.S. Senate, in 1992 and 1998, she lost both races.[37]

In 1987, during the preliminary presidential campaign, Democratic candidate Gary Hart (1936–) stated in an interview with the *New York*

Times, "Follow me around. I don't care. I'm serious. If anybody wants to put a tail on me, go ahead. They'd be very bored." The challenge came after the media responded to rumors that Hart had been in-

volved in extramarital affairs. In response to Hart's challenge, several reporters observed that the senator from Colorado had females visit overnight in his Washington, D.C., apartment. Plus, a photograph of Hart on the deck of a yacht named *Monkey Business* was published, showing an attractive blonde sitting in his lap—she turned out to be Donna Rice, a model. At first Hart responded to ques-

Donna Rice at a 1987 press conference. *AP Images*

tions about his relationships by denying anything he did had been illicit, but the escalating scandal eroded his standing in the polls—he had been leading the presidential race—and he soon withdrew from the contest.[38]

Clifford P. Kelley, an alderman in Chicago, was convicted and sent to prison in 1987 for using his influence to help companies win contracts with the city. Kelley and others were caught in an elaborate sting operation organized by federal authorities. Dubbed "Operation Incubator," it relied on an undercover agent who solicited illegal activity from elected officials. Alderman Kelley's charges included counts of mail fraud and failure to pay tax on the income he obtained from bribes. In 1988, Wallace Davis Jr., another alderman, was also convicted as a result of this investigation. His charges included bribery, extortion, racketeering, and perjury. In one case, he had taken $11,000 from his own niece, a city employee, as a kickback from her salary. The prosecutor in the case stated, "This is not the case of a man just straying once or walking close to the line. This is a man who strayed repeatedly." He was sentenced to eight and a half years in prison. Davis began his political career in 1983, several years after he had been shot in the back by Chicago policemen who thought he was a burglar. A legal settlement of $352,000 and the publicity surrounding this incident helped get him elected. On August 25, 1989, Morgan Finley, a former circuit court clerk in Cook County and a former state senator, became yet another victim of the sting. Finley was sentenced to ten years in prison for racketeering and extortion. The judge in the case addressed Finley at the sentencing: "What an honor it was to hold your office, but you made it a monument of corruption." The investigation resulted in fifteen convictions, including four aldermen.[39]

In 1987, Harold Eugene Ford (1945–), Democratic U.S. representative from Tennessee, was charged with mail fraud, bank fraud, and tax fraud. The charges related to personal income of $1.2 million that was allegedly masked as business loans from local banks. The banks in question were run by two brothers who were convicted of fraud after $20 million in deposits was misused. The prosecutors contended that some of this was money given to Ford in exchange for

Harold Ford (right center) celebrating after his acquittal in 1993. *AP Images*

political favors. Ford, the first black member of Congress from Tennessee since Reconstruction, denied the charges, which he described as racially and politically motivated. In 1990, the case went to trial but the jury was unable to agree on a verdict. In 1993, he was acquitted.[40]

In September 1987, Senator Joseph Robinette Biden Jr. (1942–) withdrew from the 1988 presidential race. Biden, a Democrat from Delaware, suffered from negative publicity revolving around revelations that one of his speeches had borrowed heavily and without attribution from the writing of Neil Kinnock, the leader of the British Labour party. The similarities were the target of a videotape created by aides to Governor Michael Dukakis, his leading Democratic opponent. Reaction to the tape turned up other allegations of plagiarism in

1980 1999

Biden's speeches as well as in research from law school days. The fall-out not only sank the Biden campaign, it led to the resignation of two Dukakis aides because they initially covered up their involvement in the "dirty tricks" caper.[41]

Stanley Friedman, head of the Democratic party in the borough of the Bronx in New York, was convicted of racketeering, mail fraud, and conspiracy in 1987. He was sentenced to twelve years in federal prison on March 11, 1987. The case developed from an investigation into organized bribery and extortion activities in the city's Parking Violations Bureau. Several key people controlled lucrative municipal contracts and awarded them to companies in return for kickbacks. Others convicted in the same scandal included the commissioner of transportation, the deputy director of the parking violations bureau, the director of the Parking Violations Bureau, and several businessmen. One of the key players in the private sector half of the scandal committed suicide during the investigation. Upon his release from prison, Friedman commented that the problem with his position had been "the longer you're in, you acquire a proprietary interest in the position. Because you justify you're doing a good job governmentally you rationalize that you're above the law. You feel you own the job. It begets arrogance."[42]

On January 22, 1987, R. Budd Dwyer (1939–1987), Pennsylvania state treasurer, shot and killed himself during a televised news conference. Dwyer's troubles began in 1984 when he was implicated—but not charged—in a case that involved a no-bid award for a state contract. In 1986, Dwyer and a former chairman of the state Republican party were indicted in a statewide bribery case that was tied to this previous investigation. On December 19, 1986, both men were convicted of bribery after a federal trial. Both declared their innocence, and there were reports that Dwyer had been offered a plea bargain, but had turned it down in anticipation of a favorable verdict. He killed himself a few

Budd Dwyer holds a revolver during a deadly press conference.

AP Images

| PROFILE | Wedtech Scandal |

In New York City, the Wedtech Corporation was the focus of a major scandal that surfaced at the end of the 1980s. Wedtech posed as a minority-owned business to qualify for federal defense contracts, and during a major growth phase it went from a private to a public company. Between 1981 and 1986, profits ballooned from $8 million to more than $72 million. Key legal services the company used to advance its interests came in part from several members of the U.S. House in New York, and connections between the company and politicians included city, state, and national officials, some with ties to the Reagan administration. Following an investigation, a number of trials ended in twenty convictions. Robert Garcia (1933–), Democratic U.S. representative from New York, was charged with bribery, extortion, conspiracy, and influence peddling. The congressman and his wife were reported to have received $75,000, a no-interest loan of $20,000, and an emerald necklace valued at $1,900, among other payments. Garcia's trial in 1989 resulted in conviction—after which he resigned his seat in the House—and he served 104 days in prison before the conviction was overturned in 1990. According to the appeals court, "By paying the Garcias, Wedtech was purchasing an advocate, not buying off a thug." In 1993, prosecutors announced they would not retry the congressman. Garcia was the first person of Hispanic descent born in New York to become a member of Congress. Mario Biaggi (1917–), Democratic U.S. representative from New York, resigned on August 5, 1988, after being tried and convicted for racketeering. In a previ-

1980 1999

days before sentencing. Dwyer, a Republican, had been a state legislator before his election as treasurer.[43]

In 1987, Daniel Walker (1922–), former Democratic governor of Illinois, pleaded guilty to charges of bank fraud. Walker was accused of misusing funds during a previous period when he had been in charge of a suburban Chicago savings and loan company. While in this posi-

Mario Biaggi (left) at a press conference after he resigned his position. *AP Images*

ous career, Biaggi was one of the most decorated policemen in New York and insisted that he never took a bribe, "not a single penny." In his trial, prosecutors referred to him as "a thug in a congressman's suit." The ex-congressman served twenty-six months in federal prison, and in 1992 tried unsuccessfully to regain his former position. Lyn Nofziger (1924–2006), assistant to President Reagan, was convicted in 1988 of using his position in the White House to influence a decision awarding a Defense Department contract to Wedtech. His involvement actually occurred after he had resigned in order to become a consultant. Nofziger's appeal resulted in the conviction being overturned. Before his position with Reagan, he was a member of President Nixon's Committee to Re-Elect the President and led election campaigns for Steve Forbes and Pat Buchanan. Edwin Meese, U.S. attorney general, was implicated in the scandal because of his relationship with E. Robert Wallach, an attorney and Wedtech lobbyist who had been friends with Meese for several decades. Although Meese was involved peripherally in using White House influence for a military bid, he was never charged. A three-judge panel investigating his alleged wrongdoing did not recommend further action. But in the face of rising negative public opinion, he resigned on August 12, 1988.[44]

1980 1999

tion, it was charged he had used fraud to obtain loans to finance the development of a chain of automotive oil change outlets. He had camouflaged the transactions by funneling them through a friend and his son, and lied about his activity during the investigation. Walker was sentenced to seven years in federal prison and required to pay restitution of $231,000.[45]

Evan Mecham at his 1988
impeachment trial.

AP Images

On April 4, 1988, Governor Evan Mecham (1924–) of
Arizona was expelled from office by an impeachment
conviction. The Republican governor's problem began
in 1987, when a grand jury uncovered a questionable
loan made to him by an attorney who was under investigation in an illegal stock case. A previous financial
disclosure statement from the governor, submitted under oath, did not reveal this income. The main issue in
the impeachment hearing involved Mecham's obstruction of justice and his filing of false statements. The
governor was also the target of a recall election because of several unrelated issues, one being his cancellation of the Martin Luther King Jr.
paid holiday for state workers and another related to insensitive public
statements. Some of his comments and actions were deemed racist and
led to a national boycott, adding to his public disfavor, but too few signatures were collected to trigger a recall election. After he left office,
the former governor was cleared of criminal charges in a parallel case
dealing with the loan. Before entering politics, Mecham owned a successful automobile dealership.[46]

On September 6, 1988, Fofó Iosefa Fiti Sunia (1937–), Democratic
U.S. representative from American Samoa, resigned his seat in
Congress. He had been charged with conspiracy to defraud the U.S.
government—specifically, adding names to his office payroll so that he
could pocket the paychecks, a total of $130,920. He pleaded guilty and
was sentenced to five to fifteen months in federal prison and asked to
pay restitution of $65,000.[47]

Patrick Lynn Swindall (1950–), Republican U.S. representative from
Georgia, was charged with perjury in 1988. During a grand jury investigation into money laundering associated with drug dealing, the congressman was videotaped negotiating a loan with an undercover IRS
agent. The tape indicated he knew the money was from a illegal drug
deal, a fact he lied about to the grand jury, but the congressman was
not charged with the greater offense of money laundering. He was
convicted and on August 28, 1989, was sentenced to one year in prison

and a fine of $30,450. During the sentencing, Swindall began to read a statement professing his humility, but the judge cut him off, stating "You don't know the meaning of the word 'humility,' Mr. Swindall. I thought you were beginning to learn it, but apparently you are not." The congressman was defeated in a bid for reelection.[48]

On July 31, 1989, Marian Humes, former alderman in Chicago, was sentenced to two years in prison after a conviction for accepting bribes. Humes was the first female elected official in Chicago to be sent to prison for corrupt practices. Despite pleas for compassion and support from prominent local people, the judge responded to the prosecutor's description of Humes—she was involved with a "cesspool of corruption in Chicago's city council"—by declaring it necessary to "erase the public's distrust of its elected officials." Humes was sentenced to two years in prison but was released early.[49]

On October 18, 1989, the Ethics Committee of the U.S. House issued a note of reproval against one of its members, Jim Bates (1941–), Democratic U.S. representative from California. Bates was charged with making unwanted sexual advances toward two female members of his staff. In reaction to the House reproval, Bates stated, "I think I made a mistake. I didn't really know what sexual harassment was." The scandal contributed to Bates' loss in his next election.[50]

On May 31, 1989, Louis V. Messercola, former mayor of Wayne, New Jersey, was found guilty of extortion. Messercola pleaded guilty to a charge that he attempted to get money from a local real estate developer in exchange for city business. He was sentenced to thirty-three months in prison. In a signed statement to the court, Messercola said, "I admit that I do a lot of wheeling and dealing; I know that it's wrong." Messercola was elected in 1985 on a platform promising to control "haphazard development" but resigned in 1988 when he faced a recall drive because of his unethical activities.[51]

In October 1989, Alcee Lamar Hastings (1936–) was impeached and convicted by the U.S. Senate and removed from his position as a U.S. district judge in Florida. Hastings, a Democrat, had been tried in civil court in 1983 on a charge involving a bribery scheme intended to influence the sentence in a criminal trial he presided over. Another person involved in the scheme was found guilty, but Hastings was acquitted by a jury. An additional investigation, however, was instigated by a panel of judges concerned about Hastings' testimony in this case, and their report eventually triggered a formal inquiry in Congress, leading to his impeachment and removal. Hastings, the first black federal judge in Florida, claimed racial bias and maintained his innocence. In 1992, he ran for and was elected to the House and has been in office since.[52]

Alcee Hastings *AP Images*

1980 1999

On September 5, 1989, President Bush made a major speech on drug policy. During the presentation, he held up a baggie filled with crack

President Bush displays cocaine confiscated in a bust in Lafayette Park across from the White House. *AP Images*

and announced that it had been seized only a short distance away, across the street from the White House, in Lafayette Park. The announcement turned into a minor scandal, however, when it turned out the bust had only taken place after Drug Enforcement agents lured a dealer to the park just so they could make this high-profile arrest. According to officers, their task was made more difficult because when

they attempted to lure the dealer to the location, he did not know where the White House was.[53]

On November 3, 1989, Walter Louis Nixon Jr. (1928–), U.S. district court judge from Mississippi, was removed from his position by impeachment. The Senate convicted him on two of three articles, both involving perjury in a federal trial. At the time, Nixon was serving five years in prison after a 1986 conviction in a federal trial. That case involved his intercession in a drug case against the son of a businessman who had previously helped Nixon with an investment. Nixon denied he had acted improperly, even though he admitted having a conversation with the prosecutor in the case. Regardless, the defendant pleaded guilty but was never sentenced. Nixon served sixteen months of his sentence before release.[54]

Walter Nixon testifies at his impeachment hearing. *AP Images*

On June 30, 1989, James Claude Wright Jr. (1922–), Democratic U.S. representative from Texas and Speaker of the House, resigned his seat. A year earlier, he was the target of an ethics investigation focused on financial deals in which he allegedly used his political clout as influence in exchange for personal gain. Some of the charges that surfaced involved years of misconduct, but the timing of the investigation was likely affected by political infighting within Congress as well as the disclosure of a specific deal involving an autobiography of Wright published by a company in his home state. He was paid a royalty rate of 55 percent for this work, *Reflections of a Public Man*, even though typical royalty rates only ranged from 10 to 15 percent. Critics suggested that this arrangement allowed Wright to improve his cash flow without violating an income cap Congress had placed on speaking fees. Instead of charging a fee for his appearance at events—a category that fell within the outside income rules—the congressman could benefit financially by selling his books to an audience, an activity that was not subject to the cap. An investigation by the House Ethics Committee uncovered numerous additional cases of extracurricular income earned by Wright, but none of these turned out to be a violation of the rules currently in place. Nevertheless, the publicity generated by House activity became increasingly negative, and Wright was eventually forced to end his political career.[55]

| PROFILE | The Keating Five |

Until 1982, savings and loan institutions were restricted from making loans
on commercial real estate. After that date, their status was altered by dereg-
ulation legislation intended to improve their competitive status in the financial
industry. Soon after the change, irregularities began to arise as some of the
S&Ls pushed investments into ventures that were both expensive and risky.
One of these was the Lincoln Savings and Loan Association in California,
run by Charles Keating, who became the target of blame when it went bankrupt in 1989 because of high-risk investments in real estate. The business focus to the story widened when a subsequent investigation by the Federal
Home Loan Bank Board (FHLBB) uncovered allegations of political interference from the failed company. Other investigations were also launched, including one from the Ethics Committee of the U.S. Senate, because Keating
was the source of large campaign contributions to several senators as well
as free vacations and other gifts. At the time, Congressman Jim Leach, a
member of the House Banking Committee, stated, "Keating is at fault because he is a bank robber, but we in Washington made it, in part, a legal
bank robbery." Five senators in particular were singled out in the probe for
their suspected role in pressuring the head of the FHLBB to quit or reduce
the scrutiny of the Lincoln's risky activities. The Senate committee voted to
give an official reprimand to one senator, Alan Cranston, and milder rebukes

Anthony Lee Coelho (1942–), six-term Democratic U.S. representative from California, resigned on June 15, 1989, in anticipation of an
investigation by the House. The congressman was suspected of improper activity involving the purchase of risky bonds in 1986 and large
personal loans—more than $500,000 in five years—but he was never
charged with any illegal activities.[56]

In 1989, prosecutors indicted Peter MacDonald, chairman of the
Navajo tribe, on more than one hundred counts of corruption and
fraud. He was accused of receiving bribes and kickbacks related to

Three of the Keating Five—John Glenn (left), Dennis DeConcini (center left), and John McCain (right)—at their Senate Ethics Committee hearing in 1990. *AP Images*

to the others. Cranston (1914–2000), the Democratic senator from California, was reprimanded for "impermissible conduct." He received $984,000 from Keating. Dennis Webster DeConcini (1937–), Democratic senator from Arizona, was singled out for the "appearance of being improper" because he received $55,000. Some of his campaign aides received $50 million in loans for real estate purchases. John Herschel Glenn Jr. (1921–), Democratic senator from Ohio, was singled out for having "exercised poor judgment." He accepted $234,000. John Sidney McCain III (1936–), Republican senator from Arizona, was cited for questionable conduct after receiving $112,000. Donald Wayne Riegle Jr. (1938–), Democratic senator from Michigan, was also reprimanded for his questionable conduct, with income of $76,000 from Keating. Negative public reaction from this scandal may have played a role in ending the careers of several of these senators, although all defended themselves and denied they had done anything improper. Three did not run again. John McCain is still in office.[57]

1980 1999

Peter MacDonald
AP Images

business activities that involved the Navajo nation. He was found guilty and on October 22, 1990, was sentenced to just under six years in prison and a fine of $11,000. In 1991, MacDonald was indicted and convicted again on similar charges related to a scheme involving a large development loan. In 1993, he was sentenced to fourteen and a half years in prison for his involvement in a riot in Window Rock, Arizona, in which two people died. The riot occurred after the tribal leader had been expelled from office following his first conviction. His sentences included tribal and federal terms and were served concurrently. MacDonald was released from prison in 2001 after his sentence was commuted by President Clinton.[58]

Arlan Ingehart Stangeland (1930–), Republican U.S. representative from Minnesota, was defeated in his reelection campaign in 1990. A six-term congressman, Stangeland suffered from a scandal that surfaced during his campaign. Media coverage focused on his relationship with a female lobbyist from Virginia and 428 long-distance calls he made to her home over a five-month period, some of them after midnight. The insinuation of unethical behavior created a negative public reaction because of the conservative politician's strong stand on family values. The congressman denied he was having an affair with the woman. One popular joke at the time suggested that Stangeland was so pro-family, he decided to have two of them.[59]

During the campaign for governor of Minnesota in 1990, conservative Republican candidate Jon Grunseth resigned from the race following allegations he was guilty of sexual misconduct. Newspapers in the state quoted two women who claimed he had behaved inappropriately during a nude swimming outing several years earlier. Another newspaper exposé alleged he had a long-running extramarital affair that spanned two of his marriages. The combination produced enough negative publicity to force Grunseth from the race.[60]

In 1990, the U.S. House voted to reprimand Barney Frank (1940–), Republican representative from Massachusetts. The least severe punishment in the censure process, the vote was a response to recent revelations that Frank had used official influence to help a friend "fix" thirty-three parking tickets. The man was an ex-con, and Frank admitted as well that he made misleading statements to the parole authorities on his friend's behalf. In 1987, Frank had publicly announced his own homosexuality. In 1989, press reports revealed that the same friend had been operating a male prostitution service out of Frank's Washington, D.C., apartment. Frank was subsequently reelected multiple times.[61]

On July 25, 1990, the Senate voted to censure David Durenberger (1934–), Republican senator from Minnesota, for financial misconduct. The action came in response to a complaint from the Minnesota Bar Association alleging that Durenberger had improperly taken advantage of his ownership of a condominium by billing the government for reimbursement for rent. In addition, he was cited for receiving improper income from the publication of two books he authored, *Prescription for Change* and *Neither Madmen Nor Messiahs*.[62]

On November 16, 1990, Alderman William C. Henry of Chicago was indicted for bribery, taking kickbacks, extortion, mail fraud, and profiting from "ghost" employees on the city payroll. In all, twenty-nine counts were included in the indictment, as well as charges of income tax evasion. At the hearing, "Big Bill" Henry pleaded innocent, stating "I will fight this indictment with my every breath, if that is what it takes." In 1991, the alderman's trial was halted after he was discovered to have inoperable lung cancer. He died in 1992, and the trial was never resumed.[63]

In 1990, Floyd Harold Flake (1945–), Democratic U.S. representative from New York, was charged with fraud, embezzlement, conspiracy, and evasion of income tax. The case involved $75,000 in funds taken from a federally subsidized housing complex that was run by a church of which Flake was the pastor. The alleged illegality hinged on accounting practices, not criminal behavior, however, providing a thin case for prosecution. Eventually, criminal charges against Flake were dismissed. The congressman was first elected in 1986 and served until 1997, when he left politics to pursue a full-time career as a pastor.[64]

On July 10, 1990, Arch Alfred Moore Jr. (1923–), former Republican governor of West Virginia, was sentenced to five years and ten months in federal prison and a $170,000 fine after being found guilty of corruption in office. Moore had been governor of the state from 1969 to 1977 and again from 1985 to 1989, the most years in that position of anyone in state history. He pleaded guilty to a variety of charges, including mail fraud, extortion, tax fraud, and obstruction of justice, the latter involving an effort made to alter the deliberations of a grand jury. The major charge in the case focused on the governor's transactions with a coal company in the state, with payments made or promised to him in exchange for his support in helping it receive refunds from a state fund set up to provide benefits to miners with black lung disease. Other investigations into corruption in West Virginia political offices over the previous few years had resulted in convictions for five state legislators and other state employees as well. In 1975, the former governor was indicted on an earlier federal charge of extortion, but was acquitted.[65]

In 1990, a statewide scandal erupted in Tennessee. An FBI investigation called "Operation Rocky Top" uncovered a web of bribery and illegal cash flow associated with bingo operations around the state. It turned out that some of the nonprofit organizations licensed to run bingo games were phonies, set up as fronts to funnel income to a wide network of individuals. The scam involved a former member of the State Alcoholic Beverage Commission, members of the State Election Commission, one former legislator, one current legislator, and others. One legislator shot himself just before he was to be indicted, and Gentry Crowell, the secretary of state—whose office was also targeted—shot himself as well.[66]

In 1990, the Ethics Committee of the U.S. House issued a report disapproving of the conduct of Gus Savage (1925–), Democratic U.S. representative from Illinois. Savage was accused of making sexual advances toward a Peace Corps volunteer while on an official tour of Africa in 1989. The female volunteer quoted Savage as saying "You should know that there are rewards to people who give their all to the movement, give everything to the movement." In the House probe, the congressman was critical of the motivations that led to his investigation, describing the three Democratic representatives who initiated it as "self-appointed guardians of personal morality," a statement he later had officially removed from the *Congressional Record*. Savage later sent a letter of apology to the woman.[67]

Marion Barry *AP Images*

In 1991, Mayor Marion Barry (1936–) of Washington, D.C., was sentenced to six months in prison after a conviction in a drug case. First elected in 1978, the controversial Democratic mayor had been suspected of illegal drug activity for years, and his administration was frequently battered by charges of corruption. During his time as mayor, twelve city officials were convicted—including two deputy mayors—although Barry himself was never implicated or charged. He once stated, "If all this corruption was going on, I should be in jail." On January 18, 1990, he fell victim to an undercover police and FBI operation, during which he was videotaped smoking cocaine. After he resigned his position, he was convicted only on a single misdemeanor count that stemmed from an earlier arrest. The case involving the undercover video resulted in a mistrial. Barry was back in politics again, after serving a six-month sentence, when he was elected to the city council. In 1995, he was once again elected mayor and has served on the city council since that term expired in 1999. In late 2005, Barry took a routine test for drug use and tested positive for cocaine. At the time, he was serving probation on a charge of failing to file a tax return, and the drug test jeopardized the terms of his sentence.[68]

On September 24, 1995, David J. Shields, presiding judge of the Cook County circuit court in Chicago, was convicted of extortion. Shields was caught in a sting in which he accepted $6,000 to "fix" a civil case. In the same sting, more money went to other conspirators, including Fred Roti, an alderman. Evidence included conversations with the men implicating themselves on hidden tape recordings. Other charges in the case included racketeering, conspiracy, and bribery. Another charge involving Roti—that he had helped fix a different case in which three gang members from New York City were charged with murder—was dropped. The judge got four years in prison and Roti got three.[69]

PROFILE   Whitewater Scandal

In 1992, stories surfaced about irregular financial activities associated with the Whitewater Development Agency and the bankruptcy of Madison Guaranty Savings and Loan Company, both in Arkansas. The story, which became known as the Whitewater Scandal, became national news because it involved Bill Clinton, the Democratic candidate for president and the former governor of Arkansas. The irregularities involved loans from the government, questionable banking practices, unethical pressure from high-ranking government officials—including Governor Clinton—and ultimately, the failure of the real estate project. A three-judge federal panel headed by Kenneth Starr convened to investigate, and special committees in Congress also looked into the affair. Significant conflicts arose between these investigative parties and the White House after Clinton's election as president. It first refused to provide subpoenaed documents and on other occasions claimed to lose or misplace important evidence. At one point, Mrs. Clinton was herself subpoenaed, the first time in U.S. history that this action was taken against a first lady. Various hearings stretched into 2000 and ultimately cleared both President Clinton and his wife, Hillary. The final report stated, "…the evidence was insufficient to prove to a jury beyond a reasonable doubt that either President or Mrs. Clinton knowingly participated in any criminal conduct." Others were not so lucky. Fifteen people were convicted of federal crimes, although not all of them were directly related to Whitewater. Governor Jim Guy Tucker (1943–) of Arkansas was one. On May 28, 1996, he was convicted of fraud by a federal jury and resigned from office on July 15. James and Susan McDougal, former business partners of Bill Clinton, were convicted along with Tucker. Flotsam that emerged as the long-running scandal played out included allegations of high-level cover-ups, other improper activity by the administration, and the suicide of Vincent Foster, White House counsel and someone with apparent inside knowledge of the Clintons' business activities. As the scandal continued, details of sexual misconduct by Clinton while he was governor emerged as well, leading to the initial disclosures of his affair with intern Monica Lewinsky, a revelation that generated a scandal of its own.[70]

1980 1999

In 1991, Tai Collins, a former Miss Virginia USA, reported on national television that she had had a sexual affair with Senator Charles Spittal Robb (1939–) of Virginia. The affair had happened in 1984 while he was the governor of the state. Collins detailed various trysts with the married senator—his wife was the daughter of President Lyndon Johnson—who admitted knowing her but denied the sexual activity. According to Robb, Collins had given him a back rub in his hotel room while he was nude, but nothing more had happened. Other allegations about the senator surfaced, including sexual contact with other young women—oral activity, but not intercourse, because of "health concerns," according to a leaked confidential memo from his staff—and suggestions of recreational drug use, also while he was governor. The scandal eventually faded but in a tight political race in 1994, Robb was in the hot seat again, accused of the illegal taping of cell phone calls of his political opponent, former governor Douglas Wilder.[71]

In 1992, former Illinois state treasurer Jerome Cosentino was charged with fraud. At the time he was in office, he was also the owner of Fast Motor, a transportation company he steered loans to from a bank that was receiving millions in state deposits. A total of $23 million was involved. Using an elaborate check-kiting scheme and loans from the bank, he inflated the value of his company far beyond its worth. Ultimately, the bank failed, in part because of other shady dealings and in part because of Cosentino's fraud. He pleaded guilty to the charges brought against him and on September 23, 1983, was sentenced to five years probation and a fine of $5,000. The sentencing judge stated that Cosentino had "clearly violated the public trust" but gave him a light sentence because of his poor health. He suffered from congestive heart failure and diabetes.[72]

In 1992, Joseph Michael McDade (1931–), Republican U.S. representative from Pennsylvania, was charged with receiving contributions and gifts from defense contractors. The federal indictment included charges of bribery and racketeering. In office since 1962, McDade was denied the opportunity to be the chairman of the Appropriations Committee because of the ethics scandal, but he was reelected while the case worked its way through the legal system. In a trial in 1996, he defended his acceptance of up to $100,000 in gifts as legitimate—they included expense-paid vacations and a college education for his son— and stated his only mistake was not reporting them properly. The jury acquitted him of all charges. He did not run in the election of 1998.[73]

Brockman "Brock" Adams (1927–2004), Democratic senator from Washington, announced he would not seek reelection in 1992. He took this action in the wake of publicity triggered by a front-page story in the *Seattle Times* in which eight women accused Adams of numerous instances of sexual harassment and rape over a period of two decades.

Despite anonymity, most of the women signed affidavits with the paper agreeing to be witnesses if the newspaper was sued. In an earlier incident in 1987, a congressional secretary accused Adams of a similar offense, but charges were not filed. According to a former female staff member, "There's a pattern that Brock has. It starts

Brock Adams and his wife respond to press allegations at a 1992 news conference. *AP Images*

subtly with a hug on the shoulder. Kissing on the forehead. Eventually the hand comes up around your armpit and grabs your breast." In the 1992 scandal, no charges were filed, mostly because all of the allegations except one had happened beyond the statute of limitations. The senator denied all the accusations.[74]

In 1993, an investigation in Miami, dubbed "Operation Court Broom," ended with the conviction of two judges. Harvey Shenberg and David Goodheart were found guilty of conspiracy and racketeering in what was called one of the biggest cases of judicial corruption in state history, and one of the biggest cases in the country. Both judges were involved with fixing cases, for a total of $266,000 in bribes. In exchange for cash, they reduced bail for defendants, suppressed evidence, released confidential evidence, and other illegal acts. Others were indicted as well, but juries found them either not guilty or had split decisions.[75]

On April 16, 1993, Nicholas Mavroules (1929–2003), Democratic U.S. representative from Massachusetts, pleaded guilty to charges of misusing his office for personal profit. Mavroules, a seven-term congressman, was charged with seventeen counts of extortion, conspiracy, and tax evasion, but admitted only to accepting the free use of a car and a beach house. He was sentenced to fifteen months in federal prison and fined $15,000.[76]

Harold Guy Hunt (1933–), the first Republican governor of Alabama since Reconstruction, was convicted of a felony and removed from office on April 22, 1993, during his second term. The charge related to the unethical use of at least $200,000 in campaign funds, including the purchase of a riding lawn mower and payments on his home mortgage. Hunt, who was also a Baptist preacher, faced other charges, including use of a state-owned plane to travel to church functions and acceptance of a $10,000 payment from a man who was later appointed

H.G. Hunt *AP Images*

to a state board. He was sentenced to five years of probation and restitution of $212,350. In 1998, the state gave him a pardon, stating that he was innocent of the charges because the misuse of funds had been due to an accounting error, not fraud, and in any case, the former governor had repaid the amount in question. Hunt promptly ran for office again but lost in the primary, receiving only 8 percent of the votes.[77]

On May 21, 1993, Lawrence "Larry" Smith (1941–), Democratic U.S. representative from Florida, pleaded guilty to a charge of violating campaign finance laws and income tax evasion. He reportedly removed $10,000 from his campaign account for personal use, some of it to pay a gambling debt. Smith had earlier admitted to bouncing ninety checks at the U.S. House bank, although the bank reported the actual number was 161. The congressman served eighty-eight days in prison.[78]

On July 21, 1993, Albert Garza Bustamante (1935–), Democratic U.S. representative from Texas, was found guilty of racketeering, influence peddling, and bribery. During his multiple terms in Congress, the congressman was found to have accepted bribes in exchange for influence in the renewal of government contracts with the U.S. Air Force. Another charge related to a no-risk investment in a television station. He was sentenced to three and a half years in federal prison, fined $55,100, and, after losing a lengthy appeal, entered prison in May 1995. During his trial, his bid for reelection failed.[79]

On July 21, 1993, Charles Panici, Republican mayor of Chicago Heights, Illinois (a suburb of Chicago), was convicted along with two members of the city council of bribery and extortion. The group was found to have taken more than $600,000 in payments from businesses trying to win contracts with the city. Panici received a sentence of ten years in federal prison, was required to forfeit $259,950 in assets, and was fined $1.1 million.[80]

On August 27, 1997, Michael Albert Espy (1953–), former secretary of agriculture in the administration of President Clinton and former Democratic U.S. representative from Mississippi, was indicted by a federal grand jury on thirty-nine felony counts. The case involved accepting favors for influencing legislative issues helpful for clients, making false statements, and witness-tampering. Gifts tracked to Espy included luggage, expenses-paid travel, tickets to sports events, and a large contribution to his brother's congressional campaign. Espy's girlfriend, Patricia Dempsey, was also targeted in the probe. On October 3, 1994, the congressman was forced to resign as a result of the scandal but ended up being acquitted of all charges in a subsequent trial. Companies involved in some of the gift-giving charged in his case did not fare so well and were assessed penalties in separate trials.[81]

Michael Espy (right) appears at a press conference outside federal court after his plea of innocence. *AP Images*

In 1994, David Reinert, supervisor of Elgin Township, Illinois, was sentenced to nine years in prison and ordered to pay $5.1 million in restitution for corrupt activities. While serving in office between 1970 and 1993, he embezzled millions from the accounts of the township and used the income for personal needs and to purchase businesses.[82]

Paula Jones AP Images

On May 6, 1994, a lawsuit was filed by Paula Jones in federal court in Arkansas, claiming her federal rights had been violated in 1991 by Bill Clinton, then governor of the state. The issue in the Jones suit focused on sexual advances allegedly made by Clinton in a hotel room. A series of legal maneuvers and court decisions delayed the outcome of the case until 1998, when a settlement was made by Clinton to end the suit. The story attracted major media attention and a decision from the U.S. Supreme Court, which ruled in 1997 that the president could not delay legal action in the matter until the end of his term in office, as his attorneys had requested.[83]

1980 1999

On December 16, 1994, the supreme court in Missouri convicted Secretary of State Judith Moriarty of misconduct. She was also impeached by the state house and removed from office. The charge related to the paperwork used by her son, Tim Moriarty, when he entered an election for a seat in the state legislature. Moriarty had backdated the forms so that they would not be voided after her son missed the filing deadline. The state employee who accused Moriarty was also charged with the same violation, to which she pleaded guilty.[84]

In 1994, Oklahoma governor David Lee Walters (1951–) was indicted by a grand jury on charges of illegal campaign violations. Walters, a Democrat, received a one-year deferred sentence and a fine of $1,000 after pleading guilty to a misdemeanor. As part of his sentence, he was required to pass on the questionable money he had raised during his campaign to the Oklahoma Ethics Commission. The deal made him the first governor in state history to either be convicted or plead guilty to a crime. He left office in 1994 at the end of his term. Although

Walters did not run again for the same office, he did enter another race, for the U.S. Senate in 2002. He was unsuccessful in this campaign.[85]

In 1994, Joseph Paul Kolter (1926–), former five-term Democratic U.S. representative from Pennsylvania, was arrested and tried on charges he embezzled from the House post office. Among the theft charges: stamps, 650 pieces of china, 40 watches, and 2 gold necklaces. The total value of the merchandise was estimated to be at least $40,000. He was found guilty but appealed, claiming the items were for official use. The appeal was denied by a federal court, and he was sentenced to six months in prison.[86]

In 1994, Carroll Hubbard Jr. (1937–), former Democratic U.S. representative from Kentucky, pleaded guilty to a charge of conspiracy to defraud the government, theft, obstruction of justice, and conversion of government property. On November 9, 1994, he was sentenced to three years in federal prison and ordered to pay restitution of $153,000. In 1996, Carol Brown Hubbard, his wife, pleaded guilty to a charge of aiding and abetting the theft of government property while running for office herself (in a different House district than her husband). She was given probation and fined $27,000.[87]

In November 1995, Enid Greene Waldholtz (1958–), Republican U.S. representative from Utah and a former head of the Young Republican National Federation, faced charges of campaign finance irregularities. The congresswoman suddenly discovered that her husband, Joseph Waldholtz, whose whereabouts were unknown, had stolen money from the campaign, falsified documents, and may have embezzled money from previous campaign funds. She was not implicated but

Enid Waldholtz and husband.
AP Images

he became the target of a federal investigation. She divorced him and served the remainder of her one term under her maiden name.[88]

On March 13, 1995, Carl Christopher Perkins (1954–), Democratic U.S. representative from Kentucky, was sentenced to twenty-one months in prison. One of many congressmen caught in an investigation of House banking activities, Perkins was accused of writing 514 bad checks in one fourteen-month period, for a total of $565,615.[89]

On August 22, 1995, Melvin "Mel" Reynolds (1952–), Democratic U.S. representative from Illinois, was found guilty on a charge of criminal sexual assault, criminal sexual abuse, obstruction of justice, and solicitation of child pornography. The charges involved a personal relationship that dated to 1992 with a young woman who was sixteen years old at the time. In a separate case in 1997, he was convicted of diverting campaign funds for personal use and supplying false information in a loan application. The state and federal sentences totaled five years; in 2001, he was pardoned by President Clinton.[90]

Walter Edward Fauntroy (1933–), ten-term Democratic delegate from the District of Columbia, was convicted of falsifying a financial report in 1995. The report in question improperly listed a donation of $23,887 to a church for the wrong year. The legal issue was limited to that of a false statement made by a federal official. He was sentenced to two years of probation and a $1,000 fine. In a previous investigation by the Department of Justice, the congressman had been cleared of a charge he had employed the son of another congressman and improperly used his services for campaigning.[91]

Robert William Packwood (1932–), four-term Republican senator from Oregon, resigned his position on October 1, 1995, in anticipation of a Senate vote to expel him. An investigation by the Ethics Committee led to a recommendation that he be expelled for sexual as well as official misconduct. Specific charges included numerous cases of unwanted sexual advances on

Women who accused Robert Packwood of improper behavior hold a press conference. *AP Images*

PROFILE	Clinton Impeachment

Only two presidents have ever been subjected to an impeachment trial, Andrew Johnson in 1868 and Bill Clinton in 1999. In Clinton's case, he was already under investigation for sexual harassment and financial misdeeds dating to his previous position as governor of Arkansas, when the former became an even bigger story. The Judiciary Committee of the House began an official inquiry on October 8, 1998, regarding potential grounds for the president's impeachment. The House inquiry was triggered by testimony from the lawsuit against Clinton initiated by Paula Jones in 1994, a case that involved unwanted sexual advances the then-governor reportedly made toward Jones. One witness in this case revealed that former White House intern Monica Lewinsky had reportedly been involved in sexual behavior with the president. Questioned about this, Lewinsky initially testified, "I have never had a sexual relationship with the president." The president's testimony was also a denial that such activity had occurred. In a public announcement, he emphasized this claim, stating "I did not have sexual relations with that woman." However, Kenneth Starr, the prosecutor who had originally been charged with investigating President and Mrs. Clinton's involvement in the

Monica Lewinsky and Bill Clinton in 1995. *AP Images*

Whitewater case, expanded his probe when evidence emerged that both Lewinsky and the president had lied about the sexual activity. The evidence was provided by Linda Tripp, a friend of Lewinsky who had also

women, diary entries altered to remove or cover up evidence of malfeasance, and using his official position to obtain employment for his former wife.[92]

Daniel David Rostenkowski (1928–), eighteen-term Democratic U.S. representative from Illinois and the chairman of the House Ways and Means Committee, was sentenced to seventeen months in federal

worked at the White House. Tripp secretly taped a phone call with Lewinsky in which the activity was confirmed, triggering the involvement of the FBI, who then provided more substantive recordings that clearly contradicted Lewinsky's and Clinton's claims. This contradiction meant that the president had committed perjury, the basis for the impeachment, along with a charge of obstruction of justice. By this time, Clinton admitted his personal errors and made a public and formal apology—wide media exposure of the details of his activity with Lewinsky magnified the drama—but the congressional process continued. On January 7, 1999, the actual impeachment trial opened in the U.S. Senate. The final vote on the articles of impeachment was held on February 12. Of the two articles voted upon, neither gained the two-thirds majority of votes necessary, resulting in the equivalent of an acquittal.[93]

1980 1999

The Clinton impeachment inquiry in the U.S. House. *AP Images*

prison in 1996 and fined $100,000. In a plea agreement, he admitted guilt for misusing public funds and was convicted of two counts of mail fraud. He had originally been tagged with more crimes, including the use of ghost employees on his political payroll, embezzlement, accepting kickbacks, witness tampering, and conspiracy. When first indicted, he stated, "I will fight these false charges, and will prevail. I will wash away the mud that has been splattered upon my reputation.

Some ask, 'How could you have done these things?' The answer is simple. I didn't do them." Following his guilty plea, the congressman stated, "I have served my constituents with dignity, honor, and integrity." In 2000, President Clinton gave him an official pardon.[94]

On April 17, 1996, Walter Rayford Tucker III (1957–), Democratic U.S. representative from California, was sentenced to twenty-seven months in federal prison after he was found guilty of seven counts of extortion and two counts of income tax evasion for activities dating to his former position as mayor of Compton, California. Tucker resigned his seat in the House before it could expel him, but

Walter Tucker

claimed he was innocent. He stated that he "was not judged by a jury of my peers, and in my opinion did not receive a just verdict." One piece of evidence in the case came from a sting operation, in which a videotape showed Tucker receiving a $30,000 bribe.[95]

On April 29, 1996, William McCuen, former Arkansas secretary of state, was sentenced to seventeen years in prison and fined $30,000. In January, McCuen pleaded guilty to charges of bribery, taking a kickback, and evading income tax. One of his misdeeds was accepting a state check for $53,650 for a bulk order of state flags. The check could not be cashed because it had been endorsed by too many people and the flags were never delivered. McCuen's predecessor as secretary of state, Steve Clark, was also convicted of a felony theft charge. McCuen was released from prison early in 1999 because of cancer.[96]

On August 30, 1996, Dick Morris, the chief campaign adviser for President Clinton, resigned his position in the wake of a sex scandal. Sherry Rowlands, a prostitute, was interviewed in the *Star*, a supermarket tabloid, and on *Hard Copy*, a television program, and described an ongoing relationship with the married politician. Morris did not discuss the affair but resigned to avoid negative publicity for the Clinton reelection campaign. According to Rowlands, the weekly assignations with Morris included conversations in which he provided specific, de-

Dick Morris and his wife at a press conference on the day he resigned. *AP Images*

tailed information about activities inside the Clinton White House, some of it unflattering. As she stated on *Hard Copy*, "But wake up, America. I mean, if he told me, who else did he tell?" Rowland's diary, published in the same tabloid, figured in a later Clinton administration scandal involving hundreds of confidential FBI files possibly used by the president's staff to research Republican opponents. This episode was referred to as Filegate.[97]

In 1996, Nicholas L. Bissell Jr. (1947–1996), chief county prosecutor in Somerset County, New Jersey, was charged with and convicted of thirty counts of fraud for skimming profits from private business deals and taking kickbacks from employees in the prosecutor's office. Bissell's wife was also implicated in these activities. Bissell had been called the Forfeiture King because of his success in seizing assets from convicted drug dealers. On November 27, 1996, facing a sentence of ten years in prison, Bissell killed himself in a hotel room in Laughlin, Nevada.[98]

1980 1999

In 1997, Republican governor J. Fife Symington III (1945–) of Arizona was convicted of seven counts of fraud. He had been charged with twenty-one counts but was acquitted on three, with the jury deadlocked on eleven counts. The conviction related to the defrauding of lenders in his previous career as a real estate developer in the 1980s. On September 5, 1997, Symington resigned his office. The former governor's appeal resulted in the verdict being overturned. He was later pardoned by President Clinton.[99]

Mary Oakar *AP Images*

Mary Rose Oakar (1940–), Democratic U.S. representative from Ohio, was charged with a misdemeanor for using illegal methods of handling campaign donations in 1997. Bank accounts with false names were used to obscure $16,000 in contributions, which would have exceeded the legal limit. Her indictment was part of a House investigation dating to 1992 that led to charges for three representatives. After pleading guilty as part of a plea bargain, Oakar received probation and a fine of $32,000.[100]

On May 3, 1997, James Heiple, chief justice of the Illinois supreme court, resigned his position. Heiple faced the threat of impeachment—and escalating negative publicity—because of the disclosure he had attempted to avoid four different speeding tickets by wielding his authority as a judge.[101]

1980
1999

Ann Eppard *AP Images*

Elmer Greinert "Bud" Shuster (1932–), U.S. representative from Pennsylvania, was investigated by the U.S. House Ethics Committee in 1997. Shuster, a Republican, was the chairman of the Transportation Committee and was scrutinized for his close ties to his former chief of staff, Ann Eppard. Her new position was as a lobbyist for companies involved with transportation issues, suggesting a conflict of interest. A year later, the House committee announced it would drop its investigation because of a similar probe initiated by the Department of Justice. This action did not target Shuster so much as Eppard. She ended up being indicted for accepting more than $200,000 in a scheme to influence contracts associated with the "Big Dig" project in Boston while she worked for Congressman Shuster. Eppard pleaded guilty to a lesser charge in 1999 and was fined $5,000. Shuster resigned his position on February 3, 2001.[102]

On January 28, 1998, Donald "Buz" Lukens (1931–), former Republican U.S. representative from Ohio, began serving a thirty-month prison sentence after being found guilty of taking bribes. He also had problems of another kind. Lukens resigned from office on October 24, 1990, because of a scandal involving sexual activity with a teenage girl. The young woman in question claimed he had sex with her in the mid-1980s when she was thirteen years old, then again in 1988 when she was sixteen. The first act brought a sentence of thirty days in jail; the latter got him convicted of "contributing to the unruliness of a minor."[103]

In the California primary election of 1998, three-term Democratic U.S. representative Jay Kim's ability to campaign was limited by his circumstances. Kim (1939–) had been sentenced to two months of home detention after being found guilty of accepting $145,000 in illegal campaign contributions. In 1992, the congressman was the first Korean American elected to the U.S. House. The scandal involving the illegal contributions contributed to his defeat in the primary election.[104]

*1980
1999*

On September 17, 1998, Henry John Hyde (1924–), Republican U.S. representative from Illinois, admitted that he had engaged in an extramarital affair thirty years previously. The disclosure came after the online magazine Salon reported it would publish an article about this relationship, prompting the congressman to make his public statement. In it, he said, "The statute of limitations has long since passed on my youthful indiscretions." Some in Washington speculated that this kind of attack was intended to embarrass or intimidate Hyde and other Republicans in retaliation for the heat President Clinton and his Democratic supporters were getting from the Monica Lewinsky scandal.

Henry Hyde *AP Images*

Hyde had been appointed by the House to be one of the managers of the impeachment proceedings against Clinton, making him a target. Hyde, who was married and the father of four sons, had been a state legislator in Illinois when he was involved with Cherie Snodgrass, a hairstylist, who was also married and the mother of three. At the time, Snodgrass's husband blamed Hyde for breaking up his marriage.[105]

In 1998, Danny Lee Burton (1938–), Republican U.S. representative from Indiana, made a public admission of marital problems. Burton, the chairman of the House Government Reform and Oversight Committee, reported that he believed he would be exposed in an upcoming article in *Vanity Fair* magazine that would disclose previous problems in his marriage. The congressman chose to announce his personal issues in advance to diminish the effects, even though he did not admit doing anything illegal. The article never ran.[106]

Robert Linligthgow Livingston Jr. (1943–), Republican U.S. representative from Louisiana and the chairman of the House Appropriations Committee, expected to be selected as the Speaker of the House in 1998 but backed out on December 19. Early the next year he resigned his position. The action was precipitated when *Hustler* magazine publisher Larry Flynt placed a full-page ad in the *Washington Post* in October 1998, in which he offered $1 million as a reward

Robert Livingston

for proof of an "adulterous sexual encounter with a current member of the United States Congress or a high-ranking government official." Flynt's stated goal was to uncover evidence of hypocrisy among politicians—especially Republicans—who were out to evict Clinton from the White House. Livingston was informed he would be one of those caught in this trap, after Flynt had been given information about the congressman's prior extramarital escapades. Livingston publicly admitted these past indiscretions as he resigned.[107]

In Alabama in 1999, two aides to the governor were suspended for their involvement in fixing traffic tickets for legislators, football coaches at the University of Alabama, and the governor's wife.[108]

On December 6, 1999, Milton Holt, a Democratic state senator in Hawaii, was sentenced to one year in federal prison. He had been found guilty of mail fraud and spending campaign funds for personal use. His unethical expenditures included paying for a family birthday party and making car insurance payments. A plea bargain in the case resulted in five additional counts being dropped. Compounding Holt's problems, in the period leading up to the trial, he tested positive for illegal drugs, causing the court to revoke his bail. He was released after serving six months. In a previous incident, Holt was investigated in 1993 on charges he allegedly bribed another state politician.[109]

In 1999, Nick Wilson, a Democratic state senator in Arkansas, was charged by the state legislature with ethics violations. On November 4, 1999, he was convicted of evading federal income tax and conspiracy. In a related case involving racketeering, he was charged with hiding income due from a realty deal by creating a complicated property swap. Another charge focused on a scheme to divert funds from a state child support enforcement budget. Along with the senior legislator, indictments named several other current and former state senators, state education officials, and others. Wilson resigned his position in the Arkansas senate on the last day of the year. He was sentenced to seventy months in prison and a fine of $40,000.[110]

1980 1999

On September 10, 1999, Henry Cisneros, former secretary of the Department of Housing and Urban Development, pleaded guilty to a

federal misdemeanor. He was charged with making false statements about payments he had made to a former mistress, an affair that dated to his previous position as mayor of San Antonio, Texas. During a background report by the FBI necessary to clear him for his cabinet position, he confirmed this affair—it was long over at the time and had been publicly acknowledged—but stated he had paid the woman in question an amount that turned out

Henry Cisneros (right) leaves court with his attorney (left), after entering a plea in 1988.
AP Images

to be less than what she reported to have received. He was sentenced to pay a $10,000 fine. The estimated cost of the government's case against him was $9 million.[111]

2000–2006

In the early years of the new century, the mayor of a New Jersey city was sent to prison; a U.S. congressman was censured for campaign finance violations; another congressman was convicted of fraud and racketeering; the lieutenant governor of Kentucky was sued by the government for Medicare fraud; the former state attorney general in Texas was indicted by a federal grand jury; and Karl Rove, President George W. Bush's adviser, was scrutinized for his role in the publication of the name of an undercover CIA agent, the wife of an outspoken critic of the administration. And more. Is the situation getting better, or worse? Are politicians more scandal-prone and corrupt, or are we just paying more attention to their problems? Changes that have made an impact include more laws governing campaign activity and donations, tougher regulations for interactions with lobbyists and constituents, and the narrowing of the concept of ethical practices. At the same time, more eyes keep watch over political activity, from citizens' groups to bloggers to scoop-coveting media outlets. Law-enforcement agencies, particularly the FBI, are also watching more closely and acting more aggressively. In a single recent year, according to a spokesperson for the FBI, the agency was involved in 2,200 corruption cases involving public officials, resulting in 800 convictions. The politicians are not likely becoming more corrupt, it's just becoming more likely that their corruption will be noticed.

The national election in 2000 not only produced one of the closest outcomes in U.S. history, it ended with a result that is still being debated. Allegations of voter fraud and claims of partisan political bias on the part of the election officials tainted the outcome, whether or not they actually skewed the results. Although most of the attention focused on Florida, other states were involved as well. In New Mexico, Doña Ana County was one of several contested counties where absentee ballots were the focus of alleged miscounts and fraud, including allegations of election officials shredding ballots. Doña Ana County has a history of problems with contested elections; municipal elections there were also contested in 2002, 2003, and 2004. Issues with the primary election in 2002 ended with the indictment and conviction in 2004 of County Clerk Ruben Ceballos on five counts of election fraud. In 1997, nineteen residents of Rio Arriba County—including two city councilors, a county clerk, and a captain in the state police—were indicted for election fraud practiced in three elections.[1]

On July 3, 2001, Andy Mirikitani, a member of the Honolulu, Hawaii, city council, was found guilty of six counts of bribery, theft, extortion, wire fraud, and witness tampering. Mirikitani, a Democrat, lost his council seat as a result of the conviction. In the previous decade, he was the recipient of an award for his activities in promoting open and honest government.[2]

2000 2006

In 2001, Philip Giordano, mayor of Waterbury, Connecticut, was arrested for sex crimes that appeared lurid even by modern standards.

Giordano was charged with using a prostitute, her daughter, and the prostitute's niece—the latter eight and ten years old—for sexual acts, some inside city hall. The scandal was uncovered during an investigation of financial irregularities, which quickly paled in comparison. The mayor was convicted and sentenced to thirty-seven years in prison. The prostitute was sentenced to ten years.[3]

Philip Giordano *AP Images*

On April 10, 2002, Rene Mansho, city council member in Honolulu, resigned from office while facing charges she misused campaign funds and assigned city workers to her own political campaign activities. On June 27, 2002, Mansho, a Democrat, was sentenced to a year in prison and a $25,000 fine. She also paid an additional $80,000 in restitution.[4]

Gary Adrian Condit (1948–), seven-term Democratic U.S. representative from California, lost a primary election on March 5, 2002, and ended a long run of political service. His defeat was directly connected to events the previous year, when Chandra Levy, an intern working in a

Washington, D.C., office, disappeared. Her body was found more than a year later in a Washington area park. Condit was investigated because of a relationship he had with the young woman, although he denied any knowledge or responsibility for the crime. No charges were filed against him, but public support in his home district withered because of the appearance of impropriety.[5]

Gary Condit

On September 31, 2002, Robert Guy Torricelli (1951–), Democratic senator from New Jersey, withdrew from his reelection campaign, ending a long career in Congress. He had been a U.S. representative for fourteen years before moving to the Senate. His withdrawal came in response to negative publicity tied to several key events. For one, he had been linked to illegal campaign gifts from businessman David Chang. Chang stated that the senator had promised and done things in exchange for the gifts, which included two bronze statues, three pairs of earrings, a stereo, and a fifty-two-inch television set. The Senate Ethics Committee published a negative report about Torricelli in July 2002, adding to his declining public and political support, but he was never indicted or charged with wrongdoing. Torricelli had weathered earlier problems. In 1990, he was linked romantically to the wife of a different campaign donor; in 1992, he bounced twenty-seven checks at the House bank; in 1994, he was investigated for receiving a windfall profit of $144,000 from a questionable securities transaction; in 1998 and 1999, wealthy campaign donors were indicted for making illegal contributions to him. At the press conference announcing his withdrawal, Torricelli stated, "While I have not done the things I have been accused of doing, most certainly I have made mistakes. When did we become such an unforgiving people? When did we stop believing and trusting in each other?"[6]

On July 1, 2002, Marshall Ige, former Hawaiian state legislator, began serving a six-month prison sentence for felony counts of theft, tax evasion, and other charges. In one case, Ige, a Democrat, was accused of taking $30,000 from a couple in exchange for expunging their daughter's criminal record. He served a total of sixteen years as a state representative before being elected a senator.[7]

On June 22, 2002, Lena Swanson, former Democratic state senator in Washington, was sentenced to four months in federal prison. She was charged with receiving more than $100,000 in unauthorized payments from former prisoners of war while in a position with the U.S. Department of Veterans Affairs.[8]

Buddy Cianci (right) and his attorney at a press conference involving his case in 2001.
AP Images

On September 6, 2002, Vincent "Buddy" Cianci Jr. (1941–), mayor of Providence, Rhode Island, was sentenced to five years and four months in federal prison for racketeering. The judge commented at the sentencing, "There appear to be two very different Buddy Ciancis.... The first is a skilled and charismatic political figure, probably one of the most talented politicians Rhode Island has ever seen, someone with wit, who thinks quickly on his feet and can enthrall an audience. The second Buddy Cianci presided over an administration that is rife with corruption at all levels.... My job is to sentence the second Buddy Cianci because the first Buddy Cianci wouldn't be here." The mayor had been reelected in 1990 after serving a suspended sentence for an earlier conviction. When he was in office in 1983, he assaulted a man he thought was involved romantically with his estranged wife. He was accused of kidnapping and attacking the man with a fireplace log and burning him with a cigarette, among other charges. The 2002 case resulted from an FBI investigation of the Providence City Hall, code-named "Operation Plunder Dome."[9]

On January 24, 2002, Martin G. Barnes, the mayor of Paterson, New Jersey, was indicted by a grand jury for extortion, skimming campaign funds, filing false tax returns, and overcharging the city for travel expenses. The extortion charges related to unofficial requirements that contractors provide gifts and services in exchange for getting contracts for city business. As part of the largesse, Barnes, his wife, and more than one girlfriend were given free trips to Rio de Janeiro, England, Aruba, and the Kentucky Derby. The mayor received furniture, business suits, home improvements, and other luxury items as well. In July 2003, Barnes pleaded guilty to two of forty charges, and in April, he was sentenced to thirty-seven months in prison and fined $1,000.[10]

On February 8, 2002, Eric J. Perrodin, the newly elected mayor of Compton, California, was thrown out of office on a judge's ruling. A member of the city council was also expelled. According to an investigation, the election held the previous June had involved voter fraud, including an incorrect order of names on the ballot, inconsistent vote counts, voter signatures not matching originals, and votes cast by noncitizens and residents of places other than Compton. The judge stated, "I saw in this case ineptitude, deceit, and illegality beyond expectations."[11]

On July 24, 2002, James Anthony Traficant Jr., (1941–), Democratic U.S. representative from Ohio, was expelled from Congress following a federal conviction for bribery, fraud, and tax evasion. In office since 1985, Traficant was the fifth member in the history of the House to be expelled. He was charged with accepting kickbacks from employees in his office and taking bribes from businesses in exchange for political favors, as well as not reporting the income from these activities on his tax returns. In a previous case, in 1983, when he was sheriff of Mahoning County, Ohio, Traficant had been charged with but acquitted of a bribery charge involving a payment of $163,000 from the mob, disclosed during an FBI undercover operation. He successfully defended

James Traficant

himself on the grounds that he was actually conducting his own undercover operation at the time. In the 2002 federal case, he was sentenced to eight years in prison.[12]

On October 7, 2003, Governor Gray Davis (1942–) of California was voted out of office during a recall election. Davis, a Democrat, was the subject of increasing voter unrest related to the general economic condition of the state, an economic crash in the high-tech sector, a major crisis with electrical power supplies in 2001, immigration problems, and other issues. During the contentious election, the governor stated, "This has been an awakening for me. I know people are upset, and it's not fun hearing it day in and day out."[13]

Edward Mezvinsky (right) leaves court with his attorney after his sentencing in 2003. *AP Images*

In January 2003, Edward Mezvinsky (1937–), former Democratic U.S. representative from Iowa and a former chairman of the Democratic party in Pennsylvania, was sentenced to more than six years in federal prison after being found guilty of sixty-six counts of fraud and other charges. After he left office in 1977, Mezvinsky was involved in a number of fraudulent business ventures in which he solicited investments totaling an estimated $10.4 million. During his trial, the former congressman blamed this activity on the side effects of a drug he took on a trip to Africa to combat malaria, as well as a manic-depressive condition.[14]

Joseph Ganim, Democratic mayor of Bridgeport, Connecticut, was convicted on March 19, 2003, of corruption in office, including bribery, racketeering, and conspiracy. During a five-year period ending in 2000, federal prosecutors charged that Ganim extracted bribes from companies doing business with the city. The bribes included cash, custom suits, diamond earrings, and crates of expensive wine. He was also accused of manipulating the city's sewer department in order to build a sewer extension in his neighborhood so that he could circumvent the cost of a septic system for his home. His sentence was nine years in federal prison and a fine of $300,000, issued by a judge who stated, "There is no excuse for corruption."[15]

On June 30, 2004, John G. Rowland (1957–), Republican governor of Connecticut, resigned from office. The governor had been targeted by a criminal investigation and expected to be impeached by the state legislature on a variety of ethics and graft charges. These included accepting inflated profits from the sale of a condominium in exchange for influencing a state contract and acceptance of personal gifts, loans, and trips in return for other official favors. Scandals involving Rowland dated back several years, when allegations of improper fund-raising surfaced and others in his administration were tied to unethical activities.

Former governor John Rowland arrives at his sentencing hearing in Connecticut in 2005. *AP Images*

In 1999, State Treasurer Paul J. Silvester was convicted and sent to prison for four years for racketeering and money-laundering; he was charged with trading the management of a state pension fund valued at $20 billion for campaign contributions and other gifts. Lawrence Alibozek, Rowland's chief of staff, was also convicted of awarding contracts for state business in exchange for cash, some of it in the form of gold coins that he buried in his yard.[16]

On January 20, 2004, William J. Janklow (1939–), Republican U.S. representative from South Dakota and a former four-term governor, was sentenced to one hundred days in jail and fined $11,000. His sentence came after he was found guilty of second-degree manslaughter and reckless driving. On August 16, 2003, the governor ran a stop sign while driving at more than 70 miles per hour and hit a motorcyclist, killing him. Janklow had been in elected office for more than thirty years at the time of the accident, which he blamed on health problems associated to diabetes.[17]

William Janklow

Lorelee Byrd, state treasurer of Nebraska, resigned from office on January 6, 2004. She was charged with and found guilty of a misdemeanor for writing $300,000 in state checks, then voiding them after the end of a budget session. This activity was alleged to have been part of a plan to maintain spending levels so that the legislature would not cut her department's budget.[18]

In May 2004, Neil Goldschmidt (1940–), former Democratic governor of Oregon, disclosed that he had sexually abused a fourteen-year-old girl in the 1970s when he had been mayor of Portland. At the time he was thirty-two and married, the youngest mayor of a major U.S. city. The sexual activity continued for a year but had happened long enough ago that the statute of limitations had expired. A private legal arrangement had been made by Goldschmidt in 1994 to pay compensation as part of a settlement, but he had not previously made information about the affair public. In his 2004 announcement, he expressed remorse and shame for his activities.[19]

Legislators in Oregon ordered the portrait of former governor Neil Goldschmidt be removed from a prominent location and rehung it in a less conspicuous place, following revelations about his past. *AP Images*

On June 2, 2004, Peter Dibble, a selectman in Stonington, Connecticut, was granted a plea bargain in a case that involved a sexual relationship with a thirteen-year-old girl. The final charge was limited to reckless endangerment, a misdemeanor. Dibble was given a three-month suspended sentence and two years of probation.[20]

On November 2, 2004, election day, in Milwaukee, Wisconsin, twenty vehicles used by the local Republican party to carry voters to the polls had their tires slashed outside the headquarters of the Bush-Cheney campaign office. Milwaukee police arrested six people for this act of political mischief. Among those arrested were the son of a former act-ing mayor and the son of a U.S. representative to Congress, both paid staff members of the Wisconsin Democratic party. A plea bargain in the ensuing case ended with the perpetrators sent to jail, with a term of from four to six months each.[21]

On November 15, 2004, James E. McGreevey (1957–), Democratic governor of New Jersey, resigned his position. The governor had been under pressure to leave office after a major scandal broke, which dominated his adminis-tration. The story involved a previously secret homosexual relationship he had with Jim Cipel, a man McGreevey met when Cipel was the spokesman for the mayor of a city in Israel. After they began an affair, McGreevey arranged to have his lover employed on the state payroll. The relationship ended when Cipel accused McGreevey of sexual harass-ment and assault. McGreevey held a news

Governor James McGreevey delivering a farewell speech at his resignation in 2004. *AP Images*

conference on August 12 and disclosed the affair after he and Cipel were unable to work out a negotiation to settle Cipel's claims. McGreevey's administration was also being investigated at the time for illegally profiting from campaign donations.[22]

On August 30, 2004, Bill Campbell, former mayor of Atlanta, was in-dicted on federal charges of racketeering, bribery, and wire fraud. The indictment dated to his term as mayor, which ended in 2002. According to the charges, Campbell accepted illegal campaign contri-butions totaling thousands of dollars, as well as gifts, cash, home im-provements, and free travel from contractors in exchange for city business. He was tried only for tax evasion, and convicted. On June 12, 2006, he was sentenced to two and a half years in federal prison and fined $6,300.[23]

Galen Fox, a state representative in Hawaii, resigned his position on December 1, 2005, following a federal criminal conviction. Fox, a

Republican, was found guilty of a misdemeanor sexual offense after fondling a female passenger on an airplane flight. The previous year, another Hawaiian representative, Brian K. Blundell, also a Republican, was convicted of fourth-degree sexual assault after fondling an undercover male police officer in a public restroom.[24]

On July 19, 2005, John Doug Hays, former state senator in Kentucky, was sentenced to six months in prison after being found guilty of mail fraud. The case involved the use of false campaign reports that Hays submitted when he ran for district judge in the state in 2002. In 2006, the charges were dropped during an appeal, on the grounds that the statute pertaining to mail fraud was not valid in applications related to vote fraud.[25]

On October 12, 2005, Frank W. Ballance (1942–), former Democratic U.S. representative from North Carolina, was sentenced to four years in federal prison for misuse of public money. Ballance, who pleaded guilty, took an estimated $100,000 for personal use from a nonprofit organization he started in 1985, the John A. Hyman Memorial Youth Foundation. It was named after one of the first black congressmen from North Carolina and received most of its funding from the state. Ballance resigned his seat in the House the previous year, on June 11, 2004.[26]

2000 2006

Frank Ballance

On August 18, 2005, Republican governor Bob A. Taft II (1942–) of Ohio became the first sitting governor in the history of that state to be convicted of a crime. The governor entered a plea of no contest to a charge he had failed to report gifts. The Taft family in Ohio includes a former president, a former chief justice of the U.S. Supreme Court, and two U.S. senators. The four counts in his indictment noted several unreported golf outings and meals paid for by lawyers, consultants, and businessmen. Similar gifts to the governor had been disclosed as part of Ohio's ethics rules. Taft's sentence included a fine of $1,000 for each offense, court costs, and a required message of apology sent to every state employee. Other ethics violations linked to the governor—but not involving him—resulted in the indictment and conviction of several aides and a major coin dealer, Tom Noe. Noe, a well-known fund-raiser for the Republican party, was found guilty of accepting up to $50 million in investments from clients with the purpose of funneling it to the election campaign of President George W. Bush. Noe received a sentence of eighteen years in prison for his activities.[27]

Don Siegelman (1946–), former Democratic governor of Alabama, was indicted in federal court on October 26, 2005. He was charged with receiving bribes while he was governor and also while he was lieutenant governor. Indicted at the same time was Richard Scrushy, a former president of HealthSouth—a company tied to the bribery activity—Siegelman's former chief of staff, and the former director of the state department of transportation. The indictment was one episode in a long-running legal attack on the governor, targeting attempts to rig bids between HealthSouth and the state. Siegelman, a Democrat, stated that the attacks were politically motivated and the work of a Republican prosecutor. In 2006, a federal jury acquitted both of Siegelman's former political colleagues but found him and Scrushy guilty on counts of bribery, conspiracy, obstruction of justice, and mail fraud. The outcome of an appeal is pending.[28]

On December 1, 2005, Randall "Duke" Cunningham (1941–), eight-term Republican U.S. representative from California, pleaded guilty to bribery charges. He received mortgage payments, antique furniture, a Rolls-Royce, and other items, totaling $2.4 million, in return for helping companies obtain government contracts. Cunningham, who was decorated for his action as a fighter pilot during the Vietnam War, stated, "I cannot undo what I have done, but I can atone." He resigned his position on November 28, 2005, and following a plea arrangement was sentenced to eight years and four months in prison.[29]

Duke Cunningham

In March 2006, former Atlanta mayor Bill Campbell was tried on charges he accepted payoffs and bribes during his two terms in office. A jury acquitted him on these charges but did find him guilty of tax evasion. His prosecution was connected to a federal investigation of other local officials and businessmen, a probe that resulted in the convictions of ten people. The former mayor, a Democrat, was sentenced to two and a half years in prison.[30]

On June 9, 2006, Thomas Dale DeLay (1947–), Republican U.S. representative from Texas and the majority leader in the House, resigned. He faced mounting pressure from allegations of violations of election rules and an ethics scandal linked to an escalating story involving lobbyist Jack Abramoff. The congressman had been indicted in Texas the previous year for campaign finance irregularities associated with a controversial redistricting action. In an unusual case that developed after his resignation in 2006, DeLay's name was legally required to stay on a ballot for the upcoming election despite his resignation and stated intent not to run.[31]

Thomas DeLay

On September 6, 2006, George Ryan (1934–), Republican governor of Illinois, was sentenced to seventy-eight months in prison after being found guilty of racketeering and fraud. He was the third Illinois governor to be convicted of a crime since 1973. The original charges dated to his service as the secretary of state and spanned his term as governor. He was accused of receiving income and gifts in return for political favors. The first indictment, in 2003, was the result of an investigation that began in 1994 after a traffic accident killed six children. During the inquiry that followed, evidence was uncovered of widespread corruption in various state departments, including transportation, vehicle licensing, and the secretary of state's office. A total of seventy-five convictions resulted, including state employees, managers, supervisors, owners and employees of trucking companies, lobbyists, and other businessmen.[32]

On September 29, 2006, Mark A. Foley (1954–), Republican representative from Florida, resigned his seat in the House. A rising tide of criticism pushed him to this action after disclosures indicated a pattern of inappropriate behavior. This related to his sexual attraction to young men, particularly one underage youth working as a Capitol page. An investigation disclosed e-mail and text messages that contained provocative content—ammunition for his political opponents as well as former political allies, especially when it was disclosed that the congressman's problems were already known within Congress, although no action had been taken against him.[33]

2000 2006

On November 4, 2006, Robert William Ney (1954–), Republican representative from Ohio, resigned his seat. Ney faced the potential of an expulsion hearing in the House because of federal charges that he made false statements in an investigation of his involvement with illegal campaign donations and other unethical activities associated with convicted lobbyist Jack Abramoff. Ney pleaded guilty to the charges in October and was sentenced in early 2007 to thirty months in prison.[34]

Robert Ney

...to be continued.

A political cartoon entitled "Promise and Performance." On the left, the caption reads "Before Election—Of some consequence. Well taken care of." On the right, the caption states "After Election—'Hey, look out for yourself!'" *Puck*, October 15, 1884.

SUPPLEMENT

CORRUPTION BENCHMARKS 1779–2005

Number of individuals who have been president 42

Number of individuals who have been vice president.....................46

Number of individuals who have been U.S. senators 1,889

Number of individuals who have been U.S. representatives....10,546

Number of individuals who have been federal judges.................3,102

Number of individuals who have been state governors..............2,190

U.S. House members censured...22

U.S. House members reprimanded..8

U.S. House members expelled...4

U.S. senators censured 7

U.S. senators convicted of crimes 4

U.S. senators expelled 15

Federal judges impeached 13

Federal judges convicted after impeachment 7

Number of governors impeached..15

Number of governors convicted after impeachment 7

Number of governors ousted by recall elections................................2

U.S. HOUSE CENSURE HISTORY

DATE	MEMBER	PARTY-STATE	ACTION
7-11-1832	William Stanberry	(AJ*-OH)	Censured

Insulting the Speaker of the House.

| 3-22-1842 | Joshua R. Giddings | (R-OH) | Censured |

Resolution introduced by Member deemed "incendiary."

| 7-15-1856 | Lawrence M. Keitt | (D-SC) | Censured |

Assisting in assault on a Member.

| 2-27-1857 | Orasmus B. Matteson | (R-NY) | Censured |

Defamed character of House by accepting money to support bill.

| 7-13-1861 | John B. Clark | (D-MO) | Expelled |

Disloyalty to the Union; taking up arms against the United States.

| 12-2-1861 | John W. Reid | (D-MO) | Expelled |

Disloyalty to the Union; taking up arms against the United States.

| 12-3-1861 | Henry C. Burnett | (D-KY) | Expelled |

Disloyalty to the Union; open rebellion against the Government.

| 4-9-1864 | Benjamin G. Harris | (D-MD) | Censured |

Treasonous conduct in opposing subjugation of the South.

| 4-14-1864 | Alexander Long | (D-OH) | Censured |

Supporting recognition of the Confederacy.

| 5-14-1866 | John W. Chanler | (D-NY) | Censured |

Insulting House, resolution containing unparliamentary language.

| 7-24-1866 | Lovell H. Rousseau | (UU*-KY) | Censured |

Assault of another Member.

| 1-26-1867 | John W. Hunter | (?-NY) | Censured |

Unparliamentary language.

| 1-15-1868 | Fernando Wood | (D-NY) | Censured |

Unparliamentary language.

| 2-14-1869 | Edward D. Holbrook | (D-ID) | Censured |

Unparliamentary language.

| 2-24-1870 | Benjamin Whittemore | (R-SC) | Censured |

Selling military academy appointments.

| 3-1-1870 | John T. DeWeese | (R-SC) | Censured |

Selling military academy appointments.

| 3-16-1870 | Roderick R. Butler | (R-TN) | Censured |

Accepting money in return for academy appointment.

| 2-27-1873 | Oakes Ames | (R-MA) | Censured |

Bribery in Credit Mobilier case.

| 2-27-1873 | James Brooks | (D-NY) | Censured |

Bribery in Credit Mobilier case.

DATE	MEMBER	PARTY-STATE	ACTION
2-4-1875	John Y. Brown	(D-KY)	Censured

Unparliamentary language.

| 5-17-1890 | William D. Bynum | (D-IN) | Censured |

Unparliamentary language.

| 10-27-1921 | Thomas L. Blanton | (D-TX) | Censured |

Unparliamentary language.

| 7-29-1976 | Robert L. F. Sikes | (D-FL) | Reprimanded |

Office used for personal gain; not disclosing interest in legislation.

| 10-13-1978 | Charles H. Wilson | (D-CA) | Reprimanded |

False statement before Standards of Official Conduct Committee.

| 10-13-1978 | John J. McFall | (D-CA) | Reprimanded |

Failure to report campaign contributions from Korean lobbyist.

| 10-13-1978 | Edward R. Roybal | (D-CA) | Reprimanded |

Failure to report campaign contributions; false sworn statement before Standards of Official Conduct Committee.

| 7-31-1979 | Charles C. Diggs | (D-MI) | Censured |

Payroll fraud; conviction.

| 6-6-1980 | Charles H. Wilson | (D-CA) | Censured |

Improper gifts; ghost employees; personal use of campaign funds.

| 10-2-1980 | Michael J. Myers | (D-PA) | Expelled |

Bribery conviction for accepting money in return for promise to use influence in immigration matters.

| 7-20-1983 | Gerry E. Studds | (D-MA) | Censured |

Sexual misconduct with House page.

| 7-20-1983 | Daniel B. Crane | (R-IL) | Censured |

Sexual misconduct with House page.

| 7-31-1984 | George V. Hansen | (R-ID) | Reprimanded |

False statements on disclosure form; conviction for false statements.

| 12-18-1987 | Austin J. Murphy | (D-PA) | Reprimanded |

Allowing another person to cast his vote; maintaining on his payroll persons not performing official duties commensurate with pay.

| 10-5-1987 | Richard H. Stallings | (D-ID) | Reproval letter |

Improper use of campaign funds.

| 10-18-1989 | Jim Bates | (D-CA) | Reproval letter |

Sexual harassment; improper campaign activity in congressional office.

| 7-26-1990 | Barney Frank | (D-MA) | Reprimanded |

Using political influence to fix parking tickets and to influence probation officers for personal friend.

| 1-21-1997 | Newt Gingrich | (R-GA) | Reprimanded |

Allowing a Member-affiliated tax-exempt organization to be used for political purposes; providing inaccurate information to the ethics committee.

DATE	MEMBER	PARTY-STATE	ACTION
10-4-2000	E. G. Shuster	(R–PA)	Reproval letter

Relationship with lobbyist; intervention on behalf of constituent.

6-20-2001	Earl Hilliard	(D-AL)	Reproval letter

Improper loans, expenditures, disclosures by campaign committee.

7-24-2002	James A. Traficant	(D-OH)	Expelled

Convicted of bribery, obstruction of justice, racketeering, tax evasion.

10-6-2004	Tom DeLay	(R-TX)	Reproval letter

Improper campaign activity.

* AJ= Anti-Jacksonian party. UU= Unconditional Unionist party.

U.S. SENATE CENSURE HISTORY

DATE	MEMBER	PARTY-STATE	ACTION
7-8-1797	William Blount	(R-TN)	Expelled

Anti-Spanish conspiracy, treason.

5-10-1844	Benjamin Tappan	(D-OH)	Censured

Released private presidential message to the Senate.

7-11-1861	James M. Mason	(D-VA)	Expelled

Disloyalty to the Union; support for the Confederacy.

7-11-1861	Robert M. T. Hunter	(D-VA)	Expelled

Disloyalty to the Union; support for the Confederacy.

7-11-1861	Thomas L. Clingman	(D-NC)	Expelled

Disloyalty to the Union; support for the Confederacy.

7-11-1861	Thomas Bragg	(D-NC)	Expelled

Disloyalty to the Union; support for the Confederacy.

7-11-1861	James Chesnut	(D-SC)	Expelled

Disloyalty to the Union; support for the Confederacy.

7-11-1861	Alfred O. P. Nicholson	(D-TN)	Expelled

Disloyalty to the Union; support for the Confederacy.

7-11-1861	William K. Sebastian	(D-AR)	Expelled

Disloyalty to the Union; support for the Confederacy (reversed in 1877).

7-11-1861	Charles B. Mitchel	(D-AR)	Expelled

Disloyalty to the Union; support for the Confederacy.

7-11-1861	John Hemphill	(D-TX)	Expelled

Disloyalty to the Union; support for the Confederacy.

7-11-1861	Louis T. Wigfall	(D-TX)	Expelled

Disloyalty to the Union; support for the Confederacy.

12-4-1861	John C. Breckinridge	(D-KY)	Expelled

Disloyalty to the Union; support for the Confederacy.

1-10-1862	Trusten Polk	(D-MO)	Expelled

Disloyalty to the Union; support for the Confederacy.

DATE	MEMBER	PARTY-STATE	ACTION
1-10-1862	Waldo P. Johnson	(D-MO)	Expelled

Disloyalty to the Union; support for the Confederacy.

| 2-5-1862 | Jesse D. Bright | (D-IN) | Expelled |

Disloyalty to the Union; support for the Confederacy.

| 2-28-1902 | Benjamin R. Tillman | (D-SC) | Censured |

Fighting in the Senate.

| 2-28-1902 | John L. McLaurin | (D-SC) | Censured |

Fighting in the Senate.

| 11-4-1929 | Hiram Bingham | (R-CT) | Censured |

Employed representative of trade association in Senate office.

| 12-2-1954 | Joseph R. McCarthy | (R-WI) | Censured |

Abuse and noncooperation with Subcommittee on Privileges and Elections.

| 6-23-1967 | Thomas J. Dodd | (D-CT) | Censured |

Improper financial conduct, improper reimbursements, improper reporting of campaign finances.

| 7-25-1990 | David F. Durenberger | (R-MN) | Censured |

Unethical conduct.

| 7-30-2002 | Robert G. Torricelli | (D-NJ) | Reproval letter |

Receiving improper gifts.

Senators who faced expulsion or censure but resigned or had their terms end before action was taken:

DATE	MEMBER	PARTY-STATE
1862	James F. Simmons	(R-RI)

Resigned while facing a charge of corruption.

| 1873 | James W. Patterson | (R-NH) |

Term expired while facing expulsion on a charge of corruption.

| 1905 | John H. Mitchell | (R-OR) |

Died before expulsion on a charge of corruption.

| 1906 | Joseph R. Burton | (R-KS) |

Resigned while facing a charge of corruption.

| 1922 | Truman H. Newberry | (R-MI) |

Resigned while facing a charge of corruption.

| 1982 | Harrison A. Williams Jr. | (D-NJ) |

Resigned while facing a charge of corruption.

GLOSSARY

attack ads. Advertising used during political campaigns that involves one or more negative facts or themes about an opponent. Also called *negative advertising* and *mudslinging*.

ballot farming. The use of selective registration lists or other sources of voter information to ensure voting activity in favor of a specific candidate or party. This activity may include hand delivery or mailing of absentee ballots, personal assistance in filling out absentee ballots, and signing ballots in place of the designated voter.

ballot fraud. Determination of the outcome of an election by controlling the vote count. Where vote counting is overseen by election officials, this activity begins with the deliberate appointment of counters, judges, and observers to be manipulated by the party. During the counting process—or when the counts are delivered to a central headquarters—the tally figures are adjusted to create the desired result, up for the supported candidates or down for the opponents. This can be accomplished by adjusting the figures on a tally sheet, altering the marks made on individual ballots, or substituting pre-fixed ballots for unwanted ones. A variety of tricks can also be used to invalidate individual ballots in order to reduce the number of undesirable votes, such as marking, tearing, or defacing such a ballot so that it does not meet the requirements for a clean ballot.

ballot rigging. The process of altering a ballot design or contents to favor one candidate or party, or to cause a disadvantage for a candidate or party.

ballot stuffing. A box or container used to deposit finished ballots is filled, or "stuffed," with additional ballots pre-marked to favor one candidate.

boodle. An old-fashioned term for bribe or illegal payment, something received in exchange for political favors. A person involved in this activity is called a *boodler*.

boss. The official or unofficial head of a precinct, ward, city, county, regional, or state-wide political machine. Bosses traditionally held elected positions but can also be the appointed or elected heads of political organizations. In some cases, bosses have been neither, working behind the scenes to run organizations. Some of the most notorious bosses used corrupt activities to generate income for themselves, their colleagues, or their parties, but not all bosses have used their power to acquire wealth. These positions of power are also associated with control over political positions, selection of candidates, and awarding of contracts for public works.

bounty hunter. A person used by a candidate or political party to register new voters and paid per new registration. In the past, some registrations gained by this process have come from obituaries, prisons, or other irregular sources, used by bounty hunters to pad their income.

bribery. In a political environment, a payment or gift made to a politician or political staff member in exchange for a vote or other favor such as a political appointment, government contract, or patronage job.

campaign spending limits. Rules or laws that govern expenditures by candidates and parties.

carousel voting. One or more voters travels from one polling station to another on election day, submitting a new absentee ballot at each stop.

censure. A condemnation of a member voted by a legislature, indicating disapproval of specific activity. There is no definitive statement or list of actions that can result in censure in the U.S. Congress, but in general it may include improper language, insults to other members, physical violence to other members, conflicts of interest, violations of law, accepting improper gifts, bribery, payroll fraud (related to congressional staffs), or other activities that may be considered disrespectful to Congress. During the Civil War, support for the Confederacy was also considered just cause for censure. Censure is a form of discipline that can result in the loss of chairmanship of a committee, loss of other rights of seniority, suspension or loss of other privileges, and/or fines or restitution. In the House, the least severe censure is a "letter of reproval," which can be issued by the Committee on Standards of Official Conduct and does not require the involvement of the complete body of the House. All other forms of censure require a majority vote of the House. The same is true in the Senate. The most extreme censure is a vote to expel, which in either body requires a two-thirds vote to pass. Rules listed in the House Committee on Standards of Official Conduct state: "... reprimand is appropriate for serious violations, censure is appropriate for more serious violations, and expulsion of a Member or dismissal of an officer or employee is appropriate for the most serious violations. A recommendation of a fine is appropriate in a case in which it is likely that the violation was committed to secure a personal financial benefit; and a recommendation of a denial or limitation or a right, power, privilege, or immunity of a Member is appropriate when the violation bears upon the exercise or holding of such right, power, privilege, or immunity." In the House, levels of censure are: 1. letter of reproval, 2. reprimand, 3. censure, 4. expulsion. In the Senate, there is a less structured reaction, but the results are similar to that in the House.

chain voting. Voting fraud linked to the use of paper ballots, in which a voter brings a pre-marked ballot into a voting booth and swaps it for a blank one already placed there. After submitting the pre-filled ballot, the blank one is slipped out of the voting place, where it is given—or sold—to a vote controller, who fills it out in preparation for the next voter.

colonizing. A voter fraud tradition in which citizens—or even noncitizens—from one ward or precinct are "imported" to another to cast votes, paid for in advance. In extreme cases, groups of people were transported from county to county and even from state to state for this purpose. In New York City, the practice was once known as "pipe laying" because of the claim used to support the presence of unusual crowds of people—laying pipe for the city's new aqueduct.

conflict of interest. A stated or implied clash or irreconcilable difference between the public duties of political officers and their actions in support of an individual or group. Conflict of interest provides a personal benefit to an official derived from normal duties. In the Credit Mobilier scandal, politicians were guilty of a conflict of interest because they accepted stock in a company that benefited from their influence.

contempt. An official charge brought against anyone, such as a witness in a congressional hearing, who "obstructs the business" of Congress. This includes a refusal to answer questions or to provide relevant documents.

cooping. In previous years, a form of election fraud. For a few days in advance of an election, hired men kidnapped people from bars and flophouses, held them in secret rooms, and kept them well supplied with alcohol. On election day, they were led—or sometimes carried—to polling places and supplied with a preselected list of candidates to vote for.

corruption. One or more activities that represent illegal or unethical use of an official position. Corruption can include bribery, fraud, extortion, embezzlement, and similar actions, or any combination of these, as long as the action breaks a law or rule. Corruption can involve interactions between politicians and individuals or between politicians and other politicians. In the early political eras of the United States, the term was sometimes used in a broader sense, to refer to the abuse or breaking of morals, ethics, or social codes.

cronyism. A type of favoritism in which individuals or groups are given advantages, jobs, or contracts because of their connection to or support for a politician or political party, rather than because of their qualifications.

dirty tricks. Activities designed to annoy, amuse, or otherwise divert attention from major campaign issues. At one extreme, these include calling voters very late at night to urge support for a candidate, posting bogus notices for campaign meetings, ordering C.O.D. pizza deliveries for an opponent's campaign offices, publishing false backgrounds or histories about candidates, and similar antics. The other end of the dirty tricks' spectrum can include monitoring cell phone calls from campaign insiders, planting "moles" inside opponent's headquarters to monitor election plans, and stealing documents pertinent to an opponent's campaign strategies.

disclosure. Presentation or publication of sources, donors, connections, or other pertinent information related to a campaign or campaign donations. Official rules of disclosure are part of campaign and election rules from the IRS and other state and federal organizations.

dynamiting. A smear tactic used to discredit a political opponent. This may be in the form of rumor or printed material such as flyers, pamphlets, or books, or advertisements. Dynamiting generally falls short of slander or libel, being slanted to produce negative impressions from carefully selected and edited quotes or facts.

election fraud. The use of illegal or unethical methods to influence or change to outcome of a campaign or vote. This may include bribes, intimidation, vote buying, ballot stuffing, and other actions.

exclusion. In the U.S. Senate, a simple-majority vote for a member to vacate his or her position. Exclusion votes occur when formal objections are presented to the results of an election, suggesting fraud or other reasons why the results are not valid.

expulsion. A vote for an elected member of either the House or the Senate to be removed from office. A minimum of two-thirds of the members must agree to this action. Expulsion is a version of impeachment and exists because impeachment is reserved for use for the executive and judicial branches. Expelled members retain their pensions—unless they are nullified for other reasons—and can run for office again.

fagot voting. Dating to an era when only landowners could vote, candidates or political parties purchased undeveloped lots for otherwise landless citizens in exchange for a vote. After the election, the temporary landowner returned the property to the original owner.

floaters. People who vote more than once on election day, moving from precinct to precinct to cast their votes. Also referred to as *repeaters*.

four-legged voting. A form of fraud in which election officials such as precinct workers pull voting levers in place of registered voters.

ghost voting. A form of election fraud in which nonexistent, deceased, or otherwise unregistered people are added to voter registration rolls and/or actually used to register votes.

gratuity. A payment made as a reward for an action beneficial to the payee, as opposed to a bribe, which is a payment made in advance to influence a desired outcome.

hacking. In earlier political eras, a form of voter intimidation in which groups of men—on foot or on horseback—moved around on or before election day, firing weapons into the air, creating noise, and otherwise producing a noticeable and threatening display. The effect was intended to let people know that their voting behavior would be under scrutiny. In the modern electronic era, "hacking" refers to illegal manipulation of a computer system that controls votes in electronic voting machines, with the goal of adding or subtracting vote totals for a candidate or candidates.

hard money. Legitimate political donations falling within the limits designated by federal campaign finance rules and disclosed to the Federal Election Commission.

high crimes and misdemeanors. This phrase, originating with English common law and as part of the U.S. Constitution, refers to the standard by which public officers (legislators, presidents, federal judges, etc.) are to be judged for impeachment. There is no clear definition of the phrase, but "high crimes" generally refers to significant offenses, such as the violation of national or international laws. "Misdemeanors" literally meant "bad behavior" in earlier eras, but now refers to corruption or neglect of duty. In some interpretations, the combined sense could also mean an offense to a system of government, suggesting moral rather than legal misdeeds.

immigrant votes. In cities with large number of newly arrived immigrants, local politicians and political parties routinely corraled votes by organizing and helping the new arrivals, in exchange for their votes.

immunity. Legal protection for members of Congress. As stated in the U.S. Constitution, Article I, Section 6: "They shall, in all cases except treason, felony and breach of the peace, be privileged from arrest during their attendance at the session of their respective houses, and in going to and returning from the same; and for any speech or debate in either house, they shalt not be questioned in any other place." The current interpretation of the Constitution does not protect members of Congress from arrest or imprisonment for criminal activity.

impeachment. The accusation or charge that an official has committed a specific category of offense known as "treason, bribery, or other high crimes and misdemeanors," as stated in the U.S. Constitution. Federal officials subject to impeachment include presidents, vice presidents, and appointees such as cabinet officers and federal judges (the impeachment standards for federal judges are slightly different than for the other branches of government). Officially, impeachment is only the process of making a charge, which at the federal level initially involves the U.S. House of Representatives. The process begins with a debate and vote to consider specific articles of impeachment, which spell out what the accused official has done to be liable for this action. The votes on the articles of impeachment—a separate vote on each article, if there are more than one—are passed or rejected by a simple majority. If the articles are passed, the process moves to the Senate in a trial format. The vice president presides in the role of judge, unless the person under impeachment is the president, in which case the Chief Justice of the Supreme Court takes this position. The process concludes with a vote for or against conviction; the vote must result in at least a two-thirds majority to pass. In the case of a tie, the vice president casts the deciding vote. Andrew Johnson and Bill Clinton are the only two presidents to be impeached, but both were acquitted in the Senate. Impeachment is intended as a means to remove an official from office; state constitutions typically provide a parallel process. Both branches of Congress can also achieve this end for their own members by voting for expulsion, a process different than impeachment, but intended for the same purpose. Between 1789 and 2006, Congress has begun the impeachment process a total of sixty-two times. Seventeen federal officers received a final vote to impeach; fourteen of these were tried in the Senate (three resigned before the Senate action, resulting in dismissals). Of the fourteen impeachment cases tried in the Senate, seven resulted in acquittals and seven resulted in convictions (all were federal judges).

influence peddling. Political power exercised on behalf of an individual, group, or business, in exchange for something of value to the politican exercising this power, such as the awarding of government contracts. Influence peddling can be practiced by an elected politician, a party member, or a go-between.

jamming. With mechanical voting machines, fraud perpetrated by mechanically blocking the lever next to a targeted candidate, making it impossible for voters to generate a vote for that person.

kickback. A share of a contract, payment, or paycheck returned to the source. Politicians typically get kickbacks when they arrange for government contracts to be awarded to a specific party, award a patronage job, or make a political appointment. Kickbacks can be one-time or ongoing payments. In previous eras, organized kickback schemes for political hirees required specific amounts to be returned, typically 2 to 5 percent.

kidnapping. An election-day ploy from earlier political eras, where party workers physically captured voters, election judges, or poll watchers, with the goal of stopping them from voting or observing vote fraud.

malfeasance. Conduct by a public official that is considered immoral or unethical but may or may not be illegal.

muckraking. Research and reporting in the media aimed at uncovering immoral, unethical, or illegal political activity or connection to such activity by politicians, political parties, or political machines. Although criticism of political wrongdoing in the media dates to colonial days, muckraking first came to prominence in the late 1800s, but the term was not applied until 1906, when President Theodore Roosevelt first used it in a speech. It was derived from "muckrake," a word used by English author John Bunyan in his book *Pilgrim's Progress*, published in 1678.

mudslinging. Verbal or written political attacks aimed at a candidate or elected official and containing specific allegations of wrongdoing.

nepotism. A form of favoritism in filling positions or employment—including political positions, appointments, and so on—in which the person hired is related to the politician doing the hiring or appointing.

opposition research. A form of background check that scrutinizes the personal, business, and political history of candidates in order to uncover scandals. This activity typically relies on public records, but in some cases, internal leaks, interviews with friends and colleagues, and sifting through discarded papers and trash are also employed.

padding (registration padding). In advance of an election, political parties operating at the precinct level add the names of fictitious people to the list of legitimate registered voters. Padding is typically done by using false names and addresses or false names and real addresses. In the past, these names have sometimes been created by copying names from cemeteries, mental hospitals, or jails. Once registered, any of these names can be used to vote a ballot, and the more padding, the more votes.

patronage. The employment or appointment of people to positions by a politician or political party, with the selection based on political support or other forms of favoritism rather than ability or experience.

payroll padding. Extra income gained by adding a nonexistent employee to a payroll or by adding a real, nonworking person who kicks back some or all of his or her income to a boss or elected official. Kickbacks and "ghost" employees have been used by politicians to increase their personal income, pay debts, or provide income for campaigns.

perjury. An answer, statement, or statements that are knowingly false and given while under oath in relation to a specific question.

poll shifting. A method of election fraud used to disrupt and diminish votes in areas with anticipated support for an opposing candidate. Election officials move poll sites just before an election or alter the time that a poll site is open in order to reduce the number of votes cast.

purging. A list of eligible voters can include names of people who have moved away, died, or are otherwise no longer legitimately able to vote. A purge is the official activity used to remove these names from a list by matching current information with that on a list following specific rules. In some cases, purges have been designed and conducted to target legitimate voters of one party—removing them from a list because of minor discrepancies in registration information—thereby decreasing the potential vote count for a candidate or party. The reverse action has also been used, "loosening" requirements to increase the number of voters.

push poll. A survey of public opinion in which a specific question (or questions) is used to gauge support or reaction to certain issues. Push polls can be a tactic in dirty politics if used to deliberately discredit or cast doubt on a candidate, but they are often used to help a campaign discover and focus on issues that generate the strongest positive or negative support.

repeater. A person who voluntarily or for a payment votes repeatedly using a different name each time. The names used match those on official registers; the lists may be padded to accommodate the practice. Occasionally, a repeater might use names of legitimate voters, beating them to the polls. In areas where the practice was particularly well developed, repeaters were often men who grew beards just for the occasion. By a succession of shaving and trimming, one repeater could go back to the same polling place as many as four times with a different appearance each time. At times, car-, train-, or busloads of repeaters have been brought in from outside locations, with participants recruited from rooming houses, barrooms, and even mental asylums. New immigrants were also frequently used.

reprimand. Used in the House of Representatives as the lowest level of official censure. In practice, a letter of reprimand is sent to a member by an ethics committee after an investigation if it has been determined the member has done something wrong, such as insulting another member or accepting inappropriate gifts. A letter of reprimand can be made public or kept private and rarely has a significant negative effect on voter support.

resignation. The voluntary termination of an elected or appointed position before the end of a term. Politicians may resign in order to accept other positions, because of health or personal reasons, or in order to avoid publicity or punishment from an anticipated investigation. In Congress, members who resign are usually no longer subject to censure action. In the presidency, resignation circumvents impeachment, as in the case of President Nixon, when he faced this action following Watergate.

ring. A group involved with a political organization, either loosely or formally bound together to control bribes, graft, patronage jobs, and other business involved with a city, county, or state.

roorback. A bogus publication about a candidate created to produce negative reactions from voters. Roorbacks can be pamphlets, letters, newspaper articles, flyers, or books. The term comes from a noted early version of this negative campaign format, a letter from a slave owner named Roorback in 1844 who supposedly came across slaves branded with the name of presidential candidate James Polk.

scandal. An event, activity, position, or allegation that creates publicity that is potentially damaging to a political candidate or elected official. Whether or not allegations of political corruption turn out to be true, for example, the publicity creates a scandal that can lose votes or erode power.

shoe-polish fraud. Shoe polish or a similar material is used to paint the button or lever of a specific candidate on a voting machine. After voting, voters are approached by a political party member or other person who shakes their hand, in the process determining if they voted for the candidate in question because of the polish that rubbed off, or didn't. This method is used to target voters for intimidation.

short pencil men. Using a shortened pencil hidden in the palm of the hand, a vote counter adds extra marks to a ballot that has been turned in. Voting rules typically allow the voter to mark only one preference per category; if a ballot has votes for two candidates in the same position, it is considered an invalid ballot and none of the votes on it are allowed. Short pencil men used their hidden stubs to invalidate unwanted votes.

smear campaign. Also referred to as mudslinging, a tactic used in politics to destroy or diminish the reputation or status of a candidate, elected official, or political party, by publicizing negative information.

smoke-filled room. A meeting place out of the public eye where political decisions are made or support for political candidate or positions are determined. So called because in earlier eras, such rooms were dense with cigar smoke.

soft money. Contributions to political parties that are designated for general use by the party and not by a specific candidate nor the campaign of a specific candidate. Soft money is different than hard money in that the rules on federal campaign finance do not include any limit on amount. The concept is controversial—and the target of reform—because political parties have found ways to use such money indirectly to support individual candidates, thwarting the intent of the law.

spoiling. The act of marking a ballot after it has been filled out so that the ballot is disqualified. Most commonly, a ballot is spoiled by adding a vote for a second candidate within the category for one office, thereby making it void under the "one vote per office" rule.

spoils system. A local, regional, or national use of patronage to fill political positions when one candidate or party obtains power.

suspension. A condition in the U.S. House for a member who has been convicted of a crime that may include a sentence of two or more years. In such a case, the member is expected to voluntarily refrain from voting in any committee of which they are a member or in the House as a whole.

telegraphing. A form of ballot stuffing in which a designated voter or election official marks ballots for one or more other registered voters.

treating. An election practice dating to Washington's day, in which voters were plied with alcohol in expectation that they would vote for the candidate who had supplied it to them.

two percent club. An unofficial group whose members are employees or appointees working in city, county, or state government and are required to "donate" a stated amount of their salary or wages to the political party that arranged for their job or is currently in power. This amount has often been set at two percent, hence the term, but variations include one percent, three percent, and other rates.

vote buying. Voters are either paid to vote for a certain candidate or in some cases, to not vote for one. The practice may involve standardized cash payments from a few dollars to more than fifty dollars per person, haggling, or payment in trade, such as food or alcoholic beverages.

vote fraud. see *election fraud*.

voter intimidation. A method of influencing the outcome of an election by reducing votes for the opposition through threats, bullying, or other scare tactics. Voter intimidation in older eras was often visible, in the form of organized groups of armed men. In recent eras, intimidation has been wielded through the telephone or mail, with messages that deliver real or suggested threats. In the South and Midwest, the Ku Klux Klan played a prominent role in voter intimidation aimed at African American voters, using parades, night rides, and lynching symbols (in handbills, posters, and graffiti) as their weapons.

walking around money. Cash distributed to precinct captains or other local organizers who "walk around" to support a campaign on or before election day. It is used for last minute expenses and has also traditionally funded incentives that support and encourage individual votes, including payments for babysitters and taxi fares, not to mention drinks at local bars. Like other kinds of slush funds, walking around money typically is not included in formal accounts and is often prohibited.

BIBLIOGRAPHY

Abels, Jules. *The Truman Scandals.* 1956, Henry Regnery Company.

Alterman, Eric. *When Presidents Lie: A History of Official Deception and Its Consequences.* 2004, Viking.

Altschuler, Glenn C.; Blumin, Stuart, M. *Rude Republic: Americans and Their Politics in the Nineteenth Century.* 2000, Princeton University Press.

Amick, George. *The American Way of Graft.* 1976, Center for Analysis of Public Issues.

Anderson, Jack. *Confessions of a Muckraker.* 1979, Random House.

Anderson, Jack. *Washington Exposé.* 1967, Public Affairs Press.

Arthur, Anthony. *Radical Innocent: Upton Sinclair.* 2006, Random House.

Ashman, Charles R. *The Finest Judges Money Can Buy: And Other Forms of Judicial Pollution.* 1973, Nash Publishing.

Bailey, Thomas A. *Presidential Saints and Sinners.* 1981, Free Press.

Barrett, Grant (editor). *The Oxford Dictionary of American Political Slang.* 2004, Oxford University Press.

Bean, Walton. *Boss Ruef's San Francisco.* 1952, University of California Press.

Beatty, Jack. *The Rascal King: The Life and Times of James Michael Curley.* 1992, Addison-Wesley.

Benson, George C. S. *Political Corruption in America.* 1978, Lexington Books.

Blakey, G. Robert. "The Rico Civil Fraud Action in Context." *Notre Dame Law Review,* 1982, Vol. 57.

Bollens, John C.; Schmandt, Henry J. *Political Corruption: Power, Money, and Sex.* 1979, Palisades Publishers.

Boller, Paul. *Congressional Anecdotes.* 1991, Oxford University Press.

Boller, Paul F., Jr. *Presidential Campaigns.* 1984, 1985, Oxford University Press.

Boller, Paul F., Jr. *Presidential Inaugurations: Behind the Scenes—An Informal, Anecdotal History from Washington's Election to the 2001 Gala.* 2001, Harcourt, Inc.

Bonomi, Patricia U. *The Lord Cornbury Scandal: The Politics of Reputation in British America.* 1998, University of North Carolina Press.

Boulard, Garry. *Huey Long Invades New Orleans: The Siege of a City, 1934–36.* 1998, Pelican Publishing.

Bowers, Claude. *The Party Battles of the Jackson Period.* 1922, Houghton Mifflin.

Britton, Nan. *The President's Daughter.* 1927, Elizabeth Ann Guild Inc.

Bryce, James. *The American Commonwealth.* 1914, Macmillan.

Burns, Eric. *Infamous Scribblers: The Founding Fathers and the Rowdy Beginnings of American Journalism.* 2006, Public Affairs.

Burrows, Edwin G.; Wallace, Mike. *Gotham: A History of New York City to 1898.* 1999, Oxford University Press.

Buschel, Bruce; Robbins, Albert; Vitka, William. *The Watergate File: A Concise, Illustrated Guide to the People and Events.* 1973, Flash Books.

Butler, Anne M.; Wolff, Wendy. *United States Senate Election, Expulsion and Censure Cases 1793–1990.* 1995, U.S. Government Printing Office.

Campbell, Tracy. *Deliver the Vote: A History of Election Fraud, an American Political Tradition 1742–2004.* 2005, Carroll & Graf.

Congressional Quarterly. *American Political Leaders 1789–2000.* 2000, CQ Press.

Cornog, Evan; Whelan, Richard. *Hats in the Ring: An Illustrated History of American Presidential Campaigns.* 2000, Random House.

Diamond, Robert A. (editor). *Congressional Quarterly's Guide to U.S. Elections.* 1975, Congressional Quarterly.

Dickson, Paul. *The Congress Dictionary: The Definitive Collection of the Words, Jargon, Quotations, Anecdotes, Customs, and Symbols that Shape American Politics.* 1993, John Wiley & Sons.

Dorman, Michael. *Dirty Politics: From 1776 to Watergate.* 1979, Delacorte Press.

Dorman, Michael. *Payoff.* 1972, Berkley.

Douglas, Jack D.; Johnson, John M. (editors). *Official Deviance: Readings in Malfeasance, Misfeasance, and Other Forms of Corruption.* 1977, J.B. Lippincott.

Eberling, Ernest J. *Congressional Investigations.* 1928, Columbia University Press.

Eisenstadt, Abraham S.; Hoogenboom, Ari; Trefousse, Hans L. (editors). *Before Watergate: Problems of Corruption in American Society.* 1979, Brooklyn College Press.

Etzioni, Amitai. *Capital Corruption: The New Attack on American Democracy.* 1984, Harcourt Brace Jovanovich.

Felknor, Bruce L. *Dirty Politics.* 1966, Norton.

Felknor, Bruce L. *Political Mischief: Smear, Sabotage, and Reform in U.S. Elections.* 1992, Praeger.

Fischer, Roger A. *Tippecanoe and Trinkets Too: The Material Culture of American Presidential Campaigns, 1828–1984.* 1988, University of Illinois Press.

Foner, Eric; Garraty, John (editors). *Readers Companion to American History.* 1991, Houghton Mifflin.

Ford, Paul Leicester. *The True George Washington.* 1896, J.B. Lippincott.

Ford, Worthington Chauncey. *The Spurious Letters Attributed to Washington.* 1889, privately published.

Franklin, Allan. *The Trail of the Tiger.* 1928, Allan Franklin.

Gardiner, John A. *The Politics of Corruption: Organized Crime in an American City.* 1970, Russell Sage Foundation.

Gardiner, John A.; Olson, David J. (editors). *Theft of the City: Readings on Corruption in Urban America.* 1974, Indiana University Press.

Geelan, Agnes. *The Dakota Maverick: The Political Life of William Langer.* 1975, Agnes Geelan.

Glasscock, C.B. *The War of the Copper Kings.* 1935, Grosset & Dunlap.

Green, A. Wigfall. *The Man Bilbo.* 1963, Louisiana State University Press.

Gregory, Charles Noble. *The Corrupt Use of Money in Politics and Laws for Its Prevention.* 1893, Historical and Political Science Association/University of Wisconsin.

Grossman, Mark. *Political Corruption in America: An Encyclopedia of Scandals, Power, and Greed.* 2003, ABC-CLIO.

Hatfield, Mark O. *Vice Presidents of the United States 1789–1993.* 1997, U.S. Government Printing Office.

Hagood, Wesley O. *Presidential Sex: From the Founding Fathers to Bill Clinton.* 1995, Birch Lane Press/Carol Publishing Group.

Holli, Melvin G.; Jones, Peter d'A. (editors). *Biographical Dictionary of American Mayors, 1820–1980.* 1981, Greenwood Press.

Holt, Michael F. *The Rise and Fall of the American Whig Party.* 1999, Oxford University Press.

Holzworth, John M. *The Fighting Governor: The Story of William Langer and the State of North Dakota.* 1938, The Pointer Press.

Hughes, R.E.; Schaefer, F.W.; William, E.L. *That Kentucky Campaign.* 1900, The Robert Clarke Company.

Jamieson, Kathleen Hall. *Dirty Politics: Deception, Distraction, and Democracy.* 1992, Oxford University Press.

Jonas, Frank H. *Political Dynamiting.* 1970, University of Utah Press.

Juno, Andrea; Vale, V. (editors). *Pranks!* 1987, Re/Search.

Kendall, John. *The History of New Orleans.* 1922, Lewis Publishing Company.

Kessler, Ronald. *Inside Congress: The Shocking Scandals, Corruption, and Abuse of Power Behind the Scenes on Capitol Hill.* 1997, Pocket Books.

Kessler, Ronald. *Inside the White House: The Hidden Lives of the Modern Presidents and the Secrets of the World's Most Powerful Institution.* 1995, Pocket Books.

Key, V.O. Jr. *Politics, Parties, and Pressure Groups.* 1950, Thomas Y. Crowell Company.

Kirwan, Albert D. *Revolt of the Rednecks: Mississippi Politics, 1876–1925.* 1965, Harper Torchbook (originally published University of Kentucky Press, 1951).

Klotter, James C. *History Mysteries: The Cases of James Harrod, Tecumseh, Honest Dick Tate and William Goebel.* 1989, University Press of Kentucky.

Lasky, Victor. *It Didn't Start with Watergate.* 1977, Dial Press.

Lee, R. Alton. *The Bizarre Careers of John R. Brinkley.* 2002, University Press of Kentucky.

Lindberg, Richard C. *To Serve and Collect: Chicago Politics and Police Corruption from the Lager Beer Riot to the Summerdale Scandal.* 1991, Praeger.

Marszalek, John F. *The Petticoat Affair: Manners, Mutiny, and Sex in Andrew Jackson's White House.* 1997, Free Press.

McDaniel, George William. *Smith Wildman Brookhart: Iowa's Renegade Republican.* 1995, Iowa State University Press.

Mee, Charles L., Jr. *The Ohio Gang: The World of Warren G. Harding, An Historical Entertainment.* 1981, M. Evans and Company.

Melder, Keith. *Hail to the Candidate: Presidential Campaigns from Banners to Broadcasts.* 1992, Smithsonian Institute Press.

Miller, Hope Ridings. *Scandals in the Highest Office: Facts and Fictions in the Private Lives of Our Presidents.* 1973, Random House.

Miller, Lillian B. *If Elected: Unsuccessful Candidates for the Presidency 1796–1968.* 1972, Smithsonian Institution Press.

Miller, Nathan. *Stealing from America: A History of Corruption from Jamestown to Reagan.* 1992, Paragon House.

Mitchell, Greg. *The Campaign of the Century: Upton Sinclair's Race for Governor of California and the Birth of Media Politics.* 1992, Random House.

Mitchell, Jack. *How to Get Elected: An Anecdotal History of Mudslinging, Red-baiting, Vote-stealing and Dirty Tricks in American Politics.* 1992, St. Martin's.

Moore, John W. *School History of North Carolina.* 1879–1888, A. Williams & Company.

Morris, Roy, Jr. *Fraud of the Century: Rutherford B. Hayes, Samuel Tilden, and the Stolen Election of 1876.* 2003, Simon and Schuster.

Noonan, John T., Jr. *Bribes.* 1984, Macmillan.

O'Brien, Cormac. *Secret Lives of the U.S. Presidents.* 2004, Quirk Books.

Orth, Samuel P. *The Boss and the Machine: A Chronicle of the Politicians and Party Organization.* 1920, Yale University Press.

Payne, Robert. *The Corrupt Society.* 1975, Praeger.

Pearson, Drew; Anderson, Jack. *The Case Against Congress: A Compelling Indictment of Corruption on Capitol Hill.* 1968, Simon and Schuster.

Pollard, James E. *The Presidents and the Press.* 1947, Macmillan.

Poore, Benjamin Perley. *Perley's Reminiscences of Sixty Years in the National Metropolis.* 1886, Hubbard Brothers.

Powell, Gene. *Tom's Boy Harry: The First Complete, Authentic Story of Harry Truman's Connection with the Pendergast Machine.* 1948, Hawthorn Publishing Company.

Rehnquist, William H. *Grand Inquests: The Historical Impeachments of Justice Samuel Chase and President Andrew Johnson.* 1992, Quill/Morrow.

Remini, Robert V. *The House: The History of the House of Representatives.* 2006, HarperCollins.

Ross, Shelley. *Fall from Grace: Sex, Scandal, and Corruption in American Politics from 1702 to the Present.* 1988, Ballantine Books. (republished 1989, Washington Babylon, Allison & Busby).

Sabato, Larry J.; Simpson, Glenn R. *Dirty Little Secrets: The Persistence of Corruption in American Politics.* 1996, Times Books.

Seale, William. *The President's House: A History.* 1986, White House Historical Association.

Seitz, Don C. *The Dreadful Decade: Detailing Some Phases in the History of the United States from Reconstruction to Resumption 1869–1879.* 1926, Bobbs-Merrill Company.

Seitz, Don C. *Famous American Duels.* 1929, Thomas Y. Crowell Company.

Shearer, Ernest C. *Robert Potter: Remarkable North Carolinian and Texan.* 1951, University of Houston Press.

Smith, Gene (editor). *The Police Gazette.* 1972, Simon and Schuster.

Sobel, Robert; Raimo, John (editors). *Biographical Directory of the Governors of the United States 1789–1978.* 1978, Meckler Books.

Southwick, Leslie H. *Presidential Also-Rans and Running Mates, 1788–1980.* 1984, McFarland & Company.

Sparks, W.H. *The Memories of Fifty Years.* 1870, Claxton, Remsen & Haffelfinger.

Stark, Andrew. *Conflict of Interest in American Public Life.* 2000, Harvard University Press.

Steward, Dick. *Duels and the Roots of Violence in Missouri.* 2000, University of Missouri Press.

Sullivan, Michael John. *Presidential Passions: The Love Affairs of America's Presidents—From Washington and Jefferson to Kennedy and Johnson.* 1991, Shapolsky Publishers.

Swanberg, W.A. *Sickles the Incredible.* 1956, Scribners.

Swint, Kerwin C. *Mudslingers: The Top 25 Negative Political Campaigns of All Time.* 2006, Praeger.

Tinkman, George H. *California Men and Events.* 1915, Stockton, California.

Todd, Charles B. *A Brief History of the City of New York.* 1899, American Book Company.

Trager, James. *The New York Chronology.* 2003, Harper Resource.

Unger, Harlow Giles. *The Unexpected George Washington.* 2006, Wiley.

Van Devander, Charles W. *The Big Bosses.* 1944, Howell, Soskin, Publishers.

Van Tassel, Emily Field; Finkelman, Paul. *Impeachable Offenses: A Documentary History from 1787 to the Present.* 1999, Congressional Quarterly.

Wendt, Lloyd; Kogan, Herman. *Big Bill of Chicago.* 1953, Bobbs-Merrill.

Wilson, James Grant; Fiske, John (editors). *Appleton's Cyclopaepia of American Biography.* 1888, D. Appleton and Company.

Woodward, C. Vann (editor). *Responses of the Presidents to Charges of Misconduct.* 1974, Delacorte Press.

Young, Donald. *American Roulette: The History and Dilemma of the Vice Presidency.* 1965, 1972, Holt, Rinehart and Winston.

Zink, Harold. *City Bosses in the United States: A Study of Twenty Municipal Bosses.* 1930, Duke University Press.

SOURCE NOTES

Several resources have been used extensively because they have provided a long and continuous source of reliable news about political events. Plus, they currently provide a beneficial service with public access to their archives online (although this may include a subscription fee). These major resources are: *The New York Times*, *Time* magazine, and *Encyclopaedia Britannica*. The author has also made extensive use of online subscription databases, accessed through public and academic libraries, which provide the full text of daily newspapers, newsmagazines, and academic journals. The primary authorities used for the spelling of politicians' names, dates of births and deaths, dates of service, and dates of formal actions are: *The Biographical Directory of the United States Congress* (U.S. Congress), *American Political Leaders* (Congressional Quarterly Press), and *The Biographical Dictionary of American Mayors* (Greenwood Press).

Library of Congress
www.loc.gov

U.S. National Archives and Records Administration
www.archives.gov

America's Historic Newspapers 1690–1900
Newsbank, Inc., and the American Antiquarian Society
www.newsbank.com

Colorado's Historic Newspaper Collection 1859–1923 (86 papers)
Collaborative Digitization Program, Colorado State Library
www.coloradohistoricnewspapers.org

Academic Search Premier
EBSCO Publishing
www.ebsco.com

The Nineteenth Century in Print (full text of twenty-three periodicals from the 1800s and early 1900s, including *Harper's New Monthly Magazine*, *Atlantic Monthly*, *United States Democratic Review*, *The Century*, and others)
American Memory/Library of Congress http://memory.loc.gov

Biographical Directory of the United States Congress
http://bioguide.congress.gov

American Heritage (access online to articles published in *American Heritage* magazine since 1954)
www.americanheritage.com

Biographical Directory of Federal Judges
Federal Judicial History Office/Federal Judicial Center
www.fjc.gov/history/home.nsf

SOURCES

One or more major sources is listed for each entry in the chronology. Full listings for book titles cited are included in the Bibliography. Abbreviations: *NYT* is *New York Times*; *EB* is *Encyclopaedia Britannica*, online edition; U.S. is United States.

Pre–1776. 1 "Corruption," Burrows, *Readers Companion to American History.* **2** *Gotham*, p. 79; *Scribner's History of the US*, Vol. II, p. 345. **3** *Appleton's Cyclopedia of American Biography*, Vol. 1, p. 77; *EB*, 15th ed., Vol. 1, p. 366; *Royal Government in America*, p. 175. **4** *Ships and Shipping of Old New York*, p. 22; *William and Mary Quarterly*, 10-1963, pp. 527–542. **5** *Royal Government in America*, pp 123–125. **6** *New York Chronology*, pp. 18-20; *Royal Government in America*, p. 42. **7** *Appleton's Cyclopedia of American Biography*, Vol. I, p. 223; Interactive Statehouse/Massachusetts; *Atlantic Monthly*, 8-1893, pp. 209–218; *Royal Government in America*, pp. 364–365. **8** *School History of North Carolina*; *Charlotte Observer*, 7-24-1904, p. 17. **9** *Royal Government in America*, p. 126.

1776–1799. 1 *Biographical Directory of the U.S. Congress*; *Dictionary of American Biography*, Vol. IV, p. 65. **2** *Scandals in the Highest Office*, pp. 23–54; *The True George Washington*; *Presidential Sex*, p. 10. **3** *Biographical Directory of the U.S. Congress*; *History of Camden County*. **4** *Vice Presidents of the U.S.*, p. 52. **5** *Fall From Grace*, pp. 22–28. **6** *U.S. Senate Election, Expulsion, and Censure Cases*, p. 3. **7** *U.S. Senate Election, Expulsion, and Censure Cases*, p. 6. **8** *U.S. Senate Election, Expulsion, and Censure Cases*, p. 13. **9** *The House*, pp. 62–63; *U.S. House of Representatives Ethics Manual.* **10** *Federal Gazette* (Brattleboro, VT) 10-20-1798, p. 3; *Biographical Directory of the U.S. Congress.* **11** *EB*. **12** *Scandals in the Highest Office*, pp. 50–53; "The Syphax Family," National Park Service.

1800–1819. 1 *Scandals in the Highest Office*, pp. 56–107. **2** *The American Past*, p. 33. **3** *Famous American Duels*, p. 76; *Biographical Directory of the U.S. Congress*; Swartwout Family Organization. **4** *Biographical Directory of the U.S. Congress*; *Dictionary of American Biography*, Vol. IX, p. 419; *New York Herald*, 9-29-1802, p. 7. **5** *Famous American Duels*, pp. 107–122. **6** *U.S. Senate Election, Expulsion, and Censure Cases*, pp. 35–37; *Responses of the Presidents to Charges of Misconduct*, pp. 35–37; "Commanding Generals and Chiefs of Staff," Center of Military History. **7** *Vice Presidents of the U.S.*, p. 44; *Biographical Directory of the U.S. Congress.* **8** *U.S. Senate Election, Expulsion, and Censure Cases*, p. 18. **9** *The House*, p. 88. **10** *Vice Presidents of the U.S.*, p. 56. **11** *U.S. Senate Election, Expulsion, and Censure Cases*, p. 41. **12** *Responses of Presidents to Charges of Misconduct*, p. 34; *The American Past*, p. 42; *Famous American Duels*, pp. 77–106; *Vice Presidents of the U.S.*, p. 39; *Duels and the Roots of Violence in Missouri*, p. 122. **13** *U.S. Senate Election, Expulsion, and Censure Cases*, p. 22. **14** *U.S. Senate Election, Expulsion, and Censure Cases*, p. 8; *New Hampshire Patriot & State Gazette*, 8-6-1827, p. 3; *Biographical Directory of the U.S. Congress.* **15** *Biographical Directory of the U.S. Congress*; *Dictionary of American Biography*, Vol. V, p. 550. **16** *U.S. Senate Election, Expulsion, and Censure Cases*, pp. 39–40; *Political Corruption in America*, p. 69; *Bribes*, pp. 435–442. **17** *U.S. Senate Election, Expulsion, and Censure Cases*, p. 42; *Biographical Directory of the U.S. Congress.* **18** *Duels and the Roots of Violence in Missouri*, pp. 47–48. **19** *Vice Presidents of the U.S.*, p. 75. **20** *Duels and the*

Roots of Violence in Missouri, pp. 66–73. **21** *Biographical Directory of the U.S. Congress.* **22** *Duels and the Roots of Violence in Missouri, Biographical Directory of the U.S. Congress; EB;* America's Historic Newspapers. **23** Biographical Directory of Federal Judges; *Impeachable Offenses,* pp. 91–100. **24** *EB; Impeachable Offenses,* pp. 101–107.

1820–1839. 1 "Bloody Island"/East St. Louis Action Research Project. **2** *Presidential Also-Rans and Running Mates,* pp. 62–65. **3** *U.S. Senate Election, Expulsion, and Censure Cases.* **4** *Vice Presidents of the U.S.,* p. 90. **5** *Famous American Duels,* p. 22. **6** *Biographical Directory of the U.S. Congress.* **7** *Biographical Directory of the U.S. Congress;* Old State House Museum (Arkansas); *Arkansas Times.* **8** "The Rise of Jacksonian Democracy," White House Historical Association; *Famous American Duels,* p. 123, pp. 125–155. **9** *Vice Presidents of the U.S.,* p. 95; *The Petticoat Affair.* **10** *Vice Presidents of the U.S.,* p. 125. **11** *Responses of the Presidents to Charges of Misconduct,* p. 57. **12** *Biographical Directory of Federal Judges; Connecticut Courant* (Hartford, CT), 5-4-1830, p. 2; *Baltimore Patriot,* 2-1-1831, p. 3. **13** *New England Magazine,* 10-1831, p. 367, 1-1892, p. 591; *Diary of Philip Hone, 1828–1851,* Vol. 1., p. 36; *Biographical Directory of the U.S. Congress; Eastern Argus,* 9-20-1831, p. 4; *Duels and the Roots of Violence in Missouri,* p. 122. **14** *Biographical Directory of the U.S. Congress; Presidential Also-Rans and Running Mates,* p. 151. **15** *U.S. Senate Election, Expulsion, and Censure Cases,* p. 38. **16** *Robert Potter, Richmond Enquirer,* 9-30-1831; *Farmer's Gazette,* 2-13-1835; *New Hampshire Patriot & State Gazette,* 4-14-1842. **17** *Biographical Directory of the U.S. Congress;* "Murder of Cilley," Library of Congress (109030); *The House,* p. 126. **18** *Portsmouth Journal of Literature & Politics* (Portsmouth, NH), 9-15-1838, p. 3; *Waldo Patriot* (Belfast, ME), 11-2-1838, p. 2. **19** *Responses of the Presidents to Charges of Misconduct,* p. 69; *Party Battles of the Jackson Period,* p. 69. **20** *Creating an Old South,* p. 185. **21** *Responses of the Presidents to Charges of Misconduct,* p. 69; *Party Battles of the Jackson Period,* p. 69. **22** *Creating an Old South,* Baptist, p. 185.

1840–1859. 1 *The Rise and Fall of the American Whig Party,* p. 111. **2** *Biographical Directory of the U.S. Congress; Hudson River Chronicle,* 5-25-1841, p. 3; *Patriot and State Gazette* (Concord, NH), 4-9-1841, p. 2. **3** *The Century Magazine,* 9-1887, pp. 366–397; *Biographical Directory of the U.S. Congress; Illinois History,* 2-1995, p. 48. **4** *Famous American Duels,* pp. 283–309. **5** *Perley's Reminiscences,* Vol. 1, p. 300; Index to the 29th Congress; *Farmer's Cabinet,* 12-28-1843, p. 2; *Berkshire County Whig* (Pittsfield, MA), 9-17-1846, p. 2. **6** *Berkshire County Whig,* 3-20-1843, p. 2; *Biographical Directory of the U.S. Congress.* **7** *U.S. Senate Election, Expulsion, and Censure Cases,* p. 47. **8** *Biographical Dictionary of American Mayors,* p. 49. **9** *Newport Mercury,* 4-27-1844, p. 2. **10** *New Hampshire Patriot* (Concord, NH), 9-26-1844, p. 2; *Barre Patriot* (Barre, MA), 10-11-1844, p. 3. **11** *Biographical Directory of the U.S. Congress; The Rise and Fall of the American Whig Party,* pp. 526–527. **12** *Southern Patriot,* 1-16-1845, p. 2; *Famous American Duels,* pp. 310–316. **13** *Vice Presidents of the U.S.,* p. 158. **14** *Ohio Statesman,* 11-4-1848, p. 2. **15** *Biographical Directory of the U.S. Congress.* **16** *Duels and the Roots of Violence in Missouri,* pp. 131–132. **17** *Farmer's Cabinet,* 3-7-1850, p. 2. **18** *Biographical Dictionary of American Mayors,* p. 57. **19** *Biographical Directory of the U.S. Congress.* **20** *New Hampshire Patriot & State Gazette,* 4-11-1850, p. 2; *Biographical Directory of the U.S. Congress; The Rise and Fall of the American Whig Party,* pp. 497–498. **21** Lawrenceville Historical Society; *Biographical Dictionary of American Mayors,* p. 15. **22** *Biographical Directory of the U.S. Congress,* p. 1124; *Daily Missouri Republican,* 9-15-1852, p. 2; *The Annals of San Francisco,* Chapter XXI. **23** "Henry Meiggs," *Mendocino Redwood Company; Macon Weekly Telegraph,* 11-21-1854, p. 2. **24** *American Political History,* pp. 207, 211; *Civic Wars,* p. 142, p. 152; *Deliver the Vote,* pp. 27–30, 46–48. **25** *Biographical Dictionary of American Mayors,* p. 216. **26** *Biographical Dictionary of American Mayors,* p. 163. **27** *Biographical Dictionary of American Mayors,* p. 35. **28** *Biographical Dictionary of American Mayors,* p. 85. **29** California Supreme Court Historical Society; *NYT,* 4-15-1890, p. 1. **30** Administrations of the Mayors of New Orleans/New Orleans Public Library. **31** *Charleston Mercury,* 5-26-1856, p. 2; *Biographical Directory of the U.S. Congress.* **32** *Presidential Campaigns,* p. 97; *Presidential Also-Rans and Running Mates,* pp. 222–223. **33** *NYT,* 1-16-1856, p. 4; 3-11-1856, p. 1; 1-21-1880, p. 4;

Deliver the Vote, pp. 43–45. **34** *Duels and the Roots of Violence in Missouri*, pp. 156-162. **35** *NYT*, 6-20-1857, p. 2. **36** *NYT*, 2-20-1857, p. 4; 3-3-1857, p. 2. **37** *NYT*, 2-24-1857, p. 2. **38** *NYT*, 2-20-1857, p. 4. **39** *Villains and Vigilantes.* **40** *NYT*, 3-2-1857, p. 1; 3-7-1857, p. 4; 3-30-1857, p. 6; *Pittsfield Sun* (Pittsfield, MA), 4-2-1857, p. 2. **41** "The Know-Nothing Riot of 1858"/*History of New Orleans.* **42** *America and the California Dream*, p. 122. **43** *NYT*, 2-28-1859, p. 1; 4-27-1859, p. 1.

1860–1879. 1 *Biographical Dictionary of American Mayors*, p. 42. **2** *The House*, p. 155; *Congressional Anecdotes*, p. 39. **3** *Biographical Directory of the U.S. Congress.* **4** National Governors Association; *NYT*, 6-30-1862, p. 5. **5** *EB*; *Biographical Directory of Federal Judges.* **6** *Biographical Dictionary of American Mayors*, p. 115. **7** *Vice Presidents of the U.S.*, pp. 213–219. **8** *Presidential Also-Rans and Running Mates*, p. 229; *Biographical Directory of the U.S. Congress*; "The Strange Death of Mr. Dayton," Noirsain. **9** *Vice Presidents of the U.S.*, p. 213. **10** *Biographical Dictionary of American Mayors*, p. 30. **11** *Biographical Dictionary of American Mayors*, p. 146; *American Heritage*, 12-1986. **12** *Biographical Dictionary of American Mayors*, p. 244. **13** *NYT*, 3-24-1869, p. 3; Virginia State Capitol/Library of Virginia. **14** *Biographical Dictionary of American Mayors*, p. 368; *Biographical Directory of the U.S. Congress*; *NYT*, 2-23-1870, p. 4; 3-1-1870, p. 4. **15** *Biographical Directory of the U.S. Congress.* **16** *Hooded Americanism*; *Rude Republic*, pp. 174–176; *Deliver the Vote*, pp. 18–19, 20–21, 35–36, 46–48, 58–60, 101–102. **17** *NYT*, 4-11-1870, p. 1; 11-3-1868, p. 8. **18** *NYT*, 5-27-1870, p. 5; 12-21-1870, p. 1; 3-23-1871, p. 1; 2-26-1873, p. 1; *Memoirs of W.W. Holden*, pp. 88–89. **19** National Governors Association; *NYT*, 8-20-1870, p. 5; 11-2-1871, p. 1. **20** *NYT*, 4-20-1871, p. 1; 10-10-1872, p. 5; 8-14-1900, p. 7. **21** *City Bosses in the U.S.*, pp. 96–112; *Political Corruption in America*, pp. 35–41, 48–49. **22** *NYT*, 1-29-1871, p. 1; 8-26-1913, p. 8. **23** *U.S. Senate Election, Expulsion, and Censure Cases*, pp. 170–172; *Biographical Directory of the U.S. Congress*; *NYT*, 2-27-1873, p. 5. **24** *NYT*, 4-16-1874, p. 5; 5-10-1874, p. 6; 5-25-1874, p. 1; 5-30-1874, p. 2; 1-15-1875, p. 4; *Encyclopedia of Arkansas History Culture.* **25** *Biographical Dictionary of American Mayors*, p. 75. **26** *U.S. Senate Election, Expulsion, and Censure Cases*, p. 190; *Biographical Directory of the U.S. Congress*; *Appleton's Cyclopedia of American Biography*, Vol. 1, p. 197; *U.S. Senate Election, Expulsion, and Censure Cases*, pp. 189–195; *The House*, pp. 220–221. **27** *NYT*, 11-9-1868, p. 1; 11-26-1868, p. 1; National Governors Association. **28** Louisiana Secretary of State; National Governors Association. **29** *Biographical Dictionary of American Mayors*, p. 174; *NYT*, 3-29-1904, p. 2. **30** *Biographical Dictionary of American Mayors*, p. 176. **31** *NYT*, 4-2-1874, p. 5; 9-13-1902, p. 9. **32** White House History Association. **33** *Political Corruption in America*, p. 81. **34** *U.S. Senate Election, Expulsion, and Censure Cases*, p. 204. **35** *NYT*, 1-26-1876, p. 8; 1-31-1875, p. 1; *Bribes*, p. 779. **36** *Georgia Weekly Telegraph*, 8-15-1876, p. 4; *Charlotte News*, 4-26-1889, p. 2. **37** *Responses of the Presidents to Charges of Misconduct*, pp. 150–152. **38** National Governors Association; *NYT*, 5-8-1879, p. 1; 4-30-1884, p. 4; 5-24-1884, p. 3. **39** *Responses of the Presidents to Charges of Misconduct*, p. 153. **40** *Responses of the Presidents to Charges of Misconduct*, pp. 154–158; *Political Corruption in America*, pp. 81–82. **41** *Biographical Directory of the U.S. Congress*; National Governors Association. **42** *Deliver the Vote*, pp. 72–78; *Fraud of the Century.* **43** *The House*, p. 224. **44** *U.S. Senate Election, Expulsion, and Censure Cases*, pp. 211–212. **45** *NYT*, 12-17-1877, p. 2; 12-7-1878, p. 1; *EB.* **46** *Presidential Also-Rans and Running Mates*, p. 343. **47** *Macon Weekly Telegraph*, 12-16-1881, p. 4. **48** *Police Gazette*, 12-13-1879, p. 11; *Philadelphia Inquirer*, 12-3-1879, p. 8. **49** Chronicle Publishing Company history.

1880–1899. 1 "The First Shakespeare Administration,"*History of New Orleans.* **2** *National Police Gazette*, 2-21-1880, p. 3. **3** *National Police Gazette*, 1-17-1880, p. 13. **4** *Macon Weekly Telegraph*, 5-25-1881, p. 2. **5** *NYT*, 6-12-1874, p. 8; 4-8-1878, p. 5; 3-30-1882, p. 8; 10-2-1885, p. 1; 6-4-1887, p. 1; National Governors Association. **6** *NYT*, 3-24-1882, p. 5. **7** *National Police Gazette*, 5-12-1883; *American Journal of Legal History*, 4-1988, pp. 157–172. **8** *NYT*, 2-2-1883, p. 5; *Columbus Daily Enquirer*, 2-1-1883, p. 1. **9** *NYT*, 4-24-1882, p. 8; 4-14-1883, p. 3. **10** *Biographical Dictionary of American Mayors*, p. 23. **11** *History of New Orleans*; *Biographical Dictionary of American Mayors*, p. 142. **12** American Political Items Collectors Association;

Hail to the Candidate, p. 48. **13** *Civic Wars; EB; The Big Bosses*, pp. 11–62; *City Bosses in the U.S.*, pp. 85–164. **14** *Macon Weekly Telegraph*, 9-26-1884, p. 2. **15** *NYT*, 11-30-1884, p. 7; 2-25-1885, p. 8; 11-1-1885, p. 2. **16** *Columbus Enquirer-Sun*, 4-2-1887, p. 5; *NYT*, 10-16-1887, p. 17; 5-20-1890, p. 1. **17** *NYT*, 4-7-1875, p. 7; 10-27-1881, p. 1; 3-6-1884, p. 4; *Responses of the Presidents to Charges of Misconduct*, pp. 170–173, 177–183. **18** "Althea and the Judges," *American Heritage*, 6-1967; *NYT*, 12-25-1884, p. 1; 5-15-1889, p. 1. **19** *The Ungentlemanly Art.* **20** *NYT*, 10-24-1888, p. 1. **21** *NYT*, 8-9-1890, p. 1; 9-27-1897, p. 1; *Dallas Morning News*, 3-22-1888, p. 2; *Macon Weekly Telegraph*, 3-24-1888, p. 2. **22** *NYT*, 11-4-1888, p. 3. **23** *Columbus Enquirer Sun*, 1-8-1889, p. 1; *Omaha World Herald*, 12-12-1895, p. 10. **24** *Kentucky Post*, 10-15-2002; *Biographical Directory of the U.S. Congress*. **25** *NYT*, 6-6-1890, p. 5; 12-16-1892, p. 3; 8-3-1898, p. 4. **26** *NYT*, 12-12-1890, p. 1. **27** *NYT*, 4-20-1891, p. 1. **28** *Presidential Sex*, pp. 64–65; "Frances Cleveland," National First Ladies' Library. **29** *Biographical Dictionary of American Mayors*, p. 168; *City Bosses in the U.S.*, p. 292; *NYT*, 4-8-1895, p. 1. **30** *NYT*, 8-13-1893, p. 2; 4-15-1894, p. 2; 11-20-1904, p. 3. **31** *NYT*, 3-29-1893, p. 5; 4-12-1893, p. 4; *U.S. Senate Election, Expulsion and Censure Cases*, p. 248. **32** *Duluth News*, 2-26-1893, p. 1. **33** *Biographical Dictionary of American Mayors*, p. 118; *History of New Orleans; Kansas City Star*, 3-14-1895, p. 1. **34** *NYT*, 5-14-1895. **35** *NYT*, 9-27-1896, p. 12; 10-23-1896, p. 6. **36** *Philadelphia Inquirer*, 4-24-1895, p. 5; 10-23-1893, p. 2. **37** *NYT*, 2-22-1895, p. 1. **38** *NYT*, 4-8-1896, p. 1. **39** *U.S. Senate Election, Expulsion, and Censure Cases*, p. 263; *Biographical Directory of the U.S. Congress*. **40** *NYT*, 3-21-1897, p. 1. **41** *NYT*, 11-16-1918, p. 13. **42** *U.S. Senate Election, Expulsion, and Censure Cases*, p. 256; *Kansas City Star*, 1-11-1898, p. 10. **43** *Vice Presidents of the U.S.*, p. 292. **44** *The Shame of the Cities*, pp. 134–136; *Biographical Dictionary of American Mayors*, p. 10; *NYT*, 5-10-1903, p. 24. **45** *NYT*, 12-9-1899, p. 1; 12-23-1899, p. 1; 1-31-1900, p. 1; 5-22-1900, p. 5; 8-19-1900, p. 1.

1900–1919. 1 *NYT*, 4-10-1901, p. 1; *Denver Post*, 4-9-1901, p. 1; 4-19-1901, p. 1. **2** *NYT*, 2-23-1902, p. 1; *U.S. Senate Election, Expulsion, and Censure Cases*, p. 269. **3** *Biographical Dictionary of U.S. Mayors*, p. 320; *NYT*, 4-27-1905, p. 1; *NYT*, 7-13-1906, p. 4; *NYT*, 11-29-1906, p. 1; *NYT*, 3-28-1907, p. 1. **4** *To Serve and Collect*, pp. 126–134; *NYT*, 11-13-1908, p. 2; 11-12-1938, p. 15; *Time*, 7-13-1942. **5** *Biographical Dictionary of American Mayors*, p. 405; *NYT*, 6-1-1902, p. 3. **6** *NYT*, 6-7-1902, p. 1; 8-10-1902, p. 21; 9-12-1903, p. 9; *NYT*, 1-30-1904, p. 2; *Grand Forks Daily Herald*, 7-12-1902, p. 1; *City Bosses in the U.S.*, p. 338. **7** *NYT*, 1-16-1903, p. 1; *Morning Herald* (Lexington, KY), 10-19-1903, p. 2. **8** *Biographical Directory of the U.S. Congress; NYT*, 6-25-1903, p. 1; 1-8-1904, p. 1. **9** *Bribes*, pp. 625–626; *NYT*, 10-1-1904, p. 8; *Responses of the Presidents*, pp. 215–223. **10** *Biographical Directory of the U.S. Congress; NYT*, 2-16-1904, p. 8; 2-20-1904, p. 5. **11** Mayor Martin Behrman Records/City Archives/New Orleans Public Library; *Biographical Dictionary of American Mayors*, p. 24. **12** *NYT*, 7-17-1894, p. 5; 9-27-1904, p. 16; 1-29-1905, p. 8. **13** *NYT*, 12-11-1904, p. 1; 12-24-1904, p. 5; 7-8-1906, p. 2; Governor Alva Adams Collection/Colorado State Archives. **14** *NYT*, 2-12-1905, p. 2; 2-14-1905, p. 5. **15** *NYT*, 4-5-1905; 4-21-1905, p. 3; 5-19-1905, p. 5; 2-15-1906. **16** *NYT*, 3-23-1904, p. 2; 2-28-1905, p. 8; 1-25-1905, p. 1; 2-28-1923, p. 17. **17** *U.S. Senate Election, Expulsion, and Censure Cases*, p. 275. **18** *Biographical Dictionary of American Mayors*, p. 23. **19** *NYT*, 11-23-1906, p. 3; 10-13-1907, p. 16. **20** *Biographical Dictionary of American Mayors*, pp. 116–117; *How to Get Elected*, p. 83; *American Heritage*, 8-1968. **21** *NYT*, 12-9-1906, p. 2; 12-4-1907, p. 3. **22** *NYT*, 9-10-1911, p. SM4; 5-11-1909, p. 1; 12-4-1910, p. 3; 2-2-1913, p. 1. **23** *Biographical Dictionary of American Mayors*, p. 37; *NYT*, 7-12-1907, p. 1. **24** *Biographical Directory of the Governors of the U.S.*, p. 1367; *NYT*, 2-24-1907, p. SM11; 3-10-1907, p. 11; 8-5-1907, p. 4. **25** *NYT*, 3-13-1909, p. 4; 3-16-1909, p. 1; 3-28-1909, p. 1; 7-27-1909, p. 2. **26** *NYT*, 9-5-1909, p. 1. **27** *NYT*, 7-15-1910, p. 2; 7-23-1910, p. 4. **28** *NYT*, 6-13-1910, p. 1. **29** *Biographical Directory of the U.S. Congress; NYT*, 5-3-1910, p. 7. **30** *U.S. Senate Election, Expulsion, and Censure Cases*, p. 285. **31** *U.S. Senate Election, Expulsion, and Censure Cases*, p. 281; *NYT*, 7-14-1912, p. 1. **32** *NYT*, 7-27-1912, p. 1. **33** National Governors Association; *Biographical Directory of the Governors of the United States*, p. 1097. **34** *Biographical Directory of Federal Judges*, Federal Judicial Center.; *NYT*, 1-14-1913, p. 1; 7-10-1924, p. 6. **35** *NYT*,

5-18-1912, p. 7; 1-25-1914, p. 9; 3-26-1916, p. 16. **36** *NYT,* 12-25-1910, p. 1; 1-3-1911, p. 20; 1-10-1911, p. 6. **37** *Biographical Dictionary of American Mayors,* p. 324; *NYT,* 9-3-1916, p. 8. **38** *Ambitious Brew,* p. 171; *NYT,* 3-4-1916, p. 13. **39** *NYT,* 9-27-1917, p. 8; 10-12-1917, p. 12. **40** *Biographical Directory of the Governors of the U.S.,* p. 1533; National Governors Association. **41** *Biographical Directory of the U.S. Congress.* **42** *U.S. Senate Election, Expulsion, and Censure Cases,* p. 302.

1920–1939. 1 *EB,* p. 233; *Biographical Directory of the U.S. Congress; Time,* 9-4-1933. **2** *Biographical Directory of the U.S. Congress; NYT,* 8-16-1920, p. 1. **3** *NYT,* 6-2-1910, p. 4; 3-11-1913, p. 3; 5-21-1926, p. 3. **4** *NYT,* 3-10-1936, p. 23. **5** *Biographical Directory of the U.S. Congress; NYT,* 2-12-1921, p. 1; 4-1-1921, p. 15. **6** *NYT,* 3-31-1921, p. 14; 3-4-1922, p. 7; 3-4-1924, p. 2; 3-8-1938, p. 19. **7** *NYT,* 4-21-1921, p. 15; 8-10-1921, p. 1; 12-30-1921, p. 16; 6-25-1922, p. 1. **8** *Bribes,* pp. 565–567; *Responses of the Presidents to Charges of Misconduct,* pp. 269–274; *The Ohio Gang; American Heritage,* 8-1965. **9** *NYT,* 8-10-1921, p. 1. **10** *Political Corruption in America,* pp. 99–100; *NYT,* 12-2-1927, p. 5; 2-3-1931, p. 8; 3-20-1944, p. 17; 3-31-1944, p. 23. **11** *U.S. Senate Election, Expulsion, and Censure Cases,* p. 306; The Handbook of Texas Online/University of Texas at Austin. **12** *NYT,* 8-7-1922, p. 8. **13** *Biographical Directory of the Governors of the United States,* p. 1244; *NYT,* 4-8-1923, p. 3; 11-20-1923, p. 1; 8-10-1924, p. 30. **14** *NYT,* 2-3-1923, p. 2; 2-17-1923, p. 12; 3-15-1923, p. 1; 10-25-1923, p. 1; 7-11-1925, p. 11; *Time,* 11-5-1923. **15** *U.S. Senate Election, Expulsion, and Censure Cases,* p. 312. **16** National Governors Association. **17** *NYT,* 1-11-1925, p. 9; 1-18-1932, p. 15; 1-18-1932, p. 15. **19** *Time,* 10-18-1926; 9-17-1928. **18** Biographical Directory of Federal Judges; *NYT,* 11-5-1926, p. 1. **20** *U.S. Senate Election, Expulsion, and Censure Cases,* p. 323. **21** *Biographical Directory of the U.S. Congress; United States Senate Election, Expulsion, and Censure Cases,* p. 330; *Time,* 2-20-1928. **22** *Biographical Dictionary of American Mayors,* p. 268; *NYT,* 6-12-1926, p. 23; *Time,* 12-23-1929. **23** *NYT,* 12-6-1926, p. 21; 12-8-1934, p. 15; *Time,* 12-6-1926. **24** *NYT,* 6-2-1931, p. 1. **25** *NYT,* 3-5-1927, p. 1; 5-8-1929, p. 40; 2-3-1933, p. 8. **26** *NYT,* 10-7-1926, p. 2; 9-13-1927, p. 9; 10-29-1927, p. 1. **27** *NYT,* 5-7-1927, p. 19. **28** *NYT,* 11-5-1928, p. 1; 11-8-1928, p. 26; 5-1-1929, p. 12. **29** *NYT,* 5-18-1928, p. 2; 11-1-1928, p. 1. **30** *NYT,* 9-10-1927, p. 1; 2-17-1928, p. 1. **31** *NYT,* 12-1-1928, p. 3; 4-20-1930, p. 51. **32** *Biographical Dictionary of American Mayors,* p. 36; "Jerry Buckley, A Victory Short Lived," *Crime Magazine.* **33** *NYT,* 4-2-1929, p. 19; 5-9-1929, p. 1; 10-22-1929, p. 25; 1-26-1930, p. 1. **34** *U.S. Senate Election, Expulsion and Censure Cases,* pp. 336-338; *NYT,* 11-5-1929, p. 1. **35** *NYT,* 11-20-1929, p. 1; 3-14-1931, p. 12. **36** *NYT,* 3-21-1929, p. 1; 11-10-1932, p. 14; *Time,* 1-28-1929. **37** *Biographical Dictionary of American Mayors,* p. 86; *NYT,* 10-31-1931, p. 24. **38** *Huey Long Invades New Orleans; EB; Time,* 4-15-1929; 5-27-1929. **39** *Biographical Directory of the U.S. Congress.* **40** *The Bizarre Careers of John R. Brinkely.* **41** *U.S. Senate Election, Expulsion, and Censure Cases,* p. 343. **42** *Vice Presidents of the United States,* p. 386. **43** *NYT,* 3-2-1930, p. 29; 6-1-1930, p. N2. **44** *NYT,* 11-19-1946, p. 1. **45** *NYT,* 7-13-1927, p. 12; 2-14-1931, p. 3; 4-15-1931, p. 20; 4-16-1931, p. 52. **46** *NYT,* 1-18-1931, p. 58; 6-9-1931, p. 3; 6-10-1931, p. 26; 7-3-1934, p. 19; *Time,* 6-8-1931. **47** *U.S. Senate Election, Expulsion, and Censure Cases,* p. 351. **48** *World Almanac and Book of Facts for 1934,* p. 92. **49** *U.S. Senate Election, Expulsion, and Censure Cases,* p. 366; *NYT,* 4-24-1940; *Time,* 7-10-1939. **50** *Biographical Directory of Federal Judges; NYT,* 1-19-1933, p. 2; 5-25-1933, p. 2. **51** *World Almanac and Book of Facts for 1934,* p. 95; *NYT,* 2-4-1933, p. 1. **52** *World Almanac and Book of Facts for 1934,* p. 99; *Time,* 5-23-1932. **53** *World Almanac and Book of Facts for 1934,* p. 100; *NYT,* 1-23-1939, p. 5. **54** *The Numismatist,* 8-1977, pp. 1610-1613; *NYT,* 9-3-1933, p. 3; *Time,* 9-11-1933. **55** *NYT,* 6-3-1934, p. 1; *Time,* 12-4-1933. **56** *World Almanac and Book of Facts for 1934,* p. 108. **57** *Presidential Also-Rans and Running Mates,* p. 523; *Time,* 8-21-1933; *Topeka Capital Journal,* 12-6-2000. **58** *NYT,* 8-12-1933, p. 18; *Time,* 9-4-1933. **59** *The Campaign of the Century; Time,* 10-15-1934, 10-22-1934, 11-12-1934. **60** *NYT,* 2-17-1935, p. E6; 6-14-1936, p. 3; 9-10-1948, p. 23. **61** *NYT,* 11-24-1935, p. 26; 6-14-1936, p. 2. **62** *The Big Bosses,* pp. 232–258; *Time,* 4-9-1934. **63** *NYT,* 4-24-1936, p. 23; 5-19-1936, p. 25; 5-27-1936, p. 25; 6-2-1936, p. 6; 8-8-1936, p. 1; 8-9-1936, p. 16; 8-12-1936, p. 10; *Time,* 5-4-1936; 5-11-1936; 8-17-1936. **64** *NYT,* 2-20-1935, p. 16; 6-

28-1935, p. 3; *Time*, 8-12-1935. **65** National Governors Association; *NYT*, 12-28-1934; 1-19-1935, p. 1; 2-3-1935, p. 1. **66** *NYT*, 1-11-1936, p. 32; 11-7-1936, p. 18. **67** *Biographical Directory of Federal Judges*; *NYT*, 3-29-1936, p. E7; 4-10-1936, p. 10. **68** *NYT*, 9-21-1938, p. 20. **69** *NYT*, 1-8-1942, p. 22; 6-7-1942, p. 26; *Time*, 5-6-1940, 6-1-1942. **70** *Biographical Dictionary of American Mayors*, p. 328; *NYT*, 8-23-1938, p. 20. **71** *Time*, 7-24-1933; 10-14-1940; 10-2-1944. **72** *NYT*, 3-15-1938, p. 21. **73** *NYT*, 4-13-1940, p. 11; 11-22-1966, p. 1. **74** National Governors Association. **75** *NYT*, 5-23-1939, p. 1. **76** *NYT*, 2-3-1939, p. 7; 8-22-1939, p. 1. **77** *NYT*, 7-16-1939, p. 24; memo, U.S. government copyright office, 10-24-1972; *Biographical Directory of the U.S. Congress*; interview, Institute of International Studies, UC Berkeley, 4-17-2000. **78** *NYT*, 10-17-1939, p. 1; 6-8-1954, p. 27; 2-3-2003, p. B7. **79** *NYT*, 10-4-1939, p. 1. **80** *NYT*, 10-6-1939, p. 1. **81** *Biographical Directory of Federal Judges*; *Time*, 6-12-1939. **82** *Bribery*, p. 571; *Biographical Directory of Federal Judges*; *NYT*, 9-10-1941. **83** *NYT*, 9-30-1939, p. 34.

1940–1959. 1 *Biographical Directory of the U.S. Congress*; *NYT*, 3-23-1940, p. 3; 5-7-1940, p. 11. **2** *Vice Presidents of the U.S.*, p. 401; *How to Get Elected*, pp. 93-94; *Time*, 8-9-1948. **3** *Biographical Directory of the U.S. Congress*; *U.S. Senate Election, Expulsion, and Censure Cases*, p. 368; *NYT*, 11-9-1959, p. 1. **4** *NYT*, 6-20-1948, p. 4; *Time*, 6-14-1948. **5** *NYT*, 11-4-1941, p. 25. **6** *NYT*, 10-3-1941, p. 24; 9-20-1952, p. 15. **7** *Vice Presidents of the U.S.*, p. 454; CNN, "The Story Behind LBJ's Silver Star." **8** *Tom's Boy Harry*, pp. 146–166; *The Truman Scandals*, pp. 24–29. **9** *Biographical Dictionary of American Mayors*, p. 263; *NYT*, 3-19-1947, p. 19; 9-1-1961, p. 1; 5-24-1964, p. 94. **10** *U.S. Senate Election, Expulsion, and Censure Cases*, p. 376, 377; *NYT*, 8-22-1947, p. 1. **11** *Presidential Also-Rans and Running Mates*, p. 495; *NYT*, 2-2-1941, p. 18; 7-23-1997, p. A17. **12** *NYT*, 11-30-1941, p. 1; 9-15-1950, p. 19. **13** *Bribes*, p. 584; *The Big Bosses*, pp. 90–116; *Time*, 6-16-1947; 12-8-1947; 1-16-1956; 6-19-1971. **14** *Bribes*, p. 573; *Biographical Directory of Federal Judges*; *NYT*, 2-7-1946; 3-25-1947. **15** *Bribes*, pp. 577, 790; *EB*; *Time*, 2-25-1946. **16** *Boston Globe*, 5-15-1983; 2-25-1984. **17** *Biographical Directory of the U.S. Congress*; *NYT*, 10-17-1954, p. 1; *NYT*, 11-16-1947, p. E10; *Time*, 5-25-1936. **18** *Dirty Politics*, pp. 4–14; *NYT*, 8-28-1948, p. 28; 9-5-1948, p. 5; 10-6-1948, p. 21. **19** *U.S. Senate Election, Expulsion, and Censure Cases*, p. 391. **20** *Biographical Directory of the U.S. Congress*; *NYT*, 11-28-1949, p. 19; 9-10-1950, p. 57; *Time*, 1-5-1953. **21** *NYT*, 10-25-1950, p. 40; 6-12-1951, p. 24; 4-25-1952, p. 46. **22** *NYT*, 3-13-1965. **23** *Bribes*, p. 577; *NYT*, 2-8-1952, p. 15. **24** *Presidential Sex*, pp. 119–134. **25** *NYT*, 9-6-1952, p. 11. **26** *Confessions of a Muckraker*, pp. 275–276; *NYT*, 1-30-1964, p. 1; *Time*, 11-11-1957; *Newsweek*, 12-12-1955. **27** *Vice Presidents of the U.S.*, p. 436. **28** *NYT*, 8-2-1952, p. 6. **29** *NYT*, 2-10-1954, p. 1; 6-16-1955, p. 14; 1-27-1998, p. A10. **30** *Star Ledger* (Newark, NJ), 11-14-2004; *Time*, 6-28-1954. **31** *Confessions of a Muckraker*, pp. 270–271; *U.S. Senate Election, Expulsion, and Censure Cases*, p. 405. **32** *NYT*, 2-6-1956, p. 12; *Time*, 2-20-1956, 3-5-1956, 4-16-1956. **33** *Time*, 9-17-1956. **34** *NYT*, 7-22-1956, p. E6. **35** *NYT*, 1-5-1957, p. 8; 1-12-1957, p. 1; 2-15-1957, p. 1; 2-16-1957, p. 12. **36** *NYT*, 2-5-1954, p. 1; 2-7-1954, p. 78; 8-31-1957, p. 14; 4-10-1973, p. 25; 4-2-1975, p. 8; *Time*, 9-27-1948, 2-15-1954, 4-14-1975. **37** *NYT*, 6-29-1957, p. 26; 9-18-1957, p. 19. **38** *The House*, pp. 414–415; *Time*, 12-24-1965; 12-9-1966; 12-30-1966. **39** *NYT*, 6-13-1958, p. 12; 9-23-1958, p. 1. **40** *Time*, 6-29-1959; 7-13-1959; 5-2-1960.

1960–1979. 1 *Vice Presidents of the U.S.*, p. 458. **2** *NYT*, 1-30-1960, p. 11; 6-10-1965, p. 43. **3** *NYT*, 1-19-1960, p. 33; 1-24-1960, p. 1. **4** *Biographical Dictionary of American Mayors*, p. 103; *Time*, 6-23-1961. **5** *Scandals in the Highest Office*, pp. 252-255. **6** *Responses of the Presidents to Charges of Misconduct*, pp. 376–378; *Time*, 6-1-1962; 6-15-1962; 9-21-1962; 10-30-1978. **7** *Dirty Politics*, pp. 98–104; *NYT* 10-28-1960, p. 16; 10-31-1960, p. 23; 10-7-1962, p. 53. **8** *NYT*, 10-8-1963, p. 22; 12-22-1965, p. 28; 3-13-1969, p. 47; 4-15-1972, p. 63. **9** *NYT*, 12-12-1948, p. 80; 6-5-1962, p. 23. **10** *NYT*, 5-24-1963, p. 44. **11** *Time*, 10-9-1964. **12** *Time*, 5-8-1964. **13** *Time*, 1-23-1964. **14** *NYT*, 7-22-1956, p. E6. **15** *U.S. Senate Election, Expulsion, and Censure Cases*, p. 413. **16** *NYT*, 8-7-1968, p. 21; 6-16-1973, p. 62; 11-23-1974, p. 19. **17** *Washington Post*, 8-24-1978. **18** *Biographical Dictionary of American Mayors*, p. 6; *Time*, 11-13-1972. **19** *Bribes*, pp. 557–560; *Biographical Directory of Federal Judges*. **20** *NYT*, 12-18-1969, p. 1; 2-3-1981, p. B14; 6-15-1970. **21** *Time*, 7-25-1969; 8-15-1969; 4-6-1970. **22** *Presidential Also-Rans and Running*

Mates, pp. 640–641. **23** *Biographical Dictionary of American Mayors*, p. 61. **24** *NYT*, 1-15-1971, p. 1; 10-6-1975, p. 30. **25** *Biographical Directory of the U.S. Congress*; *NYT*, 12-17-1970, p. 1. **26** *Biographical Directory of the U.S. Congress*; *San Francisco Chronicle*, 5-5-1992. **27** *NYT*, 7-6-1971, p. 1; 6-3-1975; *Time*, 12-31-1965; 7-19-1971. **28** *NYT*, 4-1-1970, p. 33; 12-31-1971, p. 1; 3-14-1973, p. 20; *Time*, 1-10-1972. **29** *NYT*, 1-7-1970, p. 26; 3-30-1971, p. 16; 7-17-1971, p. 24. **30** *NYT*, 3-20-1972, p. 12; 4-17-1972, p. 6; 6-7-1973, p. 7; *Time*, 4-3-1972; 8-13-1973. **31** *Dirty Politics*, p. 104; *Detroit Free Press*, 10-4-1992. **32** *Presidential Also-Rans and Running Mates*, p. 633. **33** *Presidential Also-Rans and Running Mates*, p. 661–664. **34** *NYT*, 4-23-1999, p. A23. **35** *NYT*, 1-16-1973, p. 26, 85. **36** *Biographical Directory of Federal Judges*; *Chicago Tribune*, 2-1-1998; *NYT*, 2-20-1973, p. 6; 7-29-1974, p. 47. **37** *NYT*, 3-29-1973, p. 20. **38** *NYT*, 10-16-1973, p. 31. **39** *NYT*, 1-10-1975, p. 77; 6-6-1977, p. 7; 5-13-1980, p. B2. **40** *Vice Presidents of the U.S.*, pp. 481–488; *Time*, 10-1-1973; 10-22-1973. **41** *Arkansas Gazette*, 8-8-1974. **42** *Cincinnati Post*, 4-29-1998; *NYT*, 7-24-2004. **43** *NYT*, 10-10-1974, p. 31; 11-19-1974, p. 28. **44** *EB*; *Time*, 7-3-1972, 9-4-1972, 1-22-1973. **45** *Chicago Sun Times*, 3-23-2000; *NYT*, 12-9-1975, p. 20; 3-17-1987, p. A22. **46** *NYT*, 10-24-1973, p. 28; 7-20-1974, p. 65; 4-11-1976, p. 29. **47** *Biographical Directory of the U.S. Congress*, p. 1592; *NYT*, 10-10-1974, p. 23; *Washington Post*, 10-11-1974. **48** *NYT*, 7-11-1974, p. 1; 8-7-1975, p. 1; 5-23-1996, p. D25. **49** *NYT*, 7-28-1974, p. 1; 10-3-1974, p. 89; 12-9-1975, p. 27. **50** *NYT*, 8-1-1974, p. 1; *Time*, 5-14-1973; 4-28-1975. **51** "Governor David Hall"/Oklahoma Department of Libraries; *NYT*, 8-5-1975, p. 54. **52** *Biographical Directory of the U.S. Congress*; *NYT*, 2-3-1973, p. 15. **53** *NYT*, 4-19-1975, p. 15; 12-13-1992, p. 40; *Time*, 7-2-1984. **54** *Chicago Sun Times*, 12-15-2000. **55** *Chicago Tribune*, 10-3-1991. **56** *NYT*, 10-2-1976, p. 11; 12-4-1976, p. 18. **57** *Vice Presidents of the U.S.*, p. 512. **58** *NYT*, 6-15-1976, p. 26; 8-22-1976, p. 148; 7-15-1977, p. 78. **59** *NYT*, 12-9-1976, p. 31; 12-18-1999, p. A21. **60** *NYT*, 7-25-1976, p. 21; *Washington Post*, 4-18-1983. **61** *Deseret News*, 12-16-2000. **62** *NYT*, 6-12-1976, p. 1; *Washington Post*, 5-23-1976. **63** *NYT*, 2-1-1977, p. 28. **64** *NYT*, 7-19-1977, p. 20. **65** *NYT*, 2-21-1971, p. 39; 2-19-1976, p. 18. **66** *NYT*, 1-27-1977, p. 19. **67** *Time*, 8-1-1977; 10-3-1977; 5-12-1980. **68** National Governors Association; *NYT*, 8-24-1977, p. 41; 10-8-1977, p. 49; 1-16-1979, p. A12; 7-21-1979, p. 16; 11-13-1987, p. A1. **69** Associated Press, 1-4-1986; *NYT*, 5-13-1977, p. 20; 5-3-1986, p. 8; 6-14-1986, p. 14. **70** *NYT*, 9-8-1970, p. 81; 1-10-1978, p. 6; 8-2-1977, p. 61. **71** *Boston Globe*, 4-22-1982; *NYT*, 10-27-1977, p. 41. **72** *NYT*, 1-31-1978, p. 12; 3-1-1979, p. A19; 2-24-1979, p. 7; 2-26-1979, p. 13. **73** *NYT*, 4-1-1978, p. 1; 4-25-1978, p. 1; 7-13-1979, p. A8; 2-5-1980, p. B8. **74** *NYT*, 6-13-1979, p. 12. **75** National Governors Association; *NYT*, 6-10-1981, p. A19; 5-22-1988, p. 21; 11-23-1996, p. 11. **76** *NYT*, 1-21-1979, p. 17. **77** *U.S. Senate Election, Expulsion, and Censure Cases*, p. 429. **78** *Biographical Directory of the U.S. Congress*; *NYT*, 11-4-1979, p. 32; 1-5-1980, p. 19.

1980–1999. 1 *NYT*, 1-16-1980, p. 1; 4-1-1983, p. A10. **2** *Biographical Directory of the U.S. Congress*; *Washington Post*, 6-30-1979; 8-26-1998. **3** *Biographical Directory of the U.S. Congress*; *NYT*, 10-26-1980, p. E3. **4** *Boston Globe*, 3-20-1980; *Washington Post*, 10-9-1982. **5** *NYT*, 3-13-1981, p. A13. **6** *Chicago Sun Times*, 1-30-1986; 12-25-1989. **7** *Time*, 2-19-1979. **8** *NYT*, 3-9-1981, p. A18. **9** *Biographical Directory of the U.S. Congress*; *NYT*, 3-12-1982, p. B2; *Time*, 2-18-1980; 10-20-1980; 11-10-1980; 2-9-1981; 8-24-1981. **10** *Time*, 3-2-1981. **11** *Detroit Free Press*, 8-26-1982. **12** *NYT*, 12-4-1987, p. B1; 8-28-1988, p. 35. **13** *Boston Globe*, 12-10-1985. **14** *Chicago Sun Times*, 9-28-1985. **15** *Chicago Tribune*, 10-22-1985. **16** *NYT*, 11-2-1983, p. A20; 11-9-1983. p. A23; 1-16-1984, p. B7. **17** *Washington Post*, 7-21-1983. **18** *NYT*, 4-6-1993, p. A21. **19** *Washington Post*, 7-21-1983. **20** *Chicago Sun Times*, 9-12-1989; *Chicago Tribune*, 2-25-1992. **21** *Chicago Tribune*, 11-13-1985; *NYT*, 2-24-1985, p. 21. **22** *Wall Street Journal*, 6-19-1984, p. 1. **23** *NYT*, 12-27-1984, p. 36; 3-11-1985, p. 56. **24** *Dirty Little Secrets*, p. 183. **25** *Chicago Tribune*, 8-28-1985; 10-3-1991; 10-12-1995; 1-17-1997; *Washington Post*, 10-9-1984. **26** National Governors Association; *NYT*, 7-24-1985, p. B4; 8-6-1985, p. A11. **27** *EB*; *Time*, 12-8-1986; 12-22-1986; 7-27-1987; 4-16-1990. **28** *Syracuse Herald Journal*, 1-7-1988; 1-20-1988; 3-24-1988. **29** *U.S. News & World Report*, 4-16-1984; 10-15-1984; 5-27-1987. **30** *The Record* (Hackensack, NJ), 11-24-1985; *NYT*, 2-7-1988, p. A1. **31** *NYT*, 11-1-1984, p. A26; 10-6-1985, p. E4; 10-10-1985, p. A1; 10-19-1985, p. 8; *Time*, 10-28-1985. **32** *Houston Chronicle*, 12-5-1986; *San Francisco Chronicle*, 12-6-1986. **33** *NYT*, 3-1-1985, p. A1; 1-12-1986, p. 15; 5-

11-1986, p. 18. **34** *NYT*, 10-11-1987, p. E7; 12-8-1990, p. 31; 12-24-1988, p. 26. **35** *NYT*, 12-6-1983, p. B12; 9-22-1986, p. D11; 10-10-1986, p. 17; *Washington Post*, 3-10-1987. **36** *NYT*, 1-8-1986, p. A9; 5-29-1986, p. A14. **37** *Biographical Directory of the U.S. Congress*; *NYT*, 1-8-1985, p. 62; *NYT*, 10-15-1987, p. A1; *NYT*, 7-1-1988, p. B5. **38** *NYT*, 5-3-1987. **39** *Chicago Tribune*, 4-9-1988; 4-25-1987; 8-26-1989. **40** *NYT*, 2-13-1990, p. A20; 2-28-1993, p. 22; 4-10-1993, p. 6. **41** *NYT*, 10-1-1987, p. A1. **42** *NYT*, 3-12-1987, p. B14; 11-23-1992, p. B5. **43** *NYT*, 8-26-1984, p. 33; 12-20-1986, p. 9; 1-23-1987, p. A1. **44** *NYT*, 10-21-1989, p. 28; 9-16-1993, p. B3; *Post Standard* (Syracuse, NY) 8-24-1992; *Time*, 4-20-1987; 4-11-1988; 7-18-1988; *Washington Post*, 8-6-1988; 6-30-1990. **45** *NYT*, 8-6-1987, p. 13; 11-20-1987, p. 45; *Wall Street Journal*, 8-6-1987, p. 13. **46** National Governors Association; *NYT*, 3-9-1987, p. A12; 1-10-1988, p. 18; 3-8-1988, p. A23. **47** *NYT*, 10-5-1988, p. A17. **48** *NYT*, 8-29-1989, p. A16. **49** *Chicago Sun Times*, 8-1-1989; *Chicago Tribune*, 5-17-1990. **50** *NYT*, 10-19-1989, p. A24. **51** *The Record* (Hackensack, NJ), 5-9-1989. **52** *Christian Science Monitor*, 8-4-1988; *Sun Sentinel*, 2-17-1986; *Palm Beach Post*, 7-23-1989; *Sun Sentinel*, 10-6-1996. **53** *Washington Post*, 9-22-1989. **54** *Biographical Directory of Federal Judges*; *The Advocate* (Baton Rouge, LA), 2-10-1986; 12-4-1986; *Washington Post*, 11-4-1989. **55** *Time*, 6-6-1988; 4-17-1989. **56** *NYT*, 5-27-1989, p. 9; 5-28-1989, p. 28. **57** *Time*, 11-27-1989; 11-26-1990; 3-11-1991; 8-19-1991. **58** *Arizona Republic*, 2-11-2001; 5-4-2001; *Washington Post*, 10-14-1989; 3-16-1991; *San Francisco Chronicle*, 10-23-1990. **59** *NYT*, 10-30-1990, p. A1; 11-8-1990, p. B10; *Star Tribune* (Minneapolis, MN), 8-23-1990. **60** *NYT*, 10-30-1990, p. A1; 11-8-1990, p. B10; *Star Tribune* (Minneapolis, MN), 10-15-1990; 10-28-1990; 10-29-1990. **61** *Houston Chronicle*, 7-27-1990. **62** *U.S. Senate Election, Expulsion, and Censure Cases*, p. 438. **63** *Chicago Sun Times*, 11-16-1990; 10-24-1991; 5-8-1992. **64** *NYT*, 8-21-1990, p. B1; 4-5-1991, p. B5; 3-2-1994, p. B2. **65** *NYT*, 7-11-1990, p. A10. **66** *NYT*, 12-13-1989, p. A24; 1-28-1990, p. 22. **67** *NYT*, 2-3-1990, p. 12. **68** *Time*, 6-26-1989; 11-12-1990; 11-19-1990; *Washington Post*, 1-19-1990, p. A01; 1-11-2006, p. A01. **69** *Chicago Tribune*, 1-15-1993; *St. Louis Post Dispatch*, 9-25-1991. **70** National Governors Association; *EB*; *NYT*, 5-29-1996, p. A1; 7-17-1996, p. A17; *Time*, 2-15-1999; 2-6-1997; 4-19-1996; 6-12-1996; *Arkansas Times*, 7-19-1996. **71** *Daily Press* (Newport News, VA), 9-16-1994; *Richmond Times-Dispatch*, 11-6-1994. **72** *Chicago Sun Times*, 9-23-1993; *State Journal Register* (Springfield, IL), 4-30-1992. **73** *NYT*, 8-2-1996, p. A12; 12-6-1997, p. A16. **74** *NYT*, 3-2-1992, p. A1; 3-3-1992, p. A14. **75** *St. Petersburg Times*, 4-27-1993. **76** *Boston Globe*, 4-17-1993; *Washington Post*, 6-30-1993. **77** National Governors Association; *NYT*, 4-23-1993, p. A1; *NYT*, 4-8-1998, p. A12; 6-5-1998, p. A17. **78** *Orlando Sentinel*, 12-31-1993; *Sun Sentinel*, 5-22-1993. **79** *Chicago Tribune*, 10-2-1993; *San Antonio Express News*, 5-22-1995. **80** *Chicago Tribune*, 7-22-1993. **81** *NYT*, 4-26-1990, p. A29; 10-4-1994, p. A1; 1-15-1998, p. A15; 12-3-1998, p. A1. **82** *Chicago Tribune*, 2-25-1994. **83** "Clinton Impeachment," Eagleton Institute of Politics/Rutgers University. **84** *St. Louis Post Dispatch*, 12-13-1994; 12-16-1994. **85** "Impeachment of State Officials"; *NYT*, 10-29-1993, p. A12; National Governors Association. **86** *Chicago Tribune*, 11-19-1994. **87** *Chicago Tribune*, 11-10-1994; *Kentucky Post*, 9-21-1996. **88** *Rocky Mountain News*, 12-12-1995; *Washington Post*, 11-14-1995. **89** *Kentucky Post*, 3-14-1995. **90** *Chicago Tribune*, 8-23-1995; *Chicago Sun Times*, 1-21-2001. **91** *NYT*, 4-26-1990, p. A29; 8-10-1995, p. A16. **92** *Seattle Post-Intelligencer*, 5-18-1995; *Washington Post*, 9-10-1995. **93** *EB*; "Clinton Impeachment," Eagleton Institute of Politics/Rutgers University. **94** NPR Weekend Edition, 6-11-1994; *Time*, 4-22-1996. **95** *Press Telegram* (Long Beach, CA), 12-13-1995; 4-18-1996. **96** *Commercial Appeal* (Memphis, TN), 4-30-1996. **97** *NYT*, 8-30-1996, p. A1; 9-10-1996, p. A22; *Washington Post*, 9-4-1996, p. 80. **98** *NYT*, 12-1-1996, p. 1. **99** National Governors Association; *NYT*, 9-4-1997, p. A1. **100** *Tampa Tribune*, 2-23-1995. **101** *NYT*, 5-3-1997, p. 11. **102** *NYT*, 6-11-1998, p. A17; 11-15-1997, p. A10; 11-2-1999, p. A16. **103** *Journal Gazette* (Fort Wayne, IN), 2-20-1998; *San Francisco Chronicle*, 11-9-1990. **104** *Orange County Register*, 2-11-1998; 3-10-1998; *Washington Post*, 3-11-1998. **105** *Biographical Directory of the U.S. Congress*; *The Buffalo News*, 9-17-1998. **106** *Journal Gazette* (Fort Wayne, IN), 9-2-1998. **107** CNN, 12-19-1998; *Time*, 10-19-1998; 12-17-1998. **108** *NYT*, 11-3-1999, p. A22. **109** *Honolulu Star Bulletin*, 4-4-2000. **110** Arkansas News Bureau, 10-24-2006; *Commercial Appeal*, 11-13-1999; *NYT*, 4-28-1999, p. A18. **111** *Richmond Times Dispatch*, 9-11-1999.

2000–2006. **1** *Santa Fe New Mexican,* 7-1-1997; 11-9-2003; 11-5-2004; *El Paso Times,* 3-12-2004. **2** *Honolulu Star-Bulletin,* 7-4-2001. **3** *NYT,* 10-18-2003, p. B5. **4** *Honolulu Advertiser* 6-27-2002; *Honolulu Star-Bulletin,* 4-21-2002. **5** *San Francisco Chronicle,* 3-6-2002. **6** *Chicago Sun Times,* 10-3-2002; *Star Ledger* (Newark, NJ), 10-1-2002; *Washington Post,* 10-1-2002. **7** *Honolulu Star-Bulletin,* 1-6-2001; *Pacific Business News,* 5-28-2002. **8** *The Columbian* (Vancouver, WA) 6-23-2002. **9** *NYT,* 10-1-1983, p. 14; 3-6-1984, p. B11; 4-24-1984, p. A1; 11-10-1990, p. 9; 9-7-2002, p. A13. **10** *The Record* (Hackensack, NJ), 1-25-2002; 7-10-2002; 4-29-2003; *Star Ledger* (Newark, NJ), 1-25-2002. **11** *San Diego Union Tribune,* 2-9-2002. **12** *Chicago Tribune,* 7-25-2002; *Washington Post,* 6-17-1983; 7-31-2002. **13** *Time,* 9-15-2003; 8-11-2003. **14** *Chicago Tribune,* 1-10-2003; *Des Moines Register,* 8-3-2003. **15** *NYT,* 1-9-2003, p. B5; 7-2-2003, p. B5. **16** *Hartford Courant,* 6-29-2004; 6-30-2004; *NYT,* 10-28-1999, p. B5; 3-29-2003, p. A10; 12-15-2003, p. B1. **17** *Star Tribune* (Minneapolis, MN), 2-25-2005; *NYT,* 12-9-2003, p. A1. **18** *NYT,* 11-27-2003, p. A36. **19** *The Oregonian,* 5-7-2004. **20** WTNH (New London, CT), 6-2-2004. **21** *Chicago Tribune,* 4-27-2006; *Milwaukee Journal Sentinel,* 11-12-2004. **22** *Star-Ledger* (Newark, NJ), 11-7-2004. **23** CNN, 6-13-2006; *Time,* 9-13-2004. **24** *Hawaii Reporter,* 11-1-2005; *Honolulu Star-Bulletin,* 7-18-2004; 11-1-2005, p. 1. **25** *Kentucky Post* (Covington, KY), 7-20-2005; 10-12-2006. **26** *News & Observer* (Raleigh, NC), 10-13-2005. **27** *Cincinnati Post,* 8-19-2005; *State Journal Register* (Springfield, IL), 8-19-2005; *Star Ledger* (Newark, NJ), 11-21-2006. **28** *Montgomery Advertiser,* 10-27-2005; 6-30-2006. **29** *San Diego Union-Tribune,* 12-4-2005; 3-4-2006; *Washington Post,* 11-29-2005. **30** *Orlando Sentinel,* 8-4-2006; *Washington Post,* 3-11-2006. **31** *Houston Chronicle,* 6-9-2006. **32** *Chicago Tribune,* 9-7-2006; *Time,* 4-17-2006. **33** *Time,* 10-3-2006. **34** *Washington Post,* 11-4-2006; *NYT* 1-19-2007, p. 1.

ILLUSTRATION SOURCES

All illustrations are in the public domain unless otherwise designated. Some portraits or photographs of individuals have been "flipped" left to right, and some individuals have been cropped from larger illustrations. Bold numerals indicate page number in text. Dates are only included when available.

Abbreviations: *ACAB* is *Appleton's Cyclopedia of American Biography;* PPC/LC is Prints and Photographs Collection/Library of Congress; NARA is U.S. National Archives and Records Adminstration.

4 *Scribner's History of the United States,* 1897. **5** *Scribner's History of the United States.* **5** *Scribner's History of the United States.* **6** *Scribner's History of the United States.* **8** *ACAB.* **9** *ACAB.* **10** *ACAB.* **11** *ACAB.* **12** PPC/LC, 1798. **13** PPC/LC, 1798. **14** *ACAB.* **15** PPC/LC, c. 1836. **16** *ACAB.* **17** PPC/LC, c. 1904. **18** *ACAB.* **19** *History of New York,* Todd, 1899. **20** PPC/LC. **21** *A History of Georgia for Use in School,* Evans, 1900. **22** *ACAB.* **23** *ACAB.* **25** *ACAB.* **27** PPC/LC, 1817. **28** PPC/LC, c.1863. **28** PPC/LC, c. 1852. **29** PPC/LC, 1828. **30** PPC/LC, 1831. **31** PPC/LC, 1836. **32** PPC/LC, 1838. **33** PPC/LC, 1838. **34** Used with permission of: Texas State Library & Archives Commission. **37** PPC/LC, 1838. **38** *Perley's Reminiscences.* **39** PPC/LC. **40** PPC/LC. **41** U.S. Senate Historical Office. **43** PPC/LC, 1846. **44** *ACAB.* **45** PPC/LC, c. 1846. **46** PPC/LC, 1838. **47** PPC/LC. **47** PPC/LC, 1850. **48** PPC/LC. **51** PPC/LC. *Frank Leslie's Illustrated Newspaper,* 1-15-1881. **51** PPC/LC, 1854. **52** *Perley's Reminiscences.* **54** PPC/LC, 1856. **55** PPC/LC, 1856. **56** PPC/LC. **56** PPC/LC. **58** *Century Magazine,* 11-1891. **59** *Century Magazine,* 11-1891. **59** *Century Magazine,* 11-1891. **60** PPC/LC. **61** *Harper's Weekly,* 3-12-1859. **61** *Harper's Weekly,* 3-12-1859. **63** *Perley's Reminiscences.* **64** PPC/LC, *Illustrated London News,* 12-3-1864. **65** PPC/LC, *Harper's Weekly,* unknown issue, 1861. **66** *ACAB.* **66** PPC/LC, *Frank Leslie's Illustrated Newspaper,* 3-28-1868. **67** *Harper's Weekly,* 3-21-1868. **68** PPC/LC, 1866. **70** PPC/LC. **71** *Perley's Reminiscences.* **71** PPC/LC, *Frank Leslie's Illustrated Newspaper,* 12-16-1876. **74** PPC/LC, c.1869. **74** PPC/LC, *Harper's Weekly,* 10-21-1871. **75** PPC/LC, 1871. **76** PPC/LC. **77** PPC/LC, *Frank Leslie's Illustrated Newspaper,* 10-26-1872. **78** PPC/LC. **79** PPC/LC. **80** PPC/LC. **80** PPC/LC. **82** PPC/LC, *Puck,* 2-4-1880. **83** PPC/LC. **84** PPC/LC.

85 PPC/LC. **85** PPC/LC. **86** PPC/LC, *Frank Leslie's Illustrated Newspaper,* 12-26-1876. **87** *Perley's Reminiscences.* **87** *Puck,* 9-24-1884. **88** *Perley's Reminiscences.* **88** PPC/LC. **89** PPC/LC, *Harper's Weekly,* 2-17-1877. **90** PPC/LC. **91** *Scribner's History of the U.S.* **92** *Perley's Reminiscences.* **93** *Scribner's History of the U.S.* **95** PPC/LC, *Puck,* 3-2-1881. **96** From the Collections of the South Carolina Historical Society, c. 1875. **97** PPC/LC. **99** *ACAB.* **99** *Perley's Reminiscences.* **99** PPC/LC, *Judge,* 9-7-1884. **99** Photograph of Cleveland campaign pig charm (Stanhope charm). **100** PPC/LC. **100** PPC/LC, *Harper's Weekly,* 11-16-1889. **101** PPC/LC, *Puck,* 8-1-1900. **103** PPC/LC, c. 1881. **103** PPC/LC. **104** PPC/LC. **105** PPC/LC, *Judge,* 3-22-1884. **105** PPC/LC, *Puck,* 6-9-1897. **107** PPC/LC. **107** *Harper's Weekly,* 3-15-1890. **107** *Harper's Weekly,* 3-15-1890. **109** PPC/LC, c. 1886. **110** With permission of: Picture Collection, The Branch Libraries, The New York Public Library, Astor, Lenox and Tilden Foundations. **112** *The Parties and the Men,* Law, 1896. **112** *Judge,* unknown issue, 1897. **112** *Judge,* unknown issue, 1901. **113** PPC/LC, *Judge,* 9-19-1896. **114** PPC/LC, 1939. **115** PPC/LC, 1917. **115** PPC/LC, 1910. **116** PPC/LC, *Puck,* 6-27-1900. **117** PPC/LC. **117** *The Parties and the Men.* **118** *That Kentucky Campaign,* Hughes, et al., 1900. **118** *Harper's Weekly,* 1-30-1900. **119** *Harper's Weekly,* 1-30-1900. **119** *That Kentucky Campaign.* **120** *Denver Post,* 4-10-1901. **121** PPC/LC, c. 1905. **123** *McClure's Magazine,* 4-1907. **124** *McClure's Magazine,* 1-1903. **125** PPC/LC. **126** PPC/LC. **127** PPC/LC. **128** PPC/LC. **130** PPC/LC. **131** PPC/LC, 1914. **132** With permission of: Special Collections Department, J. Willard Marriott Library, University of Utah. **133** *The American Review of Reviews,* 11-1908 (from *Saturday Globe,* Utica, NY). **135** *The American Review of Reviews,* 10-1907. **135** PPC/LC. **136** PPC/LC, 1910. **137** PPC/LC, 1913. **139** *McClure's Magazine,* 11-1911. **140** Photograph of Victor Berger campaign button. **141** PPC/LC, c. 1907. **141** PPC/LC, 1934. **141** PPC/LC, 1923. **141** NARA. **142** PPC/LC, 1938. **143** PPC/LC, c. 1920. **144** PPC/LC. **144** PPC/LC. **145** AP Images, 1920. **146** NARA, 1869. **146** PPC/LC. **147** PPC/LC, 1924. **147** PPC/LC, 1924. **148** Photograph of "Big Bill Thompson" campaign button. **148** PPC/LC. **149** PPC/LC. **150** PPC/LC. **151** U.S. Senate Historical Office. **152** PPC/LC. **152** PPC/LC, 1908. **153** PPC/LC. **153** PPC/LC, c. 1910. **154** PPC/LC, 1927. **155** PPC/LC. **155** PPC/LC, 4-25-1923. **157** With permission of: Alabama Department of Archives and History, Montgomery, Alabama. **158** PPC/LC, 9-13-1926. **159** With permission of: Governors' Portraits Collection, Indiana Historical Bureau, State of Indiana. **160** PPC/LC. **160** NARA, Franklin D. Roosevelt Library, 1930. **162** PPC/LC. **163** AP Images, 1-18-1929. **164** PPC/LC. **165** PPC/LC. **166** PPC/LC. **167** PPC/LC. **169** PPC/LC. **170** NARA, Franklin D. Roosevelt Library. **171** Photograph of Huey Long washroom medal. **172** PPC/LC. **174** PPC/LC, *Kansas City Journal Post,* 9-24-1927. **178** Photograph of anti-FDR campaign buttons. **181** NARA, Jimmy Carter Library, 9-20-1977. **181** *Adolf Hitler's Own Book Mein Kampf,* Noram Publishing Co., 1939. **182** PPC/LC, 1942. **185** PPC/LC, 1941. **185** PPC/LC, 1-30-1941. **187** U.S. Senate Historical Office. **188** LBJ Library, 3-1942. **189** Truman Presidential Library, 1-19-1949. **190** PPC/LC. **191** NARA. **192** PPC/LC. **193** PPC/LC, 1925. **194** PPC/LC, 11-1-1917. **195** AP Images, 10-10-1932. **195** LBJ Library, 6-30-1948. **196** AP Images, 8-5-1938. **199** PPC/LC, *New York Times,* 1954. **199** AP Images, 9-23-1952. **200** PPC/LC. **201** AP Images, 11-30-1955. **202** AP Images. **203** NARA, c. 1946. **203** U.S. Senate Historical Office. **205** AP Images, 1-25-1957. **206** AP Images, 11-14-1965. **207** AP Images, 6-14-1954. **207** AP Images, 9-2-1959. **209** PPC/LC. *U.S. News & World Report,* 9-9-1976. **210** LBJ Library. **211** PPC/LC, *World Telegram & Sun,* 1962. **211** AP Images, 3-6-1958. **213** Photograph of Goldwater for Halloween button. **213** LBJ Library, photo by Cecil Stoughton, 5-4-1964. **214** U.S. Senate Historical Office. **216** PPC/LC, *U.S. News & World Report,* 10-4-1965. **216** AP Images, 6-16-1970. **217** AP Images. **218** PPC/LC, *U.S. News & World Report,* 6-11-1963. **218** AP Images, 1961. **219** U.S. Senate Historical Office. **220** AP Images, 3-31-1970. **221** AP Images, 3-29-1971. **221** AP Images, 4-30-1973. **222** PPC/LC, *World Telegram & Sun,* 10-26-1965. **223** U.S. Senate Historical Office. **223** Photograph of McGovern–Eagleton button. **224** AP Images, 1967. **226** NARA, 1-20-1969. **227** AP Images, 12-1-1977. **228** Photograph of Nixon reelection button. **228** NARA. **229** NARA, 2-12-1973. **230** AP Images, 12-2-1974. **231** U.S. Senate Historical Office. **232** NARA, 8-15-1971. **235** PPC/LC, *U.S. News & World Report,* 8-1976. **236** AP Images, 6-11-1976.

238 NARA, 2-7-1977. **239** AP Images, 8-17-1977. **241** AP Images, 8-14-1975. **242** AP Images, 12-22-1978. **243** U.S. Senate Historical Office. **245** AP Images, 2-4-1970. **246** NARA, 6-8-1989. **247** AP Images, 1-16-1980. **248** AP Images, NBC-TV, 10-14-1980. **250** AP Images, 9-22-1976. **252** AP Images, 6-30-2004. **252** AP Images, 7-16-1983. **253** AP Images, 7-20-1983. **254** AP Images, 10-1973. **256** NARA. **256** AP Images, 5-20-1987. **258** AP Images. **259** AP Images, 5-27-1988. **260** NARA, 9-21-1978. **261** AP Images, 5-4-1987. **262** AP Images, 4-9-1993. **263** AP Images, 1-22-1987. **265** AP Images, 8-8-1988. **266** AP Images, 3-17-1988. **268** AP Images, 9-3-1999. **268** AP Images, 9-5-1989. **269** AP Images, 9-12-1989. **271** AP Images, 11-15-1990. **271** AP Images, 1-1-1989. **275** AP Images, 10-12-1989. **278** AP Images, 3-1992. **279** AP Images, 12-19-1994. **280** AP Images, 9-10-1997. **281** AP Images, 2-11-1994. **282** AP Images, 11-8-1994. **283** AP Images, 9-7-1995. **284** AP Images, 11-17-1995. **285** AP Images, 10-5-1998. **286** Collection of U.S. House of Representatives. **287** AP Images, 8-30-1996. **287** AP Images, 3-3-1995. **288** AP Images, 11-1-1999. **289** AP Images, 9-16-1998. **290** Collection of U.S. House of Representatives. **291** AP Images, 1-8-1998. **293** AP Images, 11-29-2000. **294** Collection of U.S. House of Representatives. **295** AP Images, 4-2-2001. **296** Collection of U.S. House of Representatives. **297** AP Images, 1-9-2003. **298** AP Images, 3-18-2005. **298** Collection of U.S. House of Representatives. **299** AP Images, 6-23-2004. **300** AP Images, 11-8-2004. **301** Congressional Pictorial Directory, 108th Congress. **302** Congressional Pictorial Directory, 109th Congress. **303** Congressional Pictorial Directory, 109th Congress. **304** Congressional Pictorial Directory, 109th Congress.

ACKNOWLEDGMENTS

Special thanks to: John Flicker and Glen Edelstein at Bantam Dell; Nathan Bransford and Peter Ginsberg at Curtis Brown Ltd.; and Gregory McNamee, Ed O'Brien, Leif Smith, Bill Casey, Steve Topping, and Marilyn Auer.

Plus: Randall Lockwood, John Lehndorff, Phil Norman, Bill Mobley, Mark Rucker, Dick Tuck, Rebecca Lintz, Kris McCusker, Doug Mudd, Dick Grinolds, Rex Stark, Tom Franch, Tom Peeling, Dick Weatherbee, Elizabeth Cook, Earl Dodge, Bill Bushong (White House History Association), Joan Carroll (AP Images), American Numismatic Association, American Political Items Collectors Assocation, *The Bloomsbury Review*, Gallagher Books (Denver, CO), Clausen Books (Colorado Springs, CO), Tattered Cover Bookstore (Denver, CO), Denver Public Library, Norlin Library / University of Colorado, Special Collections / Norlin Library / University of Colorado, Stephen H. Hart Library / Colorado Historical Society, Special Collections / Dayton Memorial Library / Regis University, Auraria Library, Penrose Library / University of Denver, Tutt Library / Colorado College, Bancroft Library / University of California Berkeley, Rare Books Collection/Library of Congress, University of Arizona Library, Culver Pictures, Associated Press Photo Archive

INDEX

rings 86, 98, 166, 318
riots 41, 48, 50, 53, 62, 69, 113, 140, 182
Ritner, Joseph 36
Ritter, Halstead 177
robbery 124
Robertson, J. 144
Robeson, George 85
Robey, Alexander 81
Robinson, Charles 64
Rockefeller, Nelson 235
Roerish, Nicholas 185
Rogers, George 240
Rolph, James 169
Romanism 55, 101
Roorback 42, 313, 318
Roosevelt, Eleanor 178
Roosevelt, Elliott 178
Roosevelt, Frankin 171, 175, 178, 180, 185, 188, 191, 193, 195, 318
Roosevelt, Theodore 120, 126, 316
Ross, Robert 204
Rostenkowski, Daniel 284
Roti, Fred 275
Rousseau, Lovell 309
Rove, Karl 292
Rowbottom, Harry 166
Rowland, John 298
Rowlands, Sherry 286
royalties 201, 269, 273
Roybal, Edward 241, 308
rude gesture 235
rumors 4, 6, 8, 9, 14, 42, 55, 109, 112, 116, 117, 179, 198, 199, 210, 218, 246, 252, 261, 316
Ryan, George 303

Sackville-West, Lionel 107
safecracker 209
Saint Tammany 100
Salon 289
Samuel, Bernard 185
San Francisco Chronicle 93
Sanborn contracts scandal 82
Sands Point Country Club 170
sanity (see *insanity*)
Savage, Gus 274
savings and loan 211, 244, 264, 270, 275
scalping 63
scandals 1, 4, 10, 13, 14, 15, 16, 18, 30, 31,
37, 43, 48, 49, 53, 55, 57, 62, 65, 67, 69, 70, 78, 79, 81, 82, 85, 86, 91, 94, 99, 103, 105, 110, 116, 117, 130, 135, 142, 146, 147, 151, 159, 167, 171, 172, 176, 179, 181, 184, 194, 195, 199, 201, 207, 209, 210, 213, 217, 220, 221, 222, 224, 225, 227, 229, 232, 237, 241, 242, 244, 247, 250, 251, 252, 254, 256, 257, 259, 260, 261, 263, 264, 265, 267, 268, 271, 272, 274, 276, 277, 278, 280, 286, 287, 289, 293, 298, 300, 303, 313, 318
scapegoat 117
Schiavone Construction 256
Schmitz, Eugene 121, 133
Schrunk, Terry 205
Scott, Andrew 26
Scott, Francis 61
Scott, Robert 73
Scott, William 245
Scrushy, Richard 302
scuba diving 257
Seabury Committee 166
Seabury, Samuel 166
Seattle Times 278
Sebastian, Charles 138
Sebastian, William 309
secret fund 199
secret negotiations 256
secretaries 68, 86, 124, 197, 218, 235, 236, 278
secretary of the interior 142, 146, 147
secretary of the treasury 9, 10, 19, 24, 27, 49, 82, 86, 232
secretary of war 18, 27, 30, 49, 66, 84, 117
Sedition Act 12
seduction 15, 109, 252
segregation 21, 62, 190, 217
Selassie, Haile 201
Selden, Joseph 24, 26
self-defense 93, 108, 125
senators 10, 11, 15, 17, 18, 20, 21, 22, 23, 24, 27, 28, 32, 33, 40, 41, 43, 44, 45, 46, 48, 50, 53, 54, 56, 60, 65, 68, 72, 76, 78, 79, 83, 84, 95, 98, 102, 103, 104, 107, 110, 114, 115, 117, 121, 125, 127, 129, 130, 132, 136, 139, 142, 143, 148, 156, 160, 162, 164, 165, 167, 168, 170, 171, 174, 175, 181, 186, 190, 191, 197, 199, 202, 203, 204, 214, 217, 219, 221, 222,